W9-BWO-746

COLONIAL HISPANIC AMERICA: A HISTORY

THE MACMILLAN COMPANY
NEW YORK · BOSTON · CHICAGO · DALLAS
ATLANTA · SAN FRANCISCO

MACMILLAN & CO., LIMITED
LONDON · BOMBAY · CALCUTTA
MELBOURNE

THE MACMILLAN COMPANY
OF CANADA, LIMITED
TORONTO

Antonio de Mendoza

COLONIAL HISPANIC AMERICA: A History

BY CHARLES EDWARD CHAPMAN
PROFESSOR OF HISPANIC AMERICAN HISTORY
IN THE UNIVERSITY OF CALIFORNIA

pupil of Bolton

THE MACMILLAN COMPANY

NEW YORK 1933

Published August, 1933.

SET UP, ELECTROTYPED, AND PRINTED BY T. MOREY & SON
IN THE UNITED STATES OF AMERICA

To My Wife

Aimée Fleming Chapman

FOREWORD

The rapid spread of the teaching of colonial history is a salutary development in American education. To study only recent history is to cut the tree of civilization off at its roots. Western Hemisphere nations as separate entities are of very recent origin; indeed, with one major exception all of them have come into existence since the opening of the nineteenth century. But the formative processes of which twentieth-century Western Hemisphere civilization is the expression run far back through the colonial period, to say nothing of the still more remote origins which must be sought in Asia, Europe, and primitive America.

For some three centuries after the discovery of the New World by Columbus the whole Western Hemisphere was either untouched by Old World civilization or was colonial in status. Europeans occupied the country, transplanted their cultures, and adapted themselves to the American scene. Rival European nations devised systems for exploiting natives and natural resources, and competed for profit and possession. Some of the contestants were eliminated, leaving at the end of the eighteenth century Spain, Portugal, and England, as the chief colonial powers in America.

By this time most of the European colonies had grown up; they now asserted their majority. In the half-century between 1776 and 1826 practically all of South America and over half of North America had become politically independent of Europe, and a score of nations had come into being. Eventually the entire Western Hemisphere, with minor exceptions, has achieved independent nationality. Since separation from Europe these nations alike have been striving on the one hand for national solidarity, political stability, and economic well-being, and on the other hand for a satisfactory adjustment of their relations with one another and with the rest of the world.

Our national historians, especially in the United States, are prone to write of these broad phases of history as though they were applicable to one country alone. As a matter of fact, they are but phases common to the entire Western Hemisphere. The story of each nation will have a clearer meaning when studied in the light of the others, for much of what has been written as national history is but a thread out of a larger strand.

In this book Dr. Chapman has told the story of the Spanish and Portuguese colonies, and of their separation from the mother countries. It is a remarkable record, and one that is indispensable to the understanding of the present-day political map and of the twentieth-century civilization of the major portion of the Western Hemisphere, where Hispanic tongues and Hispanic civilization are still dominant. The tremendous colonial success of Spain and Portugal, like that of England, is attested by the stalwart nations which their vigorous colonial children established and have maintained—nations which embrace two-thirds of the entire area of the Americas, which have a rapidly growing population that has already reached a hundred millions, and which have boundless potentialities for the future.

There used to be current in English-speaking countries the strange idea that the Spaniards and Portuguese did not colonize in America, but only explored and hunted for gold. Anyone who reads this book will find himself wholly disabused of such an absurd notion, and will wonder how it became current. That is another story.

Few if any scholars are better equipped than Dr. Chapman to write the history of Hispanic America. Thoroughly trained in the best universities, he has studied and traveled widely in the world at large and especially in the Hispanic countries of Europe and America. His writings cover a broad range, and are marked by sound scholarship. His books on the Spanish archives, on Spain and Portugal, on Cuba, and on Spanish California are all authoritative treatises. Now, they are being knit together in a general history of Hispanic America. Professor Chapman's writing is both vigorous and interesting, qualities so often lacking in college textbooks.

HERBERT E. BOLTON

Berkeley, California
June, 1933.

PREFACE

One of the greatest and most growingly important factors in the world today, especially prominent in the foreign relations of the United States, is Hispanic America, embracing the twenty republics of the Western Hemisphere south of the United States. To understand this region, which is so intimately and so essentially a product of its past, one must inevitably have a broad and somewhat detailed view of those times when it was made up of colonies belonging to Spain and Portugal. There has long been a need for a one-volume survey of this field in English. That need the present work aims to supply.

Obviously, the period from 1492 to 1808—from the discovery by Columbus to the end of the old order under the Bourbons and Braganzas—must be included. If an understanding of colonial Hispanic America is necessary in order to know the meaning of Hispanic America today, ought one also make a study of pre-Columbian Europe, especially Spain and Portugal, and of the geography and native races of the New World if he is to have a secure grasp of the colonial period? Of course, the wider one's information, the more clear his comprehension should be of any particular phase within the range of what he knows. There are practical limitations, however, as to the amount of background one should seek in a given instance, and as to the methods of its presentation. For example, if one needs Spain to explain colonial Spanish America, so also Rome and Arabia are needed in order to interpret Spain. Furthermore, if background chapters on the history of Spain are necessary prior to 1492, they are just as necessary after that date, since Columbus did not bring with him the Spanish life of succeeding centuries as well as his own. In this way one could go on to all-knowledge as an indispensable framework for any one portion of human history. Such a thoroughgoing preparation is impossible, and, in point of fact, not greatly to be desired. The best way to obtain information about such closely related subjects as those mentioned above is to read a book about them or take a course of studies under some competent teacher. Fortunately, there are a number of books available in English and courses of instruction in the universities which may serve the purpose. Otherwise, it is better to rely upon the historian of the colonial period to incorporate the minimum essentials of the background data in his running account of colonial times. This volume begins, therefore, with the era of discovery.

The problem of the ultimate limit of this work is even easier of solution. The wars of independence years were clearly a transitional epoch. They marked the close of the colonial period, with the expulsion of Spain and Portugal from the American mainland, but they also contained important beginnings which belong to the history of republican Hispanic America. Bolívar, San Martín, Iturbide, and Dom Pedro wrote the last chapters in the story of the Spanish and Portuguese colonies, but not even the first in the history of the republics; one must go back of them to the initiators of the Spanish American revolts of 1810 and to the Regent John in the case of Brazil. Figuratively speaking, the colonies ended with the battle of Ayacucho in 1824—and a year earlier in Brazil; the republics had already begun by 1808 or 1810. This volume goes to the end of the period for those factors concerned with the severance of the ties with Spain and Portugal. It touches very lightly upon those which were involved in the gropings of the new nations in their attempts to set up governments and other institutions of their own.

With the field delimited as above, a number of questions arise as to the method of treatment. The colonial period lasted more than three centuries. Certainly the life of the colonies was not the same for all this era, from start to finish. On the contrary, it was ever evolving, changing. An attempt has therefore been made to present the history of this long period in movement, by portraying institutions, as well as events, in different epochs of time. The age of discovery, the ensuing Hapsburg rule, and the Bourbon century are three fairly well-marked eras for handling in this manner. Many things come out more clearly than they do where some one phase of colonial history is covered in one chapter, once for all. The wars of independence period follows, dealing with the overthrow of Spanish and Portuguese control, but reserving institutional factors for later consideration in connection with the republican era.

Furthermore, I do not care for the encyclopaedic type of historical volume, which is primarily an accumulation, on a considerable scale, of names, dates, and isolated facts. Here an attempt has been made to discuss material broadly, with only incidental detail, except as interesting occurrences are adduced to lend color to the account. At times, a general movement has been interpreted through the medium of a single detailed illustration, thus avoiding the monotonous crowding of minutiae and an inadequate explanation at the same time. If, as a result of these methods, the book turns out to be readable, then so much the better. With this in mind, I have frequently used footnotes for matter which does not demand inclusion in the text, but which is capable of engaging the attention in itself. Direct quotations are also employed, both from eyewitnesses and from later well-formulated accounts, with the idea of making the story more vivid and more authoritative. In this form it is hoped that the volume may serve the purposes of university courses having to do with Hispanic American colonial history and the general history of the Americas and that it may find its way into the library of that elusive person, the general reader; certainly the subject is important enough and the material sufficiently attractive to deserve consideration from the thoughtful public.

Special attention is directed to the fact that this is a history of "Hispanic" America. The incorrect term "Latin America" is still used to some extent, but the word "Hispanic" has been adopted by the Romance-languages and history professions, and ought to be universally employed.[1] Such terms as "the Americas," "the Indies," "the New World," and "the Western Hemisphere" appear almost interchangeably.

[1] For an interesting argument in favor of the word "Hispanic," see the remarks of Juan C. Cebrián, quoted in Chapman, Charles Edward, "The founding of the review," in *Hispanic American historical review*, I (8–23; Feb., 1918), 16–17.

One of the problems in connection with names is that of the designation of those larger areas which in colonial days had different names from those now borne by them as Hispanic American republics. In the interests of clearness, the colonial name is referred at its first use to that of the present-day republic; indeed, I have usually preferred to use the latter, even though it may not have attained to official sanction until a later time; surely "Bolivia" is much clearer to the reader than "Upper Peru," "Charcas," or "Chuquisaca," "Argentina" than "Río de la Plata," "La Plata," "Buenos Aires," or "United Provinces," "Mexico" than "New Spain," "Colombia" than "New Granada," "Ecuador" than "Quito," and "Uruguay" than "Banda Oriental," and so also with other names.[1] A name by which to characterize the people of the United States was always an annoying problem. The incorrect "American" and "Americans" have been avoided as much as possible, but accuracy has occasionally given way to smoothness where even an "American" of Hispanic America would be in no doubt as to the people meant.[2]

Names of Spanish and Portuguese persons present many difficulties, because one often has a choice of at least two family names; Hispanic persons have no consistent practice to determine by which name they shall be known, despite the general rule in favor of the father's name. The mother's name is often included as the last name, after the father's, but an individual might choose to employ either one or the other or a combination of the two. Then there are double names, separated by the preposition *de* (of), either one of which might be used. Thus, Pedro de Peralta Barnuevo Rocha y Benavides (a prominent literary figure of colonial Peru) might conceivably appear under any one of his last four names. Other things being equal, I have employed the father's name from the point where it begins, but where an individual is more generally known by some other name, that other has been preferred. Thus, students who would be puzzled by Núñez, Ximénez, Rodríguez, and Vázquez will

[1] One name which defied such treatment was that of the Dominican Republic. Cf. *infra*, 13, n. 1.
[2] For a discussion of this point, see *infra*, 17–18, n. 1.

easily recognize Balboa, Quesada, Cabrillo, and Coronado. Modern spelling is used, except in the case of especially prominent persons whose names have become standardized under what would now be incorrect forms. Thus, "Ximénez" de Quesada is retained.

Christian names of well-known historical personages, including monarchs and a few others (such as Prince "Henry" the Navigator, and "Christopher" and "Bartholomew" Columbus), are translated, in accord with usual Anglo-American practice. The name "Dom Pedro" is a recognized exception to this rule. Other names are left as in the original, but with modern spelling.

The rule of brevity has been adopted for footnote citations. Thus, "Paxson, 153" tells the reader that the volume by the author of that name is given full entry in the Essay on Authorities; "Moses, *Spanish dependencies*, I, 130" would show that this author had more than one book with full entry in the Essay; and "Edwards, Agustín, *Peoples of old* (London, 1929), 13" means that a book so cited does not appear among those items given full entry in the Essay. With two authors of the same name included in the Essay on Authorities, a further distinction (on the basis of Christian names) would usually be necessary. This comes up here only in the case of the name "Robertson." Only one Robertson is cited in the text, however, and two of his volumes are given entry, always with a brief indication of the title. So, no additional differentiation is needed.

In the long list of those to whom thanks are due, I wish to stress one group in particular: the students in my seminar. A number of them have aided with critical work on parts of the manuscript, and two of them, Mr. Lewis Winkler Bealer and Mr. Dominic Salandra, read every word of it and rendered invaluable assistance in many ways. Professor Herbert Eugene Bolton, who wrote the Foreword of this volume, also made helpful suggestions as to methods and content. My wife contributed her services in numerous ways.

CHARLES E. CHAPMAN

Berkeley, California
April 10, 1933

CONTENTS

MAPS

ILLUSTRATIONS

COLONIAL HISPANIC AMERICA: A HISTORY

CHAPTER I

AN ACCIDENT: AMERICA

A LARGE portion of that part of the world now called Hispanic America became Spanish-speaking through an accident. That accident was Christopher Columbus. Nothing in Spanish experience could have given rise to the idea in 1492 that Spain was about to embark upon a career of over-seas conquest which was to be one of the most significant movements in the history of the world. In 711, an invasion of Moslem peoples, Berbers and Arabs, from northwest Africa resulted in a conquest of the Iberian Peninsula, except for a few mountain nuclei in the north. These latter presently became bases for a Christian reconquest which was to pursue its course for a period of nearly eight centuries, until, in 1492, Granada, the last stronghold of the Moslems, fell into the hands of the Catholic Kings, Ferdinand (1479–1516) and Isabella (1474–1504). During all these centuries the most important Christian part of the peninsula, the kingdom of Castile (as at length it came to be called), centred its attention on internal affairs, with hardly a thought for maritime matters. Spaniards of the neighboring kingdom of Aragon were, indeed, to some extent, a seafaring people, but their activities were almost wholly in the Mediterranean, with no interests in the direction of the Atlantic.

To be sure, in a somewhat casual manner, Castile had already taken one step which was later to prove of great material assistance in the voyages across the Atlantic. In 1402, Henry III (1390–1406), "the Pallid," of Castile became the patron of the French adventurer Juan de Bethencourt, who had already begun a conquest of the Canary

Islands. Thus Spain obtained a claim to these islands, which were to be an important stepping-stone in the later movement overseas. These lands were little thought of, however, and the title was bandied about during most of the fifteenth century, until Ferdinand and Isabella at length saw fit to push the Castilian claim. They, of course, had no thought of the as yet undreamed of continents to the west, but were concerned, rather, with the Moslem peoples of northwest Africa. The Canary Islands might serve as a useful base in connection with possible campaigns against the African mainland. After a war lasting nearly two decades, 1478–1496, in which, so it happens, the Castilians gained much experience in methods of combating non-European foes, even including the use of missionaries, the native resistance in the Canaries was overwhelmed. The means employed, which, to be sure, were only an outgrowth from those of which the Castilians had availed themselves in the long wars against the Moslems, were later to be in evidence on a greater scale in the conquest of the Americas.

Meanwhile, the work which Henry the Pallid might have done, if only his life had not been cut short, was in fact undertaken by another Henry, who never became a king, the far-famed Prince Henry "the Navigator," of the neighboring kingdom of Portugal. This Henry was the third son of John I (1385–1433), or John of Aviz, as he is often called, greatest of the Portuguese kings. John had to fight a long war against Castile to make good his title to the throne, but at length, in 1412, his claim was recognized. This was a great moment in Portuguese history, and, as it proved, in the history of the world. The Portuguese people at this time were ripe for new adventure, and Portugal was ideally situated for activities in the unknown or little known parts of the Atlantic which might eventually carry them overseas to the hidden continents in the West. In the extreme southwest of Europe, with half its boundaries touching the Atlantic coast and possessing excellent ports, especially that of Lisbon, Portugal was nearer the western shores of Africa than any country except Spain, and even nearer than that country to the Americas. Spain, in fact, constituted no important exception, not only because of the lack of Spanish traditions of interest in the Atlantic, but also because the Atlantic coast ports of Spain were quite inferior, as compared with those of Portugal, especially the Spanish ports of the southwest, which alone were in a position to compete with those of Portugal in Atlantic Ocean developments. Those of northern Spain shared with other western European ports a disability from which Portugal was free: the ruinous storms of the Bay of Biscay, with which the ships of that period were able to cope only with the greatest of difficulty.

This accident of geography favoring Portugal joined with another to give this little country a start in European overseas endeavors: the peculiar shape of the Portuguese coastline with reference to Spain. The southern shores of Portugal run eastward, not to the Strait of Gibraltar and the Mediterranean, but into the northern reaches of Andalusian, or southern, Spain. The reconquest against the Moslems had proceeded in Portugal at about the same rate as in Castile, but by the middle of the fourteenth century when, roughly, the Castilian movement had reached the same parallel as that of Portugal, the latter had covered the last foot of Portuguese territory, and had no farther to go. That meant that the only mainland enemy of Portugal henceforth must be the much more powerful Christian kingdom of Castile, eventually Spain, and if the Portuguese were to engage in any more independent operations against the Moslems they would have to do so through the medium of a maritime campaign.

As it happened, the Portuguese were ripe for an adventure which would take them overseas against infidel Moslem enemies. The kingdom itself was then the most compact and most united in Europe, with fewer dissensions as between king and nobles, church, cities, or other outstanding elements than in the domestic life of other lands. And the people were at one and the same time exceedingly brave and venturesome and exceedingly devout, in the full vigor of their youth and imbued with the ideals of chivalry. It was at this time that the earliest and greatest of the novels of chivalry, the "Amadís de Gaula" of Vasco de Lobeira, was written, and it is significant that this volume, prototype of a literature which was to endure for two hundred years, first appeared in Portuguese, representing the ardor of that people for knightly deeds in the never-ending crusade against the infidel. This feeling was shared by the three sons of King John, who were still very young as the long war with Castile came to an end. Quite naturally they wished to win their spurs, but whom to fight and *where* were the question. Eventually, it seems, a Portuguese noble by the name of João Affonso stepped into the pages of history with a plan which the boys adopted with enthusiasm. It was for the capture of the Moslem city of Ceuta, across the Strait of Gibraltar in Africa. It is said that King John held out three years against their importunings, alleging Portugal's need for a respite from war, the great cost of such an expedition, and no doubt much else, but when his English wife, Queen Philippa, took up verbal cudgels on behalf of her sons he could resist no longer, and authorized the undertaking.

The Portuguese expedition to Ceuta in 1415 marked the beginning of those movements which were to lead in direct line to the discovery of America, and, as such, this date ought to be considered one of the most important in the history of the world. To be sure, this event, like all others, has its background. It would, for example, take in Marco Polo and his thirteenth-century travels in the Far East, and other European travelers after Polo's time, whose tales of what they saw or heard about in the scantily known Eastern world certainly had their place in the projects of Prince Henry and his successors, including Columbus. As for Ceuta, the expedition involved the building of a fleet and the training of men in seamanship. And when the voyage was made it took nearly a month for a distance which modern steamers would cover in less than a day. Prince Henry had charge of naval operations, and greatly distinguished himself in the campaign, which resulted in the capture of the city. Then King John said in effect: "Now you have your Ceuta, and I am going back to Portugal!" As a reward for his achievements Prince Henry was made lord of Ceuta and of the southern provinces of Portugal. There the affair might have rested, as merely one more isolated instance in the annals of war, if it had not been that Henry was an unusual person, in fact one of the world's great men, who made an exceptional use of the opportunities at his command.

Prince Henry's object in the Ceuta expedition was that of striking a blow against the enemies of Christendom. The next step normally to be expected would have been for him to go inland from Ceuta and attack again, in which event he would probably have been defeated, as were his successors who made similar attempts. But Henry was a man of genius and imagination, a Vasco de Lobeira in action, as was that other Lobeira in literature. He wished to strike a decisive blow, which he knew he could not do with a frontal attack, with his meagre resources. So he planned to take the Moslem enemy in the rear, and for this purpose to ally himself with a reputedly great Christian king somewhere in the East, the legendary Prester John. Nobody knew precisely where Prester John's kingdom was, for old maps and tales of travelers located it at different times all the way from central Africa to northeastern Asia. In any event there seemed to be only one practicable way to find Prester John, and that was by sea, down the coast of Africa and around that continent, if indeed one could go around. So Henry set out in quest of Prester John. If the plan were quixotic in the extreme, as viewed in the light of present-day knowledge, it was nevertheless, in the able hands of Prince Henry, to produce one of the greatest achievements in modern annals.

It is almost impossible today to realize the enormous difficulties of Henry's task. Quite apart from the mythical Prester John, the problem of making his way down the coast of Africa was serious enough in itself. European knowledge of that coast extended at that time only as far as Cape Bojador in 26° north latitude. Beyond that was the "Shadowy Sea," a region of terrific heat, ever hotter and hotter, and of supernatural monsters. It is easy now to understand how such ideas must have originated. The equatorial regions *are* hot, even though there are the cooler regions farther south, as one approaches the South Pole, but nothing of that sort was then known. And many central African animals, the elephant and hippopotamus for example, would certainly qualify as monsters to a European, unaccustomed to animals of such size. These very tales proved that somebody had penetrated Africa below Cape Bojador, and brought back information. Indeed, there were not a few portolanos, or old mariners' charts, which mapped the continent of Africa, but the trouble was that they disagreed very materially with one another. Some made the coast of Africa turn eastward about as it actually does along the shores of Guinea, but without the renewal of the southward trend thereafter. Others prolonged Africa indefinitely southward, whether from Cape Bojador or from the bend in the Gulf of Guinea. Still others showed Africa approximately as it is. And yet these larger phases of unknown geography were a mere bagatelle in comparison with other obstacles. There were the perils of uncharted seas, the inferior character of the cockleshell boats of that day, the dreaded scurvy and other diseases, and, not least of all, the supernatural evils which to the people of that day were facts, not fancy.

The correct measure of these various difficulties is to be found in the years of persistent effort on the part of Prince Henry to attain to any success at all, even to the extent of getting his boats beyond Cape Bojador, which was not passed until 1434, after nineteen years of effort! Meanwhile, he had to encounter tremendous opposition in Portugal, where the people objected to the vast cost of his operations in lives lost and treasure expended, merely in pursuit of a whim of the "Mad Prince," as they called him. It was more than a quarter of a century after the expedition to Ceuta when at last the tide turned in his favor. In 1441, one of his ships brought back some natives from the coast of Africa. This seemingly insignificant incident was in fact a matter of great account, because it opened the way for profitable voyages henceforth, since the natives who might be captured could be sold in Europe as slaves. Thus, curiously enough, one of the foundations for the eventual discovery of America was the institution of slavery. It may be said, in passing, that other captains had been ordered to seize African natives, but Antam Gonçalvez, the commander of the voyage of 1441, was the first to succeed in the attempt.

From this time forward, Prince Henry met with continuous good fortune. The voyages became a source of prosperity for Portugal, and the undertaking was engaged in with enthusiasm, carrying the exploration well around the greater part of the bend of the Guinea coast during the lifetime of Prince Henry, no longer the "Mad Prince," but generally praised and beloved. As the years went on, Henry had laid aside much of his original motive, and accepted the situation for what it was actually turning out to be: an opportunity for Portugal to enlarge her sphere of influence, along a route which might at length take his countrymen to the wealth of the East. In 1460, he died—died at the height of his glory, just as his ships were rounding the coast of Guinea to the east, with what seemed to be every prospect of continuing in the same direction to India. Perhaps it was well for him that he did not live to know that the coast of Africa was soon to turn discouragingly south!

The successors of Prince Henry continued his projects, but it was not until the time of John II (1481–1495) that they were pushed with vigor. Toward the close of the fifteenth century, rumors of the almost forgotten Prester John were revived. Travelers returning from the East said they had heard there was a Christian kingdom south of Egypt. John II now resolved to settle the question of Prester John and the route to India. Agents were sent to Egypt, and a sea-expedition was equipped under Bartholomeu Dias, who was ordered to keep on going until he assured himself whether there was a route to India or not. In 1486, Dias made his great voyage. And he did sail on—on until he had rounded the Cape of Good Hope and sailed far enough up the eastern coast to feel reasonably sure that Africa would not disappoint the Portuguese again. His reports were confirmed by the information obtained by the men who went to Egypt. So there *was* a route to India. And what of Prester John? It proved that there was a Christian kingdom, too, but not of a character to fire the imagination over its wealth and power; it was the Nestorian Christian land of Abyssinia, in the mountains of northeastern Africa, out of the channels of any lively European intercourse, as it has remained ever since.[1]

[1] It is doubtful if it was this comparatively unimportant region which gave rise to the many legends of Prester John. Much more likely India was meant,

Into this boiling caldron of Portuguese interest in routes to India and nautical matters came Christopher Columbus, probably in 1471, and resided in Portuguese territory until 1485.[1] Who was this Columbus? The answer is not quite so easy as it might appear, for the origins and early life of this man are shrouded in obscurity. The usual story is that he was a native of Italy, born near Genoa, of a family given to seafaring, and himself a sailor.[2] At any rate, for nearly fourteen years he was in Portugal, then the focal point not only for the great maritime expeditions of those times but also for knowledge of navigation and the kindred branches of learning, such as geography and cosmography. Much of the time Columbus lived on the Island of Porto Santo, one of the Madeira group, directly in the current of the discussions and gossip about sea-routes and other maritime affairs. Columbus himself made a number of voyages in Portuguese ships, and gained some familiarity with navigation and the related sciences. There was much conversation in those days about lands to the west across the seas, and there were even some maps showing islands beyond the range of definitely located regions. Many sailors claimed they had been on voyages which reached the islands of the west.[3] By this time, too, whatever may

where the priesthood and ceremonial of Buddhism had at least a superficial resemblance to Christianity. González de Clavijo, ambassador of Henry the Pallid of Castile to the court of Tamerlane in Central Asia, 1403–1406, mentioned rumors of a great Christian kingdom to the south. At any rate, Prester John, fact or myth, was an important influence in the background of the discovery of America.

[1] Like so many other incidents in the career of Columbus, there is a controversy concerning the length of his stay in Portugal. One account makes it 1477 to 1484. The dates given here are from the monumental life of the mariner by Thacher.

[2] One of the more interesting stories of the origins of Columbus makes him a Spaniard, born in Galicia of a family of Jewish converts to Christianity. On this account, because the possession of Jewish blood was an irreparable stigma in those days, and also because his father had been involved in some questionable financial transactions, so the story goes, Columbus never revealed the secret of his birth. Another account has recently appeared which makes Columbus a Catalan. Much evidence is adduced in support of these contentions, but it is not sufficiently conclusive to overcome the argument favoring Italy as the birthplace of the discoverer of America.

[3] A curious story has made its way into print to the effect that one of these early navigators actually reached the western continent, stopping at Porto Santo Island, where Columbus lived, on the return to Europe. There he met Columbus, and told him his story, whereupon Columbus murdered him, and pursued his course thereafter in full knowledge that the lands he sought really existed!

Christopher Columbus

have been the popular opinion as to the flatness of the world, men with some knowledge of science realized that it was in fact spherical in shape. The general belief of these men was that the world was much smaller than it is, wherefore a comparatively short stretch of sea must exist between western Europe and eastern Asia.

Columbus shared these views, according to the usual story, and conceived the plan of reaching "the Indies," or, in other words, Asia, by sailing due west, instead of along the route which the Portuguese had been developing since the days of Prince Henry. Other accounts hold that Columbus expected merely to find new lands. Nevertheless, when eventually he made his great voyage he carried a letter to the Great Khan of Cathay from the Catholic Kings, and he himself always believed he had reached Asia. At length he sought backing for his project at the Portuguese court, and it is somewhat remarkable that he got a hearing, both because the idea sounded altogether chimerical to the average unscientific-minded person of that period, and also because Columbus himself was a man whose personal influence, training, and even experience in navigation were not such as to demand attention. The able John II gave him an audience, however, and referred his petition to a council. When the council advised against the plan, John called in yet another council, which sustained the action of the first. Still undecided, John sent out a boat of his own to test the theories of Columbus. After a long voyage without result, this expedition returned, and John dropped the project. At any rate, it seemed as if the Portuguese were about to succeed with the route they were following, and there appeared to be no good reason why any further expenditures should be undertaken for the somewhat novel scheme of Columbus.

Disgusted with the treatment he had received at the Portuguese court, Columbus now made his way to Spain. The concluding campaigns in the war of reconquest against the Moslems were at this time taking place. Ever since 1481 the Catholic Kings had been engaged in a conflict against Granada which was in fact to continue until 1492. On this account the Spanish monarchs were in the habit of holding their court in Seville, the conveniently located great city of the south. To Seville went Columbus. It would have been difficult to find a less informed court, as far as nautical science and related matters were concerned, than that of Ferdinand and Isabella. To most men the project of Columbus seemed as fatuous as a journey to the moon, and possibly much less interesting. Nevertheless, the remarkable persuasive powers of this persistent man at length made converts to his views. Among them was the Italian banker Juanoto Berardi, who took Columbus into his home and presented him to important persons at the royal court.[1] Regarded at first with indifference or disdain, Columbus at length won the support of the royal accountant Alonso de Quintanilla, who brought him to the attention of the powerful Cardinal Mendoza, and he in turn presented Columbus to the Catholic Kings. A committee of learned men reviewed the plans of Columbus, and pronounced them impossible, but Columbus and his friends, for he had now obtained a considerable following, gained a fresh hearing before another body of men which included several Dominican friars. This time, the decision was favorable, and along with it went, henceforth, the ardent support of the Dominicans for the project of Columbus.

Impressed by the decision, the Catholic Kings promised to take action upon it as soon as the war with Granada should be concluded. This was in 1486. Columbus was satisfied, and even took part in the campaigns. The war, however, was to continue almost six years more. So, at length, Columbus tired of waiting and returned to Seville. He now found a new patron in the great Count (later Duke) of Medinaceli, who agreed to bear the costs of the expedition, but when Isabella heard of it she insisted upon handling the matter herself. Negotiations were resumed, but were broken off, not because of any lukewarmness on the

[1] An American woman, making use of the materials in the Columbian Library (Biblioteca Colombina) attached to the cathedral of Seville, has identified the house in which Columbus lived as the guest of Berardi at what is now Abades 6, or, to put it into English style, 6 Abades Street. This house, despite changes from time to time, appears to have had a continuous existence. Juan de Ribera, a prominent churchman of the late sixteenth century, canonized in the eighteenth century, was born there. In recent years it has served as a pension, or boarding-house.

part of Isabella, but because of the excessive demands of Columbus. At a time when the Catholic Kings were upholding the principle of absolutism in reducing outstanding elements in the peninsula to their control, Columbus asked for powers over such lands as he might discover as would give the Spanish crown only a very attenuated authority over him; for example, he wished to hold the rank of admiral, viceroy, and governor in perpetuity, in full charge of affairs of state. Despite the demands of the Spanish monarchs, Columbus refused to recede from this position, showing himself to be as stubborn and unyielding in this question as he was to be later in persisting with a voyage which others regarded as hopeless.

Columbus now thought of seeking the backing of other European courts. In 1488, he had sent his brother Bartholomew to England, but with no success.[1] He himself now prepared to go to France, and set out for Huelva, meaning to take passage there. On his way he chanced to stop at the convent of La Rábida, of which the father superior was a certain Juan Pérez, a former confessor of Isabella.[2] In course of conversations Columbus convinced Pérez of the truth of his views, and the latter urged him to wait until he could make one more effort to obtain the support of Isabella. Columbus consented, and a letter was despatched. While awaiting an answer, Columbus formed other connections in the neighborhood, in particular agreeing with Martín Alonso Pinzón of Palos to share with him such honors as the queen might grant, in return for Pinzón's promise to finance the voyage. Isabella's reply was most encouraging. So Columbus set out for Santa Fe, where the Spanish army was then encamped before the walls of Granada. Once again there were difficulties over terms, but at length Isabella accepted the conditions of the obstinate Genoese.[3] It seems now that

[1] Again the historians differ as to the date of Bartholomew's mission to England, but Thacher quite definitely makes it 1488.

[2] Another story has Columbus meeting Father Pérez at La Rábida when he left Portugal, intending at that time to go to France, but being dissuaded by Pérez. The version given here, taken from Thacher, is probably correct.

[3] The story that the negotiations of Columbus and Isabella were held up because of the poverty of the Castilian crown and that the queen and her ladies solved the problem by pawning their jewels is taken from another incident of those times, when this was indeed done in order to raise funds for the expensive siege of Baza. The amount of money required to finance the voyage

Columbus regretted the contract with Pinzón, and endeavored to evade it. But Pinzón had the support of the sailing men of that section, upon whom Columbus was obliged to rely, and a fresh stumblingblock in the way of the enterprise seemed about to develop. In this emergency Father Pérez again came to the fore. He brought the two men together, and a new contract was drawn up between them, the exact terms of which are not known. One feature, however, was that Pinzón consented to supply enough money to build larger ships than those originally contemplated, and it may well be that this was a factor of no little importance in the eventual success of the voyage.

With the backing henceforth of Pinzón, preparations went on rapidly and satisfactorily. The boats employed, if larger than they would have been, but for the intervention of Pinzón, were small enough in all conscience. The "Pinta" and "Niña" were respectively of fifty and forty tons' burden. That of the "Santa María," the flagship, has been variously estimated, but may have been of about 120 tons.[1] At length, on August 3, 1492, the ships left Palos, and the great voyage began. Columbus was aboard the "Santa María," with Juan de la Cosa as master of ship. Martín Alonso Pinzón commanded the "Pinta," and Vicente Yáñez Pinzón the "Niña." A stop was made at the Canary Islands, and then they turned west. Details of the voyage may be omitted. On October 12, 1492, the island of Guanahani—or "San Salvador" in Spanish, probably the modern Watling Island of the Bahama group—was discovered. The natives were referred to by Columbus as "Indians," because he believed he had reached the then known Indies, or Asia. The term became fixed, and indeed the Spaniards for the next three

of Columbus was a comparatively small affair and not a serious issue. The Spanish rulers gambled a penny, and won a billion. Never did so small an investment give greater returns.

[1] It is difficult for the non-seafaring person even to imagine the smallness of these boats. Modern ferryboats, with a tonnage of two to three thousand, are comparative dreadnaughts in size. A close comparison would be the tiny "Gjoa" on the Cliff House Beach at San Francisco, the seventy-eight ton craft in which Roald Amundsen sailed from sea to sea around the north of North America. To be sure, the boats of Columbus may have been somewhat larger than indicated in the figures given here, which were used in the reproduction of the little fleet, after thorough study by qualified experts, for the World's Fair at Chicago in 1893. Other figures are 140 for the "Pinta," 100 for the "Niña," and 100 to 280 for the "Santa María."

centuries called the western world the "Indies" far more often than the "Americas." On October 27, Cuba was sighted, and the little fleet ran eastward along the northern shore, coming on November 19 to Haiti, or Española, as the Spaniards called it.[1] All this time they were searching for gold, which they had expected to find in large quantities, but in this they were disappointed. Nay more, on Christmas Day they lost the "Santa María," which ran aground and was wrecked. So it was decided to leave some of the sailors behind and return to Spain. A colony of forty-four persons was founded at Navidad (a Spanish word for the nativity, or Christmas), near the present-day Cap Haitien in northwestern Haiti, and the others set sail for Spain. Not one of the forty-four men was ever seen again.

The voyage back was not without its drama. With Pinzón still commanding the "Pinta," and Columbus on the "Niña," the two boats went in company from January 16, 1493, when they left Navidad, until February 13, when they were separated by a storm. Columbus reached the mainland at Lisbon in Portugal, and there met his one-time friend John II again. Some of the Portuguese nobles were anything but friendly, however. When Columbus told his story it seemed that he had in one voyage made his way to that Asia which the Portuguese had failed to reach in nearly a century of effort, and Spain was to reap the advantage to which the Portuguese felt that they were most entitled. Quite possibly Columbus and all his crew might have been put to death, but for two factors. For one thing it was pointed out that the "Pinta" might yet get back to Spain, and then the Portuguese action would have availed nothing. For another, and this was the more important of the two, John II on this occasion played the part of a true sportsman,

[1] The name of this island and the eastern of the two present-day republics in it, with its capital city, has presented numerous complications. The whole island may be called Haiti (which is also the name of the western republic), or Española, or its Latinized equivalent Hispaniola, or Santo Domingo. Santo Domingo is also the name of the capital city of the eastern republic, but the republic is not, and never was, "Santo Domingo," and certainly not the barbarous "*San* Domingo," but has been since 1844 the Dominican Republic. Here the term Española is used for the colonial period as the name for the whole island, changing to Haiti (in accord with actual practice) in the republican era. Where a distinction is necessary, prior to 1844, the eastern section may be called eastern Española, or Spanish Haiti.

and would not countenance any such treatment of Columbus. He recognized that Columbus had given the Portuguese the first opportunity and they had not accepted it. So, admitting the error, he chose to receive Columbus with honors. Proceeding at length, on March 15 Columbus entered the port of Palos. And on that same day Pinzón in the "Pinta" also arrived.[1]

In some of its immediate objects the expedition appeared to have been a failure. It brought back little of the expected material wealth, and it had not in fact reached Asia. Even though Columbus thought he had done so, there were many, including the Catholic Kings themselves, who doubted it; certainly the primitive peoples he described bore very little resemblance to the traditionally rich and cultivated inhabitants of China and Japan. Nevertheless, the importance of the voyage was recognized. Whatever were the lands Columbus had visited, lands they were, and presumably of continental proportions. So the Catholic Kings made haste to secure their claims.

A Spaniard, Alexander VI, now occupied the papal throne, and he was quite willing to aid the Catholic Kings. In a series of papal bulls of the year 1493 he granted to Spain all lands she might discover beyond a line from pole to pole a hundred leagues west of the Azores Islands. Not satisfied with this decision, the Portuguese king negotiated directly with Spain, and reached an agreement in the treaty of Tordesillas of 1494. The effect of this treaty was to divide the undiscovered world between the two countries. Eager to include the allegedly rich "Spice Islands," or the Moluccas, in her portion, Spain held out successfully for a line of longitude which would be much farther west in the Atlantic than the pope had suggested, obtaining an agreement for a point 370 leagues west of the Cape Verde Islands. The result was in the nature of a historical boomerang. The extension of the line did not bring the Moluccas within the Spanish sphere of interest, although for a time Spain oc-

[1] In 1913 the writer had occasion to visit the United States consulate in Huelva. In the absence of the consul, he was received by the clerk of the consulate, who was, quite appropriately as it seemed in an American consulate, Martín Alonso Pinzón! This Pinzón, by his own account, was probably a connection, possibly a direct descendant, of the famous companion of Columbus.

cupied some of those islands, but it did give Portugal a claim to the vast and immeasurably important Brazil, which projects into the Atlantic much farther to the east than do the eastern shores of North America. This was to be a prominent factor in making a considerable portion of the western world Portuguese-speaking rather than Spanish.

Meanwhile, Spain was active in following up the initial discovery. Columbus, who had been received with honors and confirmed in his titles of admiral and viceroy, was sent out on a second expedition in 1493. He now discovered numerous other islands of the West Indies, including Puerto Rico and Jamaica, and after sailing several hundred miles along the southern coast of Cuba convinced himself that it really was the fabled mainland region of China, or perhaps Japan, with the Strait of Malacca some distance beyond. He even compelled his crews to make a declaration to the same effect, threatening them with chastisement unless they should do so. In course of this voyage, late in 1493, Columbus founded a settlement in Española, and arranged for the founding of others.

As the affairs of the colony did not get on any too well, Columbus returned to Spain in 1496, and was sent out a third time in 1498. On July 31, he discovered the island of Trinidad. The next day he recorded the discovery of "another island." For some two weeks he ran along the coast of this new land, by which time he had come to the conclusion that it was a "new world." He wrote the Catholic Kings that he had found the Earthly Paradise at the end of the East, by the four rivers of Genesis which proceeded from the Tree of Life. He had in fact touched the coast of South America, in the vicinity of the mouth of the Orinoco. This was a continent the geographers had not expected to find. North America was not "new," because that was in the position of the Asia they had believed they would reach, but there was no precedent in the tales of Marco Polo and others for a continent in the position of South America. That, then, was the "New World," which by extension included the North American continent when it became clear that Asia was far to the west.

The colony in Española, meanwhile, was still experiencing

great difficulties. In 1496, Bartholomew Columbus had founded Santo Domingo, a site which has been occupied ever since, and which therefore takes rank as the oldest continuous European settlement in the Americas. The Spaniards were now finding out what thousands of others have had to learn, from time immemorial before and since, that European establishments in new lands, far away from bases of supply, not only do not easily attain to prosperity, but may also have a hard struggle for existence. It was to take the English more than a century to found a single successful colony in the Americas. The Spaniards had either more ability or more luck, but in these early years probably did not recognize their lot as one of any particular good fortune. At any rate, there were serious hardships in Santo Domingo and much dissension, with many charges against Columbus and his brothers on account of their rigorous and allegedly unjust government. This decided the Catholic Kings, or perhaps it might better be said gave them an excuse, to strip Columbus of many of the powers they had contracted to accord him. He was relieved of his command in 1500, and the new governor, Francisco de Bobadilla, arrested him, his brother Bartholomew, and his son Diego, put them in irons, and sent them to Spain.

This treatment was harsher than the Catholic Kings were willing to sanction. So Columbus was received at court, and over the years 1502–1504 was in charge of a fourth and, as it proved, last expedition. This time he was ordered to continue his voyage westward until he should come to the real India, just recently reached in the Portuguese voyage of 1497–1499 of Vasco da Gama. Spain wished to share in the enormous profits of the trade with the East. It must be admitted that Columbus made a worthy effort. He at length reached North America along the coast of Honduras, which fitted in with his views that he was on the eastern Asiatic shore, and so he ran down to Panama, where he expected to find the Strait of Malacca. Of course, the strait did not materialize, and after enduring terrible hardships he was obliged to return to Spain. Now broken in health, stripped of his honors, and generally discredited, because he had not reached India and because the lands he had discovered were poorer than had been anticipated, Columbus faded into obscurity, and on May 20, 1506, he died at Valladolid. His family was presently accorded great honors, but never anything approximating what had been promised to Columbus.

Whatever Portugal and Spain may have agreed upon, and papal bulls to the contrary notwithstanding, the other countries of Europe were not disposed to let the two of the Iberian Peninsula have matters to themselves. The discovery by Columbus seemed to represent a new marvel in an easy route to the long dreamed of and greatly magnified wealth of the Indies—of Asia, that is. The story need not be told in any detail here. England sent out the two Cabots, John and Sebastian. Portugal, despite the treaty of Tordesillas, sent Gaspar and Miguel Corte Real in voyages to the North American coast. Somewhat later, France sponsored the expedition of Giovanni Verrazano. These were but a few out of the many. France and England, not recognizing the Spanish claim under the papal bulls, nevertheless submitted to it in so far as it covered already occupied lands, and therefore sought territories to the north of the West Indies. Portugal eventually found her proper sphere in Brazil.

Among the most noteworthy of these voyages was *one which was never made.* An Italian, named Amerigo Vespucci, who appears in fact to have shipped obscurely on voyages of 1499, 1500, and 1501 which touched the coasts of South America, wrote accounts claiming to have headed expeditions which had discovered the "New World," antedating the Columbian voyage of 1498 in his pretended achievement. These stories were published, and caused Martin Waldseemüller, a German geographer, to suggest the name "America" for the new lands. Oddly enough, the name held. Thus was the altogether more appropriate name of Columbus passed over, forgotten also when the now United States achieved her independence, and not employed until Bolívar made use of it for the great Spanish American republic he designed, and adopted later in the nineteenth century by the one-time New Granada for its present-day designation under the name of Colombia.[1]

[1] It is unfortunate that the Anglo-American patriots of '76 did not think

Spain was the most active in following up the initial discoveries. Within a generation after 1492 Spaniards had overrun the West Indies, and explored the mainland from Florida to the Río de la Plata. In 1513, Vasco Núñez de Balboa crossed Panama and discovered the Pacific Ocean. By this time it was becoming more and more clear that the Americas were not Asia, but an obstruction in the way of the route thereto. It is a curious fact, however, that many of the old ideas persisted, and none more so than that based upon the Strait of Malacca. When that was not found at Panama it was sought elsewhere, and long after the Asiatic idea of the Americas had been dropped, that of the strait remained. New names, indeed, began to be applied, such as the Northwest Passage, by English navigators, and the Strait of Anián by the Spaniards in their search along the western coasts of the American continents. In 1520 Magellan found a strait almost at the southern end of South America, the one which bears his name, but a waterway farther north was desired. For more than two centuries the Spaniards chased the Strait of Anián to the north. In 1728, a Russian voyage under Vitus Bering discovered the strait which bears this navigator's name, but this was as much to the north as that of Magellan was south, and was even more impracticable, to say nothing of the fact that the Spaniards did not learn of the existence even of Bering Strait until a long time after its discovery. This fiction of a practicable waterway through the continent, with wealthy kingdoms and fabulously rich cities along its banks, became a *fact* of importance in its influence upon actual explorations.

of the name Columbia, or at least of some distinctive name, by which to call the country which now carries on under the awkward appellation of the United States of America, which is really no name at all. The country is not America and the people are not Americans any more than the lands and peoples of other parts of the Western Hemisphere. And, to say nothing of the fact that there are numerous other countries whose full title includes the words "United States," the phrase itself is an awkward neuter plural which often has to be used in the singular and even in the feminine, and if one is to avoid "American," to which Hispanic Americans insist the people of this country have no exclusive right, or the cumbersome and somewhat inaccurate "North American," often used in Hispanic American countries, the term "United States" must needs be used as an adjective. "Anglo-American," as distinct from "Hispanic American," is perhaps correct, but deprives the people of the United States of their separate identity.

The voyage of Magellan was of especial importance, not so much because of the strait he found, as because he settled the question of the position of the Americas with reference to Asia. Ferdinand Magellan—or Fernão de Magalhães, to give him his Portuguese name—was a Portuguese noble, long attached to the court at Lisbon, who had also spent some years in the Portuguese service in the Far East. There he developed the idea that the Spice Islands might be reached by sailing west across the Atlantic. Returning to Portugal, he eventually had an interview with King Manuel (1495–1521) "the Fortunate." Whether he broached his plan at that time is not certainly known, but he did ask for an increase in his annual court stipend. Research has shown that he wanted the equivalent of *twenty-six cents a month more*, but Manuel refused his request. As a result of the saving of this slight sum (although its real value in purchasing power was, of course, much more than the same amount today) Portugal lost the credit for an achievement which is generally reckoned as, without doubt, the greatest in maritime annals.

Magellan went to Spain, like Columbus before him. There he took out naturalization papers, and in course of time petitioned the king for an opportunity to try out his project, asserting that he could prove that the rich Spice Islands were Spanish territory under the terms of the treaty of Tordesillas. Despite great opposition, not least of which was the determined efforts of the Portuguese to prevent the expedition, Charles I gave him the authorization and assistance he required.

On September 10, 1519, the little fleet of five vessels, with perhaps 268 men, set sail. The boats ranged in tonnage from seventy-five to 120 tons, but only one of the five, the "Victoria," of eighty-five tons, was to complete the great voyage, around the entire world for the first time in history, and back to Spain again. The initial great test of Magellan came at the port of San Julián in Patagonia (southern Argentina), where the fleet spent the Antarctic winter, from March to August 1520. There he had to cope with a mutiny, led by a number of his officers, some of whom may have been hired previously by Portuguese agents to attempt this very thing. Three of the five ships were soon in the hands of the mutineers. By a bold maneuver Magellan got possession of one of the three, and compelled the others to surrender. One of the leaders, who had previously been killed in the conflict, and another, whom Magellan caused to be executed, were drawn and quartered. A little later, another officer and a priest were marooned, after they were caught attempting to stir up a fresh mutiny. Thereafter Magellan had no difficulties on this score.

Before Magellan got under way again, one of his ships was wrecked. The other four entered the strait, which later was to bear Magellan's name, on October 21, 1520. Then for thirty-eight days, amidst almost overwhelming difficulties, they followed the devious windings of the strait. The largest boat of the four deserted before this part of the voyage was over. At length, to their great relief, the Spaniards came out upon a calm and open sea. After the terrible gales which they had been experiencing, it is not to be wondered at that they gave the name "Pacific" to the ocean before them, a name very far from being deserved in all parts of its waters, and one which postdated that of the "South Sea," which Balboa had given seven years earlier. Yet Magellan's name was eventually adopted.

Going northward along the Chilean coast, Magellan and his men turned northwest on December 16 at about the fiftieth parallel. It was thirty-nine days before they saw land again—a small uninhabited island of the Paumotu group. Eleven days later, they came to another uninhabited and foodless island in the Manahikis. Then for thirty days, sailing along a route which on the map appears to be studded with hundreds of islands, they did not make land again until they reached Guam in the Ladrones Islands. This was in some respects the most terrible part of the voyage, especially as concerned the state of their rations, which were

> "of biscuit which was no longer biscuit, but powder of biscuits swarming with worms, for they had eaten the good. It stank strongly of the urine of rats. We drank yellow water that had been putrid for many days . . . and ate some ox hides that covered the top of the mainyard . . . Rats were sold for half a ducat apiece, and even then we could not get them."

So spoke Pigafetta, one of those who made the voyage, and its most famous chronicler.

After refreshing themselves a few days at Guam, they went on to the Philippines, which they first touched at Samar Island on March 16, 1521. Twelve days later, on the 28th, they came upon some natives who could understand the language of Magellan's Malaccan slave. This proved that they were in Asiatic waters. The rest of the story may quickly be passed in review. Magellan himself was killed on April 26, when he rashly engaged in a battle in support of one group of Philippine natives against another. The survivors abandoned one of their vessels, and made their way to the Spice Islands, or Moluccas, in the south. There, indeed, they got a rich cargo, but the larger of the two vessels was now so full of leaks as to be unseaworthy. The remaining ship, the "Victoria," was placed in command of Juan Sebastián del Cano (often rendered "El Cano" or "Elcano"), and after many trials and tribulations it cast anchor at Seville on September 8, 1522, almost three years to a day from the time the expedition had left San Lúcar. Only eighteen Europeans were still on board. A few others of the original party, not to mention those who had deserted in the Strait of Magellan, eventually found their way back, too, but the great majority had given their lives in the enterprise. And yet the cargo of the "Victoria" more than paid the costs of the expedition, if finances alone are considered.

The voyage of Magellan, supplemented by the voyages of earlier navigators, gave the Spaniards a fair idea of the Atlantic coasts of the two Americas, and definitively proved them a new world—not Asia. It remained to do something with the territories they had discovered. The vital beginning had already been made in the West Indies. By 1513, there were already seventeen Spanish settlements in Española, and one of them, the city of Santo Domingo, had a population of fifteen hundred inhabitants. And this was *Spain* doing all this, a country without previous experience of great moment in over-seas colonization! Ponce de León began a conquest of Puerto Rico in 1508, founding San Juan in 1511. Jamaica was soon occupied, with the first settlement there dating from 1509. Velázquez invaded Cuba in 1511, and founded Santiago in 1514 and Havana in the next year. The significance of these conquests can hardly be overstated. The West Indies are a valuable domain in themselves, but they are infinitely more important as the key to both Americas; they were then, and have remained so ever since. They were the doorway to the narrow Isthmus of Panama, and served as the base from which the Spaniards proceeded to the conquest of the greater part of North and South America.

The real marvel of the eventual conquest, however, was, not so much that Spain made it, as that she had had the chance to do so. Spain, under the able Catholic Kings, was indeed ready to accomplish great things in the world, but it was the mere accident of Columbus which turned her in the direction of what was to prove the most important Spanish contribution to history. Portugal produced Prince Henry; Prince Henry, Columbus; and Columbus gave a vast portion of the Americas to Spanish civilization.

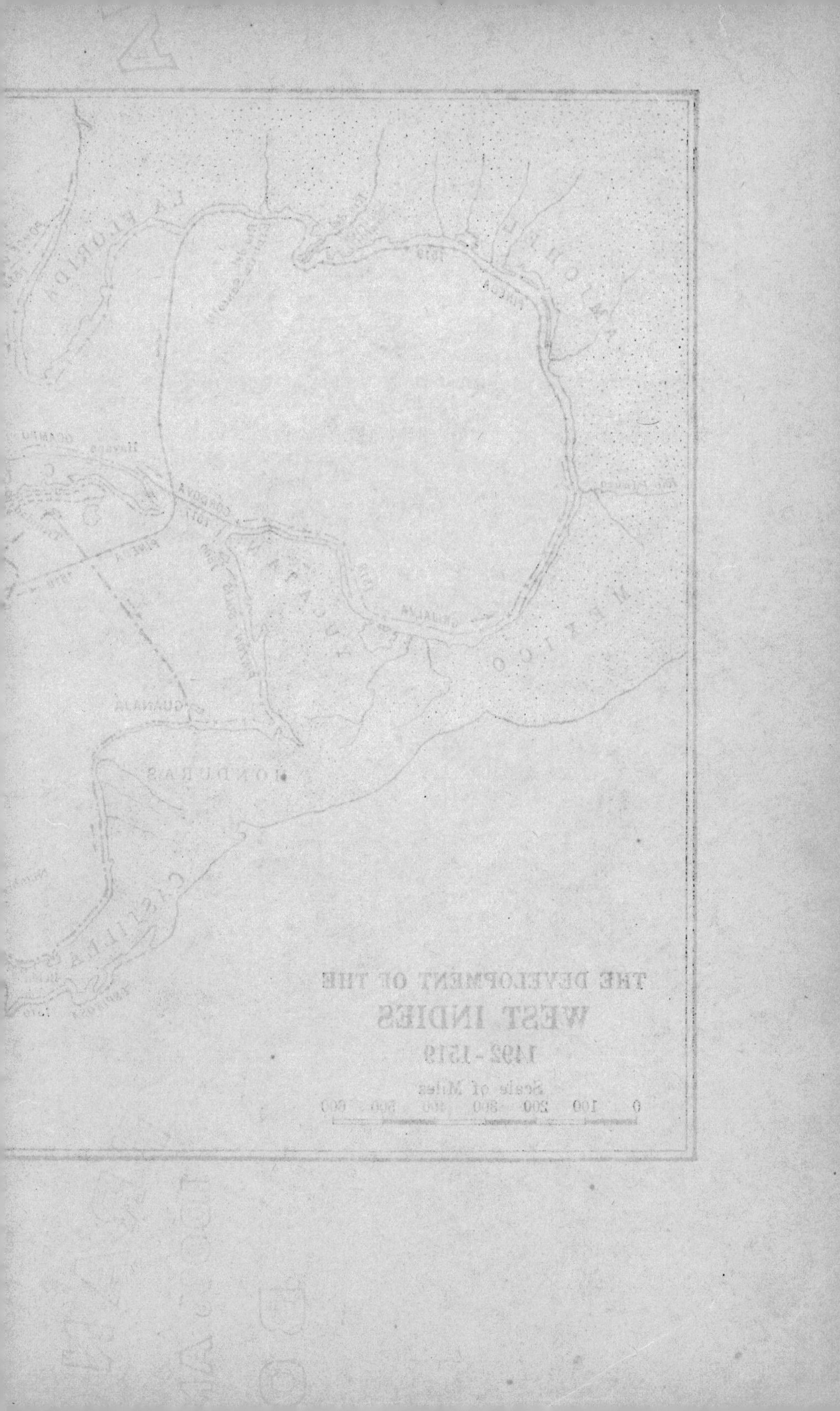

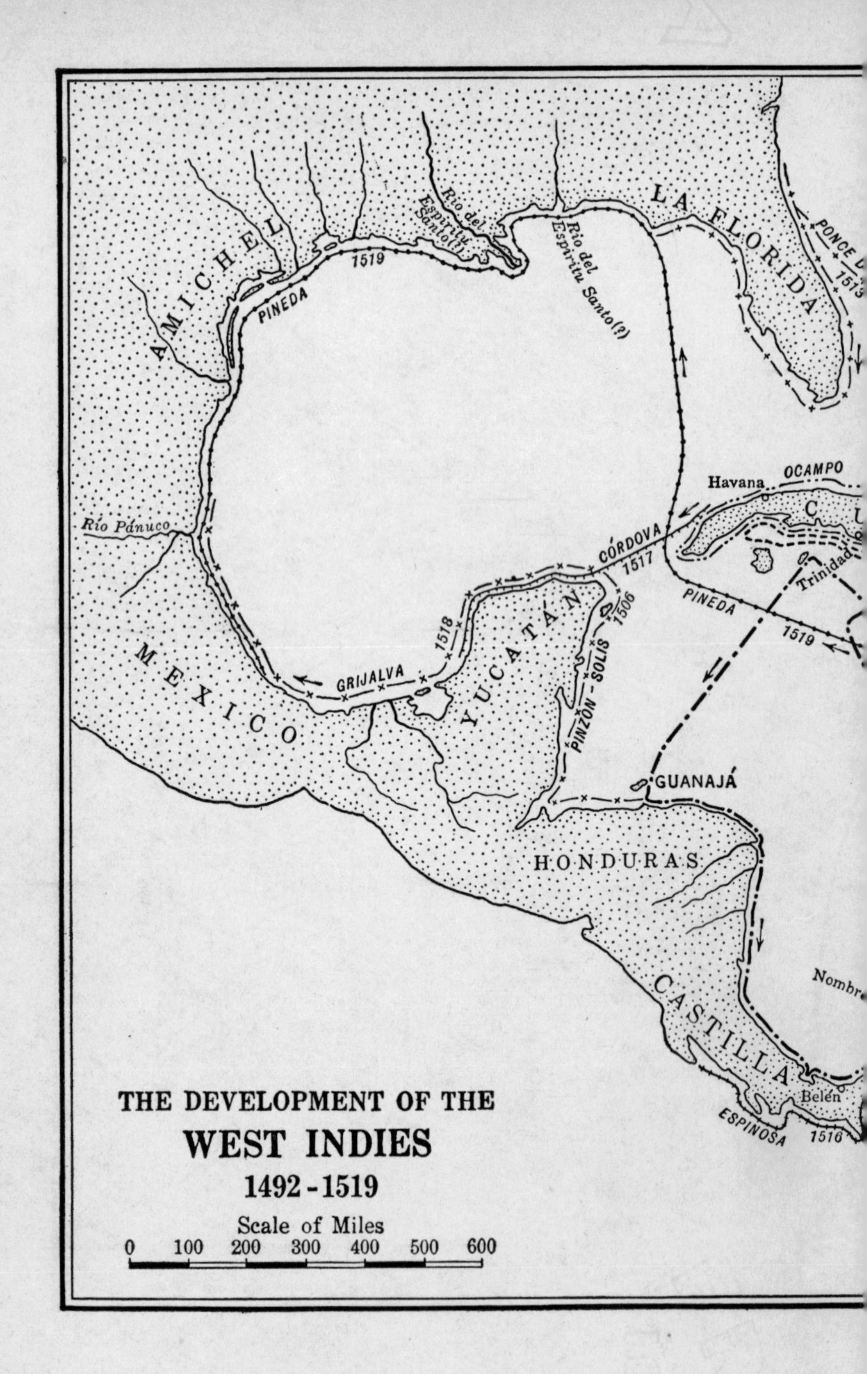
AMICHEL
PINEDA
1519
Rio del Espiritu Santo(?)
Rio del Espiritu Santo(?)
LA FLORIDA
Havana
OCAMPO
Rio Panuco
CÓRDOVA
1517
Trinidad
PINEDA
1519
1506
YUCATAN
1518
PINZON - SOLIS
MEXICO
GRIJALVA
GUANAJA
HONDURAS
CASTILLA
Belén
ESPINOSA
1516
THE DEVELOPMENT OF THE
WEST INDIES
1492 - 1519
Scale of Miles
0 100 200 300 400 500 600

LUCAYAS
U D I E N C I A
COLUMBUS 1492
COLUMBUS 1498
COLUMBUS 1505
Espiritus
Camagüey,
P. del Principe
Baracoa
Navidad
Monte Cristi
Isabela
La Plata
Santiago
S. Buenaventura
Arecibo
San Juan
Bayamo
Bonao
ESPAÑOLA
Aguado
PUERTO
RICO
Guanica
Guadianillo
COLUMBUS 1493
GUADALOUPE I.
DOMINICA
MARTINICA
SANTA LUCÍA
Santiago
O F.
Vera Paz
Azua
Higuey
Santa Maria
Melilla
Santo Domingo
COLUMBUS 1502
Oristan
JAMAICA
1509
COLUMBUS 1498
E S P A Ñ O L A
GRANADA
TABAGO
TRINIDAD
PEARL COAST
OJEDA 1499
1500
BASTIDAS
OJEDA-NICUESA
TIERRA FIRME
U R A B A
Cruz
Acla
San Sebastian
Darien
NUEVA ANDALUCÍA
EL ORO
VESPUCIUS 1504
MANHATTAN DRAFTING CO., INC. N.Y.

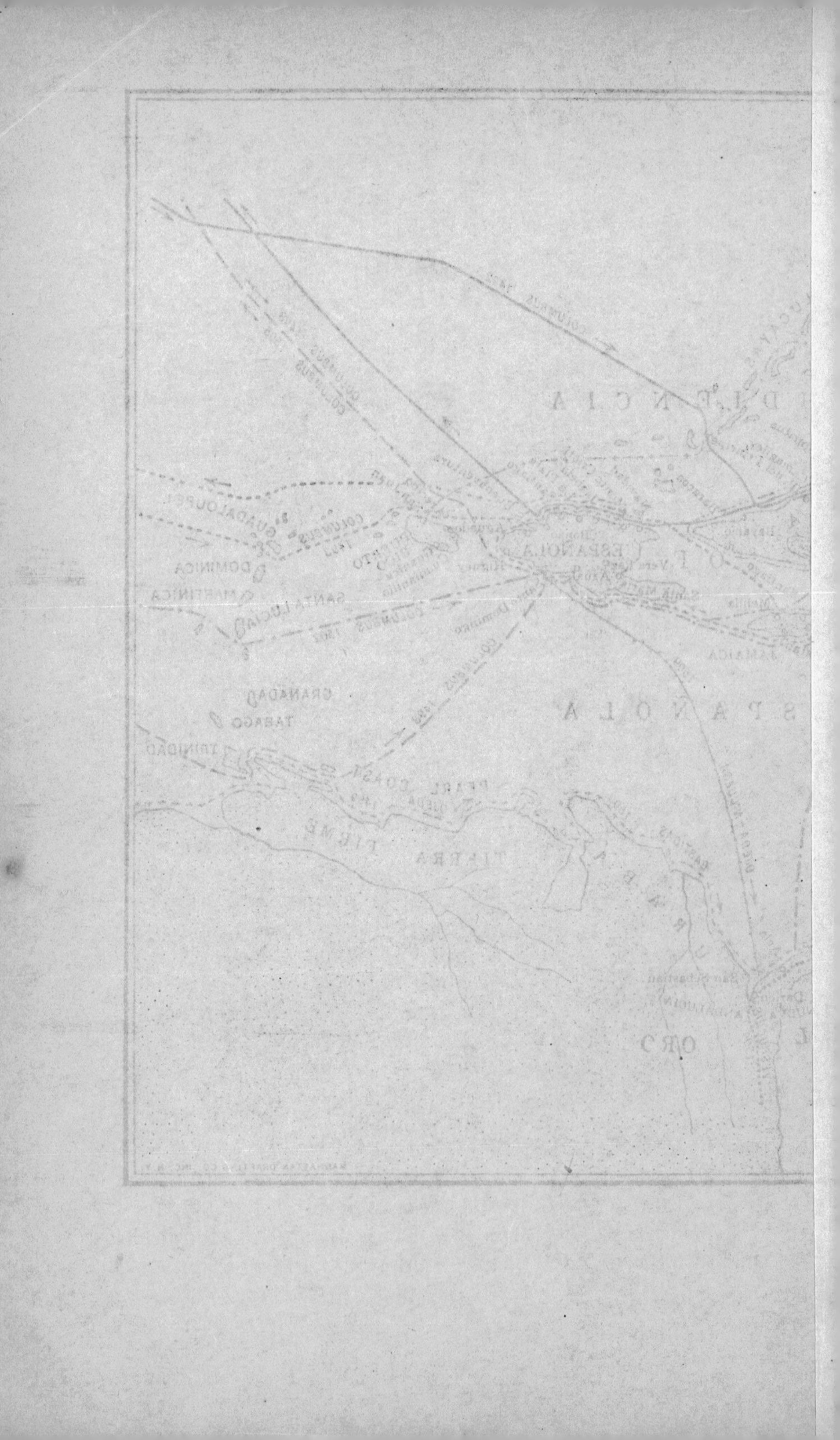

CHAPTER II

SPANISH COLONIAL INSTITUTIONS IN THE WEST INDIES, 1492–1517

WITH the founding of the first Spanish colonies in the Americas, new social, political, economic, and (remotely) intellectual institutions inevitably made their appearance. At length there developed a "Spanish colonial system," but this was by no means ready with the initial establishments, and was always a matter of growth, though along lines which were recognizably in keeping with Spanish thought and experience. The greatest contribution of the Spaniards was, of course, themselves, with all that might imply, including their Spanish speech. Over against them were the Indians, and one of the first problems to be confronted was that of relations with the conquered natives.

It was the custom of those days to consider barbarous non-European peoples as fit subjects for reduction to slavery, or some form of serfdom at the very least, and it is therefore not to be wondered at that Columbus on his first voyage brought back some Indians with him as slaves. But the Catholic Kings, more particularly Isabella, were inclined to a different policy, and gave Columbus instructions on his second voyage to effect the conversion of the Indians to the faith, always treating them kindly, however, and chastising whomsoever might be unjust to them. Nevertheless, Columbus again brought back slaves. A royal decision declared them free, and ordered them returned home.

The legal freedom of the Indians was availing them little at this time in Española, however. While Columbus was still in Española in the course of his second voyage—that is to say, in what is now the Dominican part of that island, where the Spanish establishments were—he had engaged in active warfare against the Indians. Unable to resist Spanish firearms, and terrified by the unfamiliar horses of the Spaniards and especially by their dogs, which "could kill a hundred Indians an hour," the natives submitted. Impossible terms were imposed upon them, such as *per capita* contributions in gold at stated intervals. Some chiefs asked to be allowed to give a portion of their crops instead, but Columbus, eager to prove his insistent reports about the wealth of these lands in precious metals, refused their petitions. A war, whose only issue for the Indians was extermination or slavery, followed.

Under Bobadilla a beginning was made of the system of *repartimiento* (apportionment), whereby the Indians were divided among the colonists. In theory the main objective of the laws was that the Indians might thereby be Christianized and civilized, but in fact its principal feature was that they were made to serve as slaves in the fields and mines. Sent out to succeed Bobadilla in 1502, Father Nicolás de Ovando received instructions in which there appears a note of inconsistency. The Indians were to be regarded as legally free and to be treated with kindness, *but* they were to be employed (with appropriate wages to be sure) in mining for gold, one-half of which was to go to the crown; they were to be made to live together in villages; and they were to be prohibited from bathing too often, "because this did them much harm." Furthermore, in the case of cannibal Indians away from the settlements and those who resisted indoctrination in the Catholic faith and subjection to the king, authorization was given for them to be taken prisoners and made slaves. This was an entering wedge for many abuses by the colonists, under the urge of economic necessity for cheap labor. They were successful, however, in obtaining still further sanction in royal law for enslaving the Indians. Complaints were made that the Indians would not work, not even for pay, wherefore it was impossible to "attract them to our holy Catholic faith." Perhaps the settlers understood the efficacy of religious appeal to the pious Isabella. At any rate, back came the royal order to compel the Indians to work on buildings, in mines, and in other necessary ways, though paying them wages and "treating them as free persons, which they are, and not like slaves."

This and similar enactments of the Spanish monarchs might lead one to accuse them of hypocrisy, but there seems to be no reasonable doubt of the sincerity of Isabella and her successors in their frequently expressed desire for the welfare of the Indians. The difficulty arose from the fact that they were also eager for the colonies to yield a profit to the royal coffers, or at least to be self-supporting. Their financial and their humanitarian interests proved to be inconsistent, with the result that the latter frequently gave way to the former. In consequence, as already set forth, the enslavement of the Indians was usually the most prominent feature of those arrangements whereby the Spanish settlers exercised control over large groups of the native population, ostensibly in order to Christianize and civilize them. Simpson points out that Isabella's main regard for the Indians was with respect to the fate of their souls in the hereafter. Proceeding, he has this to say:

"Isabella was an eminently practical, as well as a pious, woman. Her consent to the establishment of the encomienda [1] in the New World proves that. If the encomienda had not been economically sound it could hardly have endured for two and a half centuries. It is also difficult to avoid the conclusion that Isabella licensed and even encouraged Indian slavery, and profited by it. With a stroke of the pen she could have suppressed the traffic at any time. There is little likelihood that such a thought ever occurred to her. She acted in consonance with the practices of her day. She belonged to the Middle Ages. The soul was still the important matter. Provided that the soul was saved, the fate of the body was of little consequence, and it might as well be turned to some account by those who had been instrumental in saving the better part—and who needed the money very badly." [2]

The first seven years of Ferdinand's rule, after the death of Isabella in 1504, were, as Simpson puts it, "a dismal and sordid time for natives and colonists." According to him:

"Without the piety of Isabella to modify the dictates of necessity, the Indian policy of the Spanish Crown was simplicity itself: get money, by fair means if possible, but get it! In the royal orders the conversion of the Indians was usually mentioned as a matter of form, but with much less emphasis than under Isabella. On the other hand, no end of instructions

[1] The *encomienda,* like the *repartimiento,* was a system whereby the Indians gave their services or paid tribute to the whites. For definitions of these terms, see *infra,* 111–112.

[2] Simpson, 33.

were showered on the governors in the more urgent business of increasing the revenue." [1]

And again:

> "These seven years of Ferdinand's unrestricted exploitation of the Indies were such a hideous time that it would require a Las Casas or a Sir Arthur Helps to do justice to its description." [2]

As might have been expected, the above-mentioned royal order of Isabella enabled Ovando to return to the *repartimiento*, and this measure was approved by Ferdinand in 1508, although once again with verbal reservations. From this time forward for the next few years, the enslavement of the Indians went on apace in those islands of the West Indies already reduced to Spanish control, and along with it a quickly mounting death rate, necessitating the importation of natives from neighboring regions not yet conquered. Furthermore, the birth rate declined. The laws authorized the Spaniards to take children from their parents, the better to instruct them in matters of the faith, and encouragement was given the settlers to marry native women, with the idea of promoting the fusion of the two races and the advancement of the colonies, but in many cases the Indian women went to extremes in resisting these measures. Often they did indeed bear children, but killed them when they were born!

Much has been written concerning the cruelty of the Spaniards, both in these early settlements of the West Indies, and in their mainland conquests later on, and by none has it been asserted more than by contemporary Spaniards of those times. Unquestionably there was cruelty, but probably not more than would have been the case with any people in their position in that or any other period of history.[3] Indians required to work in the mines had to leave their families for six or eight months at a time, entailing serious burdens for the women left at home, as well as for the men in the mines. This was a harsh measure in itself, but (apart from scattered instances of specific cruelties) there was certainly no desire to bring about the death of valuable

[1] Simpson, 34.
[2] *Ibid.*, 47.
[3] For a discussion of the question of Spanish "cruelty," see *infra*, 112–114.

laborers. They passed away, however, not only on account of the conditions of work to which they were not accustomed, but also and more especially because of their very contact with the white race. It has been proved many times since then, that even the simplest diseases of white men may be fatal to people of other races. Something of this sort took place in the island colonies, with the result that the Indians were rapidly swept away. Quite apparently the problem of relations with the Indians was in no satisfactory condition, from whatever angle it might be approached.

The gentle and pious recommendations of the laws were not, however, the sole defence the Indians had. Prominent among the churchmen who had gone to the West Indies to assist in the work of Christianization were the Dominican friars, who first came to Santo Domingo in 1510. They publicly denounced the settlers for maltreating the Indians, and even refused religious services to those who had reduced them to slavery. At length a certain Bartolomé de Las Casas, who had been a civilian settler in 1502 and had later taken holy orders, placed himself at the head of the Dominican movement on behalf of the Indians. Going to Spain in 1515, he sought aid from Ferdinand without success, but in the following year he gained the support of Cardinal Cisneros, who was acting as regent until the heir to the throne, Charles, might come from Flanders to receive the crown. Las Casas was formally appointed Protector of the Indians. His every step was opposed, however, and the enemies of his policies found powerful support at the Spanish court. Even the Franciscans, who were also being employed in the over-seas colonies, favored the point of view of the civilians that the *repartimientos* were necessary. So it was many years before the activities of Las Casas began to have any effect, and they were too late as far as the Indians of the West Indies were concerned. There the Indian race virtually disappeared.

Quite early, however, a substitute was obtained. Royal instructions of 1501 authorized the Spaniards to supply the deficiency in Indian labor by introducing negro slaves from Africa. Eventually Las Casas and the other Dominicans not only did not oppose this measure but even gave it support. It must be remembered that the institution of slavery was generally accepted in those days, and negroes were looked upon as "natural slaves." Thus was the evil of Indian enslavement mitigated by the introduction of what proved to be a yet worse evil. An intermixture of the white race with the red might have worked out well, and in some places has done so, notably in Chile, but the addition of the black race has everywhere raised up difficult social problems without sufficiently counter-balancing advantages. This, however, could not have been foreseen.

Some mention has already been made of the excessive powers granted to Columbus by the Catholic Kings in the contract of Sante Fe, directly contrary to the absolutist policies being followed in Spain itself. The discoveries turned out to be of far greater importance, from the standpoint of the areas involved, than the tiny groups of islands it had been expected he might find, and it was soon recognized that a nearly all-powerful Columbus in the vast territories of the West might even vie with the Catholic Kings themselves. So the monarchs seized such occasions as offered as might permit them to diminish the authority they had bound themselves to give. One of the most important steps was taken when Bobadilla was sent out to investigate the complaints being made by the settlers against Columbus, with the result that the latter was deposed as governor. To be sure, the Catholic Kings disavowed the acts of Bobadilla. Nevertheless, they sent Ovando as their own governor to succeed him, though allowing Columbus to have a representative in the colonies to watch out for his interests. This was not unlike their legislation on behalf of the "freedom" of the Indians! In 1509 Diego Columbus, son of the great navigator, was appointed governor, not as hereditary ruler in accord with the contract of his father, but merely at the will of the king. The will of the king lasted in this instance just two years! In numerous other ways Ferdinand and his successors took steps which were not consistent with the letter or spirit of the original contract, despite the objections of Diego Columbus, who brought suit against the crown on behalf of his rights. The case continued until 1536, when a compromise was reached which was agreed to by both sides, Charles I (the Emperor Charles V) and Luis Columbus, son of Diego. The virtual effect was the abandonment by the family of Columbus of their claims in America in return for a rich pension and the hereditary title for the head of the house of Duke of Veragua.[1]

Almost from the first moments of the discovery, the Catholic Kings began to take steps with regard to the organization of the government and the economic exploitation of the new lands, and with these objects in mind they made every effort to obtain such information as they could concerning the Western world. Instructions were issued to each sailing-master and government official sent out to the Indies to draw up detailed reports of what he saw, as well in the uninhabited regions as in those which were occupied. Thus began that vast accumulation of diaries, reports, and extended descriptions which were to become one of the greatest marvels ever known in the way of archival information.[2] Finding that a single agent, such as they had at first employed, could not handle the tremendous amount of business involved in matters connected with the colonies overseas, the Catholic Kings presently devised new machinery. In 1503 the *Casa de Contratación* (House of Trade) was founded, with duties which were administrative and scientific as well as economic. It was to store in its warehouses all merchandise destined for the Americas or received therefrom, and was to preside over the purchase, sale, and shipment of goods in this trade. Later, questions concerning emigration to the Indies and the charter of boats were placed under its charge. And, like many other Spanish administrative bodies, it had its own law courts, with jurisdiction in matters peculiar to its purposes. On the technical side, pilots, cosmographers, and other experts were attached to the *Casa*. For example, there was the famous map-maker Juan de la Cosa; another was Vicente Yáñez Pinzón,

[1] The descendants of Columbus became grandees of Spain as Dukes of Veragua, so named for one of the mainland regions in Central America discovered by Columbus. In 1912 to 1914, when the writer resided in Spain, the family was one of the most widely known in the Peninsula, but for a reason quite unconnected with the exploits of its founder. The then Duke of Veragua was famous as a breeder of the Veragua bulls, among the best of those used for the bull-fight! It is said that the present holder of the title no longer engages in this industry.

[2] Cf. *infra*, 383–384.

one of the companions of Columbus in his first voyage; and even Amerigo Vespucci (1508–1512) was one of them. Instruction of the pilots who were to make the voyages to the Indies and the preparation and preservation of maps of the new discoveries were among the functions of these men.

From the outset great care was taken to see that none but Spaniards should go to the new settlements, the better to ensure their domination politically and economically. Spanish emigration was encouraged, and in this period included a number of criminals, who were pardoned on condition that they should go to the Indies. Administratively, the Spanish municipal system was transported to the colonies, and became the basis later for the rule of vast areas. A so-called Council of the Indies existed in this period, but its activities did not become of great importance until the period of mainland conquest began.[1] And religion was not forgotten. To the Catholic Kings, Pope Alexander VI in 1501 granted the "royal patronage" (*real patronato*) in the Americas in perpetuity, in consequence of which church appointments in the colonies were to be made by the royal authorities. In return the Spanish monarchs agreed to convert the conquered peoples and pay the expenses of the church. It goes without saying that this gave a vast ecclesiastical power to the crown in the colonies, with important effects, too, centuries later, in the period of the Spanish American republics.

The original economic interest in the trans-Atlantic lands was the discovery of great wealth, especially in precious metals, linked with the somewhat fantastic religious object of employing it for the reconquest of the Holy Sepulchre and in other ways for the spread of Christianity. When it became clear that the New World territories were not the expected rich lands of Asia, the royal government took charge of religious propaganda, and economic affairs had an independent development of their own. Mineral wealth continued to be a prime concern, with special attention to

[1] Many dates are given for the founding of the Council of the Indies. Some writers make it 1511, or even 1493, while others range as late as the latter part of the reign of Charles I. The writer believes that 1524 is the most appropriate date, for in that year this body began to function in an important way, at least approximating its eventual greatness.

satisfaction of the demands of the treasury. Mines were declared to be the property of the crown, but were allowed to be exploited by private individuals on terms of payment ranging from half the product in the initial stages of the work to one-third of it later on. Although the precious metals found in the island conquests were almost insignificant in comparison with those discovered on the mainland afterward, they nevertheless yielded a not inconsiderable revenue. Occasionally the finds were truly spectacular, as witness the case of a gold nugget worth 3600 *pesos*, found by an Indian woman, who exchanged it for a piece of pork.

Mineral wealth was by no means the sole royal economic interest in the Americas, however. Revenues could be derived from the colonies in other ways, and in any event there was a genuine desire, for a variety of reasons, to bring about the development of the colonies. As early as 1493 the royal instructions directed that the majority of the settlers should devote themselves to agriculture, and at different times farm laborers, gardeners, and even experts in irrigation were sent over in order to bring about an advancement in the cultivation of the soil. The *Casa de Contratación* frequently forwarded seeds and plants, as well as implements to be used in farming. In this way wheat, barley, rice, sugar, oranges, lemons, olives, grapes, and other Spanish agricultural products were introduced to the over-seas colonies. In like manner, domestic animals hitherto unknown in the Western Hemisphere were brought over by the Spaniards, such as horses, asses, cows, goats, and sheep. The first cattle were shipped to the Spanish settlements in Española in 1494. A generation later they were already abundant there. Carpenters, masons, and, in short, all the machinery of normal life, whether connected with mining or not, were included in the consignments of men and commodities sent across the ocean from the earliest days of the Spanish occupation.

Economic considerations proved to be a matter of outstanding importance as affecting the racial character of the Spanish colonies. Restrictions were placed upon trade by foreigners, who were required to have Spanish associates in any commerce in which they might engage, and, as already mentioned, were forbidden to go to the Spanish settlements themselves. In consequence they were unable to compete with Spaniards. Furthermore, only a limited number of Spaniards were allowed to participate in the trade, which at the outset was confined to long established residents of the three Andalusian cities of Seville, Cádiz, and Jerez. This was due in part to the fact that the Americas were regarded as having been conquered by the kingdom of Castile, to which Andalusia belonged. To a great degree, however, it was an administrative measure, whereby this commerce could be much more conveniently managed by the *Casa de Contratación*, and the king's revenues the more certainly collected, if handled at a few points instead of many. Seville and Cádiz became the only ports at which goods could be laden or discharged. Thus, even other subjects of Castile and other cities of the kingdom were excluded from the traffic. Quite naturally it became easier for Andalusian "Castilians" to make the voyage across the Atlantic and take the lead, in numbers at least, among the settlers of the New World. And so there developed a distinctly Andalusian tinge to the Spanish civilization in the Americas.[1]

[1] A recent study by Luis Rubio gives clear proof of the early Andalusian influence in Spanish America. In the first hundred years following the discovery, from 1492 to 1592, a total of 7976 persons went from Spain to the Indies, with the following distribution according to land of origin:

Region	Number	Region	Number
Andalusia	1915	Murcia	51
Aragon	48	Navarre	18
Asturias	50	Valencia	55
Balearic Is.	4	Vizcaya	97
Castile and León	1797	Portugal	41
Catalonia	27	Foreigners	33
Extremadura	601	Unknown	3084
Galicia	48		
		Total	7976

Rubio calls attention to the fact that the difference in favor of Andalusia is really greater than it appears. The figures for Castile and León are really for three greater provincial regions, New Castile, Old Castile, and León, and (although the editor does not say so) perhaps also for Álava and Guipúzcoa. The figures included 1115 religious (friars, Jesuits) and 289 priests, but the former were listed according to the convent from which they came, although many were natives of Andalusia and other parts of Spain. Thus, Castile was credited with 715 religious. The above information is taken from *Pasajeros a Indias*, ed. by Luis Rubio y Moreno, I (Madrid [1930?]), 41, in *Colección de documentos inéditos para la historia de Hispano-América*.

The writer would add that probably the great bulk of the "Unknown" group came from Andalusia, from whose ports the entire traffic was handled. Furthermore, the neighboring region of Extremadura, which furnished 601

The Andalusian character of Spanish colonization is a matter which cannot be too greatly emphasized. The Andalusian Spaniards gave not only their pronunciation, with its sibilant "s" for "c" before "e" or "i," instead of the soft "th" of Castilian speech, but also their racial traits to the New World colonies. That meant that the most Moslem-blooded people of Spain, with their gaiety, comparative lack of responsibility, their chance-taking recklessness and aversion to any ideal of a lifetime of toil, with, in fine, their thoroughly Arabic individualism, were to be set down in a land where their own will was to be law, where their whims were commands to the thousands of Indians and negroes, who in one degree or another became subject to them. Even the Portuguese colonization of Brazil, out of Lisbon, was much more Moslem-blooded than would have been the case with the more northerly peoples of the Iberian Peninsula. Gradually, to be sure, these northerners did sift into the colonies, and many were the individuals of Basque, Catalan, and Galician descent who were prominent in the New World, but they did not change the language or the underlying character of the people across the seas. Hispanic America, with much more opportunity for freedom of expression than had ever been the case in the home countries, became a land *par excellence* of individualism run rampant. Individualism became the social keynote. Delightful as it was in many of its aspects, it was a problem fraught with evil when at length it was to find its way into the political life of the modern republics.

Yet other Spanish institutional features had at least mild beginnings in the initial period, but they became established more solidly in the era of the mainland conquest, and may be reserved, therefore, for consideration later.

of the settlers, had a recognizably close connection with the life of Andalusia. Very likely, too, many of those registered from other provinces were residents of Andalusia. The Moslem-blooded character of Murcia, Valencia, and Portugal may also be noted.

CHAPTER III

THE EARLY CONQUISTADORES: CORTÉS AND PIZARRO

Favored by the limited territorial reach of the islands of the West Indies and the weakness of their adversaries, the Spaniards had made a rapid conquest in the Caribbean, and with the advantage of position and their island settlements as a base, they now proceeded to the mainland. The region of Panama was early acquired. From that strategic point the conquest spread out, fanlike, over much of North America and almost to the farthest extremity of the southern continent. In the sixteenth century, before the English were able to establish so much as a single successful colony, the Spaniards traversed almost the full extent of those lands which have remained Spanish American, together with other territories now part of the United States. Their expeditions and conquests were so far-reaching, so spectacular, and withal so romantic, however material their aims, and the men who made them were so remarkable for their audacity, courage, physical endurance, patience in misfortune, and unfailingly optimistic hopes, that some distinctive characterization has seemed to be necessary to set off this period from the more prosaic ages. Hence it has become customary to refer to it as the "era of the *conquistadores*," using the Spanish word for "conquerors" to lend flavor to the expression. The *conquistadores*, in the name of Spain, sought wealth for themselves—easy wealth, sudden wealth, fabulous wealth. The unknown lands of the Americas were the "stock market" of Spanish hopes, to which, however, they gave of their effort and very lifeblood infinitely more than the general run of swivel-chair fortune seekers of the present day. And, despite sordidness, violence, almost the full gamut of evil human passions, they left behind them a picture of themselves which is admirable in the main, attractive, and interesting beyond compare.

As early as 1510 the Spaniards had founded settlements in or near the Isthmus of Panama. The central figure here was Vasco Núñez de Balboa, "the fencing master," who came as a stowaway in order to avoid his creditors in Santo Domingo, hiding himself in a barrel of provisions, from which he emerged as soon as the boat had reached the high seas. A man of unusual ability, Balboa soon became the leader in the colony which this expedition founded along the western shore of the Gulf of Urabá, and proceeded to establish friendly relations with the Indians, marrying the daughter of one of the chiefs. Learning that his enemies had gained the ear of the king and that a new governor was to supersede him, Balboa resolved upon an enterprise which might restore him to favor. Thus it was that he undertook his famous expedition of 1513. Making a journey of incredible hardships through the tropical jungle, crossing swamps and rivers, Balboa also encountered native opposition, but defeated the Indian tribesmen, pursued them to their huts, and set the dogs on them. Some forty were killed by the dogs alone. What animals these Spanish dogs must have been! At length he climbed the continental divide, and he, first of all, looked out upon the "South Sea," or Pacific, which was indeed southward from Panama where Balboa beheld it. Balboa now made plans for fresh achievements, and, being confirmed in office by the king, he was in a position to accomplish his aims. The Indians had told him of rich kingdoms to the south, which he intended to explore. Before he could do so, however, he was put to death by his jealous rival in the Isthmus, the septuagenarian Pedrarias Dávila. But for this the exploit of Pizarro might have been antedated by many years. This same Pizarro had been one of the companions of Balboa, and, according to some, he was already dreaming of a conquest of Peru, of which he had heard from an Indian chief.

Very early in their explorations the Spaniards had come upon the highly developed peoples of what is now Mexico, especially the Mayas of Yucatán, and this turned their attention to those coasts, since much more wealth might be obtained from races with a superior culture than from the inferior tribesmen thus far reduced to control. Governor

Diego Velázquez of Cuba eventually decided to send an expedition to establish relations with these rich lands. The man whom he selected to command it was a thirty-four-year-old Spaniard of humble origin, Hernán Cortés, born in 1485 at Medellín in Extremadura. Bold and impetuous, a knightly figure, fond of honors and loving adventure, he was also an exceptional military leader and a born ruler, beyond a doubt the greatest of the *conquistadores* of the sixteenth century. As early as 1504, Cortés had come to Española, and had especially distinguished himself under Velázquez in the conquest of Cuba. Merriman sums up his character in these terms:

> "Calculated audacity formed the basis of it, and, coupled with a truly Napoleonic ability to seize opportunities and to estimate men, furnishes the key to his brilliant successes. Zealous, like all true Spaniards, for the advancement of the faith, determined to effect the subjugation of the Indians, and get possession of their treasures, he shrank from no means to accomplish these ends; yet there are few instances in his whole career in which he was cruel or bloodthirsty without a purpose. In his care for his person and dress, in his passion for gambling, and in the looseness of his relations with women, he was typical of the Spaniard of his day and generation; but he kept business and pleasure rigidly separate, and when he recognized the moment for decisive action, drove forward with a power that refused to be denied. His followers could not resist the magic of his appeal. Under his leadership they attempted and achieved the impossible." [1]

At the last moment, somewhat fearful lest this able young man might deny him obedience, Velázquez issued orders depriving him of his command, but Cortés successfully embarked before he could be stopped. The expedition was a great one for those days, with eleven boats, four hundred Spanish soldiers, two hundred Indians, thirty-two horses, ten cannon, and four culverins.[2] One wonders how many dogs! Nevertheless, it required not only the strength this force represented, plus later reinforcements, and all the

[1] Merriman, III, 460.

[2] It is difficult to determine exact numbers in these early expeditions. The figures given here are taken from Altamira. Merriman says there were only sixteen horses. Others make it eighteen. Exactly how many there were is not greatly material, however.

HERNÁN CORTÉS

extraordinary ability of Cortés, but also astonishingly good luck for the Spaniards to make the conquest they set out to achieve, in such a short time as it actually took them.

The Valley of Mexico was then ruled by one of the most advanced and most powerful native peoples of the Americas, the Aztecs. From at least no later than the eighth century there had been a series of migrations of Nahua peoples from the north into Mexico, culminating in the arrival of the Aztecs, early in the fourteenth century. They had conquered this territory, and instituted a harsh overlordship which at the time of the coming of the Spaniards was especially cruel and oppressive in its sway over the subject races. Burdensome taxes and hated social practices, such as human sacrifice to their insatiable war god, had reached such a stage that the Indians of that part of the world were on the point of revolt. When the Spaniards came, tribe after tribe joined them against the Aztecs, and without this assistance Cortés could not possibly have conquered Mexico with his small force. Further aid developed as a result of the superstitions of the Aztecs themselves. The mythical hero of the subject Nahua races of the valley was Quetzalcoatl, to whom legend attributed a promise to return some day as an avenger of his people. To the Indians whom Cortés and his company met it seemed probable that the Spaniards might be the agents of Quetzalcoatl, the "Fair God" of Nahua traditions. The Aztec rulers themselves credited these stories, and none more so than the weak emperor Montezuma. So it was decided that it would be better to propitiate the bearded white strangers with gifts, rather than attack them, as a few desired, for the Spaniards were *tehules*, or supernatural beings, not to be opposed.

Meanwhile Cortés had embarked upon his campaign in 1519. Early in the voyage he rescued a Spaniard named Aguilar, who had been shipwrecked along those coasts eight years before, and who had learned the Maya tongue. Landing in Yucatán, Cortés defeated the Indians in battle, and received a gift of twenty Indian maidens as a tribute from them. One of these proved to be an Aztec slave named

Marina, an intelligent young woman who knew both the Maya and Nahua tongues. Without her aid and that of Aguilar, who interpreted her communications, Cortés and his companions would probably have perished before ever reaching Mexico. Proceeding along the coast, Cortés landed at what is now Vera Cruz. It was here that he received rich gifts from Montezuma, principally gold, together with the request that he should desist from advancing farther. But gold in hand and glowing accounts, in this case justified, of the wealth of the interior were poor arguments to drive away Cortés. On the contrary, he made up his mind to effect a conquest or die in the attempt. Some of his men were not so resolute, however, and were disposed to mutiny against him, whereupon Cortés won their forced allegiance by destroying his boats. They must now survive or perish in the dangerous undertaking of Cortés.

Establishing himself on the mainland, Cortés soon learned of the real situation in Mexico, and planned to avail himself of the heterogeneous elements in opposition to the Aztecs. At length he set out on his march to the capital, following the route of the modern railway from Vera Cruz, up, up, and up, until he reached the plateau of Anáhuac. There he fought a battle with the powerful Tlascalans, enemies of the Aztecs. The cannon fire of the Spaniards was too much for the men of Tlascala, who decided to ally themselves with these "messengers from the Sun" as against the hated Aztecs. Arrived at the sacred town of Cholula, centre of the cult of Quetzalcoatl and an ally of the Aztecs, Cortés was received with an appearance of cordiality and even veneration, but plans were in fact made to destroy him and his army by treachery. Through the astuteness and cleverness of Marina the plot was discovered, and Cortés turned his guns on the natives, slaughtering them by the thousands and burning his prisoners alive, at the same time that he sent messengers to Montezuma pretending friendship. Shortly afterward, the Spaniards came in sight of Mexico City, or Tenochtitlán as it was then called, and gazed in wonderment at this city which seemed to rest on the surface of a lake, with its great towers and buildings of solid masonry.

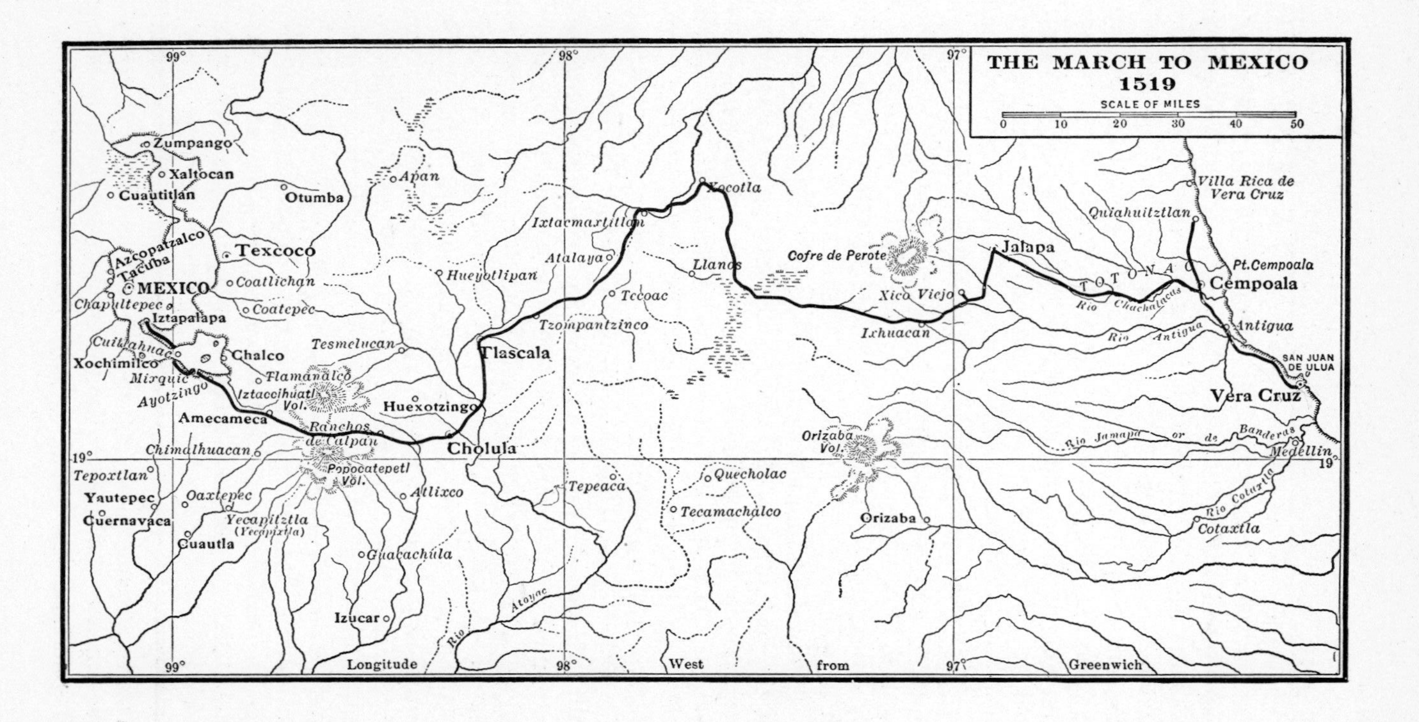
THE MARCH TO MEXICO
1519
SCALE OF MILES
0
10
20
30
40
50
99°
98°
97°
19°
Zumpango
Xaltocan
Cuautitlan
Otumba
Apan
Azcopatzalco
Tacuba
Texcoco
MEXICO
Coatlichan
Chapultepec
Coatepec
Iztapalapa
Cuitlahuac
Xochimilco
Chalco
Mixquic
Ayotzingo
Amecameca
Tesmelucan
Flamanalco
Iztaccihuatl Vol.
Ranchos de Calpan
Huexotzingo
Chimalhuacan
Tepoxtlan
Yautepec
Cuernavaca
Oaxtepec
Popocatepetl Vol.
Yecapitztla
(Yecapixtla)
Cuautla
Atlixco
Guacachula
Izucar
Hueyotlipan
Atalaya
Ixtacmaxtitlan
Xocotla
Tlascala
Tzompantzinco
Tecoac
Llanos
Cholula
Tepeaca
Quecholac
Tecamachalco
Rio Atoyac
Cofre de Perote
Xico Viejo
Ixhuacan
Jalapa
Orizaba Vol.
Orizaba
Quiahuitztlan
Villa Rica de Vera Cruz
Pt.Cempoala
Cempoala
T O T O N A C
Rio Chachalacas
Antigua
Rio Antigua
SAN JUAN DE ULUA
Vera Cruz
Rio Jamapa or de Banderas
Medellin
Rio Cotaxtla
Cotaxtla
Longitude
West
from
Greenwich

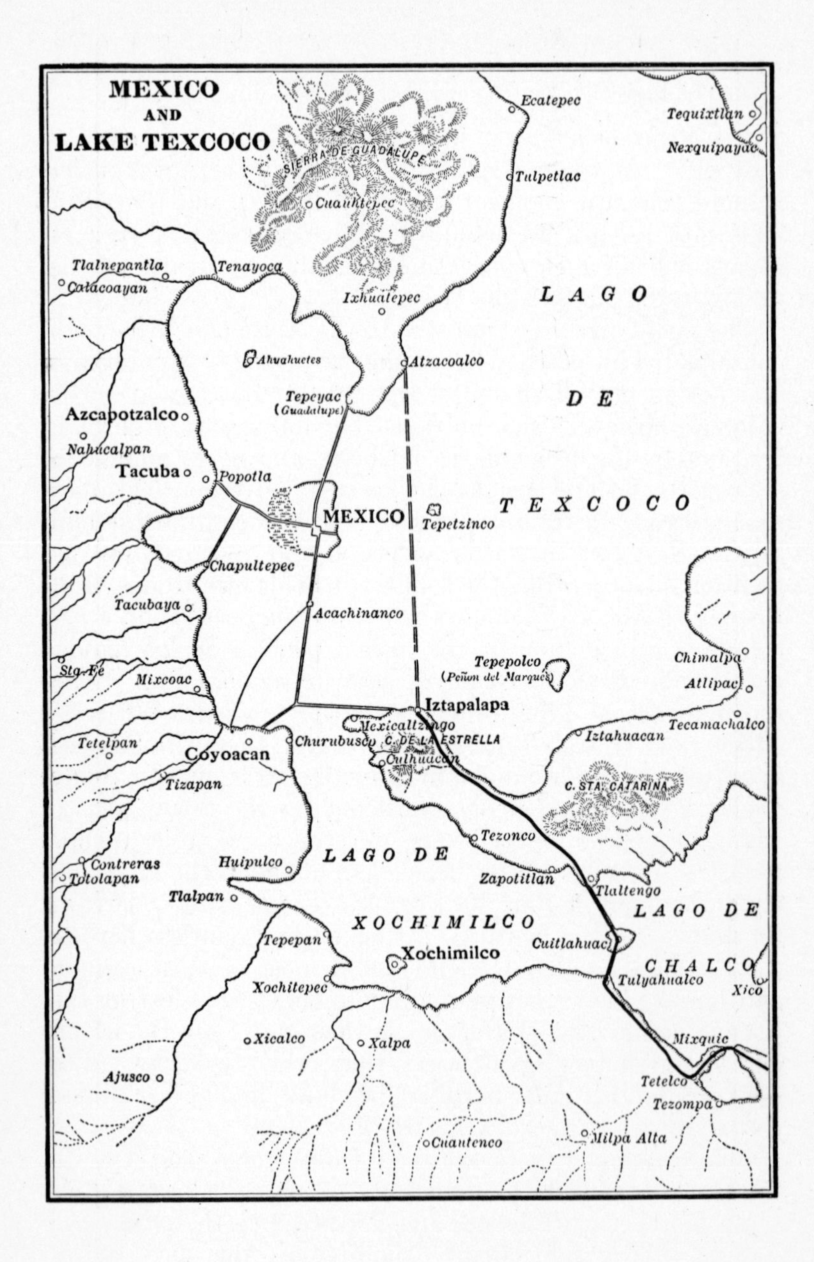
MEXICO
AND
LAKE TEXCOCO
SIERRA DE GUADALUPE
Ecatepec
Tequixtlan
Nexquipayac
Tulpetlac
Cuauhtepec
Tlalnepantla
Tenayoca
Calacoayan
Ixhuatepec
LAGO
Ahuahuetes
Atzacoalco
Tepeyac
(Guadalupe)
DE
Azcapotzalco
Nahucalpan
Tacuba
Popotla
MEXICO
Tepetzinco
TEXCOCO
Chapultepec
Tacubaya
Acachinanco
Tepepolco
(Peñon del Marques)
Chimalpa
Sta. Fe
Mixcoac
Atlipac
Iztapalapa
Mexicaltzingo
Tecamachalco
Tetelpan
Coyoacan
Churubusco
C. DE LA ESTRELLA
Iztahuacan
Culhuacan
Tizapan
C. STA. CATARINA
Tezonco
Contreras
Totolapan
Huipulco
LAGO DE
Zapotitlan
Tlalpan
Tlaltengo
LAGO DE
XOCHIMILCO
Tepepan
Xochimilco
Cuitlahuac
CHALCO
Xochitepec
Tulyahualco
Xico
Xicalco
Xalpa
Mixquic
Ajusco
Tetelco
Tezompa
Cuautenco
Milpa Alta

> "We were astonished," wrote his companion Bernal Díaz, "and told ourselves that this seemed like a thing of enchantment, such as they tell of in the book of Amadís."

Some of the soldiers were in doubt as to whether that which they saw "were not a dream." Certainly there was never a more romantic moment in the history of the Americas. This city seemed to vindicate the extravagant hopes of Cortés and his men concerning the fabulous wealth of the undiscovered lands of the West.

The Spaniards were admitted to the city, and Cortés soon consolidated his position by seizing the person of Montezuma and taking virtual charge of the government himself. His troubles, however, were only just beginning, not at an end. Irritated by the disobedience of Cortés, and all the more so in view of the latter's spectacular success, Governor Velázquez sent a strong force under Pánfilo de Narváez to arrest him as a traitor, but the latter surprised and defeated this expedition, incorporating the soldiery into his own troops. Returning to Mexico City after this campaign, he found a determined insurrection of the native peoples on his hands, with hundreds of thousands up in arms against him. Even the influence of Montezuma no longer availed. When he endeavored to address his people, urging them to obey the Spaniards, he was wounded by a missile hurled at him, dying a few days later, possibly murdered by the Spaniards, to whom he was no longer of any assistance. Unable to cope with the uprising, Cortés decided to abandon the city, and chose the night of June 30, 1520, the "*noche triste*" (sorrowful night), for the venture. Attacked by countless hordes, the Spaniards suffered terribly, and most of their cannon and horses, their treasure and equipment, were lost at the bottom of the lake, as they made their way from the island city to the shore. Nevertheless, they broke through, had to fight yet another great battle a little later, and at last gained the territories of their friends the Tlascalans.

Reinforcements were received from Cuba, and late in 1520, accompanied by thousands of native allies, Cortés again marched on Mexico, and laid siege to the city. The Aztecs, led by the gallant Cuauhtémoc, the successor of Montezuma, resisted desperately until August 1521, when at last the city was taken. There was a bloody sequel, as the Spaniards fought with one another over the spoils. The treasury officials, believing that the Aztecs had concealed a vast amount of gold, caused Cuauhtémoc and one of his nobles to be tortured by burning their hands and feet; but neither would speak, except to say that much gold had been thrown into the lake. Cortés himself at length rescued Cuauhtémoc from his persecutors. His companion died. But the Aztec treasure was never found.[1]

Thus ended the spectacular "conquest of Mexico," which was little more than a conquest of the route from Vera Cruz to the capital. The real conquest of what is now the republic of Mexico, or "New Spain" as the Spaniards called it,[2] was to be a work of many years before the domination of Spain and the implantation of Spanish institutions were measurably complete. They were preceded by a number of great land expeditions of exploration and discovery, paralleling those earlier voyages by sea. The leaders still sought wealth in gold or fabled marvels, but in the wake of their successes or failures came a stream of Spanish settlement, missionaries among the Indians, soldiers and government officials to maintain or increase the conquests, and finally civilians, who in their varied capacities made good the transfer of Spanish civilization.

By 1522 Cortés had completed the conquest of much of the heart and centre of Mexico and reached the Pacific coast. Not content with what he had already achieved, he organized fresh expeditions, hoping to overrun the territory southeast toward Panama and explore the Pacific waters to the north, perhaps finding the strait through the continent, of which so much was said, and possibly another or even richer Mexico. And there *were* such cities, if legend could be believed, especially the Seven Cities of Cíbola and those of the kingdom of Gran Quivira, located—"somewhere in the north." There,

[1] No reader who has a chance to do so should miss the opportunity of reading the account of the conquest by Bernal Díaz del Castillo, a member of the expedition. Numerous other materials are available, but the frankness and narrative qualities of the Bernal Díaz story makes it an almost unique classic among the early chronicles. Cf. *infra*, 362–363.

[2] The name New Spain (Nueva España) was applied in course of the voyage of Grijalva in 1518, on account of a fancied resemblance in the houses of masonry he saw along the coast from Yucatán to Tampico to those of Spain.

rumor had it, one might ride for miles and miles through streets which were paved with gold.

The conquest of Central America was accomplished despite sordid rivalries and internecine strife among the Spaniards themselves. As Merriman has expressed it,

> "The whole story of the occupation of the Central American lands . . . is, in fact, one of the most miserable chapters in the history of the Spanish Empire. It contains no outstanding achievements; it is but a chronicle of jealousy and self-seeking, of sordid scrambling for territory and gold. None of the characters, save possibly Gil Gonzalez, is really attractive . . . Yet no picture of the Spaniards in America would be adequate without it; the infamy of Pedrarias, his rivals and associates, makes the greatness of Cortés stand forth in clearer light. The ranks of the conquistadores contained bad men and good. Courage and persistence were their commonest virtues; brutality and self-seeking their outstanding faults. Sometimes the good qualities so prevailed over the bad ones as to make possible achievements at which the world has not yet ceased to wonder. Sometimes, when the scales were tipped the other way, we marvel that anything was accomplished at all." [1]

The initiative in the conquest of Central America came, not from Cortés in Mexico, but from the Spaniards in Panama, although the former was to have a share in the affair before it was over. Following the execution of Balboa, Pedrarias had in 1519 founded the town of Panama on the Pacific shore of the Isthmus. Later, in 1522, Gil González Dávila got off expeditions to the north, despite the opposition of Pedrarias. A small fleet went as far as Honduras. González himself marched overland across Costa Rica to Nicaragua before returning, and then left in haste for Española, in order to avoid difficulties with Pedrarias. The latter thereupon despatched Francisco Hernández de Córdoba to Nicaragua, hoping to deprive González of his claims. Córdoba founded several towns, among which were Granada and León, both established in 1523, and traditionally leaders and rivals in Nicaragua much of the time ever since. That same year Cortés's lieutenant, Alvarado, came south from Mexico, and overran Guatemala and Salvador. Olid and Las Casas followed in 1524, entering Honduras. Meanwhile,

[1] Merriman, III, 522–523.

also in 1524, González, avoiding the Isthmian territories of Pedrarias, landed on the Atlantic coast shore of Honduras, and advanced to Nicaragua, to take possession of the lands he had previously discovered. Then in 1525 Cortés entered Central America. A further complication developed when Córdoba threw off his allegiance to Pedrarias, and prepared to seize Nicaragua for himself. All Central America was soon like a bag of Kilkenny cats, with conqueror fighting conqueror, and the Indians little more than a side issue in the conflict. In the course of the fighting, Pedrarias surprised Córdoba and put him to death. Deprived of his position in Panama by royal mandate, Pedrarias was nevertheless given the rich post of governor of Nicaragua, and there at length, in 1531, he died at the age of ninety. On the basis that "the good die young," ninety was none too ripe an age for Pedrarias. Merriman calls him "one of the ablest but most repellent figures in the ranks of the conquistadores; proud, selfish, treacherous, and revengeful." [1] Eventually a semblance of order was attained to in Central America, which was made a part of the viceroyalty of New Spain, but directly subject to the *audiencia* [2] of Guatemala.

The Caribbean shores of Mexico were soon compelled to acknowledge Spanish rule, but the advance along the Pacific was considerably delayed. Like Columbus before him, Cortés found that he had powerful enemies and that the royal court itself was disposed to limit, rather than expand, his authority, though heaping him with titles and honors. Antonio de Mendoza became the civilian ruler as viceroy of New Spain, with Cortés remaining commander-in-chief of the army. Various sea expeditions sent out by Cortés explored the Pacific coasts of Mexico. One of them came upon "an island" which the Spaniards had long sought and of which Cortés had written the king in 1524 that it was

> "inhabited only by women without any men, and that at given times men from the mainland visit them; if they conceive, they keep the female children to which they give birth, but the males they throw away. The island is ten days' journey from the province, and . . . is very rich in pearls and gold."

[1] Merriman, III, 522.

[2] The *audiencias* were important judicial and administrative bodies in the Spanish colonies. For a detailed discussion, see *infra*, 134–136.

The "island," first reached in 1533 or 1534, and visited by Cortés himself in 1535, was the peninsula of Baja (or Lower) California, so named from an Amazon island referred to in "Las Sergas de Esplandián," one of the novels of chivalry, a sequel to "Amadís de Gaula." The name in itself is significant of the credulity of the conquerors. Some pearls, indeed, were found, but no Amazons.[1]

The arduous task of northward expansion was stimulated anew by the occurrence of a spectacular event in 1536. In that year out of the north came Álvar Núñez Cabeza de Vaca, a Spaniard who had been a member of a disastrous expedition led by Pánfilo de Narváez to Florida in 1528 and who had for some years been a slave of the Indians on an island off the coast of Texas. He told stories about Gran Quivira and the Seven Cities of Cíbola, which were "only a little beyond" the route he had followed in his journey from Texas. In 1539 the Franciscan Marcos de Niza was sent out to investigate these tales, and actually saw Cíbola, the smallest city of the seven, but "from a distance." To him it had looked to be larger than Mexico City. In the race to take advantage of this information Cortés sponsored yet more voyages, one of which got as far as 29° north latitude on the western coast of Baja California. The greatest expedition of these times, however, was the one sent out by Mendoza, under Francisco Vázquez de Coronado, over the years 1540–1542. This made its way up western Mexico, past the miserable Zuñi villages which Niza had identified as the Seven Cities, and on as far as present-day Kansas in pursuit of the elusive Gran Quivira. In 1542–1543 the heroic Rodríguez Cabrillo and his successor (after the former's death) Ferrelo carried the search for this legendary kingdom and the equally proclaimed and equally elusive Strait of Anián as far north as 42° 30′, just beyond the California line, opposite southern Oregon. The farthest north was attained on March 1, 1543. The account of the voyage at that point makes it perfectly clear why Ferrelo turned back:

[1] In a chapter entitled "Origin and application of the name California" the writer deals with this story in his *A history of California*, 55–69. More recently the name "Californe" of the *Chanson de Roland*, from which the word "California" was derived, has been identified with a Moslem stronghold in North Africa.

"They ran this night February 28 to the west-northwest, with great difficulty, and on Thursday March 1, in the morning, the wind shifted to the southwest with great fury, the seas coming from many directions, causing them great fatigue and breaking over the ships; and as they had no decks, if God had not succored them they could not have escaped. Not being able to lay-to, they were forced to scud northeast toward the land; and now, thinking themselves lost, they commended themselves to Our Lady of Guadalupe and made their vows. Thus they ran until three o'clock in the afternoon, with great fear and travail, because they concluded that they were about to be lost, for they saw many signs that the land was near by, both birds and very green trees, which came from some rivers, although because the weather was very dark and cloudy the land was invisible. At this hour the Mother of God succored them, by the grace of her Son, for a very heavy rain-storm came up from the north which drove them south with fore-sails lowered all night and until sunset the next day; and as there was a high sea from the south it broke every time over the prow and swept over them as over a rock. The wind shifted to the northwest and to the north-northwest with great fury, forcing them to scud to the southeast and east-southeast until Saturday the 3d of March, with a sea so high that they became crazed, and if God and his blessed Mother had not miraculously saved them they could not have escaped . . . With respect to food they also suffered hardship, because they had nothing but damaged biscuit." [1]

And yet these men, sorely beset as they were, were not altogether disillusioned. They believed there was "a very large river" in the vicinity of their farthest north.

Meanwhile, other expeditions had penetrated Florida and the northern shores of the Gulf of Mexico. Most famous of the expeditions in that neighborhood were those of Ponce de León, the discoverer of Florida. One of the objects of his first voyage in 1513 was to find the island of "Bimini," in which there was a marvelous fountain whose waters would rejuvenate all who bathed in or drank of them. Ponce de León advanced the knowledge of the New World, but for himself found, not youth, but a wasted fortune and a fatal wound. Returning from his expedition of 1521, he died shortly afterward in Cuba. But after Ponce de León, came many others, until the whole sweep of what was to be the

[1] "Relation of the voyage of Juan Rodríguez Cabrillo, 1542–1543," in Bolton, *Spanish exploration in the Southwest*, 36–37.

Spanish Empire in North America had become moderately well known and the initial steps of conquest had been taken.[1]

And what of the great *conquistador* Cortés? More and more hindered in his operations, he at length went to Spain, where he was received very coldly by Charles I, who delayed action on the protests of the conqueror for so long that the latter passed away in 1547 before they were resolved. It is said that on one occasion he attempted to get word with the king and approached the footboard of the coach in which Charles was riding. "Who are you?" Charles asked, as if he did not know him. With great dignity Cortés replied: "Sire, I am a man who has gained for you more provinces than your fathers and grandfathers bequeathed you cities!" True or not, the incident might well have happened, given the character of the two men. At any rate, Cortés went to join that great army of others who in the course of history have had to suffer from "the ingratitude of kings."

At the same time that the discovery, exploration, conquest, and settlement of North America were going on, the Spaniards were engaging in similar activities in South America, mainly from Panama as a base. The most spectacular of their conquests, in many respects paralleling the experiences of Cortés in Mexico, came with the expeditions of Francisco Pizarro to Peru.

In Peru the Incas had developed an empire and a civilization comparable to those of the Aztecs and Mayas in Mexico. About the eleventh century they began a conquest which had extended at length from north of Quito in Ecuador as far south as the river Maule in Chile, where the hard-fighting Araucanians had checked them. East and west this vast

[1] The fascinating exploits of the Spaniards within regions now part of the United States are too well known to require detailed mention here. There was, for example, the expedition of Hernando De Soto, the discoverer of the Mississippi in 1541, in whose waters he himself was buried that same year. Over the years 1539 to 1543 the De Soto party made "the most remarkable exploring expedition in the history of North America," north from Florida to the Carolinas, west to the Mississippi and across into Arkansas, and down the Mississippi in small boats and on by sea to Pánuco in Mexico. For courage and persistence in the face of extraordinary perils and hardships, there were few who equaled and none who surpassed the record of De Soto and his companions.

state ran from the coast to, and in places beyond, the Andes, ruled over by a monarch called "the Inca." Extraordinarily well organized, the empire had attained to a wealth which was certain to excite the cupidity of the Spaniards, as soon as they heard of it, and, as already set forth, word did come to the Spaniards in Panama as early as the time of Balboa. The plans of the discoverer of the Pacific were destined to be carried into execution, however, not by himself, but by a one-time comparatively obscure subordinate, Francisco Pizarro.

Francisco Pizarro was at one time almost a neighbor of Cortés, for he was born in 1470 in Trujillo, Extremadura, not far from the town in which Cortés first saw the light.[1] If the ultimate successes of these two men were to be strikingly similar, there was little in the early career of Pizarro which seemed to promise anything out of the ordinary. He was already past fifty when he first embarked upon the project which was to emblazon his name upon the pages of history, and past sixty when the decisive campaign was undertaken. An illegitimate child and brought up in humble circumstances, he was a swineherd in youth, but while still quite young he entered the army. As early as 1509 he came to the Isthmus as a soldier, and, though unable to read or write, attracted the attention of his superiors by his high qualities in other respects. A devotee of military discipline, he had a great capacity for hard work and endurance, indomitable energy, and unswerving perseverance in his tasks. He was a veritable man of steel. Withal, reserved in manner and unostentatious in dress, he was, however, astute and unscrupulous, and, while not addicted to any of the softer vices, was an inveterate gambler, never leaving the tables when he was losing, unless there came a call to arms. Nevertheless, this man, infinitely less educated, less brilliant, and less attractive than Cortés, was one who inspired confidence and knew how to make himself obeyed. Associated with him in his project were two others. One was his inseparable comrade in arms, Diego de Almagro, also of humble birth, past fifty, and illiterate, but a brave soldier,

[1] It is sometimes asserted that Cortés, whose mother's name was Pizarro, was a kinsman of the conqueror of Peru.

FRANCISCO PIZARRO

and of much more impulsive, generous, and likeable traits than Pizarro. The third in the triumvirate was a priest named Hernando de Luque, who had accumulated a considerable fortune and was to serve as the financier of the expeditions.

In 1522 a Spanish expedition reached the northern coast of the present-day republic of Peru, and brought back definite reports of the wealth of the Inca Empire. It was at this point that Pizarro and his companions took up the enterprise. A first expedition, in 1524, was a failure. In 1526 they got as far as the northern province of the Inca Empire, in Ecuador, but were not in sufficient numbers to attempt a landing. So it was decided to send Almagro to Panama for reinforcements, while Pizarro and the rest of the expedition should await their return at Gallo Island, off the coast. Like some of the soldiers of Cortés a few years earlier, so now not a few of those of Pizarro had by this time lost their enthusiasm, and registered their complaints by making Almagro the unwitting bearer of their message; they sent it in a ball of cotton which Almagro delivered to the wife of the governor as a gift of the soldiers. In consequence, two ships were ordered to the rescue, and a command was issued for Pizarro to give up the enterprise. This he refused to do, but gave permission to his soldiers to go back to Panama if they chose. Drawing a line east and west upon the sands, he harangued his men, saying "On this side you can go to Peru and get rich; on that, to Panama, and remain poor. Let every good Castilian choose what he will!" Only thirteen came over to the south side with Pizarro, while the others returned to Panama.

The next seven months was a period of terrible sufferings for Pizarro and his small company, who changed their residence by crossing to another island on a raft. At length came a relief ship, and in this Pizarro cruised southward until he reached the Gulf of Guayaquil, where he and his men saw the rich Inca city of Túmbez, with its aqueducts, temples, and houses of the virgins of the Sun. In yet further explorations Pizarro got together a quantity of gold and silver vases, vicuña blankets, and live llamas as proof of the rich lands he had discovered. Making his way back to

Panama, he was still unable to get aid of the governor, and so it was decided by the three associates that Pizarro should go to Spain to negotiate with the king.

Impressed by the story and the evidences of Pizarro, Charles I granted him authority and assistance for the conquest, and appointed him captain-general of Peru. Lesser honors were accorded Almagro and Luque, despite the promises Pizarro had made to share equally with them in the enterprise. On his way to Seville to prepare his expedition, Pizarro visited his native city of Trujillo, and persuaded his four brothers, Hernando, Gonzalo, and Juan Pizarro, and Francisco Martín de Alcántara, to go with him to Peru. Of the four, only one, Hernando, was of legitimate birth, and he alone had the rudiments of an education. But Hernando was in many respects a disagreeable person. A stout man, with a big red nose, he was excessively proud and haughty, despising the members of the expedition with whom he came in contact. Arrived in the New World, he very soon developed a feud with Almagro, who was none too well pleased, either, with the contract obtained from the king by Pizarro. Pizarro agreed to allow Almagro to conquer for himself such territories as were beyond the limits marked out by the king as within the sphere of Pizarro; only then could Almagro be induced to go ahead with the expedition.

In January 1531 Pizarro sailed for Peru, with an army of less than two hundred men and twenty-seven horses. For more than a year he operated in the vicinity of Túmbez. The time was well spent, because it gave him a chance to learn the state of affairs in the Inca Empire and provided an opportunity for a civil war in that country to develop to a point where Pizarro could take advantage of it. The late Inca, Huayna Capac, had passed away in 1525, and his son Huascar had succeeded him. Another son, Atahualpa, of illegitimate birth, had been made the ruler of the recently conquered Quito district, however. Atahualpa refused to recognize Huascar, and eventually defeated and captured him, whereupon he himself was proclaimed Inca at the capital city of Cuzco. It was just about at this time that news came of the appearance of the white strangers, and, like Montezuma in Mexico, Atahualpa was inclined to believe that they were supernatural beings, envoys perhaps of Viracocha, the supreme god of the pre-Inca peoples and identified with the Inca god Pachacamac. So he decided to propitiate them, at the same time that he believed he could overwhelm them in case of need, so small were their numbers. Learning that Atahualpa was at Cajamarca, in northern Peru, Pizarro resolved to go at once to meet him; without waiting for the reinforcements for which Almagro had been despatched, he first founded a colony at San Miguel, modern Piura, to assure his retreat in case of need and his communications with Panama, and then struck inland.

At length, in November 1532, Pizarro reached Cajamarca, which was found to be deserted. Outside the city, however, was Atahualpa and an Inca army of forty thousand men, ready to annihilate the Spaniards if it should seem to be desirable. The little Spanish force carefully occupied one of the public squares of Cajamarca, a place surrounded with walls and with only two exits to the rest of the city. Nevertheless, its position appeared to be desperate, but Pizarro planned to try the experiment which had so well served Cortés by seizing the person of the Inca. Messengers were sent to pay the respects of Pizarro to the Inca potentate and to invite him to a meeting at the Spanish camp. Atahualpa accepted, and came next day on a golden throne, which was borne on a litter. He was accompanied by thousands of his warriors. Arrived at the square where the Spaniards held possession, he was greeted by the Dominican friar Vicente Valverde, the only one of the foreign company to put in an appearance. Valverde proceeded at great length to address the Inca on the advantages of the Christian faith and the might of the Spanish king, concluding with a demand for him to give up his own gods and acknowledge the suzerainty of Charles I. Whether or no the long speech of Valverde was correctly interpreted and understood, Atahualpa seems to have become angered by the strange reception accorded him, and taking the breviary of the friar he threw it upon the ground, and began to consult with some of his followers. Valverde hurried to Pizarro, demanding vengeance for the insult to the faith, and promising absolution to those who might die in the struggle. Pizarro now gave the signal to open fire. The slaughter was terrible, and the Spanish horsemen rode down their adversaries, killing them like sheep. In the midst of the conflict Pizarro himself seized Atahualpa and made him prisoner. While protecting Atahualpa, Pizarro was wounded by one of his own men, but not another Spaniard was hurt. Thousands of their opponents lay dead—some say two thousand, some ten thousand. In utter confusion the rest of the Inca army melted away.

Hoping to rescue himself by appealing to the cupidity of the Spaniards, Atahualpa offered to fill the room in which he was lodged, with gold implements up to as high as a man could reach. The room had a surface of 374 square feet, about twenty-two feet by seventeen, and a line some nine feet high was fixed for the top of the golden treasure. Yet other gifts of silver were also offered. Pizarro accepted, probably with no intention of keeping his promise, but regarding this as a simple way in which to get together a rich booty that otherwise he might be at some pains to obtain. Meanwhile, Huascar appeared ready to pay an even greater sum if the Spaniards would recognize his rights as against Atahualpa, whereupon the latter sent messengers who procured the assassination of Huascar. Presently the ransom was accumulated, and when melted down, save for some of the more precious objects, it represented a sum the equivalent of perhaps five million dollars.[1] How much more it was worth in purchasing power than such an amount of money would be today is difficult to conjecture. Almagro and his men had arrived by this time, and demanded a share. For once there was enough to go around, if, indeed, in unequal portions. According to one early Spanish historian, some of the men on their return had so much money that they loaded down their Indian servants with gold and hunted their creditors, and whatever they owed they paid with a piece of gold worth perhaps double their debt!

Little good did the ransom do Atahualpa, however. Charges were now trumped up against him, such, for ex-

[1] Most accounts, following Prescott, say fifteen million dollars, but recent investigation has reduced the amount. See Merriman, III, 564–565.

ample, as his responsibility for the murder of his brother, of whom Pizarro was glad to be rid anyway, and he was condemned to be burned to death. Some of the Spaniards protested. Not so Father Valverde, whose uncompromising Christian spirit could find no justification for Atahualpa's rejection of his own plea on behalf of the faith. On the way to his execution, however, Atahualpa was promised by Valverde a milder form of death if he would accept baptism. Whether in order to escape torture or because he had in fact lost confidence in his own gods, Atahualpa consented, and was strangled, "while the Spaniards, gathering around, muttered their *credos* for the salvation of his soul." If the shade of Atahualpa in the next world were capable of feelings of vengeance, however, it may have had some satisfaction in ensuing years, for not one of those who took a leading part in his execution escaped a violent death himself.[1]

Pizarro now had to overcome an uprising of the native peoples, but it proved a less difficult task than might have been imagined. The Inca Empire had been shaken to its roots by the events of the past few years, and the authoritativeness and discipline of the old system no longer functioned. Different factions arose among the people, with the result that it was not possible to present a united front against the Spaniards, and in a surprisingly short time the empire was a thing of the past. Meanwhile, Pizarro had fought his way to Cuzco, entering that mountain city in November 1533, a year to the day after he had reached Cajamarca. Needless to say, the Spaniards sacked the city, obtaining another great booty in gold and silver; some say it was four times as great as the ransom exacted from Atahualpa, but the evidence is not clear. Ostensibly they were operating in the name of the Inca monarch, whose cause they had appeared to espouse, but in fact they promptly took charge of the city, organizing a government of Spanish officials.

Much of the rest of the former empire was promptly

[1] Pizarro and other military leaders were killed in course of the civil wars between the Spaniards in Peru, following the conquest. Valverde was assassinated later by Indians of the island of Puna. In relating the story the Spanish historian Oviedo, recalling the incident of Valverde's first meeting with Atahualpa, said that the Puna Indians also appeared "not to understand the Bible."

overrun, and Spanish settlements were founded. Most important of these was Lima, henceforth to be the capital, established by Pizarro in 1535, so that he might have easier communication with the sea than from distant Cuzco. Other details of government, such as the organization of the conquests, the allotment of lands and Indian laborers, the management of the mines, and the promotion of yet new expeditions, were handled by Pizarro, and very capably, it must be said. One expedition, under the command of Benalcázar,[1] penetrated to the north as far as Quito. Another, under Almagro, made the first Spanish entry into the heart of Chile. Almagro had intended to possess himself of Cuzco, which he claimed was properly within his jurisdiction, beyond that of Pizarro, but was persuaded to undertake his Chilean expedition in 1535. Disappointed in Chile, which to Almagro had paid dividends only in misfortunes, the veteran one-time ally of Pizarro returned in 1536, and now made a determined effort to seize Cuzco. This marked the beginning of a series of civil wars which were to last for nearly a generation, and which are primarily interesting in that they were symptomatic of the Spanish conquest in the Americas and of the individualistic traits of the conquering people.

A detailed study of most of the Spanish expeditions to the New World would reveal that while the *conquistadores* and their subordinates recognized the authority of the king, they conducted themselves very much as they pleased, often trying to gain royal sanction for their activities after the fact instead of before. Thus Cortés disobeyed Velázquez, and Pedrarias fought Balboa. Nowhere more than in Peru was this "I-want-what-I-want-when-I-want-it-and-I-am-going-to-take-it-if-I-can-get-it" spirit manifested. Almagro wanted Cuzco, and despite the opposition of his favorite enemy Hernando Pizarro he took it. This was in 1537. Hernando very much wanted to get revenge, and the return of Cuzco. In 1538 he had his innings, putting Almagro to death. Then he went to Spain to explain what had happened—and was imprisoned for more than twenty years. In 1541 the twenty-

[1] The real name of Benalcázar was Sebastián Moyano. He was born in humble circumstances in the Spanish village of Belalcázar, and became known in the Americas by the name of his birthplace, as Sebastián de Belalcázar, often rendered more euphoniously Benalcázar.

two year old son of Almagro headed a *coup d'état* in Lima against Francisco Pizarro himself, inflicting a mortal wound upon the old *conquistador*, who marked out the sign of the cross in his own blood and kissed it before he expired. In the following year Vaca de Castro, the agent of the king and successor of Pizarro, defeated the young Almagro and had him decapitated. Two years later, in 1544, there arrived the newly appointed viceroy of Peru, Núñez de Vela, charged with putting into effect the New Laws of the Indies, which positively forbade the use of Indians in *encomienda* or any other form of forced personal service, the long delayed result of the propaganda of the Apostle of the Indies, Las Casas. This exasperated the rank and file of the *conquistadores*, who rallied around Gonzalo Pizarro in open rebellion against the crown. The viceroy was defeated and killed. Sent out to arrange matters between the conflicting factions, La Gasca had the advantage of carrying with him the repeal of the New Laws and an offer of pardon to those who had risen against the royal authority. Gonzalo decided to hold out, but in 1548 was captured and executed. Disorder and civil war continued, however, until 1554, when at last the internecine strife of the conquerors was brought to an end.

By that time the first phase of the conquest may be said to have been complete. It had been effected almost in spite of the conquering Spaniards, who certainly had shown more of individual initiative than coöperation. In this they were merely manifesting their racial habits, here as elsewhere in the New World, and they were to pass on to their descendants the same undisciplined spirit.

CHAPTER IV

THE LESSER CONQUISTADORES IN THE SOUTHERN CONTINENT

CORTÉS and Pizarro built up a Spanish empire greater than might have been dreamed of, even in the fevered imaginations of those times, but their conquests were, in the light of history, no more important than others of the Spaniards in this same epoch, roughly corresponding with the reign of Charles I (1516–1556). In addition to the already mentioned conquest of Central America and of regions now part of the United States, other territories acquired were Ecuador, Bolivia, and Chile by expeditions from Peru; Colombia and Venezuela from the Caribbean; and Paraguay and Argentina, with a later overflow into Uruguay, for the most part directly from Spain. In romantic incident these conquests were quite as interesting and spectacular as those of Mexico and Peru, but they are less well known because less wealth was obtained and less has been written about them.

It was perhaps in the northern mainland of South America that the Spaniards were most active in the pursuit of fable, enduring hardships and suffering strange experiences which were almost more remarkable than their own weird objectives. Most persistently besought was El Dorado, the "Gilded Man," whose kingdom was so rich that his subjects painted him each day with gold, and washed him off at night. There were, of course, a Mexico and a Peru, but also there were other existing situations which could have given rise to these tales. Some of them closely approximated at least an outward semblance of the reports current among the Spaniards. Especially was this true of certain religious ceremonies of the Chibchas of the Colombian table-land, the third of the three great cultivated peoples of the Western Hemisphere whose civilization the Spaniards were to overthrow, and rivaling the Aztecs and Incas in wealth. The following is an account of one of the rites of the Chibchas:

"The most noteworthy ceremony was the sacrifice at Lake Guatavita. Every year, while the cacique of Guatavita was independent, he covered himself with turpentine, and spread gold dust over his body, thus making it resplendent in its fresh gilding. Then, surrounded by priests, he caused himself to be floated on a raft to a point indicated as the middle of the lake. During his passage to this spot, a multitude of his subjects, gathered on the shores of the lake, which rose like the seats of an amphitheatre, joined in the ceremony with music and songs. Having arrived at the prescribed point, the cacique offered sacrifice by dropping gold, emeralds, and other precious objects into the lake, and afterwards plunged into the water, offering up the gilding of his body to nature, whence it came, while the surrounding mountains echoed the applause of the people." [1]

This happened each *year*, not every day, but it was a close parallel to the eventual El Dorado tales.

But El Dorado was not alone. There were also the kingdom of the Omaguas, the treasures of the "House of the Sun," and any number of scintillating cities, such as Manoa, Enim, Meta, and Macatoa. Usually these lands were referred to as "beyond the Andes," and hidden in a thick forest, on the shores of a marvelous lake. To be sure, the Spaniards hoped to find gold and precious stones, but what were these things in themselves as compared with the dreams allied with them which Spanish fancy conjured up? What was even "another Peru," or "another Mexico"? Literally scores of expeditions went in search of El Dorado. Everywhere they met with a determined native resistance, but this was not all. The forces of nature were an even more terrible deterrent. The Spaniards waded swamps and rivers, defended themselves against alligators and man-eating fish, climbed the pathless sierras, encountered freshets and the mountain snows, crossed deserts, fought the dread and too often losing battle with disease, and, as if these misfortunes were not enough, they quarreled with one another, punctuating their peregrinations with desertion, assassination, and murder. They were still Spanish individualists, but any one of the hundreds of their expeditions, if duplicated today, would excite the wonder of the world. In danger, hardship, and interesting achievement most of them perhaps equaled or surpassed any comparable adventure of modern

[1] Moses, *Spanish dependencies*, I, 130.

times. And at least they advanced geographical knowledge, and won another considerable portion of the earth's surface for the Spanish race.

Reference has already been made to the advance of Benalcázar to Quito in modern Ecuador. After some preliminary difficulties he established himself there in 1534, and served as governor on behalf of Pizarro. But Benalcázar was a restless individual, and eager to carve out provinces for himself. So, hearing of the wealth of the Chibchas, and lured by the stories of El Dorado and the legendary city of Manoa, he marched north into the southern part of modern Colombia in 1535. There in 1536 he founded the eventually important towns of Cali and Popayán. With who could say what untold wealth ahead, however, he scorned to remain in the populous and well cultivated Cauca Valley, and pushed into the difficult country beyond. In 1538 he reached the mountain kingdom of the Chibchas. To his surprise and disgust he met there another Spanish expedition, commanded by Gonzalo Jiménez de Quesada.

Some Spanish establishments had already been set up on the Caribbean shore of the Colombian mainland. Rodrigo de Bastidas founded Santa Marta in 1525, and Pedro de Heredia followed with Cartagena in 1533. There he obtained a rich booty; on one of his expeditions into the interior he made a profit, merely through the medium of trade, of a million and a half ducats.[1] No wonder that others were soon attracted to the neighborhood!

In 1535 Pedro Fernández de Lugo, son of the conqueror of the Canaries, was made governor of the region east of the Magdalena, and struck into the wilderness with nearly a thousand men. The expedition met with many misfortunes, and "to cap the climax the governor's son, Luis Alonso, escaped to Spain with all the gold that had been found, leaving his father in a pitiable plight." Returning to the coast, the governor soon organized another expedition, giving the post of commander to Jiménez de Quesada, who heretofore had been his "chief judge."

Quesada began his explorations in 1536. Overcoming seemingly insuperable obstacles in the way of disease and

[1] A ducat is supposed to be worth \$2.28, but cf. *infra*, 152, n.

discomfort and Indians with poisoned arrows, he ascended the Magdalena for hundreds of miles, and broke away to enter the territory of the Chibchas. Going into the mountains, he and his men came to a great plateau, some seven thousand feet above sea-level, where they found a delightful and thickly populated country. He was in the land of the Chibchas, who numbered perhaps more than a million. With only 166 men and fifty-nine horses, Quesada embarked upon a stirring conquest, to the accompaniment of the usual slaughter of the natives, the frenzied search for gold, and the torture of chieftains who would not, or could not, reveal where it was hidden. One such sufferer was the ruler, or "zipa," named "Bogotá," who died as a result of the torments inflicted upon him. His name was to survive, however, in the city which Quesada founded there in 1538, after the native opposition had been crushed. This was the Santa Fe of Quesada, since called Santa Fe de Bogotá.

While Quesada and Benalcázar were still in the plateau region of Bogotá, and each more or less disposed to fight the other for his "rights," the issue was complicated by the arrival of a *third* claimant, and, like the other two who had preceded him, from a *different direction.* This was the German leader Nikolaus Federmann, from Venezuela. They did not break into triple combat, however, partly because the enterprise of each was to some extent tinged with illegality, for Benalcázar was at outs with Pizarro, Federmann with his employers the Welsers, and Quesada with Fernández de Lugo, from whom he now wished to make himself independent. Benalcázar consented to take the region of Popayán, while the other two men patched up a truce which at least averted a fight.

Who and why this Federmann? In 1520 the Spaniards had begun the settlement of Venezuela with the founding of Cumaná, following in 1527 with Santa Ana del Coro. In 1528, in return for a loan, Charles I granted rights of conquest in Venezuela to certain Germans, who transferred their rights to the Welsers, a rich German commercial house. This company took up the search for El Dorado and other marvels with fully as much enthusiasm as ever the Spaniards had done, and were not behindhand, either, when it came to cruelties perpetrated upon the Indians. For years their explorers, of whom Alfinger, Speyer, and Federmann were the principal leaders, invaded the farthest corners of Venezuela and parts of Colombia. At length, in 1546, after the contract of the Welsers had been rescinded, the Spaniards again took charge. The result of the activities of Germans and Spaniards was the addition of Venezuela to the fast-growing Spanish Empire. A number of settlements were founded of which Caracas, in 1567, was the most important.

In like manner the principal portion of what is now called Bolivia was conquered by the Spaniards by 1535, as part of the movement which overwhelmed the empire of the Incas. The most notable settlement there was the phenomenally rich mining city of Potosí, which dates from 1545. And elsewhere much of the region beyond the Andes, aside from the settlements in Venezuela, was at least explored. Two such expeditions ought at least to be mentioned, those of Francisco de Orellana and Lope de Aguirre.

Orellana was a member of an expedition headed by Gonzalo Pizarro which set out in 1539 to find the rich lands of cinnamon and precious metals reported to exist beyond the mountains to the east of Quito. Encountering the usual difficulties in crossing the cordillera and making the customary fruitless search for El Dorado, Gonzalo in 1540 sent Orellana and some of the men down a river in a boat for more supplies. Thereupon, Orellana harangued his men, told them how hard it would be to return, and pictured to them the wealth they might obtain if they would go ahead with their voyage, deserting their comrades. And on they went, down seemingly interminable rivers such as none of them had ever seen before, on for thousands of miles, fighting battles with the Indians, and meeting dangers without end. They were on the Amazon, subsequently so called because they found some villages inhabited exclusively by women. Making ropes of vegetable fibres and sails out of their own blankets, they took to sea, turned north, and were eventually rescued, late in 1541, by some Spanish pearl-fishers of the island of Cubagua, Venezuela. Altogether, they had covered more than five thousand miles! No more astounding voyage was ever made in the history of the world.

And yet the voyage of Aguirre was a close rival. Aguirre was a member of the Pedro de Ursúa expedition of 1560 from Peru, which sought the "hidden lake" and "city of gold" in the upper Amazon country. Aguirre headed an uprising of the soldiers against Ursúa, whom they assassinated, and they even went so far as to declare themselves no longer subject to the king of Spain, to whom Aguirre wrote a letter announcing himself a rebel against him "to the death" because of his "ingratitude." Turning north from the Amazon up the Negro, Aguirre struck the Orinoco, and descended it to its mouth. For cruelty, tragedy, and shedding of blood, this expedition had few if any superiors. Putting to sea, Aguirre presently landed in Venezuela, where he was attacked and defeated by a Spanish force. Deserted by his men, he stabbed his own daughter to keep her from falling into the hands of his enemies. He himself surrendered, and was soon executed.

An expedition of 1582 was the last the Spaniards made in northern South America in search of a "kingdom of gold," but at least one European people continued the hunt for El Dorado into the seventeenth century. The Spaniards had done little in the region of the mouth of the Orinoco and the Guianas, wherefore the famous Englishman, Sir Walter Raleigh, chose this territory as a field for his own operations. He headed an expedition to the Orinoco in 1595, and despite his lack of success became convinced of the truth of the legends about El Dorado and the rich city of Manoa, publishing a book in support of his beliefs upon his return to England. Expeditions of 1596 to the Guianas and the Orinoco were sent out by him, and also failed. Accused of being involved in a conspiracy against the crown, Raleigh was imprisoned for many years, but upon being pardoned he headed a great expedition in 1617 to the Orinoco. Once again, instead of finding El Dorado, Raleigh met with disaster, including the death of his son, who was killed in a battle with the Spaniards. On his return to England in 1618, he was condemned on a charge of having broken the peace with Spain, and was decapitated.

So much for the north. Meanwhile, Spain had effected a conquest of the southern part of the continent. Passing over the voyages of Magellan and other navigators to territory now part of the republic of Chile, it may be said that the first expedition into the heart of the country was the already mentioned land expedition of Almagro. With nearly five hundred Spaniards and thousands of Indian allies, the old warrior started south in 1535. Going by way of Lake Titicaca, the province of Tucumán (Argentina), the mountains of the Andes, and the deserts of northern Chile, he encountered incredible hardships—anyone acquainted with that difficult country may well wonder how even one man got through!—but at length reached the habitable part of Chile at Copiapó. Expeditions were made which covered the country between the coast and the Andes and went as far south as the Maule. No gold was found, and the land impressed Almagro and his men as poor, wherefore they decided to abandon the enterprise. They returned to Peru by way of the deserts of Atacama and Tarapacá! At length, in 1537, they came to Arequipa in Peru. In 1539 a brave and distinguished officer named Pedro de Valdivia, a native of Extremadura, obtained a contract for a fresh attempt, and left Cuzco in the following year.

To Valdivia goes the credit for the Spanish conquest of Chile, as that of Mexico and Peru belongs to Cortés and Pizarro. Less spectacular in its yield of wealth and booty, and in a sense merely an off-shoot from the conquest of Peru, it is customary to give it correspondingly less space, but the story in itself can hardly be surpassed, and the people who were to develop out of the Spanish-Indian amalgam were to become one of the leading, if not the foremost, of the peoples of Hispanic America. The harsh experiences of the Almagro expedition made it difficult for Valdivia to enlist a following, but at length he got together about 150 men. One woman also made the journey, a certain Inez Suárez, "bound to Valdivia by the ties of love." Going by way of the terrible desert of Atacama, Valdivia reached central Chile. Early in 1541, at the foot of the little hill of Santa Lucía, he founded the town of Santiago, preparing to stay in this country, which pleased him and his men fully as much as it had displeased the expeditionaries of Almagro.

The next few years were anything but easy for the Spanish

settlers. Lands and Indians were parceled out in the usual fashion, and a number of towns were founded, but little of precious metals or ready-made wealth was discovered. Furthermore, the Indians of Chile were of a different stamp from those who had submitted so easily in Peru, and proved to be perhaps the most hard-fighting race in both Americas. The Iroquois, Apaches, and many other tribesmen of the Western world have merited praise for their warlike qualities, but quite possibly the Araucanians (otherwise Mapuches) of Chile surpassed them all. In earlier years they had held back the advance of the Inca Empire. Now they battled the Spaniards, and not merely in one desperate campaign, but year after year, and century after century. In 1641 a treaty was made which left all lands south of the Bío-Bío River in the hands of the Araucanians. Later violations of the treaty by the whites caused a renewal of the wars, which did not come to an end until 1881, after a conflict which might well be called the Three Hundred and Forty Years' War. Then, what were left of the Araucanians accepted the terms of the republic of Chile. The white man's liquor had been a more potent force than gunpowder in reducing them.

In the colonial period, with their crude weapons, the Araucanians fought Spanish armies equipped with guns and cannon and the various superior devices of European military tactics, but would charge in the face of gunfire, taking cover where they could, until they came to grips with the enemy. After that, it was man to man, and not infrequently it was the Araucanian who came off the victor. At intervals there were periods of peace, when the two races mingled on more or less intimate terms. Unions were formed between Spanish men and the Indian women, from which there developed the strongest of the mixed races in the New World. Eventually, through the process of Mendelism, the Indian blood tended to breed out, and the race became white, but not a little of the old Araucanian remains in the stoically brave, sober-mannered—if, indeed, rather too dry-throated!—but thoroughly capable Chilean of today.[1]

[1] The most fascinating account of the Araucanians is to be found in the famous epic poem of Alonso de Ercilla, *La Araucana*, written by a Spaniard

In the time of Valdivia the tide of conquest ebbed and flowed uncertainly for many years. A number of colonies were founded, such as La Serena, Concepción, and far-southern Valdivia, but their life was very precarious. Even Santiago knew what it was to be destroyed. At first, to be sure, the Spaniards were successful, as they had been elsewhere in the New World, but the Araucanian tribes joined forces, and henceforth gave desperate battle.

It was the Araucanian Lautaro who gave the Spaniards the most trouble. Several years earlier, this individual proposed to himself to find out why it was that the Spaniards were so often successful in war. He therefore took service with Valdivia, and even accepted baptism, availing himself, moreover, of his opportunity to study Spanish methods. Well instructed, he later deserted to his own people, and for three years, 1554–1557, defeated the Spaniards in battle after battle. On one occasion, in order to strike terror into the Indians, Valdivia had the nose and right hand of four hundred prisoners cut off. The Indians did not forget this when eventually Valdivia himself was captured, and he suffered a terrible death. To quote from a Chilean historian:

> "Although the Indians had the swords and poniards which they had taken from their vanquished enemies, they preferred to employ sea-shells, which they used as knives. With these they cut off his arms, and after having slightly roasted them, devoured them before his eyes." [1]

The colonies were almost on the point of being abandoned, but at length the forces of Lautaro were surprised, and Lautaro was killed, fighting bravely to the very end.

Never again were the Spanish settlements in any real danger of being overwhelmed, although the wars continued. Indeed, Lautaro's successor, Caupolicán (or Quepolicán), was no mean antagonist. According to legend, he was selected because he held aloft a huge beam longer than the others were able to do. The historians doubt the story,

who participated in the early conquest. For a recent description of these remarkable Indians, see Edwards, Agustín, *Peoples of old* (London, 1929), 13–195, and *passim*.

[1] Barros Arana, Diego, *Historia jeneral de Chile* (16 v. Santiago, Chile, 1884–1902), I, 436.

however.[1] At any rate, Chile remained the principal school of the Spanish soldiery in the Americas, and the wildest of the "Wild West" of the Hispanic American frontiers.

Yet one more vast area in the Americas was added to the dominions of the Spanish king in the reign of Charles I, although its effective conquest ran over into the latter half of the sixteenth century, in the period of Philip II (1556–1598). This was the far-reaching domain of the Plata River.[2] Studied in detail, the story of the conquest has just as much of adventure, hardship, and incident as that of the others, but the results obtained were the least spectacular of the Spanish conquests in the Americas, especially from the standpoint of the acquisition of wealth in precious metals, whether through the medium of plunder, or by the more laborious processes of mining. Other regions seemed to be more attractive, wherefore this part of the Western world was in a comparative sense neglected. Such are the paradoxes of history, however, that this last and to some extent least of the colonies was to become in modern times the first in point of influence and the solidity of her institutions among the republics of Hispanic America.

The tale begins, of course, in the era of the early explorations. First to reach the Plata was the Spanish voyage of Juan Díaz de Solís, who left Spain in three little boats, one of seventy tons and two of thirty, in 1515. Touching the coast of Brazil near Rio de Janeiro, Solís continued on until

[1] The story is taken from Ercilla, *La Araucana*, canto II. According to this, the chiefs of the Araucanians held a council of war to decide who should be the leader of all their forces against the Spaniards. The venerable Colocolo, who normally might have been the leader, proposed instead that he who could hold a great beam longest on his shoulders, without resting, should be their chief. The proposition was accepted, and a beam was used which was so heavy that most of the contestants could not even move it. Lincoya, however, raised it aloft, and held it up for a day and a half. Then along came the one-eyed Caupolicán. He picked it up as if it were a light stick, and kept it on his shoulders for forty-eight hours. And so he was proclaimed the great leader of the Araucanians.

[2] This river is often referred to barbarously in English as "*the* La Plata," although the "La" is just another word for "the." To Spanish-speaking peoples it is just "the Plata," often called "*el* Plata," using the masculine article to agree with "río" (river), understood. It is no more "La Plata," or "El Plata," than the Orinoco is "El Orinoco," or the Guadiana "La Guadiana." English writers often translate "La Plata" into "the Plate," which is objectionable, not only because there is no good reason for translating such an easily pronounceable word as "Plata," but also because "Plate" is open to misconstruction as a translation of "Plata," which means "Silver."

in February 1516 he reached the Plata, which he called the Santa María, or Mar Dulce (Fresh-Water Sea). Proceeding up the Plata a few miles, Solís and a few companions landed, and were attacked by the Indians. Only one escaped. The rest were put to death.[1] The survivors of the expedition decided in favor of a return to Spain. *En route* back, one of the boats was wrecked, and the crew were stranded on Santa Catharina Island, in southern Brazil, where they had to wait ten years before they were rescued. The great expedition of Magellan, 1519–1522, came to the Plata early in 1520, and explored it with sufficient thoroughness to be able to conclude that there was no strait through the continent there.

Another voyage, also intended as an expedition to the Far East, "to the Moluccas, China, Japan, Tarsis, and Ophir," left Spain in 1526 under the command of Sebastian Cabot, an Italian who had previously been in the service of England. Arrived in Pernambuco, Cabot began to hear stories of the fabulous wealth of the Plata country. He thereupon decided to disobey his original instructions, and seek his share of the riches reputed to exist in the New World. On the way to the Plata, he stopped at Santa Catharina Island, and there came upon the shipwrecked survivors of the Solís expedition. These men definitely confirmed the stories Cabot had heard, and had in their possession some precious metals to support their tales.

The Indians had told these Spaniards of "El Rey Blanco" (The White King), whose vast dominions, far to the west, were so rich in gold that the very dwellings were constructed of that metal. Of course, they were speaking of the Peruvian Incas, famous throughout South America among the natives, but not yet known to the Spaniards at the time the Solís expeditionaries heard of them. About the year 1525 one of their number, Alejo García, and four companions resolved to test the story, and set out with some Indian allies for this purpose. On foot they traversed the modern

[1] Many accounts, relying on some of the old chroniclers, have it that Solís and his companions were *eaten* by the natives. Modern research rejects this story, on the ground that the Indians of that section were not cannibals. See Carbia, Rómulo D——, *Manual de la historia argentina* (Buenos Aires, 1917), I, 259.

states of Santa Catharina and Paraná in Brazil, and then entered Paraguay. There García got together a veritable army of two thousand Indians, and advanced into Bolivia to the vicinity of Chuquisaca (modern Sucre). By this time he had accumulated a great booty, and decided to return. From Paraguay he sent back some samples of the treasure he had found to the Spaniards at Santa Catharina, with an account of his achievements. Shortly afterward, he was set upon by his Indian allies, who killed him and the other Spaniards of the expedition and bore away the loot. It has been estimated that in this astounding journey García covered more than three thousand miles, and he and the other four Spaniards were the first white men to set foot in Paraguay and Bolivia.

The Spaniards whom Cabot picked up told him he might come upon El Rey Blanco if he should ascend the Paraná, one of the principal tributaries of the Plata. This was enough for Cabot, who promptly headed south, and entered the Plata. It was the Cabot expedition which gave the name Plata (Silver) to the great river, or really estuary, into which the Paraná and Uruguay empty their waters. Cabot did, indeed, obtain some silver trinkets from the Indians there, but the name was more indicative of hope than of fact in the way of riches discovered by him. Ascending the Paraná, Cabot founded a settlement in 1527 which he called Sancti Spiritus. Shortly afterward it was destroyed by the Indians. Having met with little success, and feeling the need of reinforcements, he returned to Spain.

The permanent settlement of the Plata region dates from the next expedition there, that of Pedro de Mendoza, which reached that country in 1536. A town was founded and named Buenos Aires, but it was able to maintain itself for only three years. At first the colony lacked provisions, and suffered so greatly from hunger that some of the soldiers went to the extreme of eating the corpses of their companions who had died. Presently relieved, the town continued to suffer, however, on account of the hostility of the Indians, who were numerous in this locality and almost incessantly attacked the Spaniards; on one occasion they burned not only the town itself, but several ships in the harbor as well.

Meanwhile, a Spanish force had gone up the Paraná, and continued its journey until it reached Upper Peru, or modern Bolivia, and in 1537 a Spanish fort was erected in Paraguay. The following year the remnants of the various Spanish colonies were gathered at Asunción, today the capital of Paraguay. This was to be the first permanent settlement in the Plata region, and, curiously enough, though far in the interior, was to serve as the principal base for the Spanish conquests toward the coast. The Indians of the lower river areas and difficulties over food supplies were entirely too great a problem for the comparatively few Spaniards in this country to handle in the earlier years.

The principal figure in the early settlement of this section was Domingo Martínez de Irala, who dominated the colony most of the time from the abandonment of Buenos Aires in 1539 until his death in 1556. At the outset of this period, however, another well-known individual was commissioned to rule the country. This was none other than that celebrated pedestrian Álvar Núñez Cabeza de Vaca. Appointed governor of the land discovered by Mendoza, Cabeza de Vaca reached the coast of Brazil in 1541, and, leaving his ships to continue the voyage, he and a number of his men went cross-country to Paraguay! Following an unsuccessful expedition of his toward Peru, he was deposed by the colonists, who elected Irala in his stead. This was in 1544. Years afterward, in 1555, Irala was confirmed as governor. Meanwhile, he and his men had established cordial relations with the Guaraní Indians in their vicinity, and had intermarried with them or formed other types of union with considerable frequency, practising polygamy quite as much as the natives. Irala himself married not merely one but all seven of the daughters of the principal Indian chief! The Indians of the neighborhood were reduced to the servitude of the *encomienda*, however. Like many of his predecessors, Irala found himself lured by Peru, but in an expedition of 1547 he was disappointed to learn that this much dreamed of land was already occupied by other Spaniards. At length, at an age of threescore and ten, this vigorous pioneer died in bed.

The government of Irala marked the beginning of Spanish success in the colonization of the Plata. Meanwhile two separate movements, one from Peru and the other from Chile, had resulted in other settlements in northwestern and western Argentina. The first was in what was then called Tucumán, but which included some seven of the northwestern provinces of present-day Argentina and part of southern Bolivia. Almagro had passed through this territory, *en route* to Chile in 1536, but did not attempt to occupy it. In 1549 Juan Núñez de Prado marched south from Potosí, and founded a settlement at Barco in 1550, subsequently moved to other sites in that vicinity. Meanwhile, an expedition of Francisco de Villagra, bound from Peru to Chile, passed through that country, and claimed it for Pedro Valdivia of Chile; Valdivia had been granted the territory for a hundred leagues east of the Pacific. Villagra took forcible possession. A new governor, sent out from Chile, abandoned Barco, and founded Santiago del Estero in December 1553 or January 1554. Later, in order to check Indian uprisings, a number of smaller towns were founded. One of them, established in 1558, was called Londres (London) by the governor, who also changed the existing name of the entire territory to Nueva Inglaterra, in commemoration of the marriage of Philip II with Mary Tudor. Thus did the first "New England" appear in a distant corner of Argentina. The name was not long retained, however, and Londres was destroyed by the Indians.

The government of Tucumán was presently separated from the jurisdiction of Chile, and subordinated to the *audiencia* of Charcas in Bolivia. New settlements were now added, including Tucumán (1565), Córdoba (1573), Salta (1582), La Rioja (1591), and Jujuy (1593). The province proved to be one of the most soundly established of all the Spanish conquests of that day. Lacking the gold of Peru and Bolivia, it was based on agriculture, the domestic animal industry, and trade. Lima and Potosí, more especially the latter, were the markets for its products. The Peruvian gentleman rode horses which came from the Argentinian *pampas*, or plains. The miners of Potosí used mules they had bought in Tucumán. Also, cotton and woolen textiles, cereals, and beef were exported to the populous communities in the north. Nevertheless, the high prices Tucumán had to pay for the goods it bought made its citizens look more and more toward the Plata, as a way of direct communication with Spain which might free them from the commercial tyranny of the Peru-Panamanian route. That idea was in the background of the eastward push in the founding of Córdoba. The Tucumán of colonial times was interesting, too, for its exemplification of caudillism, after the pattern which was to become such a fundamental factor in the history of the Hispanic American republics. The absolutism of the Spanish monarchs did not greatly disturb the dictators, or caudillos, of Tucumán.

Meanwhile, if Chile had lost Tucumán, she found compensation elsewhere across the Andes in what was then called Cuyo, also on the basis of the grant to Valdivia. It embraced the territory from 30° to 44° and as far east as the 65th meridian, including the present-day provinces of Mendoza, San Juan, and San Luis. Discovered by Francisco de Villagra in 1551, on the same march when he earlier dispossessed the Peruvian claimants of Barco, it was occupied, ten years later, by a Chilean expedition. This founded the town of Mendoza in 1561, but it was refounded at a different site the following year. In the background of this movement of colonization was the same idea eventually developed in Tucumán, that of reaching the Atlantic, so as to free Chile from dependence upon Peru and Panama. Other towns were presently founded, including San Juan (1562) and San Luis (1596). Nevertheless, the communications of Cuyo with the outside world for a time followed the route of Tucumán, by way of which province the much prized wines of Mendoza were exported to many regions. Tucumán at times argued in favor of annexing Cuyo, but the royal government left it a part of Chile until the establishment of the viceroyalty of the Plata in 1776. Then the change was made. Thus casually the destinies of South America may have been given a new direction. Chile, with Cuyo, might well have become the great country of the southern continent, rivaling or even surpassing Argentina.

All roads in Argentina pointed inevitably toward the Plata. Gradually the Spaniards from Asunción moved down the Paraná, establishing settlements along the way, notably Santa Fe (1573) and Corrientes (1588). At length, in 1580, Buenos Aires was refounded by Juan de Garay. This time it was a success, and two years later Garay wrote a letter to the king predicting that this would some day be the most important city in the Indies. This was one prediction which was to come true, though doubtless thousands of other such prophecies were made by enthusiastic Spanish captains with as good or better reason. One eventually prominent region continued for some time to be a no man's land, in doubt as to its destiny as between the Portuguese and Spanish settlers of the New World. That was the Banda Oriental (Eastern Shore) of the Uruguay, from which river that region was later to take its name.

Irala and Garay, Asunción and Buenos Aires, mark the end of that long chain of Spanish achievements which came in the era of the *conquistadores.* Columbus, Balboa, Cortés, Pizarro, Valdivia, Quesada—these are the great names—then Irala and Garay, seemingly the weakest links in the chain. But the future was to make their work (in the background of the modern Argentina), next after that of Columbus, among the most important of all.

CHAPTER V

THE FOUNDING OF BRAZIL

One of the most important facts in the history of Hispanic America is that Brazil is Portuguese, not Spanish. In many respects the people of Brazil are much the same as their Spanish-descended cousins in other parts of Hispanic America; even the language, which it is fair to say is a mere dialectal off-shoot of Spanish which hardened to a language, can easily be understood by one who knows Spanish. Nevertheless, the Portuguese and the Brazilians *feel* themselves to be a different people from the Spanish, and the separation of Portugal from the main currents of Spanish history, dating back to the twelfth century, has made this feeling to a great extent an ineradicable fact. So, while there is a certain racial affinity and unity of purpose throughout Hispanic America in the face of the rest of the world, Brazil is not whole-heartedly in the same plane of brotherhood with the republics of Spanish America. Especially is this true in so far as Argentina sets herself up as the leader of the Hispanic American nations, an idea which finds little or no recognition in Brazil. The vast size and resources of Brazil and her enormous potentialities in the way of future development accentuate the importance of her difference from the rest of Hispanic America. Here is a country as large as continental United States, with another Texas thrown in. It has more than its share of good arable land, river systems beyond anything in the world, minerals, forests, rubber, a developed wealth in coffee capable of yielding three-fourths the world's supply, and a population estimated to be already beyond forty millions, and this mostly in regions along or near the coast, a mere bagatelle in comparison with what the Brazil of the future may be. Although the supreme fact of Brazilian history is that the country was colonized by the Portuguese, other details are necessary, if one is to have a reasonably clear view of what it is, and what it is going to be.

Brazil was discovered in 1500, not by Pedro Alvares Cabral, as is often stated, but by Vicente Yáñez Pinzón, one of the companions of Columbus on the voyage of 1492. He touched the coast just below Pernambuco, thence sailing north. Another Spanish voyage reached Brazil in 1500, and still later the same year came the Portuguese voyage of Cabral. The latter's "discovery," however, was the one which was to count. Cabral, curiously enough, was headed, not for America, but for India by way of the Cape of Good Hope. Over the years 1497–1499 the Portuguese had followed up the voyage of Bartholomeu Dias by sending out the famous expedition of Vasco da Gama, which circumnavigated Africa and actually did reach India. The difficulties of navigation down the African coast were so great, however, that in the voyage of 1500 a somewhat more westerly course was steered, in hopes of better winds, if also on the chance of finding some new lands the Spaniards had overlooked. As South America projects itself into the Atlantic far to the east of North America, it did not take Cabral an exceptionally great distance out of his course to bring him to Brazil. He reached the coast at Porto Seguro, a little below 16° south latitude, and took possession for Portugal. One of his ships was sent back to report the discovery, and it carried a cargo of reddish dyewoods, for which the Portuguese word was "*brazil.*" Thus the land of "*brazil,*" or dyewoods, became "Brazil."

For a quarter of a century after Cabral, Portugal did little to make good her title to Brazil—a title based on the treaty of Tordesillas, as well as the alleged discovery by Cabral. This period, sometimes called the "era of neglect," was not wholly lacking in Portuguese voyages, however. On his return from India, Cabral met a fleet sent out by King Manuel (1495–1521) "the Fortunate." Together they went to Brazil, and explored the greater part of the coast, returning to Portugal with an unfavorable report. Here was no wealth such as Cabral's men had just seen in India—no rich cities, no spices, silk, gold-dust, or precious stones—or so they thought.

Other voyages were made, including some which continued on to India around Africa. Some ships came for the brazil wood, which was to be the first economic basis, the first article of exchange, permitting of Portuguese settlement. A number of men were marooned or stranded, whether through wreck or desertion, and many Portuguese convicts were unceremoniously dumped in Brazil to survive or perish as best they could. A few of the settlers, indeed, were voluntary and respectable colonists. Eventually, little communities of white men were established along the coast, each without organization or law, except as it had an elected captain, who was the leader in war with the Indians and influential in the other affairs of the group. At some time in this period the Bay of Rio de Janeiro was discovered, although all events of the era are shrouded in so much mystery and so lacking in clear evidences that it is almost impossible to assert any dates with conviction. Doubtless there would be much of the stirring and romantic, as well as the sordid and vicious, and certainly a great deal of the unusual, if ever the story of these early settlements could be told.

Nevertheless, the normal Portuguese attitude toward Brazil at this time was one of disapproval, as of a poor country inhabited by savage and nomadic cannibals. And so it *was*, in comparison with the East Indies, where there were cities to sack, kings to ransom or reduce to tribute, and merchandise worth its weight in gold—in that glamorous Eastern world at the end of the rainbow, the terminus of the traditional route of Prince Henry the Navigator. Thus Brazil, in course of time the greatest contribution of Portugal in the history of European expansion, was at first the most obscure Portuguese colony.

From 1525 to 1549 there came the period of an "awakening of interest." The Eastern voyages were losing some of their glitter. Portugal was beginning to find out that they were expensive—that "for every grain of pepper" she "gave a drop of blood." Indeed, the losses in ships and human lives in this traffic were appalling. And the pull of religious crusading in Morocco had dwindled almost to the point of nothingness. On the other hand, the Americas being discovered by the Spaniards in Mexico and Peru, to say nothing of the rumored Quiviras and Gilded Men, were proving to be a field of operation worthy of exploitation by even the most insatiably avaricious, and Peru was just west of Brazil! Word came, too, that some of these riches might be found in Brazil. Perhaps the principal moving cause of Portuguese settlement, however, was one which had not yet greatly affected the Spaniards in their conquests, but was to do so after Spain had fallen from her position as the foremost military power in Europe. This was the *fear of foreign danger*. Portugal was no such strong nation as Spain, and if she were to avoid losses of territory must take care to eject all trespassers before they had time to gain a secure foothold.

Reports began to come in of foreign corsairs in Brazilian waters. So Portugal acted. Afterward, when settlements had been established, there was the usual problem, which all colonizing peoples have had to face, of how to keep them going. The introduction of the sugar industry into Brazil was the saving factor, giving the country an article of exchange which necessitated a stable order of society, at the same time that it yielded good returns in trade. The Portuguese learned, too, that every cargo did not cost a battle, as might be the case in the East, for the Indians, though strong and brave, were not capable of resisting effectively.

In 1525 [1] a Portuguese fleet was sent out to test the rumors of the presence of Frenchmen in Brazil, and learned they were true. Some French boats were found in the Bahia district. These were sunk by the Portuguese, and all their crews were killed! Other corsairs were discovered in later voyages. So a decision was reached to set up a regular government. Late in 1530 Martim Affonso de Souza left Portugal for this purpose, arriving in Brazil early in 1531. After exploring most of the coast, Souza founded the first Portuguese colony in that country (not counting the tiny, unauthorized settlements of earlier times), making an establishment in 1532 at São Vicente in the present-day state of São Paulo. He now received orders to delimit Brazil into a number of *capitaneas*, or captaincies, to be held as feudal fiefs of the Portuguese crown.

[1] Or possibly 1526, as some accounts have it.

There were probably nine of these at first, and possibly as many as fifteen later on.[1] Some were never occupied by the proprietors, or captains, to whom they were granted, however. The *capitaneas* were to extend along fifty leagues, or 150 miles, of ocean front, running thence indefinitely inward to the west, to such a point as they might touch upon lands belonging to Spain. The grantees were to settle, pacify, and develop the *capitaneas* at their own expense, and were to have the hereditary rights of sovereigns, except that a certain portion of the revenues was to go to the king, who also retained the sole rights of coining money and pronouncing the death penalty. Through the medium of the *capitaneas* the Portuguese government hoped to protect the country from European invasions, as well as to effect a more solid conquest. Similar methods had been employed with success in medieval times against the Moslems and more recently in the Madeira and Azores islands.

Souza delimited the *capitáneas*, and may have been the discoverer of Diogo Alvares Correia, otherwise "Caramurú," a Portuguese sailor who had been stranded on those shores many years before. This man, whose Indian name may have meant "The man of fire" (from the efficacy of his gun) or "Big fish caught among rocks" (from the way he was found), had made a great place for himself among the Indians of his neighborhood, and must have felt that exile from his native land was not without its compensations. He was already a chief and a patriarch and the real father of a tribe. The Portuguese were helped by him in getting a footing in the country, but his greatest importance, after all, was his large family. Caramurú had taught the Indians some of the simpler arts of civilization, and even had a chapel, but he in turn had adopted at least one native practice with enthusiasm: polygamy. It would be difficult to say how many wives he had and how many more children, but there was a great plenty of both. When the Portuguese arrived, his daughters were of marriageable age, and many of them were taken to wife by the invaders, who, of course,

[1] There is a wide variance among the authorities as to the number of the *capitaneas* (often written *capitanías*, in Spanish form). There may have been nine or ten at first, and twelve or thirteen later, and seventeen in the eighteenth century.

were all men, without any white women, as these early over-seas ventures were too filled with danger and hardship for delicate femininity to engage in them.

The progeny of these unions, mathematically three-quarters white, tended, over several generations, through the process of Mendelism, to become all white or all native, with the former joining the group of the conquerors, and the latter dropping back into the masses. It was the women who went up in the scale, while the men fell down, for a part Indian woman might marry a white man, where a half-caste male could not expect to win a white, or nearly white, woman as a life partner. Thus Caramurú in a sense became, if not the "Father of his country," at least a kind of "Grandfather" to the Brazilian nation. In point of fact, however, he was probably only representative of a prevailing situation. There was many a "Caramurú" at that time in Brazil. One well-known case was that of João Ramalho in the São Paulo district, who also had a fine supply of marriageable daughters, and who assisted the Portuguese in yet other ways in the conquest of the country. Among them, however, the Caramurús and Ramalhos and their Indian wives provided one branch of an ancestry for great numbers of present-day white Brazilians whose family history goes back to colonial Brazil.

The *capitaneas* rendered great service in the Portuguese effort to acquire the country, but did not prove to be a bonanza for the proprietors. In the Madeiras and Azores, with their limited land areas, one-man proprietorship had been feasible, but a 150 mile wide stretch nearly across a continent was too much for a single individual to handle. In addition to the immensity of the territory, there were problems of climate, the excessive vegetation, the resistance of the natives, danger from foreign pirates, and, not least of all, the tremendous distance from the base of supplies in Portugal, or even from settlements on the Brazilian coast. The importance of the need for a base of supplies, and in fact for what may be called an advancing base, cannot be overestimated. The Spaniards, for example, were able to overrun the populous and more cultivated portions of Mexico in a comparatively short time, for there they could develop bases of supply near at hand. But, despite earnest effort, it took them more than two centuries before they made a success of colonizing California, a land which in itself offered every inducement for an easy maintenance of life. It was more than a century before the English could so much as make an enduring settlement on the Atlantic coast of North America, and it was almost two centuries more before their Anglo-American descendants could push a single explorer across the continent.

Brazil was perhaps a more difficult conquest than the Anglo-American portions of the North American continent. Little wonder that most of the Brazilian proprietors were ruined, eventually giving up their *capitaneas*. Meanwhile, however, they had brought over thousands of settlers—officers, soldiers, priests, artisans, tradesmen, clerks, sailors, farmers—all men, and they were among the sturdiest stock of the then vigorous Portuguese. Many died on account of the hardships from which they suffered, while only the strongest survived. These latter were the white ancestors of the modern Brazilian people. There was one further curious result of the *capitanea* system. Brazil was settled separately at many points, and the effect of history has been to continue the original separation. So Brazil is still *many* Brazils, and will remain so until communications have been more thoroughly developed. In colonial times the districts of Bahia, Minas Geraes, Rio de Janeiro, and São Paulo became the most important, and have retained their leadership ever since.

Important as were the historical services of the *capitaneas*, they were a source of grave concern in those days to the authorities, because of their inability to maintain themselves without help. One difficulty was the lack of a sufficient labor supply, wherefore the Portuguese followed the same course as the Spaniards, enslaving the Indians. The Indians resisted them, and were aroused also as a result of cruelties and indignities which they suffered at the hands of the colonists. One phase of this was the outrages of white men upon Indian women, a condition which seems to be an inevitable part of a wifeless white conquest of native lands, and which has been just as true of English settlers as it has been of the Spanish and Portuguese. Evidently in Brazil there were not enough daughters of Caramurú to go around! So, war with the Indians became chronic. This and other problems were too much for the proprietors, who began gradually to yield their position, until by the close of the seventeenth century all the *capitaneas* had become royal.

The first royal *capitanea* was founded in 1549, with the idea of sustaining and holding together the others. Thomé de Souza was sent out as captain-general, with judges, a few Jesuits, and some thousand or more soldiers and deported criminals—but again no women. It was Souza who founded the town of Bahia in that same year. Thomé de Souza was one of the great men of colonial Brazil, the one who saved the original settlements from failure, establishing them on a secure foundation. In accord with the policies of that age, and following government orders, he saw to it that there should be no intercommunication among the *capitaneas*, and no commerce except at such points where a custom-house had been erected for the collection of revenues. All his other more noteworthy measures were recognizably valuable steps in the development of the colonies. As Brazil lacked domestic animals, he had cattle imported from the Azores, the forbears of vast wild herds. He encouraged the cultivation and manufacture of sugar, which gave the new settlements a very much needed article of commerce, to be sold in Portugal, with the proceeds applied for commodities which could not be produced in Brazil. Sugar, indeed, became the prime basis of prosperity, which dates from the arrival of Thomé de Souza. In fine, Souza gave a vigorous impulse to colonization, especially in the Bahia district, and saved Portuguese Brazil. With the establishment of a bishopric at Bahia in 1552, ordinary civilized life may be said to have begun.

Sugar meant prosperity, but it also meant slave labor. The Indians did not yield willingly; so there were organized hunts for them to serve as slaves. The agents of the Portuguese in these campaigns were half-castes, or "Mamelukes" as they were called in Brazil—the sons of the sons of Caramurú, one might say. And the Indians did a little hunting on their own account. They hunted the Portuguese, for revenge and *food*, for the Indians of Brazil were cannibals. The Tapuyas, of whom there were some seventy-six tribes, were out-and-out cannibals and savages, but the Tupí, or Guaraní, tribes, of which there were sixteen, were a more advanced people and merely occasional cannibals. They ate only their prisoners of war, but to the Portuguese, who were in almost incessant conflict with both Tapuya and Tupí, it made very little difference by which of the two they were eaten. At the time of Thomé de Souza's arrival there was already grave danger of a general Indian uprising which might have overwhelmed the colonies. Steps were taken to avert it, and one of the most important proved to be the importation of the Jesuits, to Christianize the Indians and reduce them to Portuguese control.

By some considered the greatest of the Jesuits, the "Serra" of Brazil (in terms of a comparison with the Franciscans of California), was Manoel de Nobrega, who came with Thomé de Souza in 1549 and established his headquarters in the north, out of Bahia. The head of the order in Brazil, he founded what have come to be regarded as the typical Jesuit missions, perhaps more widely known in the later Paraguayan and Baja Californian institutions. The Indians were brought into villages and put to work under the Jesuits, raising sugar and engaging in the various economic tasks of the period, with the product of their industry being employed by the Jesuits in commerce. White men, except for the missionaries and a guard of a few soldiers, were excluded from the missions. A thoroughgoing control by the Jesuits was exercised, which made these settlements, or "reductions," as they are sometimes called, virtually a state within a state, for the Portuguese officials of the white towns had little authority over them. The Jesuits, of course, aimed to Christianize the Indians and to rescue them from barbarism, using kindly and paternalistic methods which won the affection and allegiance of the Indians. And yet the greatest contribution of the mission system, here and elsewhere in the Americas, was that it aided in an important way in the conquest of the territory by the whites. The Indian resistance was overcome, and the colonies were saved from a danger which might easily have overwhelmed them.

Father Nobrega converted the Indians in the north, and uprooted the institution of polygamy among them, but, curiously enough, was not equally successful in doing away with cannibalism. Almost as important as Nobrega, and perhaps an even more famous figure in the annals of colonial Brazil, was Father José de Anchieta, the great Jesuit of the south, in the São Paulo district, sometimes called the "Saint Francis Xavier of the West," in a comparison with the famous Jesuit missionary of China and Japan.[1] He was not only a learned and eloquent man, but also a lovable character and an untiring worker, at one and the same time a priest, doctor, artisan, philologist, and political leader. Acquiring an ability to speak a number of the Indian tongues, he at length composed the first Guaraní grammar. The Jesuits also founded several schools, the most notable of which was the College of São Paulo, established by Anchieta and dating from 1554; this also marked the beginning of what is now the great city of São Paulo.

Relations of the white settlers with the Jesuits were to take their place with race problems, the foreign peril, and Portuguese expansion into the interior as the leading factors in the history of colonial Brazil. The Portuguese were strongly pro-Jesuit at first, when help was needed in order to bring the Indians into subjection. But as the Indian danger decreased, the Portuguese attitude quickly changed, primarily because the missions were business competitors of the colonists. The Jesuits had the advantage of an ample and fairly contented labor supply, augmented by the Indians who escaped from the white plantations and took refuge in the missions. Ever in need of labor, and relying on the raids of the Mamelukes for their supply, the Portuguese were hampered even in this resource as a result of Jesuit action. The Jesuits were able to procure a decree, in 1570, abolishing Indian slavery in the Bahia district. This enraged the whites, and it enraged the Mamelukes even more, as it cut off their means of livelihood. Their feelings were further inflamed when it was observed that the Jesuits profited by the measure, as they had plenty of labor, obtained without

[1] Retaining the parallelism with the California missionaries, Anchieta might be likened to the amiable, highly intelligent, but able Lasuén, as Nobrega would be to the first Father-President, Serra.

cost and maintained at no more expense than were the slaves of the white plantations. The Jesuits unquestionably were sincere in their devotion to the Indians in sponsoring this measure, and proved it by suggesting negro slavery as an alternative, an institution rarely condemned as wrong in those days, when negroes were regarded as "natural slaves." The suggestion, whether originally offered by the Jesuits or not, was taken up, and negroes began to be imported from Africa in 1574. This was a momentous event in Brazilian history!

The Jesuits were also accused of endeavoring to establish a supreme political authority in Brazil, and undoubtedly they would have liked to do so, as they did later in Paraguay and Baja California. This "danger," as the white colonists regarded it, increased in the seventeenth century. Then the Jesuits, who had aided greatly in enthroning the House of Braganza (which came into power with the war of Portuguese independence against Spain in 1640), were rewarded by being given an almost dominant position in Brazil. The nucleus of the white resistance was the São Paulo district in the south, where the most vigorous of the Portuguese settlers lived. Opposing the economic advantages of the Jesuits, they had continued their slave-hunts, and from about 1562 went so far as to raid the missions themselves. This was no easy matter to do, as the missions had now in a sense become military posts, as the Fathers had made soldiers of their charges, as well as training them in more peaceful tasks. In 1640 the royal decree of 1570 was expanded to include all of Brazil, emancipating the Indians from slavery, but of course not touching the mission Indians, who were not considered technically as slaves. This was the signal for the outbreak of a most remarkable colonial civil war. The whites rose against the Jesuits, and expelled them by force of arms. The Jesuits returned in 1653, and the conflict was renewed. Beaten in the south by 1679, the Jesuits held out in the north until 1688, when once again they were driven from the country. Here was a near "half-century of conflict" which might well deserve to have its Parkman.[1] In

[1] The reference is to Parkman, Francis, *A half-century of conflict* (Boston, 1892), an interesting account of the wars in North America between England and France, down to 1763.

later years the Jesuits came back to Brazil, but thenceforth were of secondary importance. Expelled from Portugal in 1757, as part of a European movement, they were in 1758 also required to leave Brazil.

Sincere in their desire to Christianize and civilize the Indians, the Jesuits were only measurably and temporarily successful in realizing these hopes. The Indians did learn a rote Christianity, and acquired the attributes of civilization in a crude form, to the extent of their abilities perhaps, but in the end the missions were a failure. Those Indians who escaped some form of servitude under the whites reverted to their old habits, their idolatry and nomadic life, their polygamy and cannibalism. Most of them died off, or were absorbed in their intermingling with the negroes and whites. The Jesuits temporarily checked the destruction of the native races, but they are gone today; only a small fraction of Brazil's present known population is recognizably Indian. The Jesuits rendered other services of a more permanent character. For one thing they introduced a moral element into a colonial society, which was notoriously weak in the standards of good conduct. And yet their political contributions were the most substantial of their gifts. They saved colonial Brazil from the Indians. And not only this, they were also an important factor in overcoming the foreign peril, especially from the French. Before dealing with this, however, one other racial problem, that of the negroes, ought first to be taken up.

For a time, northern Brazil, in the equatorial belt, had to carry Brazil economically, on the basis of sugar and slave labor. The south, with its temperate climate and lack of adaptability for sugar, lived precariously for a number of years, raising tobacco, selling some brazil wood, and engaging in the Indian slave trade. Later, precious metals, domestic animals, and a diversified agriculture were to give a means of support, but the greatest of present-day Brazilian products, coffee, was of no importance in the colonial era. This backwardness of the colonial south rendered one great eventual service. It kept the region primarily white; slavery in any form never flourished there.

Beginning in 1574, the importation of negro slaves into

Brazil was carried on for about three centuries. Through the efforts of England, the slave trade was abolished early in the nineteenth century, but was continued clandestinely for a number of years. Usually about twenty thousand a year were imported, and it is estimated that a total of six to eight millions were brought in, most of them from Portuguese-controlled Angola in Africa. Absolutely against modern notions of right and wrong, and even of economic desirability, slavery seemed in colonial times a *sine qua non* of Brazilian prosperity and development; without slaves, no labor, and without labor, no Brazil. At any rate, the actual success of the Portuguese there is traceable to the institution of slavery, at length wholly negro.

Slaves were treated well or ill, according to circumstances —worse in the mines than in agriculture—worse on the plantations in the interior than on those of the more populous white districts along the coast—and worse where the negroes were more numerous than where they were not, in order to intimidate them. It was customary to brand them with an "F" (for "*Fugido*," or "Runaway") if they attempted to escape, and for the second offence to cut off an ear. Negroes were allowed to earn small sums for themselves, and might purchase their own freedom, or be liberated by grant of their master. Liberty was rare, however, except as the negroes took to flight, and found a means of existence out in the woods, away from the whites. Many a negro village, or "*quilombo*," was established in the Brazilian forests, and one of them in the Pernambuco district had a remarkable history, rising to such prominence as to threaten the safety of the white settlements in that neighborhood.

In 1650 some forty Guinea-born negroes of the *capitanea* of Pernambuco escaped, with arms in their hands. Forming a *quilombo*, they became a nucleus for a community which rapidly grew, as other slaves escaped to it, and as even some free negroes threw in their lot with these men of their own race. To avoid attack, they decided to go farther into the interior, and at length built a town called Palmares. Straightway they proceeded to encounter the usual problems of new settlements. One was a lack of women. So raids were organized against the colonies of the coast, and women of all colors—black, red, white, and intermixtures—were captured and distributed. And then there was the problem of some economic basis of life. At first, this was solved through marauding; later, agriculture developed, and was supplemented by some trade, even with the whites of the coast. A regular government was devised, at the head of which was a *zombe*, or chief, who held office for life. There were other magistrates of war and peace, and there was a crude system of law. Murder, adultery, and robbery, for example, were crimes punishable with death. Oddly enough, these escaped slaves based their economic activities on the institution of slavery. Slaves who escaped from the white colonies became free, but those who were captured while in a state of slavery remained slaves in Palmares.

This negro experiment in colonization had a life of nearly half a century, and it was through no fault of Palmares that it failed then. In course of time Palmares expanded until it was merely one of a number of towns, the capital city of the republic, with a population said to have been as great as twenty thousand. It is a tribute to the capacity of these negroes that they were able to solve the problem of an adequate water supply for so large a city. The city was fortified with a wall made of the trunks of great trees, with three gates. To the rear of the city was a precipitous cliff. In all the republic there was a total of some ten thousand warriors.

The authorities in Pernambuco became alarmed by the success of Palmares, and in 1696 Governor Mello decided to destroy it. He raised an army of *seven thousand men*—such an army as the Anglo-American colonies rarely saw, in even the greatest of conflicts!—well equipped with artillery, with which the negroes could not cope. At length Mello reached the walls of the capital city itself, which he had to besiege in the face of a desperate defence. When the fall of the city appeared certain, the *zombe* and other leading functionaries threw themselves over the cliff, rather than submit. No quarter was given to the others! Doubtless the Portuguese hesitated to make slaves again of these negroes, who had shown a capacity which is probably the most extraordinary instance in the history of the negro race in the Western

Hemisphere. This was the last notable resistance of the negroes to enslavement. The negro problem was to be more prominent as one of race, a social factor involving intermixture with reds and whites, than as an element of political danger.

Meanwhile, the Portuguese had been obliged to battle with other Europeans, especially the French, English, and Dutch, for the right to the exclusive possession of the territory they had occupied. The earliest in point of time was the French peril, which, indeed, had given an impulse to the initial Portuguese settlement. Just as they were later in Canada, the French were traders rather than planters, and were able to keep on good terms with the Indians, who became attached to them, a feeling which was accentuated by their hatred for their slave-seeking enemies, the Portuguese. The early French traders exchanged numerous small articles for brazil wood.

In the middle of the sixteenth century, during the period of the ascendancy of the great French colonial genius, Admiral Coligny, steps were taken to erect French settlements in Brazil. The plan was suggested by Nicolas Durand de Villegagnon, a Catholic, who proposed that these establishments might serve as a refuge for French Calvinists, or Huguenots, an idea which appealed strongly to Coligny, himself a Calvinist. The story of the enterprise is obscured by the shadows of religious controversy. It would seem that Villegagnon gave Coligny and Calvin (a boyhood friend) reason to believe that he had become a Calvinist. Nevertheless, both Catholics and Protestants made up the expeditionary forces, and the Villegagnon apologists claim that his real idea was to establish a haven for persons of different beliefs, on the basis of religious toleration. At any rate, in 1555 Villegagnon founded his colony at Rio de Janeiro. It is a commentary on the Portuguese neglect of Brazil up to this time that this harbor, which is one of the best in the world, should have been unoccupied by them. The French soon found that the new settlement was no easy matter to maintain, and they quarreled among themselves over religious questions. Villegagnon took the Catholic side, and reduced the Protestants to the same code of discipline provided for the convicts who formed part of the colony. In an attempt to leave, all the Protestant clergymen but one were drowned, and with affairs in a hopeless state Villegagnon himself soon returned to France. In the realm of the "might have been" the failure of the Villegagnon project looms prominently. One writer comments as follows:

> "It is interesting to conjecture what would have been the history of Brazil if Villegagnon had stuck to the Huguenot side. In all probability re-enforcements would have been sent, and St. Bartholomew's Day—fourteen years later—might have been followed by a great emigration like that which went to New England during the Laud persecution. Rio and perhaps the whole of South Brazil would have become a French possession or a French-speaking state." [1]

After some delay, the Portuguese took advantage of the weakness of the French, and attacked them. In 1560 Governor Mem de Sá defeated the French, and drove them into the interior, where they took refuge with the Indians, who were still friendly to them. Presently they were able to organize a general Indian uprising against the Portuguese, and it was in this emergency that the Jesuits saved the situation. Some tribes followed the Jesuits into the war on the Portuguese side, and Nobrega and Anchieta by their personal efforts persuaded most of the hostile natives to make peace. The French and some of the Indians continued the conflict, however, even reoccupying Rio de Janeiro. In 1565, Eustaquio de Sá, cousin of the governor, greatly assisted by Father Nobrega, assembled a fleet, and founded a Portuguese settlement in another part of the Bay of Rio de Janeiro from the French. It was not until two years later that the French were defeated and destroyed. All who were captured were put to the sword, and only a few escaped into the wilderness. French corsairs continued to harry the coasts during the remainder of the century, and occasionally gained a foothold on the mainland in the north, but were driven out as they had been in the south. Not until 1614 were they finally expelled, bringing to a close somewhat more than another "half-century of conflict."

[1] Dawson, I, 334. Some accounts hold that Villegagnon turned Lutheran, thus explaining his quarrel with the Calvinists. This can hardly have been the case, however.

The English peril, while it seemed important enough at the time, did not prove to be so serious as that of the French or Dutch. It was confined, in the main, to the activities of freebooters, although supplemented by plans for actual settlement. Many were the annoyances suffered by the Portuguese, however, at the hands of the English. In the later years of the sixteenth century Cavendish, Hawkins, Lancaster, and Witherington sacked and burned cities along the coast. And when Francis Drake returned from his voyage around the world, eager to found an English colony in California, which he had visited in 1579, the project was diverted into one for an establishment in Brazil, but it came to naught. The English difficulties at home held them back from any aggressive policy in the first half of the seventeenth century, and treaties between England and Portugal then began to be made which were to bring about lasting friendly relations. These gave Englishmen such commercial privileges in Portuguese-owned territories that there was no longer any great incentive for a conquest.

The Dutch peril was to be the greatest of all. This had its origin in events which for sixty years brought Portugal under the dominion of the kings of Spain, from 1580 to 1640. This era of the "Babylonian captivity" of Portugal, as it is sometimes called, is often held by Portuguese writers to have been the source of all their ills, in particular with respect to the loss of their empire. Although this is a debatable point, since the empire would probably have fallen to stronger European powers anyway, it did serve as an entering wedge for conquests by the Dutch, who availed themselves of their wars against Spain to pick up the Portuguese territories of the Spanish monarch. In the Far East they met with success, but in Brazil they failed, though only after a desperate conflict.

Dutch freebooters had annoyed the Portuguese in Brazil, much as the English had done, but presently the Dutch made a serious and temporarily successful effort at colonization. In 1621 a charter was granted to the Dutch West India Company, giving it territories in South America and Africa, together with a twenty-four year monopoly of trade. Holland did not own these lands thus so generously given away, but that was a matter of small consequence in those times; they did belong to the Spanish-Portuguese monarchy, and Holland was at war with Spain. In 1624 an expedition of twenty-six Dutch ships, some 3500 men, and five hundred cannon was sent out. Bahia was taken and sacked, but in the following year was recaptured by the Portuguese, aided by a Spanish fleet. In 1630 a still greater Dutch expedition of thirty-eight ships and nearly seven thousand men established itself in Pernambuco, and maintained itself against repeated attacks of the Portuguese. Presently the Dutch were able to expand their holdings until much of northern Brazil was in their possession.

To consolidate and improve their position the Dutch sent out one of their greatest generals, Count Maurice of Nassau, in 1637. He did advance the conquest, but being a wise and capable administrator, as well as a good general, he wished to stop and organize the existing territories, before adding new ones. And certainly Dutch Brazil was vast enough, as matters were. This was no mere New Amsterdam. At its greatest extent, about 1644, it measured some four hundred thousand square miles, an area almost as great as that of the seventeen states of the United States lying between the Appalachians and the Atlantic Ocean.[1]

Maurice was not allowed to follow his own inclinations, however. Orders came from Holland for him to take Bahia, and he did make a desperate but unsuccessful attempt, at a cost in lives of some three thousand of his followers. Thereafter he confined himself to administering the territories already occupied, showing himself to be a man far ahead of his times. He declared for freedom of commerce, aided agriculture, returned to various Portuguese proprietors the sugar estates which had been confiscated from them, formed a legislative body, and even proclaimed religious toleration in an age when Protestants and Catholics were fighting one another like wild beasts. His work was not appreciated, however. Stockholders in the Company wanted profits more than just administration, the Protestant Dutch

[1] Dutch Brazil included the present states of Maranhão, Piauhy (about half), Ceará, Rio Grande do Norte, Parahyba, Pernambuco, Alagóas, and Sergipe. The combined area of these states is 472,000 square miles.

clergy objected to the liberty granted to Catholics, and the patriotic Portuguese preferred even a bad government by themselves to a good one by a Dutchman. Unable to hold out against all these elements, Maurice resigned in 1644, and returned to Europe. Many Dutchmen rejoiced, but this in fact marked the swing of the pendulum definitively in the direction of the Portuguese.

The Portuguese had already begun their war of independence, 1640–1668, against Spain, and in 1641 the home government made a treaty of alliance with Holland. It was understood, however, that for one year the Dutch might continue to make conquests in the Portuguese colonies! And in fact the Dutch occupied the province of Maranhão in northern Brazil, but were driven out by the Portuguese settlers after a conflict of two years. In 1643 there was an uprising against the Dutch in the province of Pernambuco. This might have been handled by Maurice of Nassau, with the backing of the Company, but he was then on the eve of his departure for Europe. Curiously enough, the Portuguese government protested against the action of the Portuguese in Brazil, lest it might offend the Dutch, whose aid in Europe it desired at any cost. The Portuguese colonists paid little attention, and fought a thirteen-year war, 1641–1654, which resulted in the expulsion of the Dutch. After 1651, when the Portuguese-Dutch alliance in Europe came to an end, the Portuguese government gave some assistance, but in the main the conflict was sustained by the Brazilians themselves. In a sense this marked the beginning of a perhaps rather hazy Brazilian patriotism. Portugal had done little to help, but the Brazilians, including all the racial elements in the country, had won a great victory. João Fernandes Vieira, the principal Brazilian general, was a white man, and among the other most prominent leaders were Camarão, an Indian, and Dias, a negro. But the new-born patrotism was hardly all-Brazilian, being rather of a *capitanea* type, developing local confidence and pride, and engendering something of a resentment against the Portuguese government in Europe.

Over all these years of difficulties with Indian, negro, and rival white, the Portuguese were developing and expanding the territories they possessed, especially in the more vigorous south. Slave-hunting was one of the earlier objects of the explorations into the interior. When legal obstacles were thrown in the way of this traffic, the expeditions were continued, but now with new objectives in mind, such as a search for gold, and later to carry on smuggling operations with the Spanish colonies of the Río de la Plata. One must not forget the hazards of such explorations—those of all time in a new country—the problems of life and health, the problem of necessities. A small party might conceivably live on game, but would be massacred by the Indians, if not wiped out by disease. A large party could defeat the Indians, but could not live on game, or carry needed provisions, or perhaps as effectively combat sickness. In other words, there must be the inevitable slow penetration through the medium of the advancing base of supplies, or else there must be some great profit-offering impulse, which would make men eager even to risk death in order to attain their goal. In Brazil there was that impulse, the same one which has appeared many times in history: the pull of precious metals. Gold made California—made Alaska. Centuries earlier, gold played a prominent part in the making of Brazil. For gold, thousands died, but others survived, and permanent settlement was achieved.

The most virile people of colonial Brazil were those of the São Paulo district, or Paulistas, as they are called. They were ever exploring, ever colonizing. The original impulse for gold-hunting came from the Spanish successes to the west in Peru and Upper Peru (modern Bolivia). Word came that at Potosí a mountain of silver had been found. Rumors from the Indians were to the effect that equally rich deposits existed in Brazil. The Paulistas searched for them for about a century, making only unimportant finds at first. At length, in 1692, gold was discovered in Minas Geraes, and the next three years witnessed a rush of all classes and colors to that region, mainly Brazilians and Portuguese, but also some foreigners. Forthwith there developed the wild and rough life which people of the United States associate with California and the Klondike, as if they were unique instances, when in reality this situation has been duplicated many times and many places in history. Here, as elsewhere, were lynch law, brazen women, and excess both in luxury and vice, but here was one thing more: actual war. The Paulistas, as the discoverers, claimed a monopoly, which other elements attacked. For seven years there was war, serious blood-spilling war, in which at length the Paulistas were defeated. The Portuguese central authorities finally stepped in, and established order, later making a separate province of Minas Geraes. Meanwhile, the Paulistas had been making other discoveries. Some gold had been found beyond Minas Geraes to the northwest in Goyaz in 1682 and at Reparaz in 1694, and rich discoveries in far western Matto Grosso at Cuyabá in 1718. In these cases, too, there followed a rush of gold-seekers to the scene.

The most curious discovery, however, was of the diamonds of Brazil. Miners of the region where they were found, in Minas Geraes, had known of them for years, but were unaware of their value, using them as chips in their gambling games. In 1728 or 1729 a missionary who had been in India revealed what they were, and the Portuguese crown made haste to appropriate the diamond fields as its exclusive property. From then until the discovery of the mines of Kimberley in South Africa, Brazil was the world's principal source of supply for these much prized precious stones.

The finding of gold and diamonds accomplished much more than the enrichment of those who profited directly from them. Rio de Janeiro, with its fine bay and excellent location with respect to routes to the mines, became for the first time a rich and prosperous centre. Nearly all the regions of what is now Brazil were explored and occupied, beyond any caviling over the line of Tordesillas or other would-be limitation; indeed, Portuguese Brazil got to be about double the size of what it would have been if Spain and Portugal had adhered to the line of Tordesillas. The explorations and migrations of the Paulistas into the interior were, to Brazil, what the westward movement in the United States was from 1763 to 1860 in the making of the great republic of the north. The two movements have often been compared. And, after all, the gold was only part of the lure in

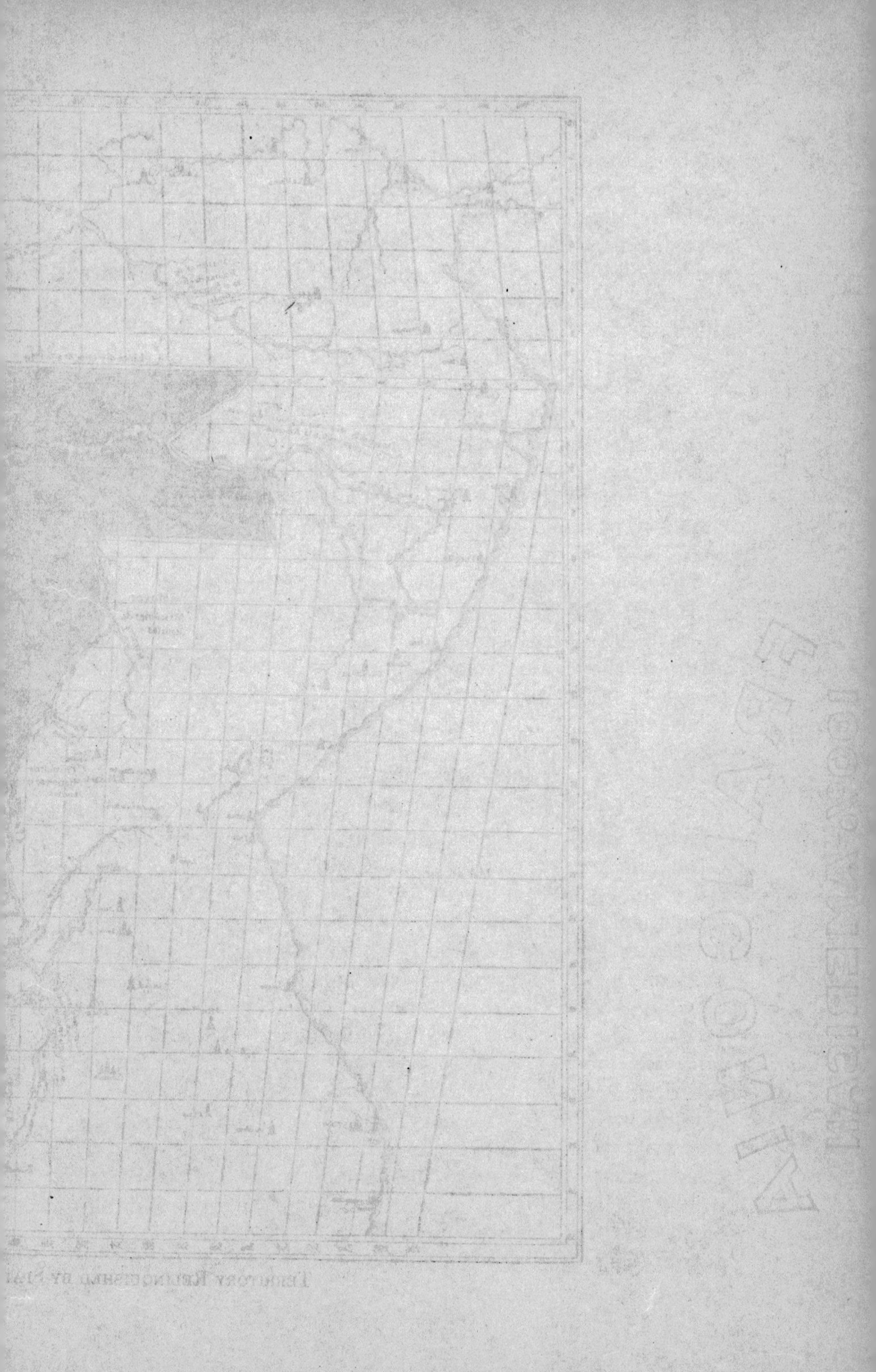

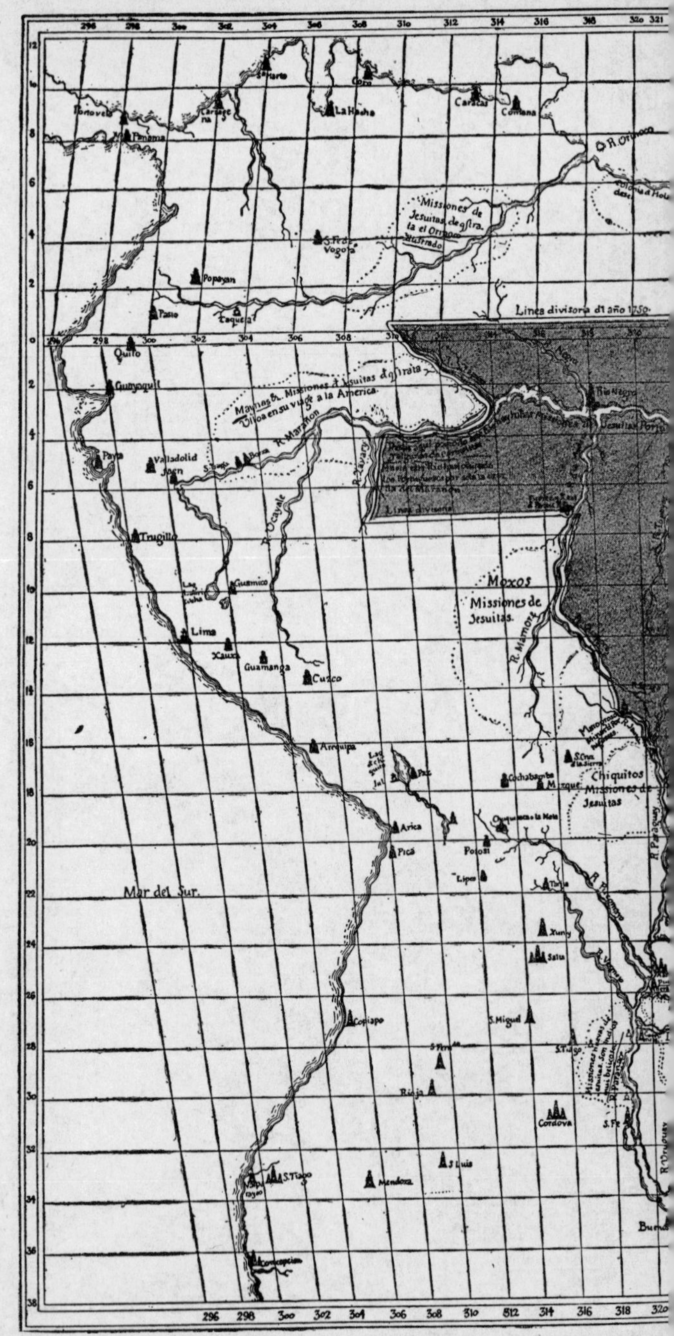

TERRITORY RELINQUISHED BY SPA

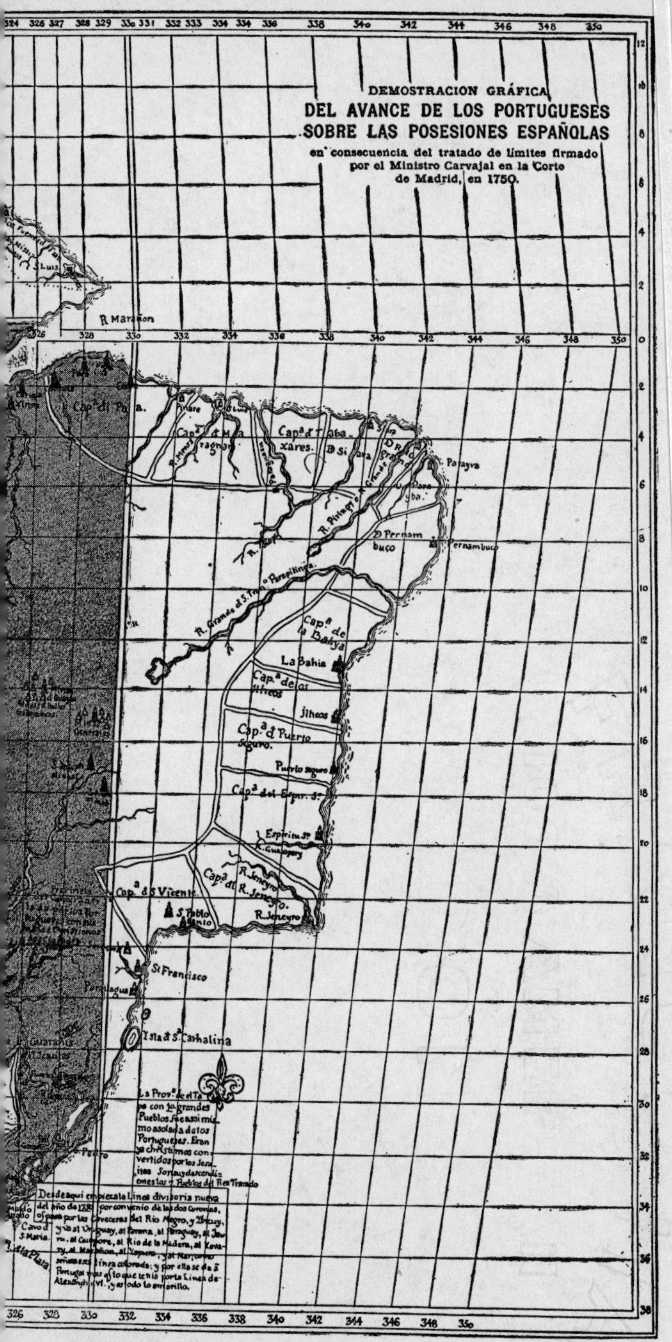

TUGUESE BRAZIL: TREATY OF 1750

Brazil. When that began to be found in diminishing quantities, other lines of industry had already been developed. In other words, thanks very largely to the Paulistas, Brazil had become *Brazil*. The only remaining question was: what would be her destiny?

CHAPTER VI

THE SPANISH AGGRESSIVE DEFENSIVE UNDER THE LATER HAPSBURGS, 1556–1700

FROM the standpoint of Spanish policy there were three broad periods in the history of the colonies in the New World. The first of these, already dealt with, was the era of the *conquistadores*, when lands were conquered because of their desirability in themselves. But a turn came in the reign of Philip II (1556–1598). Toward the close of his rule, Spain began to decline from her position of preëminence in Europe and to be put upon the necessity of defending herself against her numerous and more and more powerful enemies. Thereafter, Spain's conquests in the colonies were usually on the basis of taking territories in order to keep them from falling into the hands of another country—not so much on account of the territories themselves, as because their possession by another nation might endanger those already held by Spain—the same factor which from the beginning had been the mainspring of the Portuguese conquest of Brazil. The defeat of the Great Armada of Spain by the English in 1588 may be said to have marked the turning-point to this policy, but events had been leading in that direction for a number of years. Drake's voyage into the Pacific and around the world, 1577–1580, was such an event. Spain was awakened to the danger she ran of losing large portions of her empire. Never before had she encountered competition along the western shores of the Americas. Henceforth, Spain took the aggressive for defensive reasons. Spain pushed northwest toward California, for example, in order to protect the already conquered Mexico. The same policy was followed in other parts of the empire. Two centuries later, about 1790, the vital year of the Nootka Sound controversy with England, Spain took a further step down, when she adopted a new kind of defensive of the waiting type—waiting for an attack before adopting measures for defending herself.

The outcome of that was disintegration and loss of her colonies.[1] By way of emphasis these three periods in colonial history may be called the "aggressive aggressive," the "aggressive defensive," and the "defensive defensive."

It was in the time of Philip II that the aggressive defensive was inaugurated. The empire continued to expand, great expeditions were made as in the years before, and men lost or risked their lives. As single episodes, the stories of these various undertakings are just as interesting as those of the *conquistadores*, but a vital something has gone out of them, and the world has never given them the attention which Cortés and Pizarro and the other *conquistadores* received. Perhaps there was a little less of the flavor, less of the marvelous, the White King and Anián, less of a Mexico City, Cuzco, or Bogotá, though weird tales remained to some extent a moving cause of effort until the close of the eighteenth century. At any rate, no such startling discoveries were made as in the earlier years, the territories conquered had previously been explored, and it is difficult to feel the same enthusiasm for a defensive fighter as for one who always attacks. From the point of view of importance the era of the aggressive defensive nevertheless rivals the aggressive aggressive, because these were the years of the solid establishment of Spanish institutions, affecting the older conquests and the new alike. More space may properly be given to these institutions, however, than to the narrative of the territorial expansion of the empire. This latter phase may therefore be treated here with comparative brevity.

"Amadís de Gaula" still lived, but the more important pursuit of such wonders as that novel depicted took the direction of the Pacific. Voyages were sent across that ocean, looking for a "great southern continent" and what not; but most of these expeditions are beyond the purview of this volume. One of them, however, took the Spaniards from Mexico to the Philippines and back in 1564–1565. In consequence, the island group was conquered, and a rich trade was developed between Manila in the Philippines and Acapulco, Mexico. For 250 years, from 1565 to 1815,

[1] Cf. *infra*, 183–186.

the Manila galleons came east across the North Pacific and down past the Californias to Acapulco, before taking a more southerly route back to Manila. Drake missed the galleon, but in 1587 another Englishman, Cavendish, burst into the Pacific, and captured the rich "Santa Ana." From that time forward, the Californias became an objective of the Spaniards, as a suitable way-station where the galleon might stop to refit and to learn whether foreign pirates were lying in wait. Eventually other agressive defensive factors became more important in the advance toward California, but a beginning was made in the time of Philip II in connection with the galleon.[1]

The story of Spain's conquest toward and into California is typical of the era of the aggressive defensive, and may therefore be discussed in that light, with the details omitted or rapidly passed over in the case of similar conquests. The same tale might indeed be told with respect to the approaches to New Mexico, Texas, and Florida, the other salients in the north, and as concerns the expansion within and to the far limits of other lands in the two Americas of which the Spaniards were already in part possessed.[2]

Spain strove consciously to reach the Californias, both Baja and Alta (the latter the present-day California of the United States), by sea and land. The earlier attempts were made by sea. Some mention has already been made of the sea approaches to California in the voyages of Cortés, Cabrillo, and Ferrelo, to include only a few out of the many. The most famous voyage in connection with efforts to find a station for the Manila galleon was that of Sebastián Vizcaíno in 1602–1603. Vizcaíno made a fairly thorough survey of the coast from Cape San Lucas to Cape Mendocino, though missing the Bay of San Francisco, as all the expeditionaries did until 1769. A "wonderful harbor"

[1] For something further about the Manila galleon, see *infra*, 161–162.

[2] Without detail as to the various factors involved, the period of the aggressive defensive cannot be understood, but it should be obvious to the reader that the same detail for all sections would very greatly enlarge the volume, and make the discussion of this topic out of all proportion to its relative importance. The illustration through the medium of California is merely one from the many available, and it is not asserted that it is superior in any respect to those in other parts of the field. Those interested in other lines of the Spanish advance would do well to engage in some parallel reading at this point.

was discovered, however, in the Bay of Monterey, which is in fact not at all wonderful as a harbor. One of the ships came upon a mysterious bay and river—or so the ignorant boatswain, the only surviving officer of that particular ship, said. Henceforth, this grew in the imaginations of the map-makers until it became an almost transcontinental stream, or at the least a great western sea. Just what could have been the foundation for this story has never been determined. Many men died in course of the voyage—for example, one boat started back with thirty-four men on board, and when at length it reached its destination only nine were still alive—but the legend of the desirability of California was maintained, especially on account of its great port of *Monterey!*

For more than a century and a half after Vizcaíno, Spain intermittently continued her efforts to get to California by sea, though diverted at first by a search for a more suitable way-station for the galleon in the wealthy islands of Rica de Oro and Rica de Plata—islands of the fabled type, since they did not in fact exist. Thus the favorable moment of the Vizcaíno expedition was lost, even though Spain never forgot her interest in California. A declining power in the seventeenth century, however, Spain was unwilling to undergo great expenditures unless in case of an emergency, and tried for many years to accomplish her purposes through the medium of private voyages, paid for by the organizers, who hoped to profit from the discoveries they were authorized to make. The difficulties of settlement by sea, without the aid of the advancing land bases of supply, were so great, however, that no progress was made in more than three-quarters of a century under private initiative. Late in the seventeenth century, the government itself, under the urge of the frequent appearance of "Pichilingues," or foreign pirates, in the Pacific, decided to bear the expense. A settlement was made in Baja California which lasted two years, 1683–1685, and when this failed, Spain was still ready to make a fresh effort, but Indian troubles in Mexico and the life and death struggle of the European wars with Louis XIV of France proved to be too heavy a financial deterrent. If the Californias were to be colonized in normal course, it had to be done by land, from post to post and base to base. Meanwhile, Jesuit missionaries were sent into Baja California in 1697, and their establishments constituted an occupation until such time as Spain might take more thoroughgoing steps for the acquisition of the peninsula and the richer Alta California to the north.

It was primarily through overland conquests that Spain took effective possession of the principal territories in her vast colonial dominions and advanced from them to the outposts of her empire, such as the two Californias. The first great conqueror after Cortés in the direction of the last-named salients was Nuño de Guzmán. Over the years 1529–1531 he reduced the country northwestward of Mexico City as far as Sinaloa, and much of it remained definitively conquered. Coronado, in 1540–1542, passed through Sonora, and turned off toward New Mexico and Kansas. Great overland expeditions to the northwest now ceased for more than two centuries, although one such venture along a more easterly line of advance had ramifications which took it to the Colorado in 1604–1605. This was the expedition of Juan de Oñate, who conquered New Mexico in 1598.

Cortés, Guzmán, Coronado, and Oñate had rendered great service by effecting a permanent conquest of large areas and developing a preliminary knowledge of much of the field along the line of the northwestward advance. Other *conquistadores* had done the same service in other parts of the Americas. These men were followed, perhaps in the wake of other expeditions of lesser note, or sometimes preceding them, by a stream of Spanish soldiers, missionaries, and civilians. Thus began a second phase of the conquest—that of the frontier. Along the land route to the Californias the civilians in this stage were mostly miners, although there were not a few engaged in stock-raising and other pursuits characteristic of frontier life. Eventually, in a portion of the field, would come a third phase, with the missionaries and soldiers moving on, the secular clergy replacing the regular, and civilians entering in greater numbers and taking part in a greater variety of occupations than before. That particular region then ceased to partake of the attributes of a frontier province, and entered upon what may be called a settled life. In all three stages the Spanish elements were a small minority—certainly along the northwestward route from Mexico City, and in greater or less degree everywhere else—but were the ruling class. The masses, from first to last, were Indian, or at best *mestizo* (mixed Indian and white). Some of the Indians were driven away or killed, but most of them usually submitted, and, though strictly ruled and perhaps enslaved, were permitted to remain.

Military, religious, and civilian: these were the three elements which effected the Spanish conquest. Of the three, perhaps the most vitally essential was the military, for without its aid neither of the others could proceed very far, even though the two latter contributed most to the eventual pacification and settled development of a region. The number of soldiers was always small, but their presence in the first and second stages of conquest was a *sine qua non* of the Spanish occupation. Their expeditions into unoccupied territory, whether for punitive objects or for purposes of exploration, were the most important preliminaries of the conquest; even in the frequent journeys of missionaries into the interior, soldiers were usually taken along as a more or less indispensable escort. Once occupation of a region had taken place, a presidial force of forty or fifty men was a sufficient garrison for a wide area, so superior were they in fighting equipment and military methods to the natives, however brave the Indians might be. A mission guard of from one to five or six soldiers also served to keep hundreds of mission Indians, or even a thousand, in check, while without this military support the missions could not be sustained. To a certain extent, too, the military contributed to economic development through the great presidial stock farms, but these were in no small degree more a hindrance than a help; Indian trouble too often became an asset of the presidial capitalist, who might thereby rid himself of the competition of civilian rivals, while utilizing the troops to protect his own stock.

Rivaling the military as an agency in the subjection of the Indians, and much more prominent as a constructive social and economic factor, were the religious of the missionary orders. Neither the missionaries nor the secular churchmen acted on their own initiative, for under the already mentioned institution of the *patronato real* the church was almost as completely subordinate to the king as the soldiery were. It was the king or his sub-delegates who appointed church dignitaries and lesser functionaries, from an archbishop down to a priest or friar; he also made provision for their salaries, built their churches, approved or ordered their policies, and paid the score. The missionary was a direct royal agent; not a mission could be founded or a missionary go to the frontier without the assent of the royal authorities, and indeed the religious were sometimes thrust into an enterprise against their pronounced objections. Usually, however, the zeal of the Fathers outran the royal will for their employment, for missionaries and missions involved expenditures, and the government was none too lavish with its funds, unless it could see a likelihood of advantageous returns. Naturally, the *patronato real* did not include a right to intervene in the realm of the spiritual, but there was little else which the popes reserved.

The missionaries accompanied the troops in the first two stages of the conquest. They went with them on their military expeditions, or even preceded them into new territory on journeys of exploration, although, as already stated, they were usually attended by a small escort of soldiers. The principal function of the religious, however, came in the second stage of the conquest, through the institution of the mission. The mission system employed by the Spaniards was much the same in all of their dominions, being subject to the same laws and the same body of officials. The principal objects, as stated by the laws, were to convert the natives and lift them out of their savagery and barbarism to a state of civilization. These were indeed the primary objects of the missionaries themselves, but they were secondary to other factors in the attention of the royal government. The mission was an effective support of the troops in keeping the Indians of a particular region in subjection, and in this way contributed, through the security it gave, to the protection of the royal domain from other Indians and from foreigners beyond the frontier. Thus it assisted in actual conquests—and much more cheaply than the soldiers necessary to take their place would have cost. Ultimately, too, the Indians would become a source of profit to the crown, for those who had submitted to Spanish authority were required by law to pay an annual tribute, although this was remitted for the Indians still in the missions.

A mission was founded through a process of voluntary conversion, by gathering the Indians of a community or limited region into a "reduction," or mission village. No Spaniards other than the missionaries, the mission guard, and an occasional civilian official could stop at the mission or reside there. Persuasion, usually to the accompaniment of gifts of food, clothing, and tobacco, or trinkets which appealed to the childlike fancy of the natives, was generally employed to induce acceptance by the Indians of the mission idea. Once they entered the mission, however, there was no legal escape for them until such time as the royal government should give them their release, and emancipation meant taxation in the shape of the annual tribute. The salaries of missionaries and a certain initial sum were provided at state expense, besides military protection, but the mission was supposed to procure all else it needed, by means of its own industry or through the gifts of pious individuals. Usually there were two religious at a mission, and a corporal at the head of four or five soldiers, but at times a single missionary and fewer troops were employed. Beyond the limits of the mission proper, but within a day or two's journey at the farthest, there were *pueblos de visita* (villages of visit), or *visitas,* where the missionaries went occasionally to perform religious services. In the *visitas* there was a representative of the missionary in the person of the Indian "master of doctrine," but in other respects the *visita* Indians retained their liberty. On the other hand, they did not share in economic benefits, such as the receipt of tobacco, food, and clothing, to the same extent as the Indians of the mission.

Except for a certain amount of independence on the part

of the military escort, which, however, was in most respects under the orders of the religous, the missionaries were like absolute monarchs in their narrow realm. They were the spiritual, and political, and even economic masters of the mission, subject only to their superiors in the religious and political hierarchy. In theory the mission belonged to the Indians, who owned it in common, but it was administered under the direction of the missionaries, whose word was law. The Indians indeed elected their own petty political officers, but the missionaries in fact decided for whom they should vote. There can be no question but that the missionaries were devoted to the welfare of the Indian, but it seemed to them necessary, if his soul were to be saved and his intelligence quickened, that his body should first be enslaved. The spiritual training of the Indian resolved itself into learning the catechism and the vocabulary, or outward forms and ceremonies, of religious services; it was hardly possible for his undeveloped mind to grasp the philosophical tenets of the Christian faith. Services were frequently held—perhaps two masses a day on week days and more on Sundays, at all of which attendance was compulsory. The Indian was also required to work. The men tended flocks, or engaged in agriculture, while the women and children were taught weaving and spinning. Indeed, there was an extraordinary variety of tasks performed, for the missions were intended to be economically self-sustaining; not infrequently they produced a surplus which might be applied to assist more backward missions. Discipline was strict and severe. Native officials inflicted whippings or other penalties upon the recalcitrant, by order of the missionaries, but the more serious offences were turned over for punishment to the corporal of the guard. Unaccustomed either to working or to submission to discipline, the Indians often endeavored to run away, but were pursued and brought back. To lessen the opportunity of escape, walls were constructed around the mission, and the Indians were locked up at night. All in all, the institution of the Spanish mission was one of the most interesting examples of "benevolent despotism" which human history records.

By law a mission was supposed to endure for a period of

not longer than ten years, but in practice the term was much greater—even a century or more. In fact the end of mission rule depended more upon civilian colonization of a region than upon the instruction afforded in the mission; when a region had filled up with whites sufficiently to be safe for the crown, the mission might be dispensed with. The objects of the missionaries, benevolent though they were, were foredoomed to failure, for the Indians were rarely capable of absorbing civilization in any real sense of the term; indeed, the close of mission rule usually saw the Indian revert to his former state, if he were not killed off or absorbed by the white man; the mission at least prolonged the lives of many of the Indians. Its real importance, however, was as an agency of Spanish conquest. In this respect its effects were permanent.[1]

The civilian whites began to make themselves felt in the second stage of the conquest, and no conquest was complete until they had taken it over in the third stage as the controlling element.[2] The history of their activities while a given region was still in a frontier state has never been adequately presented or even much studied. Most of what is known of them has been derived from the works of the religious, who were primarily concerned with their own achievements and not interested in the civilian element, except as they found occasion to pronounce against them. Unquestionably the most important of the civilians along the northwestward line of conquest from Mexico City were the miners. Indeed, the route of the conquerors followed that of mineral wealth in precious metals. These men generally did their work by means of Indian labor in a state of virtual slavery. Traders, stock-raisers, and farmers came in to some extent, but the two latter were at a disadvantage, for they had to meet the competition of presidial and mission ranches. As already stated, the civilians took entire possession when it became time for the military and the religious to move on. With the civilian element should be included the secular church,

[1] The best presentation of the mission system in brief scope ever written is Bolton, Herbert Eugene, "The mission as a frontier institution in the Spanish-American colonies," in *American historical review,* XXIII, 42–61; Oct., 1917.

[2] Cf. *supra*, 96–97.

with its hierarchy of officialdom ranging from an archbishop or bishop down to the curate, or priest. The secular church entered a region only in the third stage of conquest, and sometimes rather late in that; indeed, the friars were often obliged to serve as curates, after the mission had disappeared, before the secular church came on the scene. When this arm of the church arrived, it was time for the soldier, missionary, and civilian pioneer to depart.

The crucial stage of the conquest, then, was the second, and this was the period when the greatest variety of widely differing elements came into play. These elements, to be sure, were controlled by the same fountain-head, the king (acting through his various officials), but they were rarely able to work together in entire harmony. In particular, the military and the civilians were constantly disputing with the religious. Questions of jurisdiction and relative authority were always to the fore as between the military and the religious; political rule was invariably given in charge of the former, but in some respects the missionaries were not subject to them. The civilians were opposed to the religious on economic grounds. The missionaries had been first on the scene, and had therefore had the first pick of the lands. The civilians wanted the mission lands and the Indian labor upon them. Arguments frequently turned on other matters than those which were in fact uppermost in the minds of the parties to the conflict. The civilians, for example, accused the religious of ill-treating the Indians and of retaining the missions much longer than was necessary. As for the Indians, who after all were the persons most vitally concerned, the restraints and punishments of the mission were indeed irksome to them, wherefore many, with their minds on the objectionable thing nearest at hand, supplied evidence for the civilians. Perhaps the majority realized, however, that their lot under civilian control would be far worse, and it is no doubt true that a great many were devoted to the missionaries and content with mission life, to which in course of time they became accustomed.

Coming now to the details of the advance toward the Californias, by way of illustration of the process of Spanish expansion everywhere in the New World, the age of the *con-*

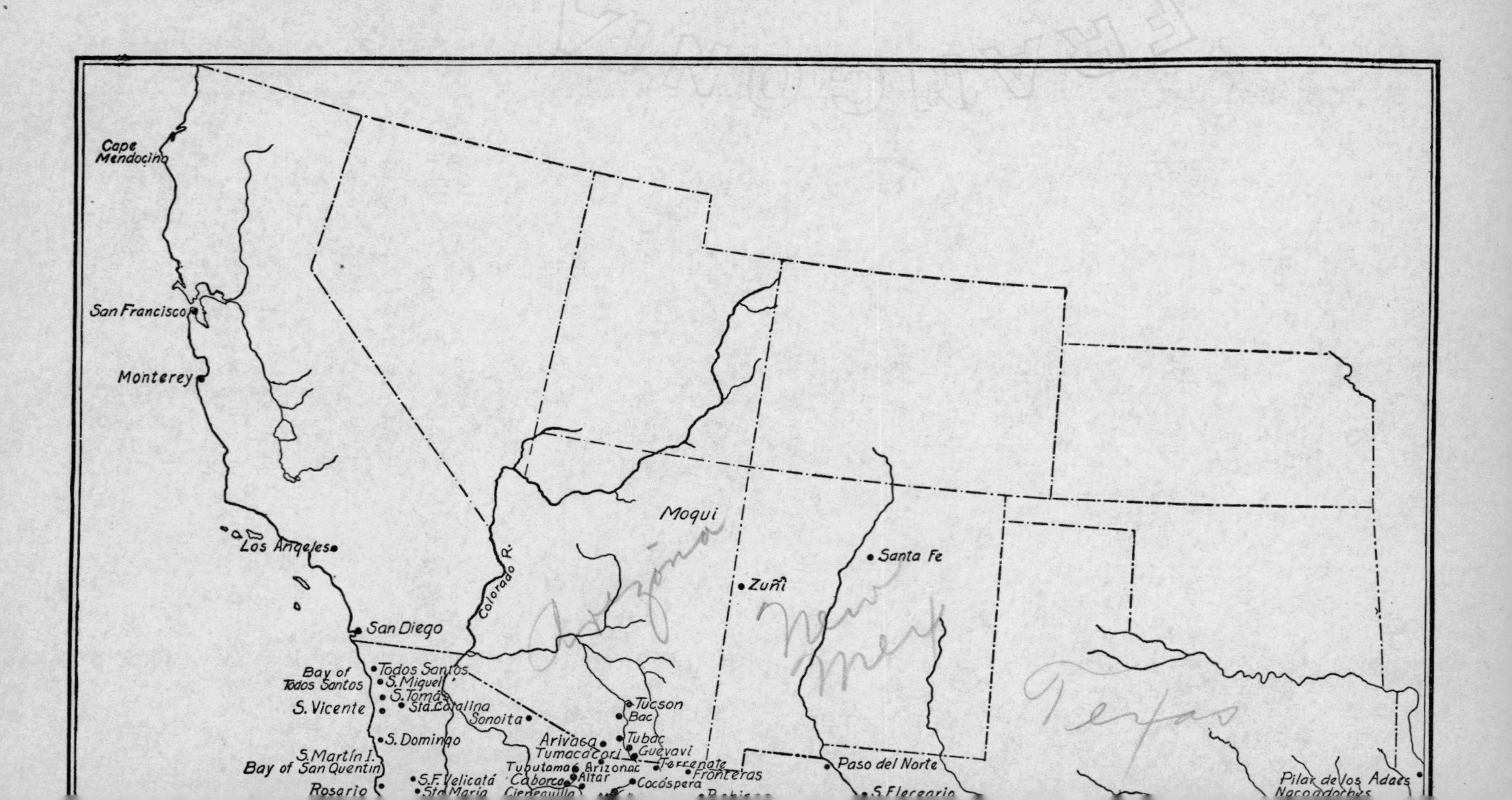

Cape Mendocino
San Francisco
Monterey
Los Angeles
San Diego
Colorado R.
Moqui
Zuñi
Santa Fe
Paso del Norte
Bay of Todos Santos
Todos Santos
S. Miguel
S. Tomás
Sta. Catalina
S. Vicente
Sonoita
S. Domingo
S. Martín I.
Bay of San Quentin
Rosario
S.F. Velicatá
Tucson
Bac
Tubac
Arivaca
Tumacacori
Guevavi
Terrenate
Fronteras
Tubutama
Arizonac
Caborca
Altar
Cocóspera
Pilar de los Adaes

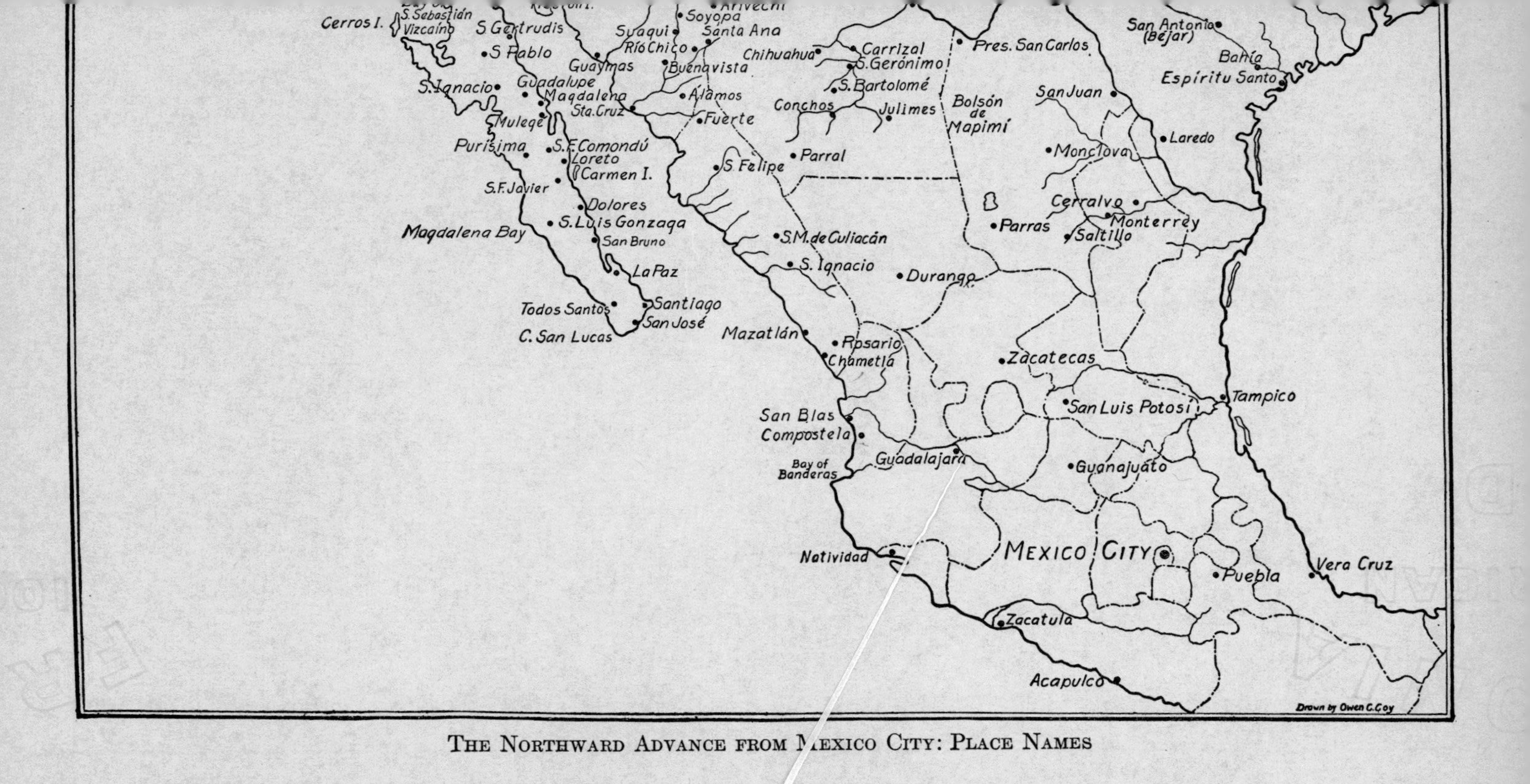

THE NORTHWARD ADVANCE FROM MEXICO CITY: PLACE NAMES

quistadores was soon over, and the work of the conquest in its second, or frontier, and third, or settled, phases came steadily to the fore. In the sector northwestward from Mexico City, Guzmán founded a settlement at Culiacán, Sinaloa, in 1531. By 1550 an *audiencia*,[1] or court, for the government of Nueva Galicia, as the Guzmán conquests were called, was established. Located for a time at Compostela, this was afterward moved to Guadalajara. Writing between 1571 and 1574, López de Velasco says that there were as many as 1500 Spaniards in Nueva Galicia, which at the time included most of the occupied country north of Mexico City. There were thirty-one or thirty-two settlements, of which fifteen or sixteen were mining camps. Guadalajara was the largest town, with a Spanish population of 150. The only settlement in what later became Sinaloa was Culiacán, with about thirty Spaniards. There were no Spaniards in Sonora. An increase in the population of Sinaloa came in 1596, when the presidio of San Felipe de Sinaloa, the first in that province, was established, with a garrison of twenty-five men. Meanwhile, the Franciscans, Dominicans, and Jesuits had been making converts, so that the region south of Sinaloa had become Christian, nominally at least, by the end of the sixteenth century, and after some futile revolts it was definitely reduced to the Spanish crown. The erection of a bishopric in Michoacán in 1537 may be regarded as a first step in the third phase of the conquest. So, despite the scant white population of Nueva Galicia, that part of it lying south of Sinaloa was fast losing the characteristics of a frontier province.

Up to 1591 not many conversions had been made in Sinaloa, but in that year the Jesuits reached there, and the real work began. Father Zapata's report of 1678 shows that by the close of the seventeenth century Sinaloa had been thoroughly reduced. The province had been Christianized, and had a white population of six hundred. In addition, there were many more of part Spanish blood; at San Felipe de Sinaloa alone there were 1200 of Spanish or mixed blood. The missionaries and civilians were supported by two presidios; Fuerte de Montesclaros had been added 1610. The

[1] For a definition of the *audiencia*, see *infra*, 134–136.

occupation of Sonora did not begin until early in the seventeenth century, when the successful military campaigns of Diego Martínez de Hurdaide paved the way. The Jesuits took charge of the mission work and made rapid progress. By 1678 there were twenty-eight missions in Sonora, serving seventy-two villages with a combined population of about forty thousand. There were perhaps five hundred persons of Spanish or part Spanish blood, a large proportion of whom were engaged in mining. Thus, by the end of the seventeenth century Sinaloa had attained to the comparative freedom from frontier characteristics which the region to the south of it had reached a hundred years before. The latter was now definitely off the frontier. Sonora, however, was in the midst of the second stage of conquest, and had such problems in the shape of hostile Indians that its early emergence into a settled state could not be expected; indeed, events were to prove that it was much more than a century behind Sinaloa in this respect.

By the close of the seventeenth century the conquest had been carried almost to the limits of modern Sonora by way of the Sonora Valley. This route led the Spaniards somewhat inland, leaving a large stretch of coast to the south and west as yet unoccupied. In this district were the Seri Indians, destined to cause trouble during the greater part of the eighteenth century. Northeast of the Sonora Valley was a little known region whence was to come an even more terrible enemy—the savage Apaches. Due to the hostility of these two peoples, Sonora was fated to remain a frontier province. Until near the close of the seventeenth century a third district of Sonora lay open. It seemed to offer fewer difficulties than the other two, though by no means an easy field for conquest. This was the region between the Altar and Gila rivers, known as Pimería Alta, beyond which to the northwest was Alta California. In 1687 Father Eusebio Kino of the Jesuit order crossed the Altar River and founded the mission of Dolores. This marked the first step in the last stage of the conquest toward the Californias, but the obstacles in the way of this further advance were perhaps greater than any which had yet been faced.

So much, in detail, for the slower phases of Spanish expansion in one part of the field. Elsewhere the story was much the same. By the central north Mexican route the Spaniards conquered New Mexico, and filled in much of the country along the way. By the more easterly route, they advanced through Coahuila and Nuevo León into Texas, where some missions were established temporarily toward the close of the seventeenth century, followed by more successful settlements early in the eighteenth century. In both of these sectors, in which the conquest went ahead at about the same rate as in the one leading to the California border, there were similar moving factors of Indian warfare and fear of foreign danger, in these cases of the English and French. In the Floridas, which then represented rather indefinitely all the mainland territory Spain claimed, or was able to acquire, to the northeast of her dominions in Mexico, the fear of foreign danger developed into a potent reality. Nevertheless, it was the prime reason for such settlements as Spain was able to make. Menéndez de Avilés landed in Florida in 1565, and destroyed a French colony already established there. A Spanish occupation of Georgia and the Carolinas followed. Intrusions of the English, French, and Dutch early in the seventeenth century caused the Spaniards to expand their holdings westward along the Gulf of Mexico. In the latter half of the seventeenth century, they began to give way in the Carolinas in the face of the English advance out of Virginia, and early in the next century the English took Georgia, too. And just at the end of the seventeenth century the French gained a foothold in "Louisiana,"—which then included as far east as Alabama, or as much territory as the French could wrest from the Spaniards—and in ensuing years built up their important colonies at the mouth of the Mississippi. Spain, however, held the Floridas, up to a point just short of the French settlement in Mobile Bay.

The Spanish colonies in southern Mexico, Central America, Venezuela, Colombia, Ecuador, and Peru were consolidated in much the same fashion as already described with respect to the conquest northwestward from Mexico City to Sinaloa and Sonora. Those regions along the Gulf of Mexico were strengthened in part because of the persistent attack of the English, French, and Dutch corsairs, who also made occasional sorties into the Pacific. In the Caribbean, however, the foreigners began in the seventeenth century to pick up islands which had not been effectively occupied by the Spaniards or were inadequately defended by them. Thus, the lesser islands of the West Indies came to fly a heterogeneous collection of European flags, and these mid-Caribbean ports were often used as bases for an attack on the Spanish mainland and the Spanish treasure fleets. As time passed, the islands became convenient points from which profitable smuggling operations with the Spanish colonies could be undertaken. A portion of the South American mainland, today represented by English, Dutch, and French Guiana beyond the mouth of the Orinoco, went into foreign hands, while in these same years the Dutch, in succession to the earlier efforts of the French, were making their already mentioned and temporarily successful inroads into Portuguese Brazil. The Dutch also were especially active in the Pacific during much of the seventeenth century, attacking the coast at different points, lying in wait for the Manila galleon, and making a serious but unsuccessful effort to establish themselves in Chile. The great island of Jamaica was lost to the English in 1655, the first territory of importance to slip away, among those which Spain had actually occupied. In 1697 France formally took over the western part of the island of Haiti, already settled for some years by French buccaneers. With such examples of losses at foreign hands, little wonder that the Spaniards responded to rumors of any new threat, however remote it actually proved to be.

In Upper Peru, or Bolivia, it was still the lure of precious metals, more than the fear of the foreigner, which invited settlement, and the Spaniards attained to remarkable good fortune in the mines they discovered there, notably in the mountain of Potosí.[1] Elsewhere in Peru and Upper Peru, gold and silver were found, just as they were in Mexico, and the logical sequel was a secure occupation of the country. Paraguay became, in the main, a region of Jesuit missions, where

[1] Cf. *infra*, 148–150.

some extraordinary establishments were founded.[1] From Upper Peru and Chile, as already set forth, the Spaniards filtered through the high passes of the Andes to expand the colonies in the Plata region and the great plains of present-day Argentina. In the seventeenth century there began to be disputes with the Portuguese over territorial limits. At length, in 1680, the Portuguese went so far as to found a settlement at Colonia del Sacramento, better known as Colonia, on the Plata itself, in present-day Uruguay. The Spanish governor of Paraguay captured this post the same year, but it was later returned to Portugal, and no decision was reached as to the boundaries between the Spanish and Portuguese colonies. In Chile the Spaniards continued the spectacular wars with the Araucanians, but gradually gained somewhat the better of the conflict, pushing definitively into southern Chile as far as Osorno, but failing in attempts to colonize and fortify the Strait of Magellan.

Thus, by the end of the period of the Hapsburg kings of the House of Austria, Spain had a much challenged, but fairly secure, grip on all that part of the Americas which was to remain Spanish-speaking. The first phase of the occupation, the era of the *conquistadores*, had long since passed; the second, or frontier, stage, had gone beyond the greater part of the territories of present-day Spanish America; and the third phase, of orderly civilized life, was already threatening the remaining frontiers. The implantation of Spanish institutions, if not yet complete, was measurably under way.

[1] Cf. *infra*, 114–115. Many of the missions were in a region now part of Argentina.

CHAPTER VII

SPANISH COLONIAL SOCIETY UNDER THE HAPSBURGS

THE vital period in the development of Hispanic American institutions was from about the close of the era of the initial great conquests to about 1700, corresponding with the end of the Hapsburg kings of the House of Austria as rulers of Spain. During about a century and a half, in comparative isolation, the American colonies of Portugal and Spain had a chance to work out an adjustment between the native customs of the conquered peoples and the habits of the conquerors in a new environment. Before then the Indians were too numerous, the Spaniards and Portuguese too few, the *conquistadores* themselves too independent, and the time too short to overcome already established institutions and set up new ones. After 1700 the Bourbon monarchs of Spain began to imitate the practices of other nations, departing in some respects from the old Spanish order, although there was a less noticeable change in Brazil. Leaving aside Brazil for the moment, the three principal racial elements in the other parts of Hispanic America were the whites of Spanish blood, the Indians, and the negroes. It is difficult to say which of the two former have been the more important in the creation of Spanish American character. On the whole, however, despite the modifying effect of Indian and negro traits, it is probably the whites who have been primarily responsible for the tone and direction of Spanish American institutions, just as Spanish has become the tongue of the lands of the *conquistadores*. It is fitting, therefore, to speak first of the conquering race.

Something has already been said about the predominantly Andalusian nature of the conquest.[1] It is probable, too, that the Andalusians, in addition to their own Moslem-blooded traits of individualism, exemplified in the most marked degree some of the noteworthy weaknesses in the Spanish social life of those times. Indolence, disdain for manual

[1] *Supra*, 32–33.

labor, and an excessive desire for noble rank, or at least for the appearance and trappings of nobility, were characteristics which circumstances had thrust upon Spaniards.

There were three principal groups of Spanish society, widely separated one from another: the ultra-aristocracy of the court, wealthy and privileged, but no longer vigorous or constructively important; the thousands of the lesser nobility and the untitled rich; and the masses. Except for an occasional official of high rank, only the two latter groups were concerned in the settlement of the Americas. In Spain both of them were for the most part in a wretched state in the sixteenth and seventeenth centuries. The masses might better hope to escape from poverty and rags through beggary and crime than through honest labor. The *hidalgos* and *caballeros* were forbidden by force of custom even to think of industry or commerce, at the same time that they must make a show of being the cavalier, no matter if their clothing were in tatters and their stomachs empty. It was this class primarily, together with ambitious young lawyers and clerks, which furnished the Spanish population of the Americas, supplemented by the more ambitious and more daring of the third group, not to mention the criminals who in the earlier periods were deported to the colonies. In the New World many of the nobles soon found an opportunity to strut with importance as holders of vast estates, with Indian or negro slaves upon them. The consequences in the formation of Spanish American character were none too favorable, as will appear presently.

Philip II and his successors made an effort to preserve the purity of the Catholic faith of the colonists, rigidly restricting emigration to the New World to those of whose uncompromising Catholicism there could be no doubt. There was by no means any boat-crowding migration to the Americas, nor was it desired. As late as 1550 it has been said that there were only fifteen thousand Spaniards in the colonies. Special permission of the king or other qualified officials had to be obtained before one might go to the Indies, and one had to prove his Catholicism as of several generations, besides giving full details of why and where he wanted to go. Even then he was usually required to return to Spain within a limited time, generally two years. Since a similar caution was exercised in the colonies, it was not so difficult for one to remain there, once he had reached them. Prohibitions were soon raised against the entry of any foreigners whatsoever, and the few who drifted in were ever in danger of being denounced as heretics or witches. Even the coming of a foreign ship to a Spanish American port was looked upon as a crime, and the crews of such vessels were often killed or sent off to the mines for life. Thus cultivated, there developed in Spanish American character a certain antipathy against the foreigner which has its survivals even at the present time.

After the flush days of the *conquistadores*, when there was plenty of ready-to-hand plunder as a quick road to wealth, the Spaniard had to depend upon some slower form of industry or upon official graft if he were to make his fortune. This inevitably involved the labor of Indians or negroes, as the Spaniard, with his real or pretended rank, could not lower himself to create wealth by his own efforts. The Indians were the first material available, and were always the more important element employed, except in the islands and the South American mainland of the Caribbean. The question of the adjustment of the relations of the conquerors with the natives had by no means been solved in the Columbian era already dealt with. The problem continued, with much the same characteristics as before, throughout the era of the House of Austria. On the one hand were the whites, controlling the Indians in various forms of servitude, disregarding the laws or minimizing their force in so far as they affected the employment of the natives. Opposed to them were the humanitarians, including many of the missionaries, who were indignant over the bad faith with which the laws were administered and constantly denounced the slaveholding class before the royal court. Yet a third element was the crown, which made and remade laws favoring the Indians, setting up safeguard after safeguard, but not insistently enforcing its own legislation. Indeed, both the humanitarian and the king fell a little short of the ideal, where their own interests were concerned, for the former held the Indian willy-nilly "for his own good" in the missions, and the latter saw to it that there should be no release from forced labor where the royal government profited, for example in the mines. The vast bulk of law-making with respect to the Indians is perhaps more important as showing the evils in the relations of the whites with them than it is as indicative of the protection afforded. There was always, too, a marked legal distinction as between Indians who were to be considered free and those who could be enslaved, giving an opening for an evasion of the laws, while the system of "reductions," by which the Indians were concentrated into mission towns, and the *repartimiento* and *encomienda* were continued in one form or another.

The only whites allowed in the reductions were the religious and the *corregidor* or other royal official. The *corregidor* was a type of royal agent who had many functions, ranging from those of a governor to that of merely an observer on behalf of the king,[1] but in the reductions he served the double purpose of being a protector of the Indians and the collector of tributes from them; at the same time he also had charge of the provision of supplies for their needs. This gave an opportunity for profits which all too few of the *corregidores* were able to resist. The royal officials quarreled with the religious, too, over questions of jurisdiction and other matters, and the Indian usually paid the penalty. Little wonder that the reduction of this type declined.

There were many fine legal distinctions spun around the terms *repartimiento* (distribution) and *encomienda* (literally "recommendation"), but both came virtually to the same thing: the enslavement of the Indians. The *repartimiento* was an allotment of Indians to individuals of the conquering class, who thenceforth had a right to their services, in whole or in part. The holders, usually called *encomenderos*, were to see to it, however, that the Indians were converted and civilized and generally protected. The *encomienda* was a grant in recognition of distinguished services to an individual, also called an *encomendero*, who was to have the right for his own life and that of his heir to the collection of tributes for himself from the Indians of a given district.

[1] For a discussion of the *corregidores*, see *infra*, 137, n. 1.

Some *encomiendas* ran for as many as four generations in the original grant, while many continued indefinitely, with or without official authorization. Though usually limited to the collection of tributes, some of the *encomiendas* also gave rights to personal services, and many of them evolved to that character, the laws to the contrary notwithstanding. Thus, the Indians might be compelled to work in undertakings considered necessary, such as mining, road-making, some forms of agriculture, and cattle-raising, though in theory for a fair wage and under good conditions. The *encomenderos* took full advantage of loopholes such as these.

And yet the Spanish system, which treated the Indians as minors for life, making them the wards of the king, did at least preserve the Indians much more surely than was the case with the other colonizing nations in North America, the English, for example. In Anglo-America the Indians were driven away or killed. In Spanish America, where, to be sure, there were proportionately many more of them, they survived, whether in the full blood, or as a part in the mixed races which have been so prominent a factor in Spanish American life. The stories of cruelties against the Indians, which may have had even more *raison d'être* in the case of the English colonists, attained to such proportions as they did, because of the very vigor and, indeed, the exaggeration of the Spanish humanitarian denunciations of existing practices. The leader in this respect was the already mentioned Dominican friar, Bartolomé de Las Casas, who had begun his efforts on behalf of the Indians in the last years of King Ferdinand, and carried them on with even greater insistence in the reign of Charles I. Despite opposition, which included that of many churchmen, Las Casas at length prevailed at court. His great moment of success came with the enactment of the New Laws of the Indies in 1542, as one part of which Indian slavery was abolished. Something has already been said about the difficulty of enforcing these laws in Peru. The same thing happened elsewhere.

Las Casas himself, named bishop of Chiapas (then in Guatemala, but since added to Mexico), found that the laws were not being executed in his own district. So he renounced his bishopric, returned to Spain, and devoted himself to exposing the evils of the system against which he had fought for so many years. In 1552 he published his *Brevísima relación de la destrucción de las Indias* (very brief account of the destruction of the Indies), in which he charged that fifteen millions of Indians had perished on account of the cruelties of the Spaniards. The book was translated into the principal languages of western Europe, and was welcomed as an exact picture of conditions and of the inherent qualities of Spaniards, who were hated by the Protestant peoples of that day as the leading Catholic power, and by all others as the then strongest nation of Europe. The answers to Las Casas, some of them by men who agreed with his anti-slavery principles but pointed out his mistakes and exaggerations, were overlooked, and the legend of Spanish cruelty toward the Indians became established. On the other hand, the pendulum should not be allowed to swing too far in the opposite direction. There was a great deal of cruelty, inevitable under the circumstances of the general exploitation of the Indians. On the whole, however, the treatment of the Indians was humane, or at least not excessively harsh, if only because their lives were valuable to those who were virtually their masters, the Spanish-blooded whites.

No one has given a sounder judgment with respect to Spanish "cruelty" to the Indians than Simpson. According to him:

> "A thesis on Spanish barbarity is irresistibly easy to support, and irresistibly attractive to a foreigner. This hoary tradition dates from the publication in 1552 of the *Brief Relation of the Destruction of the Indies* by Bartolomé de Las Casas. In the pages of the 'Apostle of the Indies' one reads an indictment of his countrymen so complete, so circumstantial, so blasting, so thoroughly satisfactory, in short, that ever since his day it has been the indispensable handbook of the historians of America.
>
> "Let us admit at the outset that there is little to be said from a humanitarian point of view in favor of the exploitation of weaker races by the stronger. However, if the Spaniards achieved earlier and greater notoriety in it than their European rivals, assuredly it was not because Spain's villainy was the blacker. Rather was it due to the extraordinary fear, hatred, and jealousy which in the sixteenth and seventeenth centuries she evoked

beyond the Pyrenees . . . Thus when Spain was at the apogee of her political power and all good Protestants were shuddering at the thought of the dungeons of the Inquisition, the *Brief Relation* came as a veritable godsend to those most interested in believing it. Better still, it was written by a Spaniard of unquestioned authority, by a bishop! Wherever the Spanish name was hated the *Brief Relation* found a ready sale and a readier credence, and its numerous reprints show that the popular appetite for bloody horrors was fully as great then as now. Sabin's *Dictionary* lists, for the sixteenth and seventeenth centuries, three Italian editions, three Latin, four English, six French, eight German, and eighteen Dutch." [1]

And again:

"It must be admitted that the Spanish treatment of the Indians was abominable, but meanwhile the equally nefarious activities of the other exploiting nations should not be forgotten. India, China, the Guinea Coast, the Congo, the United States, could all furnish their 'Brief Relation.' Whether the motive has been to turn an honest penny, to take up the white man's burden, or whether it has been downright, unabashed greed, the price of exploitation of the weak by the strong has been suffering, hatred, blood, and brutality the world over. It was not new in the sixteenth century. It is not rare in the twentieth." [2]

As for Las Casas, he continued to the end of his days fighting for the rights of the Indians. At length in 1566, at ninety-two years of age, the indefatigable "Apostle of the Indies" passed away.

Meanwhile, beyond the reach of civilian white exploitation, the missionaries were engaging in their activities in the frontier districts. The usual character of the missions has already been described. Something may well be added with respect to the Jesuit missions of Paraguay (most of which were in a region now part of Argentina), which had "the most extensive and intensive development" of any in the New World. To quote from Roscher:

"Usually the affairs of the mission were divided between two monks; the elder had the spiritual oversight, the younger the secular economic control. With great shrewdness the Indians were formed into military companies and, by the means of splendid uniforms and titles and such like, became a well-

[1] Simpson, 1–2.
[2] *Ibid.*, 18.

organized machine. All foreign necessities were paid for by the sale of Paraguay teas which the order managed 'because the Indians are too timid.' Then, too, the laborers and such people worked under the direction of the priest, and even the slaughter-house was managed by him. Work on the *conuco* claimed two days of every week. The beginning and ending of a day's work were regulated by church ceremonies; likewise the hour and manner of meals, dress, and so on were arranged once for all by the mission . . . In every mission there was a special house, called beaterio, where women of bad repute were kept under control; here also resorted childless married women during the absence of their husbands. In similar cloistered seclusion young maidens (*monjas*) were kept until marriageable age."[1]

The Jesuits had more than thirty missions among the Guaraní Indians of Paraguay, and seven more in the dangerous Chaco district. The inhabitants of the former traded with one another, and communications were facilitated among them by good roads, which joined them with the mission of Candelaria, where the Jesuit Father Superior resided. The Jesuits themselves accumulated a vast store of knowledge with respect to the Indians under them. At the time of the expulsion of the Jesuits in the eighteenth century, nine thousand volumes were found in nineteen of the missions, of which more than a thousand were in Guaraní, and in addition there were quantities of manuscripts containing scientific observations. The Indian militia was organized in the second quarter of the seventeenth century, following the destructive raids of the Paulistas from Brazil. Thereafter, the mission armies rendered important service, not only against the Paulistas, but also against the savage tribes of Indians and the Portuguese forts at Colonia on the Plata. These splendid missions were maintained at their height, however, only so long as their isolation from the world under the Jesuits endured. To get ahead to the close of the colonial period, soon after the expulsion of the Jesuits, nothing was left of the mission towns but ruins.

The characteristic traits of the Spanish law with respect to the Indians were its aims for the conversion of the natives and the suppression of their barbarous customs and its absence of anything in the nature of repugnance for the

[1] Roscher, 15–16. The *conuco* was a term for lands common.

mixture of races, which, indeed, was facilitated, rather than hindered, by the laws. Quite apart from the illegitimate unions formed, there were many marriages—all the more so, since unmarried women were forbidden to go from Spain to the Indies, unless by express permission of the king. Sex relations with the black race followed the same course as with the Indian. In consequence, the caste system, inevitable in any conquered colony, was accentuated by differences in color, with the result that Spanish colonial society was extraordinarily lacking in homogeneity. There were seven principal castes: Spaniards born in Spain; the creoles, or native-born whites of Spanish blood; *mestizos*, descendants from mixed unions of Indians and whites; mulattoes, or those of part white and part negro blood; *zambos*, of mixed Indian and negro blood; pure Indians; and negroes. Naturally there were many gradations and shades in the mixed groups. Socially and politically they fell into four categories: the Spanish official aristocracy; the creole nobility; the proletariat; and the slaves.

If a man wished truly to be of the super-elect in Spanish America, he had to make certain that his mother was in Spain at the time of his birth. In the first place, the Spaniards from Spain held nearly all of the best government jobs. Only twelve of the first 369 bishops were creoles, and only one of the fifty viceroys of New Spain, or Mexico. Altogether, in 160 viceroys there were only four creoles. Only fourteen creoles were numbered among the 602 captain-generals or other local governors.[1] Furthermore, the Spaniard's social precedence was quite on a par with his political preferment. The creole women offered good evidence on this point, for, like the women of many another country, they sought the more socially prominent as husbands, and the merest Spanish clerk had a better chance to win the fairest of the fair than the richest and generally most eligible creole noble. It was claimed, too, that the Spaniards deserved their higher rank, because man tended to degenerate from long life in the "tropics" of the New World. Quite naturally the

[1] Different accounts show slight discrepancies in numbers. For example, Moses says there were "166 viceroys and 588 captain-generals, governors, and presidents" in the colonies, but agrees that there were only eighteen creoles among them. Moses, *Spanish dependencies*, II, 398.

Spaniard despised the creole, and the creole hated the Spaniard. This, indeed, was a characteristic attitude from class to class, for the creole in turn despised those lower in the social scale than himself, as they hated him; perhaps for that very reason, they clung the more loyally to the Spanish crown, obsessed as they were by their disapproval of the oppressor nearest at hand. It is possible that the Spanish government itself encouraged these class differences, on the well-known theory of "divide and rule."

These antipathies had many ramifications beyond the mere difference in class. Those of the seashore and those of the plateaus and mountain districts hated and despised one another with a cordiality which the Anglo-American might find hard to understand, and similarly those in the hot regions and the cold. Given the peculiarly mountainous character of Spanish America, as a result of which one may change quickly from level to level and climate to climate, ample opportunity near at hand was provided for the exercise of these animosities. It must be remembered, too, that Spaniards then and since have not been one great happy family by any means. Catalans and Basques carried with them to America their disapproval, for example, of the Andalusians. Indeed, the strongly individualistic tendencies of all Spaniards made them distrust one another, however close the resemblance might be in their blood and living conditions, even to the extent almost of affecting those beneath the same roof. The difficulties of communication from region to region hardened these natural inclinations into a nearly impenetrable and ineradicable racial characteristic, not a little of which has been carried over into Hispanic American life today.

The creole nobility were of two kinds. Many of them were in fact descendants of Spanish nobles, although in a country with such a numerous nobility as Spain this was not nearly as noteworthy as it would have been in an Anglo-American land. In Lima in the eighteenth century, from a quarter to a third of the whites were of noble blood, including forty-five families of marquises and counts. In addition, the descendants of the conquerors were regarded as nobles, and, indeed, were usually possessed of a title. Given the natural Spanish pride, it must have rankled in the feelings of the creoles to be considered inferior to the over-seas Spaniard, who certainly in the majority of cases did not demonstrate in achievement any remarkable superiority. So the creole hated the Spaniard, but he did not rise against him, as he would have needed the assistance of the lower classes, who hated him and whom he loftily despised.

The proletariat included white vagabonds and the various free colored groups. These latter had all of the vices and few of the virtues of the races from which they had sprung. The *mestizos* and mulattoes were strong and vigorous, mentally quick and sagacious, but passionately devoted to gambling, inclined to drunkenness, and fond of a wild, free life. There were various gradations of social recognition among them, depending on their relation to the higher social groups and also on color. They hated the upper classes, however, without distinction as to whether they were Spaniards or creoles, and obeyed the laws only because they were afraid of punishment and saw no hope of improvement in their lot. Thus there developed the *peones* (peons) of Mexico, the Chilean *rotos* (broken or ragged masses), the *llaneros* (plainsmen) of Venezuela, the *gauchos pobres* (poor cowboys) of Argentina, and the Peruvian *plebe* (plebeians or populace), which have their survivals at the present time. Many of them depended absolutely on the upper classes, in a state which at least approximated servitude, so scanty were the fare and the wages meted out to them. If some of the men of these classes prospered, or, more likely, if the women advanced through marriage with a member of the white upper classes, they and their children proceeded to despise the lower groups from which they had come, and endeavored to include themselves among the white creoles. Not accepted on account of color or other social distinction, they might purchase a royal decree declaring them to be white. The sale of these "*cédulas de gracias al sacar*" (royal decrees of thanks on getting out of, i.e. out of the colored ranks into those of white men) were bitterly opposed by the creoles, who bowed meekly in the face of political and economic oppression, but resisted this invasion of their social group. The crown needed money, however, and the decrees continued to be sold.

As for the negroes, they began to be introduced within a generation from the discovery. Las Casas himself, carried away with enthusiasm on behalf of the Indians, was one of those who suggested negro slavery as an alternative, although later repenting of his views. As early as 1518 a license was granted by Charles I for the introduction of four thousand negroes into America, and the laws recognized the principle of hereditary slavery for negroes. Great problem that they were in Portuguese Brazil, they were of importance in Spanish America only in the Caribbean area. Elsewhere the institution of negro slavery did not take deep root. In the Caribbean islands and the northern mainland of South America, however, the negroid elements eventually became a majority of the people. The laws were as humanitarian as they had been in the case of the Indians, but some of them may be taken as evidence of occasional specific cruelties, such as one prohibiting mutilation of the genital organs of negroes in case of rebellion, and another against branding them with an iron like beasts. There were a number of negro uprisings and cases of negro banditry, but the royal government never let them get far out of hand. It availed itself, too, of the prevailing social ideas, for the mulatto despised the negro as he hated the white, but if he were nearly white himself he might buy, or even be given, a patent declaring him white. Thus were the mulattoes, like the *mestizos*, deprived of those who might have been their natural leaders in a conflict with the aristocracy or against Spain herself. On the whole, however, the negroes of the Spanish colonies were treated perhaps better than in any white land where black slavery has existed; at any rate, that appears to be the verdict of the historians, some of whom ascribe it to the lack of importance attached by the Spaniards to their plantation colonies. Negro slaves might indeed emancipate themselves by purchase, and the means afforded them were probably at least as easy as in any other modern slave-holding region. Perhaps the great majority of the negroes were faithful to their masters and loyal to the church and the Spanish régime, especially those who were out-and-out blacks and not mulattoes.

The Spanish laws gave scant opportunity for any change in the existing social situation through contacts with the outside world. The restrictions against foreigners have already been mentioned. Nature assisted by raising up barriers against easy communication, and the royal government availed itself of, and improved upon, the existing obstacles. Spanish America possesses few good harbors, and many of them are commanded strategically from one or two points; thus, Havana was the key to the Caribbean. Many of the coast regions were unsuited to white habitation, whether on account of excessive heat, with its accompaniment of yellow fever, as in the case of the mainland ports of the Caribbean, or because of arid dryness, as in Peru and northern Chile. Some ports were deliberately founded, for purposes of defence, many miles up the rivers instead of along the sea. Where this was not feasible, the roads between an important town in the back country and its outlet along the coast were unimproved and difficult of access. Such was the case with the road between Caracas and La Guaira. Other regions which might naturally have been easily approached were neglected, or even handicapped, by the laws. The most glaring instance of this was the case of the colonies of the Plata, which were not allowed to communicate with Spain or other parts of the world by sea. Instead, one had to make use of the arduous and impossibly expensive route over the Andes to Peru, and thence to Panama, across the Isthmus, and so to Europe. Buenos Aires was a port of which even its own citizens could not avail themselves.

Through the medium of the Inquisition, a close censorship was also maintained against the entry of foreign ideas, especially those which might weaken the faith of the king's subjects in the Americas. It did not take a great deal to have a book included in the forbidden list, and the agents of the Inquisition might enter a person's house at any hour of the day or night to look for such volumes. Comparatively few books were allowed to circulate in the colonies which did not at least have a religious tinge of the approved orthodox type, and printing was not encouraged. Nevertheless, the restrictions were probably not so insistently enforced as many writers have made them out to have been. The records of the *Casa de Contratación* show that the Spanish novels of chivalry and other of the lighter forms of literature were among the books shipped to the Americas in considerable quantity. Such works, to be sure, were in no respect heretical.

Nor was education sufficiently developed to bring about any profound modification of the social system. Spain gave what she herself then had in the way of instruction, but that was not very much. At least a dozen universities were established in different parts of the colonies, with patents being issued as early as 1551 for Mexico and Lima, followed shortly afterward by the founding of these the two oldest universities of the Western Hemisphere. The universities were primarily schools of theology for the training of priests, although a number of other than purely religious subjects were taught, such as medicine, law, Indian languages, and scholastic methodology. The importance of the universities to society as a whole was in point of fact very little. Many secondary schools were established by the Franciscans, Dominicans, Jesuits, and other religious orders. There also were a number of primary schools, in which instruction was limited, as a rule, to religious doctrine, reading, writing, and the rudiments of arithmetic.

Nevertheless, the sum total of education was very slight. Not a few members of leading creole families, particularly the women, were illiterate. The student of the Spanish colonies will find a vast array of materials in histories, diaries, reports, descriptions (of regions, native peoples, languages, and products), and even scientific or literary treatises, although only a small proportion of these works, perhaps, were published by their authors. They constitute an important storehouse of information. But most of the more valuable among them were the writings of Spaniards and foreigners, and they are in no respect to be considered as an index of any general high level of intellectual achievement. The reverse of that situation was the rule among the creoles and other elements of the native-born, who contributed very few names to the list of distinguished persons in literature, science, or art. The poetess Sister Juana Inés de la Cruz and the Mexican savant Carlos de Sigüenza y Góngora are about the only creoles demanding mention in the field of literature in this period, while those who did noteworthy work in architecture, painting, sculpture, or music might easily be indicated by the fingers of one hand. Writing of Sigüenza y Góngora, Leonard has the following to say:

> "Despite the fact that he lived in one of the most important and the most advanced of Spain's possessions in the New World, this son of seventeenth-century Mexico found himself in an atmosphere which was essentially medieval. The society of the capital as in the provinces was in many respects feudalistic; the venerable University with which he was associated during the most active years of his career was an interesting and curious survival of European medievalism particularly in the matter of its government and curriculum. The 'Athens of the New World,' as the city proudly termed itself, was far removed from the centers of learning in Europe and was only slightly touched by the currents of thought which were beginning to circulate there. Indeed, the men of learning of the viceroyalty were almost wholly dedicated to the study and to the perpetuation of a doctrinal theology which, elsewhere, was gradually becoming obsolete. The seventeenth century in New Spain gave rise to some literature, to be sure, but this was almost entirely in the form of religious guides, the chronicles of missionaries, theological tracts, and an almost uninterrupted flood of gongoristic poetry, unutterably dull and tedious for the most part with its cloying artificiality and inanity. This relatively slight literary activity was cultivated by an infinitesimally small and select group of intellectuals, standing like a tiny edifice upon a vast foundation composed of an ignorant and hopeless native population." [1]

These remarks, by a competent scholar who has made a detailed study of the literary history of seventeenth-century New Spain, are applicable to all Hispanic America, revealing the essential backwardness of the colonies.[2]

Under these circumstances Spanish America developed

[1] Leonard, 182–183.

[2] It would be quite as easy to write a chapter on intellectual factors in this era as about social, political, and economic conditions, but in the writer's opinion that would amount to giving a false perspective. Other volumes, which do not have to consider proportions so rigidly as this, often give interesting accounts.

a set of social customs, scantily influenced by the outside world, which were an adjustment, or one might say a compromise, between the Spanish and the native Indian or negro life. The Spanish, through its official control and its Spanish-speaking aristocracies, peninsula and creole, was the dominating force, but in the lesser incidents of day-to-day existence the subject peoples imposed their customs, and fixed them to such an extent that they have survived to the present time. Naturally, there were differences from region to region, but along certain broad lines Spanish American habits resembled one another from northern New Spain to southern Chile.

The life of the free proletariat and the servile classes was probably more Indian or negro than Spanish in its daily routine. Homes were of the simplest, often nothing more than a one-room, grass-covered, windowless hut, and varying from that to a three-room (single bed-room, living-room, and kitchen) house, with a narrow slit or two in the walls for light and air. Furniture ranged from a wooden bench to a few chairs and rough beds and perhaps a table. Possibly a crucifix or some other reminder of the prevailing religion might be found as the sole adornments within the home. Dirt was everywhere, and joined with lack of bodily cleanliness and the insanitary habits of the people to promote disease and a general weakening of the physical fibre of the Spanish American race. Another contributing factor in this direction was sexual laxity, which in the case of the lower classes was noteworthy even among the women as well as among the men. Food was of the simplest, and was much the same from day to day. Thus, in Mexico the corn fritter, or *tortilla,* was nearly the equivalent of another word for "food," so much was it eaten, almost to the exclusion of everything else, but only because other things could not be as easily and cheaply procured. Naturally, the clothing of people in this class was of the most inexpensive type, and often lacking in such comparative luxuries as shoes and hats. People of the Indian-blooded masses led a sad and sombre life, broken only on Sundays and holidays, when raw native liquors or maybe a cock-fight proved the only means of escape from their otherwise humdrum existence. One may go to many parts of Spanish America today, and he will find the same type of people—in Central America, for example. The negroid masses differed little from those of Indian blood, though much more gay and noisy.

At the top, society aimed to imitate Spain, which provided the most approved standards of those times, but in many respects there were striking resemblances to the life of the lower classes. Houses were usually grouped around one or more open courts, or *patios*, with scant pretence of architectural excellence, either inside or out. Rooms were dark and damp, and ideas with respect to hygiene within the home were not greatly superior to those of the masses. Even among the aristocracy bathing was infrequently indulged in, and many a proud beauty or young gallant went to a social function dressed in the height of the prevailing fashions but amid an aroma of body odors. Dress, indeed, occupied an important place in the life of the wealthy, who followed the Spanish modes as closely as possible, never tolerating the introduction of any novelty of their own. Of course, the food of this class was much better than that of the masses, but was in some respects unwisely chosen. In particular, Spanish Americans went to excess in eating meat and other heavy foods, and in most of the countries below the Rio Grande the same thing is true today. People of the aristocracy, like their Andalusian and other Spanish forefathers, were courteous, amiable, and hospitable, but self-indulgent. The men gave undue attention to the charms of the opposite sex, drank a great deal more wine than their ancestors had done, and gambled whenever and by whatever means opportunity offered. These same traits manifested themselves in greater or less degree among the other groups in the social scale.

The Spanish Americans were fond of many simple pleasures, such as sitting around in amiable colloquy and discussion with others of their kind, talking of everything in general and nothing in particular. They liked to take a late afternoon stroll around the *plaza* of the town, or a ride along the avenue, at which time the young women, or *señoritas*, might also be expected to appear. Aside from such functions as this, however, and from the inevitable church-going, the women of the aristocracy rarely were seen in public, being kept away from too dangerously admiring eyes, as the women of Moslem Spain had been, centuries before. They were indeed protected, as the women of the masses were not, and with numerous servants to assist them they had little or no work to do, but their life was of very limited scope. They gossiped with other women, usually relatives, within the home, did a little fancy needlework, went to church on all conceivable occasions, and kept their eye out for the *novio*, or sweetheart, who was expected to appear as early as possible in the offing. Unless a young woman were married before she had reached twenty-five, her life was a failure. She therefore chose her future lord and master quickly, if not always too wisely and well. Thereafter she was as faithful and devoted to him and his children, as he was faithless, though also "devoted," to her. Taken all in all, life in the Spanish colonies moved slowly and monotonously, yet not unhappily, within the narrow confines of a small circle, repeating itself over and over again until habits became fixed, transmitting themselves to later generations.

CHAPTER VIII

THE SPANISH COLONIAL POLITICAL SYSTEM UNDER THE HAPSBURGS

WHAT difference does it make just what the governmental machinery of the Spanish monarchy was in the Americas, if it were to be swept away in the establishment of the republics of the nineteenth and twentieth centuries? Is an account of it anything more than a dry relation of a hierarchy of officialdom? It *does* make a difference. In the first place, even where the names of political agencies have been changed, the methods and the spirit of colonial institutions have remained. One of the festering sores of Hispanic American political life today is the corrupt and autocratic character of government, and this had its roots in the era of the House of Austria, more particularly under the later Hapsburg kings. Even Brazil was directly affected, as she came within the sphere of the Spanish system from 1580 to 1640, when the kings of Spain were also kings of Portugal. It is probable that Brazil would have reached a similar basis in any event, however, as Spanish and Portuguese habits in government ran along parallel lines in those days. While it is impossible to omit the details concerning the various instrumentalities of royal control, one must always bear in mind the underlying spirit of government, for it was that, more than mere machinery, which was to transmit itself to later times. Another point is that colonial institutions were not fixed, given over ready-made and remaining unchanged, but were always in process of evolution. Many admirable features in the early stages were corrupted under the weak kings of the seventeenth century, and reappeared only in part as a result of the eighteenth-century reforms of the Bourbon monarchs. Under the Catholic Kings and the sixteenth-century Hapsburgs, Charles I and Philip II, the main features of the system itself were set up, leaving it to the later Hapsburgs to stamp it with those inner qualities which were to be one of the most unfortunate of the Spanish legacies to the New World.

One should not forget the great initial Spanish achievement, however. In the course of the sixteenth century a comparatively small and poor country of not more than seven or eight million inhabitants, such as Spain then was, was able to discover and explore most of the Atlantic and Pacific coasts of the Americas, to conquer rich and long established empires like those of the Aztecs, Incas, and Chibchas, and to overrun a great part of two continents. According to statistics of the closing years of the sixteenth century, Spain had already founded more than two hundred towns, in which there were 150,000 Spaniards, and had dominated some eight or nine thousand native settlements, in which a million and a half Indians had been reduced to tribute and converted to Christianity. As an evidence of the thoroughgoing organization required, it may be mentioned that at that time there were in the Spanish colonies nine *audiencias*, thirty different governments, twenty-four establishments of royal treasury officials, three mints, four archbishoprics, twenty-four bishoprics, and 360 monasteries or convents. No other country of Europe could even remotely compare with Spain in the tremendous sweep of colonial conquest.

Although the machinery of Spanish colonial government was a development over the entire course of Spanish rule, the different institutions eventually attained to an essential character which did not vary strikingly with the passage of time. It is therefore possible, as it is also necessary in a brief treatise, to deal in one discussion with the political life of the colonies as it usually was. For convenience the subject may be divided into two branches: colonial machinery in Spain: and the governmental agencies in the New World.

With the claims of the family of Columbus disposed of, the fountain-head of the whole system was the absolute Spanish king. It was not until the time of Charles I that the importance of the Americas was realized. As one historian puts it:

"At his accession he had probably regarded the American continent, in so far as he had any conception of it at all, chiefly in the light of a vexatious barrier, impeding his access to the Spice Islands beyond. At his abdication he realized that it was his principal source of wealth, the financial foundation on which the power of the house of Austria reposed; that his territories there were vastly more extensive than all the rest of his Empire put together; and that the Christianization and civilization of the Indians who inhabited them constituted a problem and a duty far more difficult than he had originally supposed. Small wonder if his reign witnessed an enormous development and ramification of the colonial system of the Catholic Kings." [1]

Just as the Catholic Kings had discovered that a single representative of the monarchs could not handle the vast business of the colonies, and so created the *Casa de Contratación*, so Charles I found it necessary to add yet new machinery in Spain. The most important governmental body set up was the Council of the Indies. This existed in name during the era of the Catholic Kings for the officials in Spain in charge of colonial affairs, but was not formally organized and in operation until 1524, in the reign of Charles I. From that time forward, this was one of the great Councils of the kingdom. All of its members, whether among the higher officials or the numerous lesser employees, were required to be "of approved customs, nobility, and purity of lineage (*limpieza de sangre*),[2] men who fear God and are a select group from the standpoint of learning and prudence." Subject only to the king, this was to be the supreme legislative, executive, and judicial body for the colonies. Every official of the Indies, from the highest to the lowest, civilian or ecclesiastical, came within the purview of the authority of this body, which made and unmade laws, appointed or removed government employees, handled inspections of the conduct of colonial officials,[3] intervened in military matters, and heard appeals in important cases from the courts in the Indies; indeed, it might act in any matter of colonial affairs, great or small, and its decisions were final, save in rare instances where the king himself might choose to have the last word. In fact, of course, there was never any such instant obedience to its commands as the system would seem to

[1] Merriman, III, 618.
[2] That is to say, freedom from any taint of non-Catholic ancestry.
[3] See *infra*, 141, for a discussion of the method of these inspections, through the medium of the *visita* or the *residencia*.

have required. Officials in the Indies often gave lip service to its orders, at the same time that they were acting directly contrary to them, but the Council of the Indies was nevertheless important enough and sufficiently powerful to deserve its ranking as the principal governmental machinery for Spain's empire overseas. It was the Council of the Indies which was primarily responsible for that vast body of the laws which regulated the management of state and church in the colonies. It accumulated great archives, rich in information about the Americas, and its activities are certainly one of the most noteworthy sources of information for an understanding of Spanish America of pre-independence times.

Next in importance to the Council in Spain was the *Casa de Contratación*, whose fundamental purpose continued to be in connection with trade and travel to and from the New World. Residing at Seville, the port of communication between Spain and the Americas, its activities very greatly increased as the colonies themselves developed. To lighten its labors, some supplementary machinery was created, such as the *Juzgado* (Court) of the Indies and the *Consulado* [1] of Seville. The former made it possible for boats to load and unload at Cádiz, instead of undertaking the somewhat difficult ascent of the Guadalquivir to Seville. The latter, representing the merchants of Seville who were engaged in the American trade, relieved the *Casa* of many of its earlier responsibilities, especially in its handling of suits at law as between the merchants themselves.

The connecting link between Spain and the colonies were the ships of Seville and Cádiz which crossed the seas; these took on an especial importance in connection with the system of great treasure fleets, or *flotas*, eventually developed. As already mentioned, the Catholic Kings had restricted commerce with the Indies to Castilians and to a single port, at first Cádiz, then Seville. The Flemish Charles I threw open the trade to a number of other Spanish ports, and even proposed to permit foreigners to engage in it, but as he became

[1] The term *consulado* is often rendered "consulate" in English, but it does not even remotely fit the dictionary meaning of the word "consulate." The phrase "commercial tribunal" would be nearer the truth, but even that is inexact. Cf. comments *infra*, 164.

more and more Spanish in his point of view he reverted to the system of the Catholic Kings, which was established definitively by the reign of Philip II. In early years, before the wealth of Mexico and Peru had become so large a factor in the shipments from the New World, the voyages were made by individual ships or in small groups, as occasion called, but the dangers from foreign pirates, noteworthy from the very first, were even more pronounced as the richness of the traffic increased. So, in 1537, a large war fleet was sent out to convoy the merchant ships of that season to and from the New World. Employed again several times during the reign of Charles I, this method was adopted by Philip II as the only one to be followed. Single ships henceforth were forbidden to go to the Indies, except for the royal "information boats" (*navíos de aviso*), which carried the mails, but no passengers or cargo. Like most of the Spanish laws, this requirement was not always observed, sometimes being waived, while also it was often evaded, especially through the connivance of venal Spanish officials. Two fleets a year of from forty to seventy boats were sent out from Spain, one destined for Vera Cruz in Mexico, and the other for Nombre de Dios, but after 1584 for Portobelo,[1] both in Panama.[2] At different points along the route, some of the ships broke away from the main body to go to their particular ports of destination in the West Indies or along the mainland of the Caribbean. Supplementary voyages were also necessary, the most important of which was the run down the west coast of South America from Panama to Callao, the port of Lima. Santo Domingo was in early years the port of reunion in the West Indies for the fleets going to and from Spain, but Havana presently replaced Santo Domingo, and became an outstandingly important point

[1] Most writers in English give this name as "Porto Bello," or sometimes "Portobello," either of which terms is a barbarism in Spanish. An interesting investigation by Dominic Salandra reveals that Columbus called it "Puerto Bello," but the name presently took form as "Portobelo," occasionally rendered "Portovelo." And "Portobelo" it is today. This is hardly a widely enough known name to justify an anglicized spelling different from the original. So "Portobelo" it ought to be.

[2] The term *flota* was ordinarily applied to the Vera Cruz fleet, as distinct from *galeones* (galleons), used for the Portobelo fleet. The more powerful "galleon" type of armed vessel of the latter squadron accounts for the difference in the name.

in the strategic defence of the Spanish colonies in the Americas.

Whether in large groups or small, the Spanish ships were harassed almost incessantly in the sixteenth and seventeenth centuries by foreign pirates. Not infrequently, at least in times of war with Spain, they had the backing of foreign governments in their depredations. The French corsairs were perhaps the most persistent enemies of the Spaniards, but the English were a prominent factor during the later sixteenth century, and the Dutch during most of the seventeenth. Whatever their nationality, they gave the authorities many an anxious hour, and inflicted great losses on the Spaniards. Not only did they attack isolated ships, or even the fleet itself, but also they made their descents upon Spanish ports in the Indies, murdering, plundering, and destroying. Even the most important seaport cities were not free from danger. Henry Morgan, for example—later *Sir* Henry—with the backing of the English governor of Jamaica, seized Portobelo, sacked Maracaibo, and crossing the Isthmus captured and plundered the city of Panama, retiring to Jamaica with a rich booty. Although the Caribbean was the principal centre of these operations, all of the possessions of Spain in the New World, and of Portugal as well, whether in the Atlantic or the Pacific, at one time or another had occasion to defend themselves. Along the coasts of the Americas the foreign pirates, corsairs, freebooters, buccaneers, *pichilingues*,[1] or (as they were sometimes regarded in their own countries) the gallant "sea-dogs," or perhaps respectable "business-men," took toll from their much hated or envied Iberian enemies. Toward the close of the seventeenth century the foreign pirates began to attack the ships and ports of other nations than Spain. That was where they made their big mistake. The European navies joined forces, and the traffic was soon very nearly suppressed.

To the damage caused by pirates must also be added the losses as a result of storms or other maritime accident. By

[1] Occasionally, and perhaps more properly, *pechilingues*—obviously to denote those North Europeans whose voices appeared to the Spaniards to come from out of their "chests."

way of illustrating the prominence of this factor it may be observed that in 1601 fourteen ships were lost at Vera Cruz, with their immensely rich cargoes and more than a thousand men. This is but one instance out of many. Despite recurring disasters, the treasure fleets of Spain were an important medium, not only for the replenishment of the never-ending needs of the royal coffers, but also for the development of Spanish institutional life in the Americas.[1]

Chronologically first in the evolution of Spanish government in the colonies—apart from the conquerors themselves—was the municipality, just as it had been in the long years of the war in Spain against the Moslems. Usually the first official act of the *conquistadores* was to found a town, as did Cortés, for example, at Vera Cruz, acting thenceforth under the authority of the town. As for the inhabitants, they were allowed to gather afterward; the town was ready from the outset. In the earlier years the colonial municipalities had an active political life and a great deal of independence, electing their own officials, and controlling the country for miles around, far beyond the normal limits of the city itself or town. Chief among their officials were the *alcalde ordinario*, whose functions were those of a mayor and judge, and those of the *cabildo*, or *ayuntamiento*, a municipal council, to which were attached the *alcalde* himself and the councilors, or *regidores*, and indeed some other local officials. The whole body had functions which were in part administrative and judicial as well as legislative. In the case of matters considered of grave importance prominent men of the city were called in to sit with the *cabildo* in sessions which were called *cabildos abiertos*, or open meetings of the *cabildo*, the nearest approach to the town meeting of Anglo-America which the Spanish colonies ever had. These bodies were a vital factor in the outbreaks inaugurating the wars of independence in the nineteenth century, but were of less account in earlier times. Indeed, leaving aside their activities at the beginning of the Spanish American revolutions against Spain, it is possible that the importance of the *cabildos abiertos* has been overemphasized by some writers. There were a num-

[1] For something about the economic importance of this maritime traffic between Spain and the Indies, see *infra*, 156–167.

ber of such meetings in regions which the Spaniards regarded as of lesser account in the empire—in Buenos Aires, for example—but fewer of them elsewhere. Rarely did their activities in any way impinge upon the powers exercised by the officials of the crown. If a *cabildo abierto* wished to make a gift of money to assist the king in his European wars, or to celebrate the birth of an heir to the throne, or even to take steps against Indian depredations in the neighborhood of the town, then its deliberations were welcomed. Not so if it dared to assume functions of government which the royal officials had taken over as their own.

The comparative unimportance of the *cabildo abierto* was, however, a late development, paralleling the decline in the political authority of the towns. Even before the close of the reign of Charles I the normal centralizing and absolutist tendencies of the Spanish monarchy had made themselves felt in the municipalities. Appointment of *alcaldes* by crown officials and hereditary tenure in office of the *regidores* at length made their appearance, and in course of time many of the positions in the *cabildos* were sold freely, like any other commodity. Meanwhile, the royal officials of the provinces, under various titles (*alcaldes mayores, corregidores, gobernadores*),[1] had taken over the actual power, leaving the local officials to play at government, or usually, indeed, not even that much in political functions.

And yet the municipality was to be a fundamentally important factor in the development of Spanish American political life. Municipal posts were almost the only positions in the political hierarchy to which creoles might aspire, and they took full advantage of their opportunities to obtain them, gaining therefrom little or nothing in governmental authority, but great prestige in creole society. Holders of these places were regarded as of the higher ranks of the creole nobility and the natural leaders of their class. And it was possible for the creoles to outnumber the Spaniards in the municipal bodies. It is not surprising, therefore, that the *cabildos* were eventually to take the lead in the nineteenth-century wars of independence against Spain and that the revolutions organized by them should reach far out into

[1] For the functions of these provincial officials, see *infra*, 137, n. 1.

the country to the earlier limits of the municipality and beyond. Both then and since, the influence of the greater towns and cities of Spanish America has far surpassed that of the larger communities in Anglo-American life. In Spanish America everyone who can do so goes to the city, which is the recipient of most of the favors, political, economic, social, and intellectual, which the nation has to offer, whereas in the United States the cities have a fair conflict on their hands to hold their own against the "embattled farmers" and others beyond their limits. For this difference in the Spanish American municipalities the traditions of the Spanish peninsula are responsible, a force so potent that it lived on through centuries, even though the powers of the municipal officials in government itself seemed utterly to have passed away.

The most important agencies of the crown in the Americas for ruling the colonies were the *audiencias* and the viceroys. The Spanish monarchs early wished to place some check on the almost arbitrary authority of the *conquistadores*.[1] Gradually they worked out a system which not only accomplished this purpose, but also enabled them to have more direct control over the later conquests themselves. The sending of Bobadilla to replace Columbus as governor in Española may be regarded as the first step in this direction. But something more than a mere individual successor was needed in order to dominate such great mainland conquerors as Cortés and Pizarro, who were in a position almost to vie with the crown itself.

First in point of time of the two greatest of the royal political institutions to be introduced was the *audiencia*. In Spain the *audiencia* was one of the most important of the law courts. In America its judicial duties remained its principal function, but it also had a large place in legislative and administrative affairs, very great indeed during the reign of Charles I, but less and less in later years as the viceroys and even the captain-generals increased their power. A court of

[1] Many of the *conquistadores* had an official title of *adelantado*. The *adelantado* was authorized to explore, conquer, and colonize a specifically named territory at his own expense, becoming the governor of the region, with numerous special privileges, in the event of the success of his expedition. This title was often inheritable.

three judges, afterward referred to as an *audiencia*, was set up in Santo Domingo in 1511, but the first formally constituted body of that name was established there in 1526. In addition six *audiencias* were created by Charles I, five others (including the one at Manila in the Philippines) by his Hapsburg successors, and two by the Bourbons in the eighteenth century, or fourteen in all.[1] Allocated to different cities, the *audiencias* had jurisdictions which covered immense areas. It was a common practice to refer to the different parts of the colonial empire by the names of the *audiencias*, especially those at a distance from the viceregal capitals. Eventually most of these jurisdictions were coterminous with the regions ruled over by a viceroy or captain-general.

Each *audiencia* had a number of *oidores*, or judges, usually four, but with as many as eight in such an important body as the *audiencia* of Mexico. One of them, or in later years the viceroy or captain-general, acted as president of the body, and there were various subordinate officials, such as criminal justices, bailiffs, and the important *fiscales*, or prosecuting attorneys. At Mexico City and Lima the *fiscales* were at length to become prominent for their consultative powers in association with the viceroys, apart from their legal duties as members of the *audiencia*. The *audiencias* were the highest courts of law in the colonies, and except in cases involving very great sums of money were courts of final appeal. At the outset it was intended that they should be the principal political machinery in other respects as well, representing the king more truly than did the *conquistadores*, whose activities they were designed to check. To keep its members free from outside influences, the laws forbade them to have any social or commercial contacts with the people of their districts. They could make no business deals on their own account, were not allowed to own a home or estate

[1] In order of creation the following were the *audiencias:* Santo Domingo, 1526; Mexico, 1527; Panama, 1535; Lima, 1542; Guatemala, 1543; Guadalajara, 1548; Bogotá, 1549; Charcas, 1559; Quito, 1563; Manila, 1583; Santiago de Chile, 1609 (succeeding one established in 1565 at Concepción); Buenos Aires, 1661; Caracas, 1786; Cuzco, 1787. Some others were also established in the nineteenth century. Not all of these bodies were continuous from the time of their creation. There were instances of abolition of *audiencias* and even of re-creation.

or to have more than four slaves, could not marry anyone who resided in their jurisdiction, and could not even lend their presence to marriages, baptisms, or funerals. Needless to say, these restrictions were soon forgotten or not enforced, but they do make clear how important the *audiencias* were intended to be.

With the appearance of the viceroys and captain-generals upon the scene, the powers of the *audiencias* dwindled, but they were still important in many respects. If a viceroy or captain-general exceeded his authority, the *audiencia* had the right and duty of calling him to order. The two greatest of the *audiencias*, those of Mexico City and Lima, might correspond directly with the crown officials in Spain, while the lesser *audiencias* might address themselves to the viceroys over the heads of the captain-generals. If the post of viceroy or captain-general were vacant through death or other cause, the president or other member highest in authority of the *audiencia* stepped into the place of power until a successor might be appointed. In the absence of other executive officials, the *audiencia* even conducted military campaigns. It had jurisdiction in some of the cases pertaining to the church, and might forbid the publication of papal bulls considered contrary to the rights of the king in the matter of the royal patronage, or *patronato real.* Acting as an advisory body, the *audiencia* held sessions for drawing up "resolutions," in *acuerdo* as they were called, and their decisions, or *autos acordados*, were added to the laws of the region. Naturally, the period of greatest power for the *audiencias* was prior to the arrival of the viceroys and captain-generals. Then for a few years there was some conflict of authority between them. It developed, however, that in administration and legislation the executive officials had the ear of the king and Council of the Indies, although the *audiencias* were protected in the exercise of their judicial functions. Even by the end of the reign of Charles I they had yielded to viceroy and captain-general in importance. The seemingly inevitable tendency in Hispanic life toward executive predominance had already prevailed—a tendency which was to become a fixed habit with the peoples of Hispanic America.

The captain-generals were little more than petty viceroys in jurisdictions too far away from the seat of the viceroyalty for the viceroy himself to exercise power. In a sense the captain-generals were subordinate to one or another of the viceroys, but often they corresponded directly with the Council of the Indies, and their captaincy-general was thus virtually a little viceroyalty. Broadly speaking, their functions were the same as those of the viceroys. Subject to the viceroys and captain-generals were the rulers of the lesser divisions of the jurisdiction, or governors, but frequently called *alcaldes mayores* or *corregidores*.[1]

Events proved that the *audiencias* alone were not capable of controlling the dangerously powerful *conquistadores*, of whom Cortés and Pizarro were the leading examples. As Merriman has put it:

> "Some sort of a royal representative on the spot, with the fullest powers, was an obvious necessity; yet the utmost care must be taken to make sure that the new official did not follow the same course as the conquistadores, and defy the authority of the monarch that sent him out. The Hapsburgs did not, as a rule, take kindly to subordinates of the brilliant or inventive sort, who wanted to strike out lines of their own. The official whom they preferred was the hard-working, competent, but obedient type, who would faithfully discharge the duties laid upon him, and send back for fresh instructions in any case of doubt." [2]

The first of the viceroys, Antonio de Mendoza, was just that kind of man. Member of one of the most distinguished

[1] Official names in Spanish administrative history stand for a complicated and changing variety in functions. Thus the *corregidor* in Spain evolved from a kind of royal ambassador in a considerable town to the ruler of a large district. In Spain he was more important than the *alcalde mayor*, who had charge of the smaller districts and the greater towns. In Spanish America these officials had much the same power, with jurisdiction over provinces and districts. Each of them combined in himself the functions of judge, inspector of *encomiendas*, administrator of finance and policing, collector of tributes, vice-patron in matters relating to the church, and petty captain-general, besides many lesser duties. The *gobernador*, or governor, of a province was primarily a military man, with the duty of maintaining peace, but the *corregidor* and *alcalde mayor* frequently had military functions, too. Local conditions caused some differentiation in powers in different parts of the Americas. As a rule, the area ruled by a governor was greater than that of the *alcaldes mayores* and *corregidores*. The *corregidores* eventually became especially important as royal representatives for the protection of the Indians, a function they exercised notoriously in their own interest, to the detriment of the natives.

[2] Merriman, III, 649.

families of Spain, Mendoza was of a character ideally adapted to the needs of the king. To quote Merriman again:

> "Loyalty to the crown and devotion to the church formed the basis of it; firmness and resolution stand out in everything he did. Like the Emperor he made it a rule to listen to the advice of many different counsellors, but to reserve to himself the final decision, and he showed his Spanish training and traditions when he told his successor that the secret of good ruling was to do little, and to do that slowly, since most matters lend themselves to that kind of treatment . . . Nor were the gentler virtues lacking; there are countless instances of his generosity, liberality, and boundless hospitality." [1]

Aiton calls Mendoza "the first, and, from many points of view, the ablest, of a long line of imperial agents in the New World," and continues as follows:

> "Mendoza's success was in the main due to three things: his prestige, his statesmanship, and the reasonable use he made of the wide powers of his office. He came to New Spain a great nobleman, possessed of ample wealth, from the immediate circle about the Emperor, to be his personal representative. No later word or act of his lessened the original respect this inspired. On the contrary, he bent every effort and made use of every means to enhance the prestige of his person and, by so doing, to establish a tradition of proper awe for authority. His bodyguard, his palace, and his open hospitality were all elements which contributed to this end. So well did he reflect the Imperial splendor in his entertainments that years afterward, when alluding to the celebration of the peace with France in 1538, the bluff veteran Bernal Díaz was moved to remark: 'They decided to hold great festivals and rejoicings, and they were such that it seems to me I have not seen others of the same quality [even] in Castile'[2] . . . By nature firm and just, he knew when to yield to popular clamor in order to avoid destruction, not only of his own influence but of the new society. He never antagonized the Spanish settlers unnecessarily but rather chose to obtain his ends by diplomacy, management, and, if necessary, on occasion by intrigue. The one great failure of his administration, the failure of the laws emancipating the natives, was in reality an evidence of his common sense, for he saw that

[1] Merriman, III, 650–651.

[2] According to Bernal Díaz there were over five hundred guests at this dinner. The old warrior described every phase of it vividly and in some detail. It seems that the *pièce de résistance* consisted of "huge pasties filled with live quail and rabbits which were brought on and afforded much merriment when these animals escaped."

the alternative to Indian labor was revolt and the loss of New Spain, since his own countrymen were too few, too little acclimated, and, in general, regarded work as degrading. He chose to keep New Spain and to do his utmost to protect the Indian from want or inhumanity.

"The powers he enjoyed were not abused but rather wielded in useful service. In his administration the encomenderos were brought under control, the royal authority established, and the ground laid for a period of peace. He gave a new impulse to industry and agriculture; cattle multiplied extraordinarily, new mines were opened, and exploration pushed far into the unknown north, while at the same time his vessels plied the Pacific Ocean. Under his direction the conquests of Nueva Galicia and Yucatán were extended and consolidated and the remnants of disorder which were the heritage of the conquest were almost completely eradicated. In brief, confusion gave way to the order and system of a regular state, and Mexico of the conquest became Mexico of the viceroys." [1]

Mendoza was chosen viceroy of New Spain, or Mexico, in 1529, but did not in fact enter upon his duties until 1535, holding the position until 1550. He was then ordered to Peru. Arriving in 1551, he served nearly a year more, until his death in 1552. The viceroyalty of Peru had meanwhile been established in 1542, although the first viceroy did not arrive until 1544. These were the only two viceroyalties of the Hapsburg era, but two more were to be established in the eighteenth century, that of New Granada at Bogotá in 1718,[2] and the viceroyalty of the Río de la Plata at Buenos Aires in 1776.

The viceroys were the *alter ego* of the king. This, in an absolute monarchy, in a sense tells all, but some further detail about them will, no doubt, make the picture more clear. They were to be received like royalty itself, "with pomp and circumstance," and in addition to the numerous titles and honors they already possessed were abundantly supplied with yet others. It was customary to address them with some such adulatory term as "*Excelentísimo señor*" (Most excellent sir), and, like the members of the *audiencia*,

[1] Aiton, 193–195.

[2] The viceroyalty of New Granada was first created in 1717, but the first viceroy was not appointed until 1718. The viceregal office was suspended in 1722, but revived by a law of 1739, which went into effect in 1740. By the new act the viceroyalty was to include the territory subject to the *audiencias* of Quito, Bogotá, and Caracas.

they were to hold themselves aloof from any close association with their subjects in the viceroyalty. They were not permitted to bring their families to America, to engage in business in any way, acquire estates, or visit with individuals. While the viceroys probably came nearer meeting these requirements than did the members of the *audiencias*, it must always be remembered that there was a vast difference between the law and its observance in Spanish America.

The instructions given to Mendoza were in many respects typical of those which the later viceroys received. Great emphasis was placed upon his duties in ecclesiastical and economic matters. Under the *patronato real* he was, on behalf of the king, the virtual head of the church in the viceroyalty, charged especially with the obligation of Christianizing the natives and maintaining them in their faith—a measure which not only reflected the religious ardor of the Spanish kings, but which also was recognized by them as conducive to the security and permanence of Spanish rule in America; it is more than probable that the latter was in most cases the greater reason. In economic affairs, certainly, the Spanish monarchs were frankly concerned with their own material interest, to produce or increase the revenues which might be obtained for the crown in the New World. Mendoza, for example, was to inspect the towns of the viceroyalty, and see if the financial returns from them might be improved. He was to keep a careful lookout for hidden treasure, which by law belonged to the king; was to withdraw exemptions from the *alcabala*, or sales tax, at the earliest suitable moment; and was in other ways to lose no opportunity to add to the resources of the royal treasury. In like manner, the viceroy presided over the *audiencia* of his immediate neighborhood; he was in charge of all military affairs as a captain-general; he awarded *encomiendas;* he made appointments to civil and ecclesiastical posts; and he had oversight of inspections into the conduct of the officials of the viceroyalty.

There were, however, some restrictions on the authority of the viceroys. The royal support of the *audiencias* in the exercise of judicial functions has already been mentioned, and the viceroys were required to consult the *audiencias* in important matters. In later years it is probable that these checks were not very effective; more likely the viceroys appropriated the *audiencias* to their own purposes, than that they were hindered by them, as witness the case of the *fiscales*. The government in Spain must have realized the possibility of this result, for it devised yet other machinery for a more direct check upon the viceroys in the *residencia* and the *visita*, institutions which applied also to other officials as well as to the viceroys. At the end of a viceroy's term of office, he suffered a trial, or impeachment, covering his acts during the period of his rule. The presiding judge, or *visitador*, who might have been sent out from Spain or might be designated from among officials already in the colonies, was to hear and investigate the charges of anybody who chose to make them, and make his recommendation to the Council of the Indies for sentence in the case. This institution was called the *residencia*. There was no implication of disgrace in the trial of the *residencia*, as officials were subject to it as a matter of course, but it might be dispensed with by royal order. In rare instances the institution was an effective check on the conduct of the viceroys, but in most cases probably was not. As one viceroy of Peru put it, it served only "to stir up the dirt." The *visita* (visit) differed from the *residencia* primarily in that it came during the term of office of the official "visited." The *visitador* might in this case be making an inspection into the conduct of such official, or he might be virtually supplanting him for certain specific purposes, such, for example, as increasing the revenues or carrying on a particular campaign.

If it is true, as has been stated, that the viceroys were like oriental satraps or Roman proconsuls, acting very much as they pleased, often directly contrary to the wishes of the government in Spain, it is also true that the kings accomplished their main purpose of keeping them politically subject to them. The Spanish monarchs never had great occasion to fear any movement on the part of the viceroys to establish themselves as an independent power; not one of them was a Cortés or Pizarro. This was the result of a method discovered by the kings and the Council of the Indies which was more effective than *audiencias, residencias,* or *visitas:* through the medium of corruption, not openly permitted, but rarely prevented. After Mendoza, it was enacted into law that the viceregal term should last for three years only—another intended check, but a rule which was in fact very frequently not observed. At any rate, opportunities were given to the incumbents to enrich themselves. They received great salaries and many lucrative perquisites, but their richest source of income was often through the medium of graft. Three years of rule was generally reputed time enough to accumulate a fortune, sufficient to buy off the judges of the *residencia* and leave a surplus which would enable one to live in ease and luxury for the rest of his days. The government in Spain seems almost to have connived at this corruption. Why? For one very important reason, it meant that the royal control in the colonies was safe, and a few millions in corruption was a small price to pay. Nevertheless, the consequences in Hispanic American history have been far-reaching and unfortunate. There were a number of the viceroys who were decent, reasonably competent, and financially honorable men. All, probably, were loyal to the king. Only a very few, however, could be called really great. The majority were both mediocre and corrupt. It was the last-named type of official which stamped itself upon the traditions of Spanish America, to become the norm in political life, greatly esteemed, indeed, but not so much for character and achievements as for position in society and *opportunities for wealth.* With no better model to observe during three centuries than the Spanish viceroys, it was natural that the peoples of Hispanic America should accept them as the standard of high authority and imitate them when occasion offered.

Just one other element of the governmental machinery needs to be mentioned, the *oficiales reales* (royal officials) of the treasury. Bearing in mind the vast expenses of the government in Spain, with its never-ending wars in Europe and its extravagances of the court, one will readily understand that great attention was paid to the work of these officials. They were to see to it that the Spanish investment in the Americas paid richly in dividends to the crown. The gold of the colonies was looked upon as "the nerve and spirit which gives vigor and being to the royal estate," and it was the duty of the *oficiales reales*, as tax-gatherers, treasurers, and accountants, to provide this "nerve and spirit" in great and increasing quantities. A discussion of the results they achieved belongs more properly to the field of economic considerations, but it may be said here that the normal rule of Spanish administration of the colonies in the matter of finances was to collect "as much as the traffic would bear."

It is not necessary to say that the viceroys had no monopoly of the mediocrity and corruption among the officials in the Americas. All government, from top to bottom, was permeated with these evils. Allied with graft were the twin vices of "job-mania" (*empleomanía*) and nepotism. Despicable in action though he might be—at least as judged by present-day standards—the holder of a government job was highly regarded as a member of the colonial aristocracy, to say nothing of the easy road to wealth, or at any rate to a comfortable living, which he possessed. Little wonder that there was generally an excessive number of officials in the Americas and that the relatives of those in power were provided for with the utmost generosity. "Get me a relative," says a character in a book dealing with Spain in the reign of Charles II (1665–1700); "I have an extra government job." The remark might well be applied to Spanish America—except as to the extra job! The Spanish government was aware of the defective character of officialdom in the colonies, and passed many and many a law to correct the bad features of the system, but only spasmodically did it make any earnest attempt to overcome them. Even though it meant a depletion in the revenues available for Spain, it was part of the price for the retention of the empire overseas. And it worked! It was worth the money—*to Spain!* But how great has been the cost to Spanish America in the traditions which have survived to plague the modern republics, even to the present time.

Nevertheless, it is not fair to Spain to be utterly condemnatory in referring to the political system in the colonies.

The *system*, in its main essentials, did not differ greatly from those of other colonizing powers. And Spain was far from having a monopoly of corruption. Her misfortune, perhaps, was the very fact of her extraordinary *success*. No European country had ever ruled so vast an empire, and no contemporary could compare with Spain in the reach and exercise of the royal authority. The measures employed brought seemingly good results at the time, and Spain is not to be blamed if she could not divine the future any better than her rivals. England, with only a mediocre record in comparison with Spain, eventually became one of the great colonizing nations, profiting from her mistake in connection with the American Revolution. Spain, on the other hand, was a success in colonial rule for three centuries. She therefore was less ready to adapt herself to new methods, and lost her empire. In consequence, it is perhaps too easy to observe her shortcomings, forgetting that it was almost as extraordinary an achievement to hold such an empire as it was to have conquered it.

CHAPTER IX

THE SPANISH COLONIAL ECONOMIC SYSTEM UNDER THE HAPSBURGS

In economic matters Spain transplanted herself to the Americas just as surely as she did in social and political institutions, finding conditions in the New World which were well adapted to the traditional customs of Spaniards in Europe. In the course of two centuries of Hapsburg rule these habits and methods were first transferred, and then became ingrained in Spanish American practice, with the result that the stamp of Spain was to maintain itself through the succeeding centuries, even after the separation from the mother country had taken place. Today, some of the Spanish American republics are in the mild beginning stages of striking out for themselves along new lines, but, even in them, economic life is more Spanish still, in its pattern and spirit, than it is independent. It is therefore worth while to look back for a moment to the economic factors of the sixteenth and seventeenth centuries, the better to understand the eighteenth, nineteenth, and especially the twentieth.

The Spanish crown was almost as inseparably associated with business in the colonies as it was with government itself. The king was not only sovereign, but also in theory owned all the land, granting some parcels outright to certain of his subjects, but more often giving only the user. This amounted virtually, nevertheless, to a legal title for the holder, with certain reservations which were rarely exercised. Furthermore, the regulatory spirit of Spanish administration touched nearly every branch of economic life. Throughout, one finds that curious note of inconsistency so characteristic of Spain in her management of the colonies. On the one hand, there was Spain assisting them with commendably wise and generous measures, and then there was the same Spain—a victim, to be sure, of what are now considered the false economic notions of those times—hindering the development of the dependencies overseas.

Spain found much already at hand, it hardly needs to be observed. There was an almost unlimited expanse of land, suitable to nearly every known form of occupation, if not in one place, then certainly in another. In addition, there were millions of Indians as an initial labor supply; even when their place was taken over to a great extent by negro slaves in the Caribbean area, they remained the principal element in unskilled labor in all the countries traversed by the great cordillera of the North and South American continents. The territories of Spanish America, too, were rich—rich at least in potentialities—and the capital investment for the kinds of industries which appealed to Spaniards was not great—not great, that is, for the first scratching of the surface, which was about all Spain did in the economic development of the colonies. Spain, with the crown usually an interested party, supplied little more than control and management. And yet the results were in many respects phenomenal.

Mining, the pastoral industries, and agriculture were the foundation of economic life, supplemented by the vast machinery of commerce. Manufacturing, as in Spain itself, was less prominent. If the colonies were a raw product region, the mother country was only a little less so. It is said that eventually ninety-five per cent of the manufactured goods sent to the Americas came first from England, Holland, France, and other foreign countries, and that the Spaniards themselves, apart from unlawful traffic, made only two kinds of profit from them. In the first place, the government derived a considerable revenue from tariff duties. And, secondly, Spanish middlemen took out a rich percentage, adding it to the price in Spanish America. Such use of raw materials from the Indies as there was in Spain was to be found primarily in the government-owned industries at Seville. There, for example, tobacco and bronze ordnance were manufactured, and the precious metals from America were coined.

Spaniards in the colonies, most of whom were of the real or *quasi* nobility, felt the normal aversion of their class for the mechanical industries. Even the artisans who came from Spain refused to work at their trade in the Americas, affecting to despise it, and leaving it for the Indian and negroid populations to carry on. And no wonder, considering the slight esteem in which these occupations were held in Spain. Probably the majority of the Spaniards of those times looked upon the trades of the tanner, shoemaker, and blacksmith as low and debasing, marking those who engaged in them with an ineradicable stain.

And yet there were some instances of notable manufacturing enterprises in Spanish America, although one must not forget that they were a small fraction in the sum total of economic activities. The already mentioned Jesuit missions of Paraguay were famous for their industrial life, not only in its simpler forms, but also in the more complicated occupations of silversmiths, makers of guns and cannon and numerous other instruments of war, and even those of the sculptor and painter, to mention only a few. Cotton from Tucumán was shipped to Potosí. In Mexico the textiles of Puebla were highly esteemed, and were exported to some extent. At various places in Mexico, too, furniture and carriages were manufactured on a considerable scale. In Peru bronze cannon were cast, at Lima; and Arequipa was famous for its manufacture of church bells. Ships were constructed at several ports. Some really notable work in silver and gold was done in both Mexico and Peru; at the beginning of the seventeenth century there was a powerful guild of silversmiths in Lima, with a membership of more than eighty. To be sure, the laws of the Indies forbade the colonies to have any form of manufacturing which might compete with the same industry in Spain, and this must have had some effect in checking development along these lines. A law of 1628, for example, forbade the colonists from embarking on any new manufacturing enterprise, not only without the consent of the viceroy, but also without that of the king. Enacted with the idea of checking holders of *encomiendas* from entering fresh demands for the services of the Indians, on whose account the crown continued to be solicitous, this legislation was bound to handicap industrial activity in all respects.

It is easy to overestimate the importance of this factor, however. Spain herself was so little given to manufacturing that the government even went to the length of hindering exports from the country, at the same time that it encouraged imports, on the false theory that in hoarding lay the basis of wealth. More important than governmental prohibitions was the repugnance of the Spaniards and Spanish colonials for industrial activities; they certainly were not prevented from breaking the laws in other respects, including other business occupations more nearly in accord with the Spanish spirit.

In an age when wealth was measured in terms of gold, without much thought of the fluctuating value of that commodity itself, Spain was agreeably surprised to find that her New World conquests were so rich in precious metals. In the earlier years of the mainland occupation the conquerors may fairly be said to have subordinated all else to their insatiable desire for the accumulation of fortunes in gold and silver. At first, the methods of "mining" employed were of the simplest possible, consisting in little more than robbery of temples and even graves for the ornaments they possessed, in addition to the coercion of native potentates. Charles I tried in vain to divert attention to agriculture, and even forbade emigration from the West Indian islands to the mainland, under penalties of confiscation of property and death. This law soon added itself, however, to the many others which were a dead letter when it came to execution. For a time, the colonies were little more than a "mining speculation on a gigantic scale." Actual mining operations presently took the place of plundering, and equally astonishing results were obtained. The viceroyalties of New Spain and Peru, with Upper Peru (modern Bolivia) especially important in the latter, gave yields in mineral wealth which Cortés and Pizarro themselves might have envied. Guanajuato and Zacatecas in the former viceroyalty and Potosí and Huancavélica in the latter were especially famous. A full appreciation of Spanish colonial life, socially as well as economically, cannot be obtained unless one learns something of what transpired at the great mining capitals. For purposes of illustration the story of Potosí will serve, but the reader should know that this had its parallels, though on a smaller scale, in all of the vast mineral area of the Spanish conquests.

The mountain of Potosí lies in a cold and inhospitable region in what is now Bolivia, rising some two thousand feet from a sloping plain which is itself between thirteen and fourteen thousand feet above the sea. Legend has it that when the Indians of Inca times began to dig there to extract the ore, a mysterious voice called out to them in tone of command: "Take no silver from this hill, which is destined for other owners." At any rate, it was not until Spanish days that its treasured stores began to be mined. An Indian herdsman accidentally discovered one of its veins of silver in 1545. He was dispossessed of his rights by his master, Captain Juan de Villaroel, and shortly afterward the rush of miners to Potosí started. At first, they lived exposed to the rigors of the mountain climate, but within eighteen months after the discovery there were 2500 houses and fourteen thousand inhabitants. A little later, while Francisco de Toledo was viceroy of Peru (1569–1581), a census was taken which showed a population of 120,000 inhabitants. In 1611 there were 114,000, of whom 42,000 were Spaniards or creoles, 65,000 Indians or *mestizos*, and six thousand negroes or mulattoes. In 1650 the population was 160,000, making Potosí the largest city in the Western Hemisphere.[1] Gradually the mountain yielded the greater part of its wealth, and by 1825 there were only eight thousand inhabitants there.

In the flush days of the sixteenth and seventeenth centuries, especially the former, Potosí lived a luxurious life rarely surpassed anywhere in the world. In 1556, a scant eleven years after the discovery, the city spent eight million dollars (*pesos*) to celebrate the accession of Philip II to the throne. In 1580 it was estimated that the private fortunes of the dominant class ranged from about three hundred thousand dollars to six millions. By 1593 the royal fifth on

[1] The only possible rival of Potosí in population would have been Mexico City, but as late as 1793 the latter had only 112,926, although other estimates raised the figure to about 130,000. Statistics of the seventeenth century on this point are not clear, but it is doubtful if the Mexican capital nearly approached Potosí.

silver from Potosí had already been taken on the sum of $396,000,000. At one time in this city there were "fourteen dancing-schools, thirty-six gambling houses, and one theatre, to which the price of admission ranged from forty to fifty dollars." Extraordinary sums of money were spent for the richest clothing and jewelry. As a symbol of the wealth and extravagance of Potosí the tale of a certain Doña Clara stands out. In the early days she was "the gayest, the most beautiful, the most accomplished, and the most elegant woman of the Imperial City." As the most affluent woman of Potosí she had slaves, *encomiendas*, and white servants, treasures untold of silver, gold, and precious stones, and incidentally "as many chemises of fine cambric and Dutch linen as there are days in the year, and a change was made every night"; also, she had four fine beds, moving from one to another every three months. Eventually, Doña Clara's luck turned, and many years later, when she was an old woman of ninety-two, she was discovered in a church at Potosí, begging for a living.

The Doña Clara type, of which there were a number in the history of Potosí, was not the sort of woman who would be welcomed within the circles of a modern mothers' club, but it fitted the turbulent character of mining camp society. There were comparatively few European women there, and those who were wives and mothers had less than the usual influence in developing the homely virtues among their children. In the streets of Potosí were thousands of adventurers, and the sons of the city were quickly enveloped in the currents of greed and avarice and dreams of sudden wealth which were the norm in Potosí. So they drank and gambled, followed in the retinue of the Doña Claras, and fought their duels at the drop of the hat. And the city itself caused many a difficulty for the officials of the viceroyalty. Yet who would not like to have had the opportunity to see this prodigal and restless but moving and vigorous city at the height of its fame and greatness! [1]

[1] The account of Potosí given here is from Moses, Bernard, "Flush times at Potosí," in University of California *Chronicle*, XI, 217–239; July, 1909. While the modern Mexican *peso* is reckoned ordinarily to be worth half a dollar, it is no exaggeration to translate the word *peso* of Spanish days by that of "dollar." Apparently *pesos* were not worth much in extravagant Potosí,

From the above it may already be clear to the Anglo-American reader that the familiar rushes of the gold-seekers to California, Australia, South Africa, and the Klondike were by no means unique instances of these affairs. Hispanic America knew many such a gold rush in colonial times, with all the attendant factors of a wild frontier life and ready-made lynch law to meet emergencies. About the only difference of note was that they were confined in the main to people from the mother country and the colonies themselves, to the exclusion of foreigners. Eventually, the authorities would make their influence felt, and a semblance of order would be obtained, backed up by the numerous regulations about mining in the laws of the Indies.

It goes without saying that the Spanish government took an active interest in mining. By law, all buried treasure belonged to the king, who also retained rights to the subsoil in the grant of lands to his subjects. In mines worked by private individuals, the "royal fifth" of the proceeds was required to be set aside for the king. Many mines were handled directly for the crown. If the supply of labor were not sufficient, it might be acquired by force from Indians of the neighborhood, who were obliged to work at a legally stipulated wage. This system, called the *mita*, might be used, indeed, in many necessary operations, such as road-making, the cultivation of indispensable food products, and cattle-raising, but was especially characteristic of the mining industry. And the king, so solicitous of the Indian's welfare in many respects, was as determined as any of his subjects to make use of him, with or without his consent, when the accumulation of precious metals was involved. This is not to say that the *mita* was an unduly harsh institution. Not infrequently the Indians actually applied for work under this system, for the wages paid were comparatively high. In yet other ways, too, the crown profited from the mining industry. There was, for example, the government monopoly on the sale of quicksilver, which was employed in the colonies for the separation of the precious metals from the ores. Whereas in the New World there

but elsewhere they would probably have been valued at considerably more than the modern dollar.

was but little quicksilver, Spain produced several times as much as the rest of Europe combined, which presented an ideal set-up for trade. The Spanish crown did not neglect the opportunity afforded.

Just how much was the yield of the colonies to the mother country in mineral wealth? Only scattered indications in the way of figures are available; even these cannot properly be interpreted, because the true value of precious metals and money itself in those times is not yet known.[1] Beyond all question, however, the amount of gold and silver Spain obtained from the Americas represented one of the greatest quantities of precious metals ever added to the world's supply. And Spaniards in those times were the outstanding experts in the sciences related to mining. A book by Alonso Barba, published in 1640, was the leading authority in metallurgy for more than a century, and was repeatedly translated into the different European languages. Numerous also were the inventions of Spaniards in connection with mining. Thus Spanish America, if indeed through the research activities of Spaniards, contributed greatly to the knowledge of the world.

Next after mining in Spanish interest in the exploitation of the New World were the pastoral industries, which were of traditional importance in Spain. Almost everything in these lines had to be done *de novo*, as there were no domestic animals in the Americas, except for the llama of Peru. Nevertheless, the resources of the colonies in almost limit-

[1] According to Altamira, III, 511, "Solórzano . . . says that from 1492 to 1628 there were 1,500,000,000 *pesos* registered as coming from America. Sancho de Moncada values . . . the gold and silver from the same place of origin from 1492 to 1595 at more than 2,000,000,000 which were registered and a great but indeterminate amount not registered. Father Las Casas fixed the amount of gold taken from America in the first years of the sixteenth century at 450,000 to 460,000 *pesos*. Fernández de Navarrete . . . indicates an entry of 1,536,000,000 *pesos* for the period from 1519 to 1617. Obviously, it is not easy to draw any sure conclusion."

It is even less easy to do so when one attempts to interpret the sums of money mentioned into values of the present time. One might figure the value of a *peso*, a ducat, or a piastre in terms of money itself, but what were they worth in purchasing power? This difficulty becomes especially clear when one speaks of the *maravedí*, usually reckoned at only a small fraction of a cent. And yet the *maravedí* was an eminently respectable coin a few centuries ago. It would seem that one important service the economic historians might render would be to engage in studies which would determine the real value of the different coins of all ages.

less lands and feed were so great that they soon became the world's leading exemplars in this occupation. Just a few animals brought in, here and there, would in a few years mean thousands. In the seventeenth century in New Spain there were owners of as many as forty thousand head. The Peruvian history of this industry begins in 1539 (apart from the llamas), when the first cow was brought to that viceroyalty. Other animals were presently imported, and in 1599 in Lima alone 2700 cows were killed, as well as 200,000 sheep, twelve thousand pigs, and a great quantity of turkeys, hens, and other animals. The most notable region, however, was that of the Plata. There, the mining industry did not exist. So, pastoral pursuits were easily the leading occupation of the colonists. The animals became so numerous that in the comparatively unsettled central and northern portions of what is now Argentina there were vast wild herds of cattle, so great in numbers that eighteen or twenty men could capture seven or eight hundred of them in an hour. Only the skins were taken, and perhaps the tongue as a delectable morsel of food. The rest was left for the dogs and vultures to eat, or to rot and dry as it would. From these beginnings this region was to go on, until Argentina and Uruguay today are in the forefront of the nations in the pastoral and allied industries. Spain did much to establish and assist this industry in colonial times. Not only did the government see to it that the animals were shipped over from which the flocks and herds of the Americas developed, but it also enacted helpful laws. A law of 1548, for example, favored the export of raw hides, and another of 1572 encouraged the production of raw wool.

If agriculture to some extent lagged behind mining and the pastoral industries, it was not from any lack of assistance by the royal authorities. The government repeatedly encouraged the cultivation of the soil, offering inducements of various kinds, sending seeds and plants with almost every ship despatched to the Indies, and seeking farm laborers who might be persuaded to go to the New World. Even on expeditions of conquest the essentials for the development of agriculture were not infrequently carried along. And when lands were granted to individuals by the king, there was a tendency not to recognize the title of the grantee unless he made some use of the properties. Many times lands were regranted or sold on this account as lots which had been abandoned by their earlier possessors. On the other hand, the amount of revenues collected in connection with the passing of title and various other difficulties of procedure made it impossible for persons of limited financial resources to acquire lands. In consequence, vast estates, which have become so characteristic a feature of Hispanic American rural life, very early made their appearance, unfortunately for these countries. It is not surprising that where the lands were given over to cultivation the labor was performed by negro slaves or by Indians and half-castes in a state closely approximating medieval serfdom. As for the Spaniards, actual farm labor had not appealed to them greatly in the home country, and it was even less attractive to them in the New World.

Nevertheless, agriculture developed in an important degree in the Spanish American colonies. Like the pastoral industry, it had the advantage of a great plenty of available land, often of the highest degree of fertility. Almost anything desired could be grown. Owing to the prohibitions and restrictions of the laws, however, some of the agricultural industries were handicapped, and most of them had only a local market, coterminous with the captaincy-general or viceroyalty. The Spaniards found many agricultural products already thriving in the Americas—such, for example, as cacao, maize, tobacco, and various woods and dyes, to mention only a few. To these they added much from Spain, just as they had done in the initial period of the conquest, in the Caribbean islands. Writing in 1590, Father Acosta said:

> "The Indies have been better repaid in the way of plants than in other merchandise, for those which have come to Spain are few and get along badly, while those which have been sent from Spain are many and get along well . . . Almost everything good which is produced in Spain is now over there, in some cases better than in Spain, and in others not so good: wheat, barley, garden stuff, greens, and vegetables of every sort, such as lettuce, cabbage, radishes, onions, parsley, turnips, carrots, eggplant, endives, saltworts, spinach, chick-peas, beans, lentils . . . for

those who have gone there have been careful to carry seeds of everything, and in all cases the land has responded well . . . Of trees, those which most generally have been planted there and which are especially plentiful are the orange, sweet lime, citron, and fruit-trees of this type . . . Also there are many peaches . . . and apricots . . . There is an abundance of figs . . . Quince trees are everywhere . . . The cultivation of the vine is not slight, but its product is not employed in export trade beyond the locality. Silk, which is produced in New Spain, is exported to other realms, for example to Peru. They had no silk in the time of the Indians; the white mulberry tree was brought over from Spain, and got along very well, especially in the province called Mixteca, where the silkworm is raised and taffetas are woven and made . . . Sugar is even more generally produced, for not only is it consumed in the Indies, but also a great quantity is shipped to Spain, for the sugar cane grows exceedingly well in different parts of the Indies; in the islands, in Mexico, in Peru, and in other parts estates on a great scale have been developed . . . Olive trees have been planted . . . in Mexico and Peru and in other regions, but, so far, there are no mills for the manufacture of olive oil." [1]

To this statement much else might indeed be added. Other types of cereals, vegetables, and a great variety of fruits were introduced. Rice was cultivated in the hot lowland districts. Chile and Peru developed a considerable grape industry, from which excellent wine was made. According to one seventeenth-century historian, the wine of Ica, in the diocese of Lima, was so famous that more than a hundred ships went out each year laden with this commodity, not only to other provinces of that viceroyalty but elsewhere as well. By a law of 1595 the cultivation of the vine was forbidden in the Americas, but the Peruvian industry was allowed to continue, under heavy penalties. Peru was also the leading olive colony, and, Acosta's statement to the contrary notwithstanding, had olive-oil industries. Sugar estates were first established in Española, then in Cuba, and afterward on the mainland. If some industries were prohibited by the laws, others were developed by express order of the crown. An instance of this was a royal order of 1545 for the cultivation of flax and hemp.

[1] Acosta, I, 261–265. This author goes into great detail about every phase of the productivity of the Spanish colonies, allocating each item to its most favored regions.

In fine, the efforts of the Spanish government, on the whole, deserve praise in connection with agriculture, and the results obtained were quite important from the standpoint of the future of Spanish America. Even in colonial times there were planters who attained to great wealth; in Mexico in the seventeenth century, according to the English friar Thomas Gage, there were those whose wealth was reputed to be as much as twenty to forty thousand ducats, which is as much as to say that there were a number of farmer millionaires, in language of the present day.[1]

It is in the field of commerce, however, that one sees the workings of the Spanish colonial economic system in its most characteristic forms. The main ideas of the Catholic Kings, of a rigid governmental control and a monopoly of the trade for Castilian Spaniards, were followed by the Hapsburg monarchs. These had their explanation in the prevailing political and economic views of the time. It was felt that the maintenance of Spain's dominion over such vast and distant territories could be assured only through an exceptionally close connection with the mother country, at the same time that all foreign influences were kept away. The danger from other nations, all envious of Spain, was largely responsible for the methods employed. And, finally, Spain shared in the usual opinions of those days that colonies existed primarily for the benefit of the home country, which had a right to as great a profit as could be made from them. It is easy to see now that a better yield could have been obtained with a more liberal system, but who can say that Spanish dominion in the New World might not have been just that much the more quickly cut short?

The story, indeed, runs very greatly to restrictions and handicaps. Save for a brief effort of Charles I to throw open the ports of northwestern Spain, virtually without result, the trade of the colonies continued to be restricted to Seville or Cádiz. There were some protests at first. In 1532 the *audiencia* of Santo Domingo petitioned for a right of the Spaniards in Española to trade directly with the various ports of Europe. The request was denied. Other

[1] The dictionary valuation of $2.28 for the ducat is obviously not even close to its actual value in colonial times.

similar petitions met the same fate. The crown officials believed that it would make it too difficult for the government to get all the revenues to which it was entitled, unless the traffic passed by way of a very few points, where ample machinery might be maintained to collect what was due and see to it that other regulations were being observed. Similar limitations existed with respect to the routes of colonial trade. Direct commerce between Spain and the Philippines was forbidden; indeed, there was only one port in the empire with which those islands might deal, that of Acapulco on the Pacific coast of Mexico. Trade between Mexico and Peru was limited to two expeditions a year. This might have been viewed as an exceptional privilege, because the general rule was to forbid traffic between different colonies.

One of the most oppressive of these regulations was that which prohibited direct trade between Buenos Aires and Spain, requiring the commerce of the Plata region to go by the ultra-expensive, slow-moving way of Peru and Panama! The ostensible reason was to maintain the political authority of the viceroy of Peru and to avoid competition with the Peruvian mercantile fleet and the fair at Portobelo. Of perhaps greater weight was the argument that an open port at Buenos Aires would create a wider door for the fraudulent extraction of Peruvian gold and silver, already a problem to the Spanish state, as a result of the illicit operations of the Portuguese in the Plata. It would also facilitate the illegal entry of other commodities, which could be transported to the Pacific coast more cheaply than by way of Panama, thus interfering with the monopoly of the Sevillian merchants.[1]

Yet, save for its own superior rights, the Spanish government was eager to assist at least the Castilian subjects of the king. This was partly responsible for the legislation against foreigners, although the factor of doing everything possible to avoid a foreign conquest was no doubt a superior consideration. Charles I was inclined at first to admit all subjects of the Hapsburg dominions to the privilege of trading with the Americas, but this liberal policy was

[1] Haring, 140–143.

short-lived. From the time of the Catholic Kings there was an entering wedge, however, as a result of which the foreigners played an important part in the traffic: those residing in Spain might engage in it, provided they made use of Spanish agents. So the foreign goods were brought to Seville or Cádiz, and then shipped to the Americas, with the result that the foreigners soon dominated the trade. Prices, of course, were much higher than they would have been, but for this diversion from the natural routes, and in like manner the bulk of the traffic was cut down and the development of the colonies held back.

Despite the wish of the crown to aid Spanish subjects in American commerce, there were many restrictions which hindered the interests of Spaniards as well as foreigners. There were, for example, the innumerable delays and annoyances from the inspections and appraisals of a medieval type which were still a part of Spanish methods. Then there were the government monopolies on the sale of gunpowder, tobacco, quicksilver, playing cards, salt, lead, tin, and, indeed, many other commodities. These rights were generally rented to private individuals, with the normal result of increasing the price of the goods, all of which were in the prime necessity class. The habit of speculation which this engendered was followed by those who dealt in yet other commodities, and many were the complaints against such practices and many the regulations to prevent them, seemingly without avail. With the example provided by the government, it is not strange that this was so.

One of the greatest burdens on trade, of course, was in the amount of revenues collected by the government. In the early years of the reign of Charles I, hardly any duties at all were collected at Seville on either exports or imports in the American trade. In the Indies there was the *almojarifazgo*, or import tax, of seven and a half per cent, but the receipts were applied in the colonies, and no export duty was imposed. But a change came in 1543, when more funds were needed for the war with Francis I of France. A five per cent *almojarifazgo* and ten per cent *alcabala*, or sales tax, irrespective of whether the goods were subsequently sold or not, were now collected at Seville. These levies were only a beginning. From being very light in the early sixteenth century, the tax burdens of the colonies evolved to become excessively heavy in the seventeenth century. In course of time the following were some of the principal sources of revenue in connection with the Americas, including taxes which were not directly on commerce, but which were, nevertheless, an indirect charge thereon: there were the tributes from the *encomiendas;* the royal fifth on gold, silver, and precious stones taken from the mines; the rental and sale of crown-controlled mines; the royal half of treasures found in Indian graves, tombs, and temples; all goods without an owner; the much hated *alcabala*, ten per cent in Spain and six per cent in Spanish America; the *almojarifazgos;* the *avería* (average), to pay the expenses of the ships of war which escorted the merchant fleets; the *almirantazgo* (admiralty dues), collected on behalf of the admiral of the Indies and later of Castile; the *tonelada* (tonnage duty) for the benefit of the navigators' association of Seville; tolls collected at different points; all contraband or other goods with the taint of illegality upon them; the *media anata*, or half-annates, or half of the income of the first year for all royal officers, civil or ecclesiastical; the sale or concession of public posts; the various royal monopolies; numerous stamp taxes; and the royal share in the tithe, or tenth, collected from parishioners by the church. There were many others, less important in themselves, but which helped to swell the total of Spanish revenues and heap up the financial burdens of Spanish America. There was, for example, the sale of titles and honors. The later Hapsburg governments went even so far as to sell certificates declaring half-castes white. Then there were numerous taxes imposed for a particular emergency, but allowed to remain after the emergency had passed. Examples of these were the *bula de cruzada* [1] and the *armada*

[1] The *bula de cruzada* (bull of crusade) was originally a papal bull granting indulgences to those who went on the crusades to Jerusalem. By papal *breve*, or brief, of 1578 it was extended to Spanish America, and indulgences continued to be sold there until the end of the Spanish régime. Usually the *cruzada* was in the hands of royal collectors, who obtained a percentage on their sales; for, under the *patronato real*, it was administered by the king. The revenues were considerable. In 1786, for example, 416,883 *pesos* were ob-

de Barlovento.[1] The effect was that goods cost far more than they did in Spain—not infrequently five or ten times as much.

An equally great burden resulted from difficulties in connection with money itself. There was too little specie in the colonies for their needs, and not enough facilities in coinage to supply the lack. On this account it became the practice to use pieces of metal of a specific weight, or *peso*, from which the modern word for the principal coin in many Spanish American currencies is derived. In Mexico the Indians often used cacao, a traditional money in that country, in place of copper coins. The Spanish government even went to the extreme, at times, of secretly debasing the currency, and altogether the fluctuations in the value of money were so great that business was under a constant handicap. Yet other difficulties arose from the necessities for the defence of commerce itself and even of the lives and estates of the colonists. Sailings were restricted to the voyages of the great annual fleets. And many towns were required to be built in the interior, to avoid attacks of pirates, instead of utilizing the more economically advantageous sites along the coast. Thus not a few good ports were left without inhabitants.

The general effect of these policies may be summed up in the words of Roscher as follows:

"Staples, caravans, trading companies, are exactly the institutions which serve admirably for the beginnings of trade and for the lower stages of civilization; but Spain tried to perpetuate them in her colonies. But where not only the state, but society as a whole is established upon the basis of medieval ideas and institutions—the caste system, the impossibility of a separate nationality, the great power of the church—it is practically impossible to break away from them even in trade. Highly artificial governments, which are at the same time conscious of

tained in New Spain alone. The proceeds were devoted to undertakings which had a recognizably pious tinge, but they pretty generally fitted in with the objectives of the colonial government.

[1] The *armada de Barlovento* (fleet of the Windward Islands) had to do with the coast guard fleet for protection against the buccaneers of the Caribbean. The sums applied were taken from various sources of revenue at different times, as for example the tobacco monopoly, and then again the *alcabala*, or sales tax. When the buccaneers were no longer a source of worry, the *armada* levy was nevertheless continued.

their weakness, have ever felt the need of limiting to as small an amount as possible trade which brings peoples together and which might bring, with foreign wares, foreign ideas and influences . . . What effect such an artificial adherence to the lower stages of culture must have upon the development of national wealth is self-evident. In Spanish America this was aggravated by the fact that the mother country, to which the colonies were chained in all economic matters, was, after the middle of the sixteenth century, really retrograding. For example, Caracas could not dispose of its enormous excess of hides in Spain, because she already received from Buenos Ayres and Montevideo more hides than were needed and those of Buenos Ayres were superior to those of Caracas in every respect. When the trade of Seville was at the height of its prosperity both fleets did not carry more than 27,500 tons, while, for example, in 1836 the little island of Mauritius sent 17,690 tons to England and received 18,576 tons from her." [1]

Something has already been said about the system of the *flotas*, or fleets, which Spain used for trade or other communication with her colonies.[2] During the reign of Charles I, before the *flota* system had become definitely established, there were 2421 boats which left Spain for the Indies and 1748 making the return. The annual *flotas* included thenceforth from forty to seventy boats. Apart from the handicap to commerce of a single voyage a year, at a time which might not fit all branches of business, there was the further difficulty that in periods of war there might be no fleet at all. In the last twenty years of the sixteenth century only eleven fleets came to Vera Cruz, and only sixty-six in the entire seventeenth century. The voyage itself was very long, requiring two months and a half from Spain to Mexico, two months from Panama to Callao, and another two months to the port of destination in Chile. There was, indeed, some relaxation of the system, in that the *avisos*, or information boats, were occasionally allowed to carry merchandise, as also some of the ships of war apart from the fleet, but the colonists found a better way of relieving the situation through an evasion of the laws.

Perhaps the most interesting example of the necessary voyages in addition to the regular routes of the fleet was

[1] Roscher, 35–36. Some of the examples given are taken from the eighteenth century, but the generalization nevertheless applies.

[2] *Supra*, 129–132.

that of the already mentioned "Manila galleon," or "China ship." In order to avoid too great competition by the silks of China, trade with that country was forbidden, and the sailings from Manila in the Philippines, whence the China silks were nevertheless transshipped, were restricted to one boat a year, from Manila to Acapulco, Mexico. The history of this service covers a period of two hundred and fifty years, from 1565 to 1815. The law restricted the size of the boats to five hundred tons, although some were in fact larger, and the value of the cargo was limited to a sales total of five hundred thousand *pesos* at Acapulco, but as much as double this amount was often received. The westward cargo was light, consisting mainly of small quantities of silver and articles of luxury, but the eastward cargo was remarkable in bulk, variety, and value, although silks were the chief item. Profits for a successful voyage were enormous. So the galleon was laden to the limit of its capacity; even the decks were piled with merchandise. The westward voyage by the favoring current north of the equator was comparatively easy, requiring from two to three months, but the ships of those days could not buck the current coming back, and so followed the far northerly route of the Japan Current going east. About seven or eight months was needed for this voyage, which one traveler, who made the trip in 1697–1698, rightly called "the longest and most dreadful of any in the world." Indeed, weeks before Acapulco was reached, the ship was little better than a floating hospital, with men dying and being cast overboard almost every day in the later stages, for the world had not yet learned how to combat or avoid the worst scourge of the sea in those times—the scurvy. There was no thought of abandoning the voyages, however; with men able to run a stake of ten thousand *pesos* into a profit of possibly a hundred thousand or two hundred thousand, persons could be found who would face the risks involved, which included pirates and shipwreck as well as disease.[1]

Just as in the case of Spain, so also in the Americas,

[1] For an account of the Manila galleon, see Chapman, *History of California*, 84–96. Also, cf. *supra*, 93–94.

trade was restricted to a few of the available ports. The fleets themselves, after leaving Havana, touched only at Vera Cruz and Portobelo, whence supplementary voyages might be made to designated points. The cumbersomeness of the system was somewhat relieved by the employment of fairs, after the medieval Spanish pattern, as a medium of exchange. Portobelo was "the emporium of South American commerce, the Buenos Aires of the sixteenth and seventeenth centuries." Indeed, it was in a sense more than a modern Buenos Aires, for there was no other port for the exchange of goods between Spain and South America, not even in the Plata region. As Roscher puts it:

> "The exchange took place at Porto Bello during a forty days' fair, on which occasion this otherwise quite desolate and unhealthy place was for a time enlivened to an extraordinary degree. Very small booths were rented for 1000 pesos or more, and single houses for 4000 to 6000 pesos. The remaining larger portion of the year was characteristically enough called the dead time of year." [1]

Vera Cruz was deemed too unwholesome a spot; so the principal fair in New Spain was held at Jalapa, the nearest healthy city. Among lesser fairs, the one at Acapulco was probably the most noteworthy.

An inevitable consequence of the restrictive methods thus far described was that there should be yet further difficulties in the handling of trade within the colonies themselves. Knowing that there would not be another voyage for a year, some wealthy capitalist might corner the market in a certain product, and then sell it at excessive prices. The laws endeavored to correct this evil, but were ineffectual, since all too frequently the officials themselves were in league with the speculators. The whole system tended toward monopoly. Only the wealthier merchants could pay the sums required even to obtain permission to ship goods to or from Spain, and they were, of course, in a better position to secure favors from a venal officialdom than the smaller capitalists could be. In fact, only a few houses engaged in the trade.

[1] Roscher, 33–34.

In the Americas a mercantile organization was attempted like that in Spain through the formation of *consulados*, of which the two most important were those of Mexico City (1604) and Lima (1627). Paralleling similar institutions in Spain,[1] the American *consulados* had certain administrative and judicial functions. They tended to become privileged trading corporations. Nevertheless, there were many disturbances within the *consulados* themselves, growing in part out of differences in origin in Spain of the membership, but more particularly a result of the never-ending quarrel between the wholesale and retail merchants. The former, who were the richer group, had all the better of the conflict, being favored by the laws and officials alike.

Strange as it may seem today, religious houses were often among the leading commercial institutions, despite repeated bulls of the popes forbidding them to engage in business. Something has already been said about the Jesuits in Paraguay. In the Philippines the trustees of the Pious Fund were the prime factor in the trade of the Manila galleon, acting as bankers to finance the undertaking, and charging interest at rates as high as fifty per cent. Other religious associations bought up shipments as a speculation, selling the goods later at their own price. Taken altogether, it may be said that although the volume of trade between Spain and the Indies was very greatly restricted as a result of the system employed, the profits on the part of those who engaged in it were enormous, not infrequently as much as one hundred to three hundred per cent—to say nothing of exceptional cases, like the even greater profits of the Manila galleon trade. The colonies as a whole did not by any means share in this good fortune, however.

There was yet one other source of income through trade, which may eventually have been the most lucrative of all: smuggling. The restrictive system employed by Spain led almost inevitably to violations of the laws and to a public opinion which looked with leniency, or even approval, upon these deviations from the codes. Foreigners, envious of Spanish wealth in the Americas (the glamour of which was perhaps even greater outside of Spain than in it), resentful

[1] Cf. *supra*, 129.

of their exclusion by the Spanish monopoly, urged on by internal competition in their own countries, and less and less impressed by Spanish might as Spain declined, availed themselves of opportunities to bring contraband goods into the Spanish colonies. This they did in connivance, of course, with merchants in the colonies, quite frequently in complicity with the authorities. Even the Spanish *flotas* carried quantities of goods which were smuggled into the colonies; it has been estimated that probably more than half of the merchandise of the Spanish vessels was passed through the customs without payment of duty. The foreigners, however, especially the French, Dutch, and English, managed the greater part of this traffic. The foreign-owned islands of the West Indies very largely based their economic life on smuggling into the Spanish territories in and around the Caribbean. The regions which were most neglected by Spain were their most fruitful ground for exploitation, especially Venezuela and the Plata countries. It is perhaps no mere coincidence that these lands, least bound to Spain by ties of affection and interest, were to produce the Bolívar and San Martín who were to take the leading part in the eventual separation of Spanish America from Spain.

The importance of the foreigners in the trade with Spanish America cannot be too greatly emphasized, because it was through them that the mortal wound to the whole system was inflicted. From the first they insisted on having a share in this commerce, illicitly if need be, or lawfully if it could be arranged. It was the rich Spanish mainland beyond, which drew them to the islands of the West Indies, and it was a blow to the empire when in the second half of the seventeenth century Spain was obliged to recognize the possessions which they had filched from her there. To this foreign appetite for participation in the profits accruing from Spanish America were owing the attacks of corsairs on the fleets and the Spanish American coasts; this also accounted for the unceasing desire of European nations to make yet new colonial conquests from Spain. Foreign diplomats were always eager to get some advantage for their countrymen in the Spanish American trade. The Dutch were for a time quite successful in this respect, but the

French replaced them in Spanish favor in the closing years of the seventeenth century.

One of the principal entering wedges for foreign participation in Spanish American trade was through the medium of contracts for bringing in negro slaves, under the protection of which the foreign ships would sell unauthorized goods. Under the Hapsburgs the people most often favored with this privilege were the Portuguese. For sixty years, from 1580 to 1640, the kings of Spain were also kings of Portugal, and although the two countries were governed separately, there was a natural tendency to assist Portuguese traders rather than a complete outsider. The Portuguese colonies on the African coast were the principal source, too, for the negro slaves sent to the Americas. Even after the Portuguese had withdrawn from the Spanish connection as a result of their war of independence, 1640–1668, some slave contracts with them were made, for example in 1696. Of course, the Spanish Americans themselves were very much in the picture in the matter of the foreign contraband trade, and not only those merchants and officials who profited directly from it, but also the people in general. After all, it was *their* demand for foreign goods which made the traffic possible, and as the population developed both in numbers and in quality the desire for European wares increased.

Reeling before these ever more insistent attacks, the Spanish system at length gave ground. At times the ships of the fleet were unable to dispose of their cargoes, because the smugglers had already supplied the need. The once great Spanish commerce fell apart; in the face of a growth in the population of the colonies, the *flotas*, despite their legal monopoly, dwindled in number of boats. Even though the goods which came from Spain were almost wholly foreign, the colonists were able to get what they wanted somewhat more cheaply, and perhaps in better season, through the contraband trade. The consequences were important socially as well as economically. There developed a habit of disregard for law which has been a plague in Spanish American life from that time to the present. Even the religious associations felt no qualms about defrauding the government through smuggling. For example, on the testimony of some of the religious themselves, the Jesuits of Paraguay illegally brought in foreign goods. But they felt no more reason to be ashamed than a citizen of the United States of the prohibition era buying his whiskey from a bootlegger and drinking it with a sense of right, and perhaps even some pride, as well as satisfaction.

It is obvious that while Spanish America as a whole suffered from the Spanish economic system, a few individuals profited from it very greatly, and here again was an unfortunate legacy to the later republics: class distinctions, based on the excessive wealth of a limited number and the poverty of the masses, have the sanction of centuries of tradition. The already mentioned English friar, Thomas Gage, wrote of individuals in Guatemala and Mexico who were enormously wealthy. Official fortunes might be transferred to Spain, but some of the creoles also attained to vast riches.

And what did the Spanish government itself, apart from the profits of individual Spanish subjects, receive from its economic relationships with the Indies? As one writer has put it,

> "The Spanish government officials 'passed the time in talking of the arrival of the fleets of the Indies,' and on the treasures they brought they founded their hopes and their calculations. The financial policy of the Spanish monarchs in America consisted solely in planning ways and means and introducing advantages in order to get the greatest quantity of money possible from them." [1]

It is perhaps true that the aim was to get as much revenue for the royal treasury as within reason it was possible to obtain, but to how much did this amount? The sums were very great at first, but dwindled in importance in the seventeenth century. Precise figures are not available, as no thoroughgoing study has been made, but some indications may be offered. Prior to the conquest of Mexico, about seventy thousand ducats were the normal annual yield of the revenues from the colonies. In 1556 the figures had reached seven hundred thousand, and in the time of Philip II they were more than 1,200,000. It is generally

[1] Navarro y Lamarca, II, 335–336.

believed that Philip relied principally upon the Americas as his financial backlog. Roscher has the following interesting comment:

> "These advantages to the state as well as to private individuals were naturally most important in the first century of colonization. In everything, and especially in political affairs, the period of development is fuller of spontaneous activity than maturity and the standing still that follows. The streams of gold and silver which flowed from America to Spain had in the sixteenth century a greater effect, because the value of the precious metals had not then fallen so low as was the case later. What an impression it must have made, for example, when Pizarro paid, out of the ransom of the Inca Atahualpa, to every knight of his army 8000 pesos, and to every foot-soldier 4000! The more lasting sources of wealth, trade, and industry in which England and France so greatly outstripped Spain in the seventeenth century were, in the sixteenth century, not strong enough to counterbalance Potosi and Zacatecas. Hence I do not doubt for a moment that the treasures of America essentially promoted the world-wide tremendous power of Philip II not only in an immaterial but also in a material way, although the fact may hardly allow of an exact estimate." [1]

And yet the revenues seem never to have constituted the greater part of Spanish income, even though their fractional contribution may indeed have been the "nerve and spirit" of the royal estate. As of the years 1523 to 1525 the income of Charles I has been computed to have been about four hundred thousand ducats a year. In the period from 1554 to 1560 the annual income had advanced to some 3,500,000 ducats. Under Philip III (1598–1621), at a time when the value of money had very greatly depreciated, one estimate claimed a royal revenue of nearly twenty-four million ducats, which fell to something like 17,750,000 toward the close of the seventeenth century, with the Americas then contributing a million and a half. Just what these sums mean in terms of present-day values it would be difficult to say. [2]

Whatever direct profit Spain may have made from the Indies, it is certainly true that comparatively few benefits were conferred in the way of expenditures for public works. In the development of communications her gift was almost

[1] Roscher, 41–42.

[2] The figures given for the revenues of Spain and the Americas are taken from Altamira, III, 281–283.

a minimum. The Spanish American countries in which Spain was most interested do indeed present many difficulties for road-building, but Spain made little effort to overcome these obstacles, being somewhat fearful, so it has been alleged, that good roads might facilitate the entry of Spain's enemies. Money was expended for fortifications at important ports and for certain administrative edifices, but these were more for the advantage of the mother country than for the colonies. Isolated instances of heavy disbursements may indeed be found, as for example in the reconstruction of Mexico City and the large sums of money spent to protect that city from floods, but these cases were distinctly exceptions. In the main, after the first transfer of Spanish products to the New World had taken place, and allowing for the fact that the Spanish policies were in keeping with the ideas of all European peoples of that day, there is little that can be said which is favorable to Spain concerning her economic management of the colonies, and much that is unfavorable. The verdict of the jury must therefore be "Guilty!"—but only in the second degree. And the penalty was to be the loss of the colonies.

to here
Summer 1934

CHAPTER X

THE BOURBON ATTEMPTS TO RETAIN THE AMERICAN COLONIES

UNDER the kings of the Hapsburg line Spanish America was not greatly concerned with the course of affairs in Europe, because in all circumstances there was a never-ending hostility to the foreigner in the colonies. It was really a continuous warfare, whatever may have been the periods of official peace in Europe. And meanwhile Spain had conquered vast empires in the era of the "aggressive aggressive," and picked up yet other territories under the later policy of the "aggressive defensive," though forced to yield some of her possessions in the Caribbean. In 1700 Charles II, last and feeblest of the Spanish kings of the House of Austria, passed away, having previously willed his dominions to Philip of Anjou, grandson of the powerful Louis XIV of France. Philip V (1700–1746) thus inaugurated the Bourbon line, which was to occupy the throne of Spain continuously, save for brief interruptions in the nineteenth century, until the overthrow of Alfonso XIII in 1931. The period from 1700 to 1808, however, with its Bourbon absolutism, was to be quite distinct from the post-1808 era of the pseudo-constitutional monarchy and of a Spain stripped of most of her colonies as a result of the Spanish American wars of independence, beginning in 1810. It is with the colonies in the former of these two periods with which this chapter is concerned—years in which they were more closely connected with European affairs than in the centuries before.

Down to 1790 the "aggressive defensive" continued to be a fundamental Spanish policy, but the greatest moments in the external events of colonial life were usually coterminous with Spain's wars in Europe, whether occasioned by events in the Americas or not. Pirates still caused trouble, but no longer had respectable consideration at foreign courts in times of peace with Spain. The buccaneer had become an outlaw with all nations, and was not now a political factor affecting Spain's dominions, however annoying he may have been in other respects. Most of the eighteenth century was a time of a somewhat remarkable recovery of Spain from the degradation of the last days of the House of Austria, reaching its high point with the reign of Charles III (1759–1788). Great changes were made in Spain, but even more noteworthy were the changes in the Americas. The famous reforms of the Bourbons, made with the idea of strengthening Spain as against her enemies in Europe, were the means in the colonies of an awakening from a somewhat sluggish, routine acceptance of matters as they were, to a consciousness of resources, power, grievances, and rights which was soon to produce the movement for independence from Spain.

In the background of the reforms, then, were Spain's numerous wars, some imperialistic—notably in the case of Spain's efforts to recover the position she had formerly held in Italy—but most of them arising from the unavoidable necessity of defending herself against the aggressions of other powers. France had been the great Spanish enemy of the seventeenth century, but in the eighteenth century England was the *bête noire* of Spanish policies in the international field. No fewer than eight times down to 1808 (1702–1713, 1718–1720, 1727–1729, 1739–1748, 1762–1763, 1779–1783, 1796–1802, 1804–1808) Spain and England were at war. As England made good her position as "mistress of the seas," Spain's task of maintaining communications with and protecting her colonies became more and more difficult. Under the weak monarchs of the seventeenth century many of them might have been lost forever to the Hispanic world, passing under the British flag, but the eighteenth-century Bourbons at least gave England a good battle, and saved most of Spanish America for the Spanish-speaking race, aided in no slight degree by the now greatly strengthened colonies themselves. At different times Spain had other enemies, but in many cases their potency could be ascribed to the manipulations of England in the background. This was especially true with respect to the troubles with Portugal, who had already embarked upon her career of being what has sometimes been called "an outlying province of England."

During most of the century Spain and France were friends, bound together not only by family ties of the ruling Bourbons, but also by necessities of defence against the aggressions of England. At the close of this era, however, in the reign of Charles IV (1788–1808) of Spain, the France of the French Revolution and Napoleon developed into a terrible opponent which fairly overwhelmed the Spanish state and had much to do with the eventual loss of the colonies by Spain.

The accession of Philip V to the Spanish throne, seemingly giving the Bourbons of France and Spain too great a predominance in Europe, was not accepted by many European powers, among them England, which proceeded to support the claims of the Archduke Charles of Austria. There followed the War of the Spanish Succession (1702–1713), with most of Spain enthusiastically rallying to Philip. The Bourbon powers were defeated, but saved something out of the wreck. The archduke had already become Holy Roman Emperor. So Philip was allowed to retain the Spanish throne, but renounced all rights for himself and his heirs for succession to that of France. The war had its repercussions in America, especially in the Caribbean, where there were many battles at sea and thrusts at the island or mainland possessions of the three principal combatants, England on the one hand and France and Spain on the other. The result was in the main a stalemate, although England gained one important advantage in the treaties which brought the war to a close: the negro slave-trade contract, or *asiento*, together with accompanying rights which made this a veritable entering wedge for English commerce in the Spanish colonies.[1]

The wars of 1718–1720 and 1727–1729 with England had no noteworthy consequences in Spanish America, but the intervals of peace were merely an armed truce. Hostilities were resumed in 1739, with the opening of what has come to be known as the "War of Jenkins' Ear." For a long time there had been various causes of dispute with England, the most important of which arose from the English contraband trade in the Spanish colonies. Under cover of the

[1] For something further about the *asiento*, see *infra*, 209–211.

asiento treaty, English merchants had repeatedly violated the laws, and at times met with reprisals, especially when English smugglers were caught by the more faithful of the Spanish officials in the colonies. One Englishman, a smuggler named Jenkins, brought home his ear, which he had preserved for several years, wrapped in cotton, claiming that the Spaniards had cut it off. This fitted in with English conceptions of Spanish cruelty, and furnished a pretext for war to the rising party of British imperialists, headed by William Pitt. Indemnity claims demanded by England were agreed to by Spain, but when the latter put in a counterclaim the British government threatened war, which was soon declared. This merged into the great European conflict of the War of the Austrian Succession (1740–1748), but as between England and Spain the Caribbean was the principal centre of operations. Again there were isolated battles, raids, and the sacking of cities, but Spain proved that her internal reforms had brought a recovery of strength, for she fought off the English attacks with considerable success. An outstanding instance was the defence of Cartagena.

Spain had spent more than fifty million dollars on the fortifications of Cartagena (on the Caribbean coast of Colombia), which was regarded as the principal bulwark of her colonial defences. In 1741 Admiral Vernon appeared before the city. In his preliminary attack he was unexpectedly successful, taking the forts, while the Spaniards retired to the town. Feeling sure of victory, he despatched a ship to England, announcing his triumph. "It is the Lord's doing, and seems marvellous in our eyes," he wrote, quoting scripture. When the message reached England, there were public celebrations, and medals were struck off to commemorate the taking of Cartagena. Meanwhile, "the Lord's doing" at Cartagena had veered over to the Spanish side. The British were beaten off, and compelled to reëmbark. Altogether, the Spaniards lost two hundred men killed in this famous affair, while the British losses were very much greater.[1] The entire war, however, was hardly to be

[1] Moses, *Spanish dependencies*, II, 343, says: "With respect to the losses of the British, Spanish writers are less reluctant than English to give definite

considered a decisive victory for either side. England yielded the *asiento*, but was able to exact an indemnity therefor from Spain.

Nevertheless, the disputes with England were far from settled. As Altamira has put it,

> "The English ambition to possess the greatest colonial empire in the world necessarily encountered an obstacle in the Spanish provinces of America, where, as far as commercial exploitation was concerned, the advantages obtained in the latest treaties were not sufficient to satisfy that government. Every extension of its dominions and its operations in the New World unavoidably had to be at the expense of the possessions held by Spain. The weakening of Spain was therefore a political and economic necessity for England. The conduct of the latter from 1702 responded perfectly to her consciousness of that necessity." [1]

English aggressions and especially English contraband trade had continued their serious inroads in Spanish America. Of the former the most noteworthy instance was the founding of British establishments in Honduras—the beginnings of what is now Belize, or British Honduras. This was, of course, Spanish territory, but England paid scant heed to Spanish protests. On the other hand, England refused to allow Spanish ships to engage in fishing off the coast of Newfoundland, claiming a monopoly of the seas in those waters.

Meanwhile, England and France were engaging in the so-called Seven Years' War (1756–1763, but really from 1754 in North America). In 1761 and 1762 Spain signed the treaties of the Family Compact with France, amounting

figures. They affirm that when the fleet departed for Jamaica, it had lost seventeen vessels . . . and that the total loss amounted to about eighteen thousand men." This would have been some three times as many men as Admiral Vernon had in the entire expedition. It seems that about eighteen *hundred* were lost.

It was Admiral Vernon for whom the Washington home, "Mount Vernon," was named. Lawrence Washington, an elder brother of the famous George, was an officer under Vernon and a close friend of the admiral. Through this association a warrant was obtained, in 1746, authorizing George Washington's entry into the British navy as a midshipman, but because of the opposition of Washington's mother the plan was abandoned. What his later career would have been if he had accepted the position is an interesting speculation. It was Lawrence Washington who gave the name to the now famous Washington home. Cf. Ford, Douglas, *Admiral Vernon and the British navy* (London, [1907]), 166–167.

[1] Altamira, IV, 49.

to an offensive and defensive alliance of the two Bourbon crowns, and in 1762 entered the conflict against England. The results were disastrous for the Bourbon powers. English expeditions captured Havana and Manila, which were restored, however, when peace was signed in 1763. England also agreed to destroy her fortifications in Honduras or other Spanish territories, but virtually made good her position in Honduras by receiving the right to enter that district to engage in the logwood industry. Of more account was the cession of Florida to England, together with all other Spanish territories east of the Mississippi River. As some recompense for her losses, Spain received from France what may be called a "left-handed" gift of Louisiana, embracing all French claims to the lands west of the Mississippi—left-handed not only because this region was considered of no great importance then, but also because France intended to be in a position to reclaim these territories at some future time. As matters were, Spain had to conquer the settled portion of this province, because the inhabitants objected to the transfer to Spain. And, of course, Spain had to yield all pretensions to the right of Spanish subjects to fish in Newfoundland waters.

Spain's participation in the Seven Years' War took place early in the reign of Charles III, greatest of the Bourbon kings of Spain. More than ever, England was the most dangerous enemy Spain had during these years. To oppose that country the already mentioned Family Compact treaties were signed, and continued to be the basis of Spain's foreign policy, although it soon became manifest that France would honor the treaty only when it suited her purposes. After 1763 Spain gradually improved her position, strengthening herself through the medium of sweeping social, political, and economic reforms at home and in the colonies, the immediate result of which was to provide her more amply with the sinews of war. From the standpoint of the eventual narrow interests of Spain there were some drawbacks, however. If the colonies were strengthened, it was more with a view to the production of greater revenues for Spain than for the contented development of Spanish America itself, although, in this, Charles III was merely following the precedent of three centuries of Spanish rule in the New World. Thus, growing dissatisfaction was engendered which, along with the increased strength of Spanish America and other incentives to revolt, was to lead inevitably to the wars of independence of the nineteenth century.

Even so, the officials sent to America in the time of Charles III were generally of a higher type than those of previous years. One of the best examples was Antonio Bucareli, viceroy of New Spain from 1771 to 1779. Of him a Mexican historian has written:

> "The period during which Señor Bucareli ruled was an uninterrupted sequence of peace for New Spain; it seemed as if Providence wished to reward the virtues of the viceroy by scattering upon his subjects everything that contributed to their well-being; he was one of those men whose memory will never be erased from the heart of Mexicans. His administration is a clear example of what this land was able to be, when a man of integrity and intelligence resolutely undertook the difficult task of developing its elements of wealth." [1]

An important thoroughfare in the Mexican capital still bears his name. Still more noteworthy is the fact that his grave is in the sacred church of Guadalupe. Within that veritable national shrine of Mexico, in the midst of reminiscences of the Indians who fought Cortés and of the patriots who won the independence of Mexico from Spain, the grave of Bucareli and a tablet commemorating his work are the sole Spanish representatives of the colonial era. Bucareli, however, was merely somewhat typical of the Spanish officials sent out by Charles III.

Between wars, as well as during them, England was a disturbing factor in Spanish affairs. For sixteen years, from 1763 to 1779, for example, England and Spain were officially at peace, but war was an ever present possibility. A prominent instance of this was the dispute over the Falkland Islands in 1771. This group, lying some 250 miles east of the Strait of Magellan, appears to have been discovered by Spanish navigators, but was never occupied until a French expedition landed there in 1764. Later, the French settlement was withdrawn, following a protest by Spain, but in

[1] Rivera Cambas, Manuel, *Los gobernantes de México* (2v. México, [1872]–1873), I, 422.

Antonio Bucareli y Ursúa

1765 an English establishment was made, and the name Falkland was applied to the islands. The Spaniards now founded a town on one of the islands, and in 1770, on orders from Spain, the English settlers were expelled. The British government thereupon made excessive demands for reparations on account of the "insult" to England, and insisted also upon a restitution of the colony. Spain, relying on the Family Compact, was ready to go to war over this issue, but an unforeseen event changed the whole aspect of affairs. Choiseul, the French minister who had negotiated the Family Compact and who was believed to be ready to bring France into the conflict, fell from power. It was on this occasion that Louis XV is reported to have said: "My minister wanted war, but I do not," thus calmly disregarding the treaty with Spain. Spain was obliged to yield, and the British colony was restored.[1]

Spain might justly have abandoned the Family Compact after the Falkland incident, but self-interest soon drew Spain and France together, especially after the death of Louis XV in 1774, which resulted in Vergennes becoming minister of foreign affairs in France. Vergennes was an ardent supporter of the Family Compact, although his enthusiasm was tempered in moments of crisis by a clear view of what most favored France. Recognizing the likelihood of a united Bourbon action, England tried to divert Spain from pursuing a common policy with France by occupying her with other affairs, especially by stirring up trouble between Spain and Portugal over the boundaries of their colonies in South America. This measure met with some success, but, curiously

[1] The later history of the Falkland Islands includes a strange controversy between Argentina and the United States. The British settlement was abandoned in 1774, after which the Spaniards returned. Following the winning of independence, Argentina occupied the Falklands. In 1831 the Argentinian governor seized three fishing boats from the United States, and imprisoned some of their crews. The latter were released by an American naval vessel, which dispersed the Argentinian colony. The government of Argentina thereupon protested, in 1832, against this act of aggression within its territory, but the Washington authorities denied Argentina's right to prohibit fishing near the Falklands, implying a doubt as to Argentinian sovereignty there. England promptly took the hint, and reoccupied the islands in 1833, no doubt welcoming the chance to get something for nothing and cast the odium therefor upon the United States. As late as 1887 there was an active diplomatic interchange between Argentina and the United States over the Falkland issue, without any settlement being reached, and it is still an open question between the two governments.

enough, a much greater difficulty of the British government itself was more effective in dimming the ardor of Spain for a conflict with England: the development of the controversy between England and her own colonies in the Americas.

Down to 1774 the troubles of England in the Americas were regarded by Spanish authorities as merely a device of the Whig party in England against the ruling Tories. By 1774, however, it began to appear that the Anglo-American colonials were ready to fight over the issues in which they were involved with the mother country. France and Spain now became alarmed on various scores. For one thing, England was sending thousands of soldiers overseas, and these might be employed to make a descent upon the colonies of the Bourbon powers, whether in the flush of victory or as a recompense for defeat. Then, too, if William Pitt, the imperialist, now Lord Chatham, should be returned to power, there loomed a danger from another angle, and there was even the possibility that the Tories might use the device of a war against France and Spain to win back the Americans to their allegiance; Lord Rochford, a high British official, was credited with a remark concerning the probable efficacy of this last-named measure. Spain was so much impressed by the above-mentioned factors that she consulted with France as to whether it would not be advisable to break with England immediately, but Vergennes advised against it.

A yet more startling contingency, when at length it began to be considered, was what might happen if the English colonies should chance to prevail in a war with England. Early in 1775, Escarano, the Spanish minister to England, voiced that possibility. He was of the opinion that England could not defeat her colonies, with their "three million souls, guided by the enthusiasm of liberty, and accustomed to live in a kind of independence," a people "who had given so many proofs of valor." Later that same year, the Spanish minister to France, Aranda, first raised the question as to whether the Anglo-American outbreak might not endanger the Spanish colonial empire. According to Aranda, an independent Anglo-America would be a menace, as her population was increasing, and consequently she needed lands, which she would probably seek in a region with a temperate climate like Mexico, rather than by expansion northward. Thus she might eventually dominate North America, or perhaps help Spain's colonies to become independent. On the other hand, if England should defeat the colonies, they would join with her in her wars, as in the past, and the danger would be equally great. Thus Spain seemed to be caught on both horns of the dilemma.

Up to the close of the year 1776, Spain leaned toward war with England, while France held back. In 1776, indeed, both governments appeared ready for an immediate declaration, before England could prepare to meet it, but when the Spanish minister of state said that one of Spain's objectives would be the conquest of Portugal, Vergennes lost his enthusiasm for the war. From about this time, however, Spain began to be more and more impressed by the scant advantages to be obtained by her, whatever the issue of the conflict between England and her colonies. So, Spanish ardor cooled, while that of France increased, with the latter in 1778 entering the war, which had been going on between England and the colonies since 1775. At length, in 1779, Spain was drawn into the war, but not until she was thoroughly well prepared. France and Spain planned an invasion of England, which did not materialize, but it did cause the retention of the English fleet in British waters and a diminution in the military forces sent to America—a factor of no small importance in the eventual victory of the recently established United States. Spanish troops reconquered Florida from the English, took possession of the British establishments in Honduras, and overran the Bahama Islands. When peace was made in 1783 the Bahamas were restored, but Spain retained Florida, and limited the dyewood privileges of the English in Honduras to a term of years—a term, however, which has yet to "expire," though many years have long since passed!

It was at the time of the American Revolution, too, that Spain settled her long-standing issue with Portugal over boundaries in South America, a matter which had been in dispute since the treaty of Tordesillas in 1494. Brazilian territory was used as a base by both the Portuguese and the English for smuggling goods into the Spanish colonies. The principal scenes of conflict were the Spanish-owned Paraguay and the Portuguese colony of Sacramento, more often called "Colonia" (Colony), on the Plata River directly opposite Buenos Aires in what is now Uruguay. Hundreds of thousands of domestic animals were driven away from the Spanish settlements in Paraguay by the energetic Paulistas of Brazil, and thousands of Indian families were captured and sold into slavery. Moving southward, the Paulistas pushed toward the Plata in Uruguay. The first settlement there was made as a result of a naval expedition sent out from Rio de Janeiro, however. Thus Colonia made its début in Plata history. First established in 1680, it was almost immediately destroyed by the Spaniards, but was restored and re-founded in 1683. From that time forward, Colonia became a sore spot in Spanish colonial affairs. The post was frequently taken by the Spaniards, but always restored to Portugal, largely as a result of the influence of England. When the Portuguese pushed on, however, to Montevideo, the Spaniards expelled them from there, and founded a settlement of their own in 1726—another illustration of the "aggressive defensive," comparable to the similar Spanish action in Georgia and Texas, for example. In 1750 a treaty was made whereby Spain obtained Colonia in exchange for some of the Jesuit-occupied region of Paraguay. The Indians of Paraguay, influenced by the missionaries, refused to accept the treaty, and it was necessary to reduce them by force of arms in the so-called Guaraní War, 1752–1756. Meanwhile, Portugal had not delivered Colonia. So, in 1761, Charles III annulled the treaty of 1750. In 1762 the Spaniards again took Colonia, where they also captured twenty-seven English merchant ships. They even overran Rio Grande do Sul, today the southernmost state of Brazil, but both this region and Colonia were returned in the treaty of 1763.

Nevertheless, the troubles with the Portuguese continued, with England ever in the background, profiting from contraband trade and awaiting a favorable chance for a more pointed thrust into the affairs of the Plata. Portugal was England's pawn, and under the direction of the Marquis of Pombal, the Portuguese minister of state, she was desirous of expanding her territories in South America at the expense of Spain, relying upon English support in case Spain should declare war. Pombal secretly directed officials in the Colonia region to seize desirable Spanish lands. When reports of these captures came to Europe, he pretended they were false, or that they were nothing more than inconsequential affrays between the Spanish and Portuguese soldiery, promising to order his own troops to desist from such actions. In fact he continued his aggressive designs, sending reinforcements in the hope that the Portuguese might secure posts from which it would be impossible to dislodge them by the time his duplicity should be discovered. Before the English government, he pretended that Portugal was a victim of Spanish ambitions, and, whether the English officials were misled or not, they supported Pombal with vigorous diplomatic action. Affairs were in this state, when the American Revolution broke out. That was to be the bombshell which exploded the policies of Pombal, and brought about an adjustment in the Plata region.

By the close of 1775, England was so busily engaged in the conflict with her colonies that she was far from desiring a war in Europe. So the British government announced that it would take no part in the quarrel between Spain and Portugal, provided Charles III should make no attempts against the territorial integrity of Portugal or Brazil. Pombal now made peaceful overtures to Charles III, hoping to delay the sending of Spanish troops to South America, but Charles was unwilling to trust the shifty Portuguese minister any further, and took steps to settle the issue once for all. In 1776, therefore, the region of the Plata was raised to the rank of a viceroyalty, as a defensive measure against Anglo-Portuguese military aggressions and violations of the mercantile laws through smuggling, which was now being carried on upon an enormous scale. At this time, too, an expedition of some nine thousand men, the greatest force ever despatched from Spain up to that date, was sent to South America to offer the Portuguese the "wager of battle." Once again Colonia was taken, in 1777, and the Spaniards seemed to be in a fair way to overrun Rio Grande do Sul, when in that same year hostilities were suspended.

In 1777, too, the Portuguese king died, and the regent, María Victoria, a sister of Charles III, dismissed Pombal. There followed the important treaties of 1777 and 1778, as a result of which outstanding issues between the two countries in all parts of the world were resolved, including the definitive acquisition of Colonia by Spain, who also retained Paraguay. This was not, indeed, the end of the Plata controversy, for it was to bristle forth on several occasions in the nineteenth century in the disputes of Brazil and Argentina. As will be seen, the eventual victory was to lie with Argentina, for which the treaties of 1777–1778 were in great part responsible. Back of them, however, was the American Revolution. It is interesting to speculate upon what might have happened if England had been free to act in the disputes between Spain and Portugal. Would there be a republic of Argentina? More than likely not; there would probably be different colors on the map of the Plata country, and quite possibly some of it might be *red*—the red of the British Empire, on which "the sun never sets." This was one curious result of the American Revolution to which the historians have rarely, if ever, given a thought!

The reign of Charles III marked the highest point Spain had reached in European councils since the great days of the sixteenth century, but under his successor, Charles IV, there was a rapid plunge downward. The prime upsetting factor was the change in relations with France. In 1789 the French Revolution broke out, followed a few years afterward by the execution of the French king. Then, in 1801, Napoleon Bonaparte rose to power in France, later becoming emperor. The Family Compact fell apart, and war with France became as great a threat as the wars with England had been. France and Spain were actually in open conflict only once in these years down to 1808 (from 1793 to 1795), but the latter had scant reason to feel satisfied with the state of French relations, even when the two countries were allies against England. Indeed, Spain was something of a football between England and France, being kicked by both powers until she should choose which violence to resent the more. As already pointed out, there were the wars of 1796–1802 and 1804–1808 with England, but these were little more than moments when the injuries received from that country were placed upon a formal basis. In the end it was France which inflicted the greater damage, overrunning the Iberian Peninsula and causing the abdication of Charles IV and Ferdinand VII in 1808, who were supplanted by Joseph Bonaparte, the brother of Napoleon. Right at the outset of the reign of Charles IV, however, Spain suffered a severe blow in her relations with England and France which occasioned an important change in Spanish colonial policies. This was in connection with the Nootka affair.

The northwest coast of North America below Alaska was regarded by Spain as part of her territory by right of discovery, although no permanent settlements were founded north of those in California.[1] A Spanish expedition of 1789 captured two English ships at Nootka, on the western shore of Vancouver Island, part of present-day British Columbia. Notification of this event was sent to the British government early the following year, together with complaints over the frequent usurpations of Spanish territory by British subjects and a request that England should recognize Spain's ownership of Nootka. What followed was almost a duplicate of the Falkland incident, twenty years before. England claimed that the British flag had been "insulted," and demanded satisfaction, which Spain refused to give, feeling that it might involve a doubt over Spain's ownership of Nootka. War appeared imminent, and the French government was invoked to stand by Spain under the terms of the Family Compact. The revolutionary National Assembly was then in control in France, and it acknowledged the obligation, but attached such conditions to French assistance of Spain that the latter preferred to yield to England. There followed a series of treaties over the years 1790 to 1794. Spain agreed to pay an indemnity and to permit the ships of both countries to sail the waters and make landings in regions not already settled by either

[1] The Spaniards made a settlement at Nootka on Vancouver Island in 1789, but it was presently abandoned. Over the years 1792 to 1795 the settlement was resumed, and for a short time in 1792 another was established at Cape Flattery, in what is now the state of Washington.

power, thus throwing open the northwest coast to the possibility of English occupation. The consequences, however, were much more far-reaching than the terms of these treaties, because it was from this time that Spain began her new policy of the already mentioned "defensive defensive."

The year 1790, with its inauguration of the "defensive defensive," is one of the great dates in Spanish colonial history. Spain now proposed to wait until she were attacked, before taking steps to avert the danger, hoping thus to avoid heavy expenditure and foreign complications. The new state of mind was well represented in a famous memorial of the Count of Revilla Gigedo, viceroy of New Spain from 1789 to 1794. Revilla Gigedo prepared a voluminous report on the history of the Department of San Blas and the Californias [1] since 1769. He praised the viceroy Bucareli, who had been responsible for the Spanish occupation of Alta California, but asserted that henceforth all costly enterprises of conquest should be looked upon at least with scepticism and probably with disapproval. To quote from his report:

> "From now on there ought . . . to be an end of such projects as compel us to incur heavy expenses, even if they may be recommended with the most positive assurances of advantageous results, for it is always understood that these results are to be in the future, whereas the expenditures have to come out in cash from a treasury which has a maximum of urgent matters requiring attention and which is constantly under a strain on account of its considerable debts. Once its funds and those of the money-lenders are exhausted, the projects cannot be sustained, their advantages will disappear, the return of the sums expended will be difficult, and perhaps it may be necessary to incur still greater outlays, with the almost self-evident risk of of their being yet more fruitless. In the course of twenty-five years many millions of dollars have been consumed in founding and maintaining the new establishments of Alta California, in

[1] The Department of San Blas, with headquarters at the port of the same name on the west coast of Mexico, was principally important in connection with sending supplies to the two Californias, which were considered to include all the territory along the Pacific coast from Cape San Lucas, at the southern tip of Baja, or Lower, California, to as far north as the continent ran, or at least as far as Spanish discoveries had gone. Alta, or Upper, California was understood to refer to what is now the American state of California within the area already occupied by Spain, together with the unsettled areas indefinitely to the north.

repeated explorations of its northern coasts, in the Department of San Blas, and in the occupation of the port of Nootka. But if we engage in other yet more distant and venturesome enterprises, there will be no funds left with which to sustain those we have already taken upon ourselves." [1]

With a complacency which would have been strange indeed in earlier years, Revilla Gigedo remarked in this same report that the Russians had settlements reaching southward almost to Nootka, but Spain had too few troops and ships of war and too scant funds to dislodge them. He was opposed to extending Spanish dominion to the northern coasts, and even favored ceding Nootka to the English, holding that a Spanish occupation of such distant localities could lead only to foreign complications and heavy expense. This was typical of the Spanish attitude at this time throughout the empire. The day of the "aggressive defensive," to say nothing of the vigorous "aggressive aggressive" of the era of the *conquistadores*, was gone. Waiting to be hit, Spain soon received the "knock-out blow," delivered in this case by her own colonies with the revolutions of 1810.

Meanwhile, the other countries continued to whittle down the colonial empire of Spain. By the treaty of 1795 the eastern two-thirds of the island of Haiti, the one-time Española, was ceded to France, who now possessed the whole island. Difficulties developed with the newly-born United States, at first over the navigation of the Mississippi, the mouth of which river was controlled by Spain at New Orleans. This particular issue was settled when Spain was virtually compelled to return Louisiana to France in 1800. France promised never to cede the territory to another power unless it should be Spain—and then sold Louisiana to the United States in 1803! The pressure of the United States was felt in the direction of Florida, also, although Spain postponed the issue in this case until 1819, when she was obliged to sell Florida to the United States. The treaty of 1802, ending one of the wars with England, involved the cession of the Island of Trinidad, north of

[1] Revilla Gigedo, Juan Vicente de Güemes . . . de, "Early California," tr. in *Land of sunshine* (Los Angeles), XI, 229; Sept., 1899.

Venezuela, to the English. In the last war of the era with England, Spain shared with France in the disastrous defeat of the naval battle of Trafalgar, which was to be one of the decisive factors in the background of the outbreak of the revolutions in the colonies. At the rate of disintegration which the Spanish Empire was undergoing, it was perhaps just as well for Spanish America that the wars with Spain began as early as they did. Otherwise there might not have been much left to fight for, or else the conflict would have to have been waged against stronger powers than Spain. The great imperial days of Spain in America were at end.

CHAPTER XI

INSTITUTIONAL DEVELOPMENTS OF THE BOURBON CENTURY

THE foundations in the social, political, economic, and intellectual life of the colonies had been laid and in their main features become fixed by the close of the period of the House of Austria, but some noteworthy changes were introduced under the Bourbons. More important, perhaps, than the outward differences in institutional factors was the new underlying spirit which they began to possess, *en route* to the separation from Spain and the inauguration of the republics. The creoles, for example, were still creoles, and their position in the social order was apparently much the same as before. Their attitude toward conditions evolved, however, from the comparatively mild, and one might say stagnant, acceptance of their situation as it was under the Hapsburgs, to one of resentment in Bourbon days against the inferior place accorded them in the Spanish colonial system. And yet the eighteenth century was one of considerable institutional advance, but not at a sufficient pace to overcome the forces which were making for the downfall of the empire. This has to be borne in mind; otherwise, the recital of events is a mere addition of meaningless detail. Many were the reforms, especially by Charles III, Spain's most distinguished exponent of the "enlightened despotism." Like other European monarchs of his time, he proposed measures for the benefit of the people, but within the system of absolutism, without popular participation. As one writer has expressed it:

> "In studying the reforms introduced into America by Charles III and his ministers, one must distinguish clearly the *results* which they produced from the *motives* which determined them . . . The New World, for Charles III and his ministers, had a very secondary interest. If they fostered its industry, it was to increase the royal revenues; if they gave liberty to commerce, it was simply in order to extend the monopoly of Cádiz to all the peninsula; if they created the viceroyalty of the Plata

River, it was to oppose the advances of the Portuguese and do away with their smuggling. Nevertheless, it is an undoubted fact that the reforms of Charles III prepared the work of emancipation, and marked the beginning in the colonies of an era of prosperity and progress . . . The results of the reforms introduced were diametrically opposed to the wish of the reformers. The kings abolished part of the institutions of other ages, and succeeded only in making more odious those which remained in existence. They sowed ultra-royalisms, and reaped rebellions; they sought vassals, and encountered free men; they aimed to consolidate the absolutism, and their own throne fell to pieces." [1]

Underneath the surface the most important development was the change in the social spirit. In externals, however, except for a probably considerable advance in the white and near-white population, there was little which was new in the social history of the period. Slavery continued to exist, openly in the case of the negroes, and in disguised form as affecting the Indians. As in previous centuries, the laws were solicitous for the welfare of the submerged classes. A decree of 1784, for example, abolished the practice of branding slaves, which is primarily interesting as evidence that this barbarous custom still existed. As for the Indians, the *encomiendas* and *repartimientos* and the *mita*, or forced labor in the royal mines, continued until the two former were definitively outlawed in the legislation of Charles III, and the *mita* was given up in some regions. One of the worst evils from which the Indians suffered was at least mitigated to some extent, when the office of *corregidor* in the Indian districts was abolished, for the *corregidores*, who in theory were to look out for the interests of the Indians, had in fact subjected them to grave abuses, profiteering against them unmercifully. It is said, for example, that one Peruvian *corregidor* compelled the half-naked Indians of his district to wear spectacles, which, of course, they bought from him at a good price. In like manner, illiterate natives might be required to purchase pens and ink, and those who went barefoot might have to buy silk sockings. Outrages of this character were typical of what happened throughout the colonial period. If the Spanish government made some gestures toward protecting the

[1] Navarro y Lamarca, II, 410–411.

lower classes from injury, it had no notion, however, of promoting democratic uplift. Classes were to remain as they were. As an example of this may be mentioned the legal prohibition against *mestizos* being allowed to receive academic degrees. Class was still set against class. The value of being white was to continue to be great, and more especially, of course, if one were a peninsula Spaniard.

The figures for population show that it was going to be increasingly difficult for Spain to enforce her narrowly restrictive system, however, as there were beginning to be too many people to control. Estimates for the year 1810, when the wars of independence were to begin, range from some thirteen and a half millions to fifteen millions. The well-known figures of the great German traveler and savant, Alexander von Humboldt, show nearly seventeen million inhabitants in the colonies in 1823. Humboldt tabulated them as follows:

	Whites	Mestizos	Indians	Negroes
Mexico	1,230,000	1,860,000	3,700,000	
Guatemala	280,000	420,000	880,000	
Colombia and Venezuela	642,000	1,256,000	720,000	387,000 [a]
Peru and Chile	465,000	853,000	1,030,000	
Río de la Plata	320,000	742,000	1,200,000	
Cuba and Puerto Rico	339,000	197,000	— [b]	389,000
Totals	3,276,000	5,328,000	7,530,000	776,000

[a] This figure for the negroid elements is for all the colonies except Cuba and Puerto Rico.
[b] There were in fact a few Indians in Cuba and Puerto Rico, but the number was negligible.

If these figures show that the whites constituted only some twenty per cent of the total,[1] the creoles were, nevertheless, in the overwhelming majority as compared with the Spaniards and other Europeans.[2]

[1] As of the years 1800 to 1804, Humboldt estimated that in Cuba fifty-four persons in every hundred were white, in Mexico (exclusive of the Provincias Internas, or interior provinces, of the northern frontier—see *infra*, 199) sixteen, and in Peru only twelve. Humboldt, 209.

[2] According to Humboldt, 209–210, there were only some seventy or eighty thousand Spaniards in New Spain, or Mexico, in the years 1800 to 1804, in a total white population of 1,200,000. He estimated the creole element to be

Other estimates vary considerably from those of Humboldt. Most of the others would probably give a smaller grand total and a much smaller proportion of whites. Figures of the middle years of the nineteenth century, despite the gradual whitening process in Hispanic America, set the number of whites in Mexico at only one-eighth of the total, in Central America one-twentieth, in Peru one-seventh, in Colombia a sixth, and in Venezuela a little more than a quarter. These proportions are perhaps more nearly accurate than Humboldt's. Among other interesting factors concerning population may be mentioned the habit of the whites of congregating in the cities, a thoroughly Hispanic custom. Comparatively few whites were to be found in the rural districts, although they controlled the land, usually through the medium of the *latifundia*, or vast estates, which the government itself encouraged. As Roscher has expressed it:

> "Just like the Spaniards, the Spanish creoles have an extraordinary love for city life; a landlord, there, thinks he does very well if he makes one journey of recreation in a year to his possessions, without the least business motive. Hence the white population is to be found only in the cities for the most part, and hardly at all in the country . . . The government seems to have especially feared the rise of a creole peasantry. For this reason it held the more firmly to great entailed estates the more distant the province. In Chile the only exception allowed was on the frontier. Here Pöppig found the sturdiest and at the same time the most warlike population . . . This unmistakable superiority of Chile over all the rest of the Spanish-American world, which appears also in other fields . . . may be due partly to the temperate climate of the country. The basis of it, however, is undoubtedly the ethnological preponderance of the whites themselves, who, according to Wappäus, apparently form the majority, besides the fact that the white race already predominates among the mestizos and always will do so to an increasing degree." [1]

Not only in Chile, but also throughout the colonies, the white race predominated, if not in numbers, at least in

fourteen times as great as that of the Europeans. Mexico City at that time, with a population of "more than 135,000 souls," was twenty-four per cent Indian, twenty-five per cent *mestizo*, forty-nine per cent creole, and only two per cent Spanish.

[1] Roscher, 18–19. The two men named in the quoted paragraph were German writers cited by Roscher.

prestige, power, and the force of its culture, and always in "an increasing degree." Superimposed upon a welter of colored races and intermixtures, the Spanish civilization, on the whole, prevailed, and obtained a stronger grip as the population, through the processes of Mendelism and immigration, became proportionately more white. If Spain "failed" in the Americas, as is so often asserted, the loss was merely political. She succeeded in transferring her civilization to a great and growingly important part of the earth's surface, and that was a victory whose extent in point of time, reaching certainly many centuries into the future, can hardly be approximated even in the imagination.

Unquestionably one of the most important agents in the transfer of Spanish civilization was the church, and perhaps more especially the regular clergy, without whose efforts in the rural districts the influences of Spanish culture might have been lost. To be sure, much of the service was an unconscious contribution, or the result of other motives more immediately related to the objects of the church, for it would not appear that the clergy in Spanish America, except for some of the missionaries, was outstandingly better than it was elsewhere. Indeed, it was perhaps on a somewhat lower level than in the more advanced regions of the world, if the testimony of contemporaries may be believed. There were proportionately fewer churchmen in the colonies than at that time in Spain. Humboldt estimated the number for New Spain, including both the regular and secular clergy, as fourteen thousand, or two per thousand inhabitants. Altamira believed that the same ratio would hold true for all of Spanish America, estimating the total as of the close of the eighteenth century at about thirty-five to forty thousand. The great majority were to be found in the cities. About one-sixth of all the churchmen in New Spain were in Mexico City alone. In Lima in 1778, according to Antonio de Ulloa, a famous official inspector of the viceroyalty of Peru, there were forty convents, and those of the nuns were so crowded that, as he put it, they could populate a city. The wealth of the church in the Americas was believed to be very great, and much of it was in cash, which was loaned at interest. Altogether, it is said to have owned from a third to a half of all the property in the colonies. The documents of those days, too, are replete with discussions of the internal difficulties of the church. There were quarrels of the various church groups, regulars with seculars or with other regulars, and the lesser clergy with the bishops. Also, there were numerous instances of relaxation in customs and discipline among clergymen.[1]

These things aside, however, the positive services of the church were almost incalculably great. In the more populous regions they at least maintained social practices at a higher level than otherwise they might have been, and along the frontiers the missionaries did work which merits the highest admiration and praise. The Jesuits Kino and Salvatierra and the Franciscans Garcés, Serra, and Lasuén, all famous in the advance toward and into the Californias, are only a few examples out of thousands in all parts of the Americas, who not only conquered for Spain and the church, but also modified the customs of the Indians in the direction of Spanish culture; they ripened them, as it were, for absorption into the masses of what are now called "Spanish Americans." The tasks of the missionaries were performed to the accompaniment of such hardships and self-sacrifice that these men quite properly have taken their place in history as among the great heroes of those times. The first three Bourbons (Philip V, Ferdinand VI, and Charles III) gave generous support to missionary enterprises, and their reigns were one of the greatest eras in the history of these activities. For the most part, the missionaries held their own in the frontier regions already occupied, and added important new fields in the two Californias, Texas, the lower Orinoco Valley, and southern Chile. The expulsion of the Jesuits in 1767 was a blow to the system, however, and the general decline, beginning with the reign of Charles IV, brought about a rapid disintegration of mission life. Meanwhile, the civilian absorption of the one-time frontier continued, as it had in earlier centuries; the presidial soldier and

[1] Cf. Altamira, IV, 243–244. Especially noteworthy testimony on this score is the well known *Noticias secretas* of Jorge Juan and Antonio de Ulloa, two Spanish officials who investigated conditions in Peru.

the missionary gave way, as the miner, rancher, secular churchman, and others moved in.

The Jesuits and Franciscans were perhaps the most important of the missionary orders, but the Dominicans, Augustinians, and some other orders were also prominent. In the middle of the eighteenth century, many other branches of the church and the kings of Spain themselves were inclined to be hostile to the Jesuits, who were suspected of too great aspirations for political power, although the objections to them were primarily European (and in most of the Catholic countries) rather than Spanish American in character; the ultra-regalist royal authorities could not brook what appeared to them to be a state within a state. In 1767 Charles III decreed their expulsion from all Spanish dominions, and this order was carried out in the Americas in that and the following year. Public opinion in the colonies seems to have favored the Jesuits rather than the king, and there were tumults in various places when it came time to execute the order of removal. In Mexico the Marquis of Croix published an order prohibiting conversations and commentaries on the expulsion, asserting that vassals "ought to know that they were born to keep still and obey, and not to discuss or give vent to opinions about the high affairs of government." Nevertheless, he and the *visitador* José de Gálvez had to suppress incipient revolts in Guanajuato and elsewhere on behalf of the Jesuits. It has been estimated that there were 2260 Jesuits in the Americas at the time of the expulsion, controlling 717,000 mission Indians. Many thousands of others, relatives of the Jesuits and the pupils of the numerous schools, resented the action of the Spanish government.[1]

In intellectual history the Bourbon century is of considerable importance, not on account of any great achievements, but because of the development of an instinct for rebellion in the minds of the colonials, as a result of the restrictions

[1] Navarro y Lamarca, II, 418–419, holds that the expulsion of the Jesuits was a leading cause for the development of a revolutionary spirit in Spanish America, asserting that they had been one of the strongest ties of the crown in influencing the people to have respect for authority. Other accounts claim that the Jesuits fomented the "murmurs of the populace" against the monarchy. Cf. Altamira, IV, 244. The revolts in New Spain at the time of the expulsion are described in Priestley, 210–233.

of the Spanish policy. If society continued to exist on the basis of caste, so also with education. When reforms were introduced into the universities, after the expulsion of the Jesuits, the matriculation of *mestizos*, negroes, *zambos*, and mulattoes was prohibited at the University of San Marcos, in Lima. If the Indians were not included in the prohibition, attempts were made, nevertheless, to educate them in schools of their own, where in a sense they might be kept as hostages against the danger of Indian uprisings. A notable example of these schools was the one founded at Chillán, Chile, in 1700, with sixteen Jesuit instructors, who were to prepare their pupils for the priesthood and missionary work. Following an Indian insurrection, the school found itself without pupils in 1723. It continued its existence for the education of the sons of Spaniards, but was revived in 1775 as an Indian school. The money appropriated for this institution was greater in amount than for the university, but the results obtained were very slight. Over a period of forty years it produced merely "half a dozen ecclesiastics, and an insignificantly small number of 'quill-pushers' who were to occupy themselves in the offices of lawyers or as subaltern officials in judicial or administrative bureaus." Over the Indian mass as a whole, the effect of such schools as this was said to be hardly worthy of mention, as they did not uproot native habits, for when the students went "back to the land of their forefathers they would return to a barbarous life, as if they had never known the civilized manner of living."

The Spanish authorities were none too desirous of any thoroughgoing education even for the native-born whites, or creoles, although still more opposed to general instruction of those colored groups which made up the majority of the population in the colonies. One high official of the *Casa de Contratación* went so far as to denounce education and wealth among creoles as "bad qualities in a vassal of the Indies." This attitude may be traced to the never-ending Spanish fear that something might happen to bring about the loss of the dominions in the Americas. The ideas of the French encyclopaedists of the eighteenth century and their followers were viewed with suspicion, not only on account of their attacks upon religion, but also, and very much more, because of their political and juridical opinions. These were certain to reflect unfavorably upon the Spanish state and the colonial system it employed. The numerous revolts and conspiracies of the century in the colonies [1] served only to accentuate this fear, which translated itself into the rearing of obstacles against the diffusion of culture on any broad scale. There was an almost embittered objection to the creation of a lawyer class among the creoles and even more among those of mixed race. The study of law was therefore discouraged. In 1762, when the ancient cathedral of Buenos Aires crumbled away, the governor ascribed it to divine punishment "because of the continual law-suits, hatreds, and rancors which the lawyers foment among the inhabitants."

In spite of governmental precautions, however, revolutionary ideas developed in the Americas. The Inquisition joined with the civilian authorities in attempts to check them; indeed, this was possibly a much more important feature of its work in the eighteenth century than the repression of Protestantism or other heresies, which in fact were never a matter of grave concern in the colonies. Books regarded as having suspicious tendencies were confiscated. The right to print was very carefully guarded. In Peru even the formal salutations of the university to new viceroys and the Latin orations delivered at the end of the university course could not be published without a prior license. Especial care was taken in connection with the introduction of foreign books. Books going to Peru, for example, were allowed entry only at the port of Callao, after a preliminary inspection at Panama. Foreign books nevertheless came in, but even then they were not safe from the authorities, who might enter private homes to search for them. No fewer than 5420 authors were in the black books of the Inquisition in the eighteenth century. On one occasion, as late as 1806, a certain friar was asked to prepare a report concerning the boundaries between the United States and Mexico. He requested permission to consult the works of Robertson and Raynal, which were in the Catholic Index of forbidden

[1] See *infra*, 215–221.

volumes, on account of heretical ideas, and which were also hostile to Spain. The friar said that although these books were "detestable in other respects" they had valuable materials for the subject of his report. The Inquisition denied his request, but did agree to have two of its own members look at the books and extract from them the material which the friar desired. Nevertheless, something of the reform spirit, which was so prominent a note in Spain in this era, reached the Americas also, although it is to be borne in mind that even in Spain there was not nearly the same activity in education and other intellectual pursuits as there was in political and economic institutions.

Schools in the colonies were comparatively few, and especially was there an insufficient number of primary schools. The religious orders took a leading part in such education as there was. The Jesuits were in the forefront, but the other orders also engaged in the work. Often their convents and residences were devoted in part to instruction in some of the rudimentary branches of education, and occasionally in more advanced subjects. Almost all of the schools were in the cities, but even there they affected only a small proportion of the population. In Buenos Aires in 1773, for example, there were five schools, with a total of 856 pupils, in a city with an estimated population at that time of some twenty thousand inhabitants.

Just as was the case in Spain, the colonies made a better showing in university education than in the schools of lower grade. At the close of the eighteenth century, there were eighteen universities in Spanish America, of which those of Mexico and Lima were the most important. Most of them were poorly equipped, teaching mainly the traditional subjects of other centuries. At Córdoba, in what is now Argentina, only theology, canon law, philosophy, and the Latin language and literature were taught. At San Marcos in Lima the study of mathematics was suspended at one time, because there were no students taking the subject. The University of San Felipe, at Santiago, Chile, had a somewhat typical experience. It was planned as early as 1600, formally founded in 1738, "inaugurated" in 1747, and opened for instruction in 1758,[1] but although it included mathematics in the curriculum, it never graduated a student in that field. As late as 1769 this institution did not so much as have a library. In actual practice the universities were handicapped by the methods employed, such as emphasis upon memorization of data and the use of Latin as the academic tongue; a law of Ferdinand VI went so far as to forbid the employment of any other language in university work. Religious studies continued to hold a prominent place, but some new subjects, in keeping with the tendencies of the times, found their way into a few of the universities; among them were medicine, mineralogy, and botany in Mexico, anatomy in Lima, and chemistry and astronomy in certain other institutions. Such studies as these were stimulated by the visits of scientists in various parts of Spanish America in the Bourbon period. Most widely known among these men was Humboldt, but he was preceded in point of time by a number of others.

The more ambitious among the creoles were not to be deprived of a good education, however. Some of them went to Spain, including a few who afterward were to be leaders in the wars of independence against Spain. Others developed contacts with citizens of other countries, either by travel and study abroad, or by reading the foreign books, which entered the colonies despite the laws. In consequence, there was a growing desire throughout Spanish America for a more adequate educational system, one with a broader curriculum and with greater freedom in instruction. The new subjects, already mentioned, were a partial response to these demands, but did not come even close to satisfying the creoles; they were exasperated by what they regarded, not without reason, as a deliberate attempt of the Spanish government to tryannize over them and check their progress. Foreign propaganda, eager to break down the Spanish monopoly, nourished this colonial irritation with pronouncements which were hostile to Spain. So, all in all, despite advances in intellectual opportunities during the Bourbon era, Spanish America moved a step nearer revolution.

[1] Some accounts say 1756, which was indeed the year of the formal opening, but classes did not start until January 9, 1758.

As for intellectual achievement in this period, whole volumes might, of course, be written about it, but its importance in the life of Spanish America as a whole was still very slight. There were some few contributions to science, much bad poetry enthusiastically composed, some primitive essays at dramatic representation, a genuine interest in music, and a respectable proficiency in sculpture, painting, and architecture. The church was the mainspring of accomplishment in the field of art; religious edifices were easily the outstanding examples of architecture, and scriptural themes supplied the principal motives for painting and sculpture. The greatest single artistic creation of the whole colonial era was the cathedral of Mexico, begun in 1573, but not finished until 1813. The bronze equestrian statue of Charles IV by Manuel Tolsa is regarded as an exceptional triumph in the field of sculpture. It is still standing in Mexico City. Early in the eighteenth century, a number of news sheets and a few literary and scientific journals made a semi-occasional appearance, but were usually short-lived. These publications, nevertheless, meant a great advance over the two previous centuries, but the sum total was slight, and their influence not very far-reaching. There were possibly not more than ten printing presses in all Spanish America by the end of the period. Furthermore, the Inquisition, if not altogether successful in its effort to check the influx of forbidden books, was able to hinder the development of literary production. Books of history and description about Spanish America continued to be written, and they are among the most noteworthy volumes of the period, but most of them were the work of Spaniards and other Europeans.[1]

Some political changes were made which were, on the whole, improvements. Nevertheless, the result was the same as in the innovations in social and intellectual life,

[1] Each region produced its writings of this character. For example, in that sector which led to and into the two Californias one finds the names of Eusebio Francisco Kino, José González Cabrera Bueno, Matías Ángel de la Mota Padilla, Isidro Felis de Espinosa, José Antonio de Villa-Señor y Sánchez, José de Ortega, Andrés Marcos Burriel, Francisco Javier Alegre, José de Gálvez, Jakob Baegert, Pedro Font, Francisco Garcés, Francisco Palou, Francisco Javier Clavigero, Juan Domingo Arricivita, Alexander von Humboldt, and indeed a number of others.

since the new methods in fact helped to promote the campaign for independence. The object of the Spanish crown, of course, was to make the defence of the colonies against foreign attack more effective, with also the never forgotten projects of producing more revenue.

As already mentioned, the two viceroyalties of New Granada (1718 and 1740) and the Plata (1776) were created, taking their place with New Spain and Peru to make four governments of this type. The first-named included what are now Colombia, Venezuela, Panama, and Ecuador. The virtual independence of Chile from Peru was in a sense confirmed when it became a captaincy-general in 1778. Venezuela, which had been subordinate to the *audiencia* of Santo Domingo, was made a captaincy-general in 1731; subject to the viceroyalty of New Granada after 1740, it was freed from that connection in 1777. In like manner, the captaincy-general of Guatemala became less dependent upon the viceroy of New Spain, or Mexico. Puerto Rico obtained a separate government. The government of Cuba became a captaincy-general in 1777. Both before and after that date it included the Spanish territories along the gulf coast from Florida to Louisiana, except from 1763 to 1800, when there was a captaincy-general of Louisiana, embracing the mainland possessions, which was given up with the return of Louisiana to France. Another government, called the commandancy-general of the interior provinces (Provincias Internas), was established by Charles III in 1776, comprising the Indian-infested, hard-fighting frontier of northern New Spain, or the border states of what are now the United States and Mexico. Altogether, including the older governments in Guatemala and Española, there were four viceroyalties and eight other separate jurisdictions, whether as captaincies-general, jurisdictions of a governor or commandant-general, or presidencies of an *audiencia* (Guatemala, Española, Chile, Venezuela, Cuba, Louisiana, Puerto Rico, and Provincias Internas), with a ninth in the Philippines. Still other *audiencia* districts were virtually subject to a viceroy or captain-general; three of them were eventually to become Spanish American republics: Charcas (Bolivia); Quito (Ecuador); and

Panama.[1] Except for Uruguay and Paraguay and the break-up of Central America, one may find the pattern of the modern republics in the situation resulting from these eighteenth century changes.

Toward the close of the eighteenth century a new plan of government was adopted in the establishment of the intendancies. The first of them appeared in Cuba in 1765,[2] but it was not until after the ordinance of 1786 for New Spain that the institution became general. Presently, the entire colonial empire was cut up into small jurisdictions, under the direct rule of officials called intendants. In Mexico there were twelve, presided over by a superintendent. There were eight each in the viceroyalties of Peru and the Plata, and so on down to one in smaller areas such as Cuba and Guatemala. The announced objective was to improve fiscal and financial administration, but in point of fact the intendants virtually superseded the viceroys, *audiencias*, and captain-generals in the smaller details of government. They were to be responsible for an honest, economical, and rapid administration of justice, visiting all parts of their intendancies each year for this purpose. Under the head of what was called *policía* (policing) they were to pay attention to agriculture and industry, especially mining and the raising of cotton, and also to pursue vagabonds, look after the cleaning of cities and the proper functioning of public granaries, markets, inns, bridges, and mints. Their military duties included the supply of provisions and the numerous types of equipment required, the quartering of soldiers, inspection of dépots and magazines, and a share in the councils of the viceroys and others in planning campaigns or the movement and distribution of troops. Their most important services, however, were to be in the field of the royal finances, in which they had exclusive jurisdiction and power.

The effects of this change were considerable. To some extent the abuses of local and provincial officials were corrected. The corrupt and tyrannical rule of the *alcaldes*

[1] The *audiencia* of Panama, which had been abolished and revived before, was definitively suppressed in 1751.

[2] By enactment of 1764.

mayores and *corregidores* was done away with, and the *repartimiento* abolished. Nevertheless, while the intendants were a somewhat better group of men than their predecessors, the inner spirit of the lesser Spanish officialdom did not change overnight, and not a few of the evils continued, serving to increase the hatred of the colonials for a system which prated reform but did not bring it—at least not in the measure which a growingly dissatisfied population regarded as necessary.

The intendants quite thoroughly absorbed the life of the municipalities, displacing the *corregidores*, and leaving very little for the *alcaldes* and *cabildos* to do, except as subordinates of their own. The objections to this excess of authority were so great that the once much prized positions in the *cabildos* now often went begging, as it became increasingly difficult to find anybody who was willing to serve as a *regidor*. In one respect the intendants must very nearly have approximated the wishes of the crown, although gaining no eulogies therefor from the people of Spanish America, and that was in increasing the royal revenues. Some regions, such as Cuba, Florida, Louisiana, Trinidad, Española, and the Philippines produced a deficit, but an annual surplus from the other domains made up this loss with millions to spare. New Spain yielded a profit of five to six million *pesos*, Peru about a million, Buenos Aires six to seven hundred thousand, and New Granada four to five hundred thousand. These figures do not take into account the indirect profit through the trade and investment relationships of Spanish subjects, plus the salaries received by officials of the Indies.

Nor were these the only reforms. The calibre of the men sent out as viceroys was distinctly better than in the period of the House of Austria. There was no longer any fear that one of them might turn *conquistador*, like a Cortés or Pizarro, and rival the king; so the necessity for protecting the empire through the weakness and corruption of its agents in the Americas no longer existed. These men, however, were too late to save the situation for Spain, and, after all, they were unable to make any profound change in the system and methods traditionally employed. One misstep might overcome the effect on public opinion of many meritorious acts. Such a case, for example, was that of a certain Diego de Urbea, who secured a post in the *audiencia* of Lima in 1749 as a reward for a gift of 41,000 *pesos* to the king. Changes also appeared in the direction of affairs in Spain. With the creation of the post of minister of the Indies in 1714, the importance of the Council of the Indies and the *Casa de Contratación* began to decline; in 1718, the latter was moved from Seville to Cádiz,[1] and in 1790 it was abolished. Under Charles III the great secretaries, such as Julián de Arriaga and José de Gálvez, became the virtual heads of the entire colonial empire. The advantages of these changes were lost, however, with the reappearance of graft and incompetence in the reign of Charles IV. Officials in the Indies promptly reflected the weak and inefficient character of the monarch, giving just cause for the complaints of Spanish America.

Whatever the merits of the reforms, the prime difficulty for Spain, the dissatisfaction of the colonials, was never cured. More than one Spanish thinker realized the danger in this situation, and made suggestions to meet it. Campillo, one of the ministers of Philip V, referred to the system in the Americas as one of militarism and conquest; it was suitable in the time of Charles I, he said, but ought now to be abandoned in favor of greater freedom, such as the French had accorded their subjects in Canada, with also a much wider measure of economic liberty. The most radical suggestions, however, were made by Count Aranda, one of the officials of Charles III, in a remarkable and prophetic memorial to the king in 1783. He was convinced that, on account of the vast extent of the colonies and their distance from Spain, they could not be defended successfully against any powerful attack; he feared in particular, not England or France, but the newly-born United States, predicting that the pigmy of 1783, as the United States then was, might some day become a giant, with an appe-

[1] The decree was issued in 1717, but the transfer took place the following year. An extraordinary variety of dates appears in books which touch upon Hispanic American colonial history, but the discrepancies can usually be accounted for by the difference between the promulgation of a law and its execution, or as between the beginning of an operation and its conclusion.

tite for new territories. First, the United States might be expected to take Florida, and then proceed to yet other conquests, which Spain would be unable to resist. As a means of combating this peril, Aranda proposed that Spain should give up direct control of her colonies, forming three kingdoms out of them, with the Spanish monarch retaining the title of emperor, and keeping for himself only such strategic points as Cuba and Puerto Rico and some other suitable positions in South America. The three kingdoms would then form an offensive and defensive alliance with Spain, and would endeavor to maintain the intimacy of the connection through the medium of intermarriages of the royal families. Neither Charles III nor Charles IV, to whom a similar suggestion was made in 1793, was willing to adopt it, however, and traditional policies were followed, much to the dissatisfaction of the creoles, who by this time were only too ready to pick flaws in colonial administration anyway.

This just mentioned disposition of the colonials had existed for many years. Apart from various conspiracies and uprisings, referred to presently,[1] there are numerous other evidences to the same effect. The Marquis of Linares, viceroy of New Spain from 1711 to 1716, asserted that both the creoles and the Indians of Mexico had the idea that everything the Spaniards possessed in that country was the result of usurpations from people born there. José de Gálvez, in the course of his *visita* in New Spain, observed that there was a ferment of protest in some such formula as the following: "The Spaniards will not let us have a share in the government of our own country, but carry away our money to Spain." And, indeed, the creoles of Mexico once sent a petition to Charles III, asking for the right to hold public office, but the authorities were too suspicious of them to grant the request. The clergy played no small part in fomenting the dissatisfaction against the government, despite the fact that any attack on the mother country was almost certain to affect the church disadvantageously, too. It was perhaps natural, however, in such a comparatively backward region as Spanish America that

[1] See *infra*, 215–221.

the church should provide some of the intellectual leaders. Accustomed to reading and study, many of the clergy did not disdain to peruse even the forbidden books, and shared in the usual admiration of those times for the free government of England. In 1806, when an English expedition under Sir Home Popham and General Beresford captured Buenos Aires, the religious orders there directed a remarkable memorial to the latter which contained these words:[1]

> "Although the loss of a government under which a people has been formed is accustomed to be regarded as one of the greatest disasters, it has also many times been the first step toward their glorification. We do not make bold to predict our own destiny, but do indeed assert that the gentle character of English government will console us for what we have lost." [1]

One explanation for this attitude, which was to be found throughout the colonies, was that the lesser clergy were in great degree creoles or *mestizos*, who shared the feelings of their class against the Spanish system.

Even Spaniards themselves helped to foster the spirit of liberalism and independence, especially many of those in the peninsula who were vaguely and sentimentally sympathetic for any "cause," such as that of the unjust oppression of the Americas. Eventual patriot leaders, among whom may be named Belgrano, Bernardo O'Higgins, Bolívar, and San Martín, were strengthened in their beliefs by the very contacts they had with Spaniards in Europe, influenced as they were by the encyclopaedists and other political thinkers hostile to the system employed by Spain. Many Spanish writings of those days contained such phrases as "unhappy America," and, in general, there was an undercurrent of feeling on behalf of Spanish America which was to find expression in some of the early resolutions of the famous *Cortes* of Cádiz in 1810. If Spaniards encouraged the differences between Spain and the colonies, it can easily be imagined that foreigners did so, too, and very much more. The English were especially prominent in this, eager to break down the Spanish monopoly. Not only in their writings and their private conversations, but even in the goods they sold they made propaganda against the Spanish sys-

[1] Quoted in Altamira, IV, 202.

tem; on the snuff boxes, watch covers, and other objects they brought in they frequently showed the figure of a woman waving a flag, together with the legend "Liberty for America."

Under the circumstances, it was natural that even the measures of the Spanish government, undertaken with a very different purpose, should assist in the preparation of the movement for independence. Outstanding in this connection was the creation of the colonial militia for the defence and preservation of the colonies. The ministers of Charles III felt that it was impossible for Spain to provide soldiers enough, and so established the creole militia to assist the regular army. Figures for 1804 show that there were twenty-five thousand regulars in Spanish America and some 127,900 militiamen. The Spaniards made a jest of the latter, but they had already given proofs of their capacity as warriors in repeated campaigns. When they themselves began to realize that they might possibly cope with the Spaniards in war, the conflict was not far distant; then the militia, far from defending the Spanish Empire, became one of the most important elements of the patriot armies in bringing about its destruction.

In the field of economics the eighteenth century produced vast changes in Spanish America, although mainly in commerce, in which the foreigners, more particularly the English, began more insistently to replace the Spaniards, with or without the permission of the laws. Domestic production, however, continued to be in the hands of Spanish subjects, whether peninsula or native-born, and conditions, in the main, followed the norm of previous centuries. Whatever the total number of the inhabitants of the Americas,[1] there was still a comparatively scant population, given the immense extent of the Spanish colonies. Not only were the whites a decided, though controlling, minority, but also ownership of lands was in the hands of the very few. In the Buenos Aires district, for example, according to figures for 1744, there were 327 proprietors in a population of 16,306, with 186 owners to 5897 landless laborers out in the country. Throughout Spanish America vast

[1] Cf. *supra*, 189–191.

estates, of missions and civilians alike, were the rule, and only a very small proportion of the land was cultivated or exploited.

Agricultural history followed the same lines as for the seventeenth century. Farming continued to be much less esteemed than mining. Governmental prohibitions against the cultivation of products which might compete with those of Spain were something of a handicap, although the laws were not very actively enforced. Thus, Humboldt observed a number of important exploitations of the olive and the vine. As in previous centuries, the Spaniards brought seeds and plants to the colonies, and their yield in the soil of the New World was often exceptional. Wheat, for example, produced from five to twenty times as much as under the same conditions in Spain. The native crops, such as maize, potatoes, and cacao, were still being raised. Yet there was no development of agriculture on a great scale. Nevertheless, the Spaniards were considerably interested in forest products, especially in those from which dyes and medicines might be obtained. In all forms of the cultivation of the soil the labor was either Indian or negro, which meant that there was slight opportunity for the white man of limited means to accomplish anything.

In the pastoral industry the most noteworthy feature was the development of the Plata region. It was estimated that there were some twelve million cattle and three million horses there. The most primitive methods were employed, with no attempt at improving the breed of the animals and scant effort to do much more than obtain the hides, while the various possibilities in the way of derivative industries were overlooked. Mining, as in earlier centuries, had an extraordinary development, although almost wholly in precious metals. In comparison, the production of other metals was insignificant, despite the now well-known wealth of Spanish America in copper, tin, and other minerals, to say nothing of oil, recently so prominent. As for manufacturing, it remained unimportant, and probably would have been so, even without the restrictions of the laws.

It was in commerce that the reform ideas of the century

had their widest play. The annual *flotas* were employed until 1735, and definitively abolished in 1778. In their place in the interval between these years it was the practice to authorize individual "register ships" to sail to the various ports of the Americas, even including direct voyages to the Pacific coast. The Cádiz monopoly was still in effect, however, and license fees were high, and difficult to obtain. Under Charles III reforms were introduced at a rapid pace. Beginning in 1764 a regular mail service, once or twice a month, was established with the West Indies and the Plata region, and presently extended to other parts of the colonies. The mail boats were allowed to carry some cargo. In 1765 commerce with the West Indies was thrown open to all Spaniards, not only by way of Cádiz, but also from a number of Catalan ports. Like provisions followed with respect to South America in 1775 and Mexico in 1789. In 1774 the previously existing restrictions on the intercolonial commerce of New Spain, Guatemala, New Granada, and Peru were withdrawn. Most important of all, however, was the great free trade *reglamento*, or ordinance, of October 12, 1778. In addition to the abolition of the *flotas*, this authorized direct trade between virtually all ports of consequence in Spain and twenty ports in Spanish America, besides very greatly reducing duties on the traffic. Mexico, however, the richest plum in the Spanish colonial orchard, was excluded from the benefits of this decree, as also Venezuela, but in 1789 it was extended to them.

These measures made themselves felt almost immediately in a vast increase of the volume of trade. In Mexico, for example, the average annual exports prior to 1778 amounted to 617,000 *pesos*, and jumped to 2,850,000 after that year. Early in the nineteenth century the figures for Mexican exports had advanced to some twenty-seven millions a year, at the same time that imports were twenty millions. Other regions profited in like manner. The total volume of trade between Spain and the colonies, which was estimated to amount to 171,900,000 francs in 1753, had advanced to 638,500,000 francs in 1800. As a further stimulus to business, new *consulados* were created, and private trading companies were authorized to engage in an exclusive traffic with different parts of the empire, on the analogy of similar enterprises of other European countries which had met with success, such for example as the British East India Company. The most noteworthy of these were the Royal Guipúzcoa Company of Caracas (1728) and the Royal Company of the Philippines (1733), the latter of which eventually succeeded to a share in the American trade. Plans for a canal at Panama were also discussed, as they had been, in fact, ever since the time of Charles I, but now a canal was actually made. To be sure, it was merely a barge canal, availing itself of the Atrato River in Colombia, and was open at only certain seasons of the year. A permanent canal was authorized early in the nineteenth century, but the wars of independence prevented any attempt to build it.

Nevertheless, despite the considerable expansion of trade as a result of the reform measures, it was not nearly so great as it might have been, because of continuing handicaps, such as heavy taxation, the royal monopolies, and the repeated cornering of the markets by individuals who took advantage of opportunities in part created by the laws. Not least of the difficulties was the general suspicion on the part of the state of the formation of a class of wealthy creoles, who therefore had to encounter many obstacles. Perhaps the greatest handicap, to Spanish commerce at least, was the competition of foreigners, whether through the medium of legitimate trade, somewhat grudgingly acquiesced in by Spain, or by way of smuggling. With the foreign propaganda for freedom of trade the people of Spanish America were thoroughly in accord, and it was to take its place among the many factors bringing about the movement for independence.

The French, English, and Dutch were, as in earlier times, the most active in the efforts to break down the Spanish trade monopoly in the Americas. What each of these peoples really wanted was, not free trade, but freedom for itself, to the exclusion of other nations, except the Spaniards. Thus, all attacked the idea of monopoly, but with reservations. The French were at first in the best position to obtain favors, but the kings of France were more concerned with checking the advances of the English and Dutch than over commercial privileges for their own subjects, and endeavored to prevent any infraction of the Spanish laws by French navigators; in 1716, French trading expeditions to Spanish America were forbidden on penalty of death. The French government contented itself with the grant by Spain of the negro slave trade *asiento*. In 1701 the contract of the Portuguese company was canceled, and the privilege was given to the French Guinea Company. Over a period of ten years it was authorized to import forty-two thousand slaves into Spanish America. Valuable though this privilege was, its greatest advantage was that under cover of the contract it actually gave the company a virtual free trade in any commodities in the various ports of the Spanish colonies, though, of course, by evasion of the laws. And yet the company was so badly managed that its profits were not excessively great.

English successes in the War of the Spanish Succession enabled the British government to demand the *asiento* privilege at the peace settlement in 1713. The English had for years berated the Spaniards for the injustice of the Spanish American monopoly, but now they proposed to exclude other European nations, even including their allies the Dutch. Indeed, the hopes of the English somewhat outran what they were able to obtain. They asked for territorial concessions in the Plata country, free navigation of Spanish waters in the Caribbean and the Gulf of Mexico, the right to cut dyewoods in Honduras, and permission for English boats from the Caribbean islands to enter Spanish ports to purchase provisions. It was perfectly evident that these privileges would be equivalent to English free trade with the Spanish colonies, since international good faith in the way of exactingly honest fulfilment of treaties was honored more in the breach than in the observance thereof in those days. All England obtained, therefore, was the *asiento*, plus the so-called *navío de permiso*, or "permission ship." This latter was a right for a single English ship of five hundred tons to go directly from England to Spanish America in the season when the fairs were being held, and sell its cargo in the Atlantic ports of the Spanish colonies.

This privilege was given on the express promise of the English company not to engage in contraband traffic in any manner, but in practice it was employed as a medium for smuggling on a tremendous scale, just as were the slave-trading features of the *asiento*.

Beginning in 1713 the English company, in which the kings of England and Spain were each to own a fourth of the capital (presumably with the idea of committing them to the enterprise), was to import 4800 negroes a year into Spanish America, paying a tax to the Spanish treasury of 33⅓ *pesos* per head for each slave. As a natural consequence, English traders soon established themselves in Spanish American ports, ostensibly to inspect and direct the slave traffic, but really in order to engage in a general commerce. English business houses were thereupon founded which were to outlive the duration of Spanish rule. The English were also allowed to rent lands on which they might have buildings where they could keep their slaves until they should be sold; they were even permitted to cultivate these lands, either with their own slaves or with the native labor of the colonies. In this way they established direct contacts with the Spanish Americans, obtained an exact knowledge of their tastes and needs, and very greatly increased their illicit trade. As for the "permission ship," it developed a remarkable capacity for never getting empty. In fact it was accompanied by a number of other English ships, which would anchor some distance away and renew its cargo as fast as it was discharged. And in spite of Spanish prohibitions, English vessels, and sometimes whole fleets, would enter Spanish American ports "for provisions," but really in order to bring in British goods unlawfully.

Yet the English were not satisfied, repeatedly demanding complete freedom of trade *for English ships*, and it is quite probable, as has been asserted,[1] that the war which broke out between England and Spain in 1739 was due in great measure to the desire of the former to acquire this right for the subjects of Great Britain. As far as this particular issue was concerned, England fought a losing battle. Not only did she fail to gain what she sought, but also she lost

[1] Altamira, IV, 308.

the *asiento*, which was not renewed when the treaties were signed in 1750, two years after the end of the war. Nevertheless, this did not by any means banish the English from participation in Spanish American trade. The right to cut timber in Honduras, obtained in 1763 by treaty, sanctioning a practice which had existed for many years, was availed of for an enormous contraband trade with Mexico. The Island of Trinidad, taken by the English in 1797 and ceded to England in 1802, became a base for smuggling with Venezuela; thereafter, the British purchased three-fifths of what Venezuela had to sell, and paid for it in British manufactured goods. In all parts of Spanish America, indeed, the smuggling went on, especially since the Spanish Americans themselves desired the goods at the prices for which they were offered by the foreigners. The region of the Plata, for example, witnessed smuggling operations of the Portuguese and their British friends at Colonia, and even on the part of peninsula Spaniards and communities of friars.[1]

The Dutch and the French did not leave the field clear to the English, but took advantage of their opportunities, even to the extent of making long voyages to the Pacific, as was also done by the English; the coöperation of the French government with that of Spain was not sufficient to overcome the lure of the Americas for French navigators. According to figures of 1790, less than nine per cent of the legitimate imports of Spanish America came from Spain, excluding goods coming from other countries by way of Spain, and Humboldt estimated that the contraband trade of the colonies amounted to a fourth of the whole. Along with his goods, Englishman, Frenchman, and Dutchman carried his books and his ideas, so much the more undermining Spain's grip on her colonies. In times of war with England, when the seas were not safe for Spanish ships, it was customary to throw open the ports of the colonies to the ships of other nations, and it was noticeable that Spanish American trade often flourished more in wartime than in times of peace. Inevitably, the Spanish Americans began to take sides against Spain over commercial issues. Individualists that they were, they could not fail to see that their

[1] Altamira, IV, 310.

private situation would be better under a system of free trade, and they were not so greatly impressed by the danger of a foreign conquest as were the authorities in Spain. Thus one link the more was forged in the chain which was leading to the revolutions. Spain had done much under the Bourbons for the economic betterment of the colonies, but not enough! In Spanish America it was becoming much more habitual to complain of defects and omissions than to sing paeans of praise for the grant of insufficient favors.

CHAPTER XII

THE BACKGROUND OF THE WARS OF INDEPENDENCE

THE fundamental cause of the Spanish American wars of independence was the oppression of the colonial system and the growing resentment of the creole class against its restrictions socially, intellectually, economically, and politically. Spain is not to be too greatly condemned on this account, because, after all, her ideas with respect to colonial government were substantially those of other countries of those times. It was her misfortune, however, to be more successful in establishing a system which, in the long run, was bound to react against her. The English colonial system, for example, was oppressive in its political and economic aspects, but there was the substantial difference that the English system, for a century and a half, was only very weakly enforced. Thus, the Anglo-Americans had a long period of virtual self-government and control of the main features of their economic life, and there never was any social or intellectual oppression from the mother country worthy of the name. The American Revolution came about through fear of future oppression, because it was not until after 1763 that the British government began seriously to make an effort to enforce the already existing system. In the Spanish colonies, as already pointed out, there was political and economic and also social and intellectual oppression in fact.

On the other hand, the oppression was never so great as it has often been depicted. It was, as a general rule, not harsh or cruel, but was merely the accepted thing, and, in keeping with the individualistic Hispanic spirit, it was to be found side by side with an atmosphere of personal liberty greater than the Anglo-American colonials ever had. It was some two centuries, indeed, before the creoles were awakened to the point of serious protest, and then it took yet another century to drive home the idea with sufficient force to induce them to take up arms. Even then, the revolutions began from other more casual causes, and drifted into movements for independence almost "in spite of themselves." Nevertheless, the oppression was measurably great, and must be taken as the principal underlying cause of the wars against Spain which broke out in 1810.[1]

Allied to the increasing dissatisfaction of the creoles with the Spanish colonial system were a number of other underlying factors which contributed to the movement in the direction of war with Spain. There was, for example, the already discussed dissemination of foreign ideas, English, French, Dutch, and American, against the Spanish system. There was the incitement of events elsewhere which inevitably reminded the Spanish Americans of what they might attempt themselves. In the American Revolution, beginning in 1775, thirteen of the then some thirty North American colonies of England won their independence from the most powerful country in the world. And the French Revolution of 1789 was able to overthrow one of the strongest and seemingly most firmly entrenched monarchies of Europe. If these things could be accomplished, why might not Spanish America obtain redress of grievances from Spain, which was a much weaker country than England or France? Then there was the virtual freedom, at least from economic oppression in the realm of trade, at times when England and Spain were at war. As already mentioned, there were eight such wars in the Bourbon period prior to 1810; on these occasions, with England in control of the seas, the restrictive features of the navigation laws were relaxed, to the great profit and advantage of Spanish America. The last of these wars in this era, 1803 to 1808, deserves special attention, because of its influence upon the outbreaks of 1810.

[1] It does not seem worth while at this point to interrupt the narrative in an attempt to convey what is meant by the term "personal liberty," which is more or less inherent in the "individualistic Hispanic spirit," in contrast to the inhibitions which are part and parcel of the "Puritanism" with which Anglo-Americans are endowed, the boisterous and gay and criminal as well as the pious and good, at least by comparison with the unfettered social freedom of Hispanic peoples. By way of illustration, this writer's experiences in Cuba, not separated from Spain until 1898, may be mentioned. In Cuba there had been oppression, but if the remarks of some of the old settlers there can be believed its precise character has been misunderstood by people in the outside world. As one American, long resident in Cuba before 1898, said to the writer: "Forget all they tell you about the cruelties of Spanish times. Those were the happy days!" This was typical of the statements of the pre-1898 foreigners in Cuba, not one of whom defended the Spanish system, though denying its essential harshness.

In course of the war the British fleet, in 1805, destroyed the combined French and Spanish fleets at the great naval battle of Trafalgar, with the result that Spanish America for a few years enjoyed an almost complete freedom of trade. And this time the creoles resolved that they would never go back to the old restrictive system. So Trafalgar takes its place as one of the important indirect causes of the later Spanish American independence. Ideas, however, must join with action, if such a result as a revolution is to be produced. Mere desire for a changed situation is not enough. The Spanish Americans had to do something about it themselves. They did! And the story of their efforts must inevitably be the principal feature of any account in the immediate background of the wars.

As compared with the eighteenth century, the sixteenth and seventeenth centuries in Spanish America were a period of a somewhat placid acceptance of Spanish colonial methods by a people who had been born to them and had grown up to consider them the norm of their existence.[1] In the eighteenth century, however, there were numerous uprisings against the Spanish authorities, many of them involving merely the personal ambitions of individuals or protests against the acts of certain Spanish officials, without any idea of a separation from Spain, but there were a number which were at least to some extent related to projects for independence. Disregarding the almost chronic warfare with the Indians of the frontier districts, it is in point to discuss some of the other eighteenth-century conflicts, if only because they habituated the minds of the Spanish Americans to the concept of a possible armed opposition to Spain.

One of the earliest of the insurrections worthy of note was that of the so-called *comuneros* (people of the community) of Paraguay, under the leadership of José de Antequera.[2] In course of a quarrel between the *cabildo* of

[1] This is not to say there were no outbreaks against Spanish authority prior to the eighteenth century. Apart from the outstanding instance of Gonzalo Pizarro in Peru, there were several other plots and projects of independence, but they were not sufficiently influential upon public opinion in the colonies to require mention.

[2] The term *comuneros* was employed in reminiscence of a famous uprising in Spain under that name in the early years of Charles I.

Asunción and the governor of Paraguay, Antequera was sent out by the *audiencia* of Chuquisaca [1] (Bolivia) in 1721 as judge-investigator (*juez pesquisidor*) to resolve the situation. Taking sides with the *cabildo*, Antequera was himself elected governor by the executive body of the *comuneros*, and publicly declared that by natural law there should be no distinction in privileges and that people had a right to flee from the excessive cruelties of an unjust government. With this pronouncement he put himself at the head of the *comuneros*, becoming the virtual *caudillo*, or dictator, of Paraguay—an interesting precursor of those *caudillos* who were to play such a prominent part in the history of the later Spanish American republics. Orders were sent to him relieving him of his government, but he refused to obey them, alleging that they were forgeries. When armies marched against him he seemingly placed them in the same category, for he resisted them with armies of his own. For ten years he held out against Spanish authority, defeating the royal troops, persecuting the Jesuits because they upheld the rights of the king, and executing his opponents in Paraguay, and all the time he was the idol of his partisans, the *comuneros*. At length, on orders of the viceroy of Peru, he was overthrown by the governor of the Plata in 1731. Taken into Lima, he was executed in that same year, not however before he had communicated his views and something of his own fiery spirit to a fellow prisoner, Fernando Mompó de Zayas. Mompó escaped from prison, and made his way to Paraguay, where he revived the organization of the *comuneros*, holding "that the authority of the people was superior to that of the king himself." The Spanish governor was forced to withdraw, and the war began afresh. Mompó himself was soon captured, but his followers continued the war until 1735, when they were defeated by an army which the Spaniards raised among the Guaraní Indians of the Jesuit missions. Yet another conspiracy was dis-

[1] Otherwise, Charcas. The early name Charcas was still employed in the term "presidency of Charcas" for the entire country, but when the city of that name came to be called Chuquisaca, it carried with it the title of the *audiencia*. The confusion of many books with respect to this name is still further enhanced by the fact that Chuquisaca became Sucre (after the victor of Ayacucho) in the nineteenth century.

covered in 1741, and wiped out with much spilling of blood.

Over the next half-century there were a number of minor uprisings in Spanish America, no one of which was truly separatist in character.[1] Of somewhat greater importance was the rebellion of Tupac Amarú in Peru, beginning in 1780. This was an Indian movement, growing out of abuses by some of the Spanish *corregidores*, who tyrannized over the natives and inflicted burdens upon them in connection with the *mita* and *repartimiento*. Several times before, notably in 1742 and 1748, the Indians in different parts of Peru had risen against the Spaniards in hopes of expelling them from the country. This time they found a capable leader in a member of their own race, who also held a high position in the established Spanish society. José Gabriel Condorcanquí was the man, a descendant of the Inca emperor Tupac Amarú (decapitated by the Spanish viceroy in 1571). Educated in a Jesuit school of Cuzco, he had also been honored by the Spanish authorities with the title of Marquis of Oropesa. As chief of a number of Indian villages, he endeavored to alleviate the situation of his people, but his complaints went unheeded, and he on his part incurred the hostility of the *corregidores*. Accordingly, he decided that the time had come to resort to arms. Ambuscading a hated *corregidor*, he took him to one of his towns, and executed him before a great concourse of people. This was the signal for an outbreak of the Indians and *mestizos* of the mountain districts of Peru against the Spaniards, under

[1] In 1724 the cities of Salta and Jujuy, Argentina, rose against the governor of the district, and caused him to flee. In 1749 and 1751 there were uprisings in Venezuela against the abuses of the Guipúzcoa Company, in control there. In 1752 La Rioja and Catamarca, Argentina, witnessed an outbreak of the militia against periodical compulsory military service, and in 1754 Tucumán joined with La Rioja and Catamarca in a rebellion against the governor. In 1767 it was Salta and Jujuy which rose against the Spanish governor. In 1765 a baker named Jacinto Canek got himself proclaimed in Yucatán as king of the Mayas, and roused the Indians against the imposition of tributes, the rigor of the tribunals of justice, and the state of abandonment in which it was alleged they had been left by the clergy. This movement was suppressed only at the cost of much bloodshed. The public tumults at the time of the expulsion of the Jesuits in 1767–1768, especially in Mexico, have already been mentioned, and in the same period occurred the uprising of Guanajuato, Mexico, against the financial reforms introduced by the *visitador* Gálvez. These instances of revolt are but a few out of many which could be adduced. Cf. Altamira, IV, 116–117.

the leadership of Condorcanquí, who now took the name of his ancestor, Tupac Amarú, and set himself up as the liberator of the people from the shackles of Spain. Gathering six thousand men, he swept all before him until he was beaten in the vicinity of Cuzco, but returned shortly afterward with an army of no fewer than fifty thousand. Nevertheless, the Spaniards were able, early in 1781, to defeat this enormous but disorganized force and capture Tupac Amarú and his family. Moses describes the fate of the chief prisoners, as follows:

> "They were taken to separate places of confinement, and informed that their next meeting would be on the day of their execution. The *visitador* Areche pronounced the Inca's sentence on May 15, 1781. He wished to show the Indians that even the high rank of the heir of the Incas could not deter the Spaniards from imposing the extreme punishment when they considered it deserved . . . He was condemned to witness the execution of his wife, a son, his uncle, his brother-in-law Antonio Bastides, and his captains; to have his tongue cut out; to be torn in pieces by horses attached to his limbs and driven in different directions; to have his body burnt on the heights of Picchu, and to have his head and arms and legs stuck on poles to be set up in the different towns that had been loyal to him; to have his houses demolished, their sites strewn with salt, his goods confiscated, his relatives declared infamous, and all documents relating to his descent burnt by the hangman. It was also provided that all Inca and cacique dresses should be prohibited, all pictures of the Incas destroyed, the presentation of Quichua dramas forbidden, the musical instruments of the Indians burned; all signs of mourning for the Incas, the use of all national costumes by the Indians, and the use of the Quichua language should be prohibited. This sentence in all its barbarity was carried out on the 18th of May, 1781." [1]

This exasperated the Indians, who found a new leader and continued the revolt. Capturing a Spanish town on one occasion they pitilessly beheaded the inhabitants. Soon afterward, an army of forty thousand of them laid siege to La Paz (Bolivia), which resisted desperately for 109 days, when it was relieved by troops from Tucumán (Argentina) and Cochabamba (Bolivia). Once again La Paz was besieged, however, but after three months the rebels were dispersed. Not until 1782 was the uprising suppressed, only to break

[1] Moses, *South America on the eve of emancipation*, 209–210.

out again briefly in 1783. One definite result of the rebellion was that the Indians in this section embraced the cause of the creoles against the Spaniards when the wars of independence began.

At about the same time as the Tupac Amarú affair, occurred the so-called Revolution of Socorro in New Granada. There a royal *visitador* had endeavored to increase the revenues by reviving some former imposts and raising the amount of the *alcabala* to a ruinous figure. The revolt began in Socorro in 1781, and soon spread to all parts of New Granada. Taking the traditional name of *comuneros*, the rebels, under the leadership of two creoles, one Berbeo and José Antonio Galán, advanced upon Bogotá twenty thousand strong. Greatly alarmed, the authorities capitulated, consenting to the conditions imposed by the *comuneros*, who thereupon dispersed. A few weeks later, the viceroy received reinforcements, and proceeded to violate the terms agreed upon. Galán and three other leaders were captured and executed in 1782. Berbeo escaped. Some historians claim that he took the assumed name of Aguiar, and continued to work for the cause of the *comuneros*. In 1784 three mysterious individuals turned up in London, claiming to represent Aguiar and his fellow conspirators, and endeavored to enlist the support of England. They asserted that they were allies of Tupac Amarú, and were seeking English aid on behalf of the independence of South America, announcing themselves ready to declare for freedom of religion and freedom of trade and, if necessary, to proclaim themselves subjects of Great Britain. Receiving no attention at the English court, they went to France, where two of them fell into the power of the Spanish minister and were sent as prisoners to Spain.

Contemporaneously, there were separatist plots, elsewhere in the Americas, influenced not only by the events in Peru and New Granada, but also by the success of the American Revolution. The creoles were enthusiastic over the victories of Washington and the organization of the northern republic, and it was no doubt due in part to his appreciation of this that Aranda made his proposals for the three separate kingdoms of Spanish America. In 1780, for example, a conspiracy was discovered in Santiago, Chile, which had as its object the independence of the country from Spain. Two Frenchmen, Antoine Gramusset and Antoine Berney, and a Chilean named José Antonio Rojas were the leaders. The "three Antonios" were deported. In Mexico the Indians not infrequently proclaimed a restoration of the empire of Montezuma, just as in Peru there were the rebellions in the name of Tupac Amarú. A little later, in 1799, a certain Portilla and others were caught in a plot to bring about the independence of Mexico. The influence of the American Revolution was followed by that of the political and social ideas of the French Revolution, increasing separatist tendencies in Spanish America. In Venezuela in 1797, for example, Captain Manuel Gual and José María España headed a movement of creoles and *mestizos* which intended to proclaim a republic of Venezuela. The conspiracy was discovered, and eighty-nine persons were implicated, including two Franciscan friars; three Spanish republicans, who had recently escaped from a Spanish prison at La Guaira, Venezuela, were also involved. It developed that the conspirators were imbued with the French ideas, and had been encouraged by the English governor of Trinidad. Several of the prisoners were decapitated, and drawn and quartered.

Another typical instance of creole opposition to Spain was the Nariño affair in New Granada. Antonio Nariño (born 1765) was one of the student group of the University of Santa Fe de Bogotá. As is usually the case in Hispanic countries, the students were intensely interested in current political problems.[1] In Nariño's library, adorned with a portrait of Benjamin Franklin, the young creoles were in the habit of discussing the writings of the French philosophers of the eighteenth century and the current revolution in France. In 1794 a copy of the Declaration of the Rights of Man by the French Assembly came to the hands of

[1] The intensity of student interest in politics in Hispanic America can hardly be comprehended by a person from the United States who has not observed it. Take loyalty to the football team, as one finds it in the United States, and multiply liberally; and the result is still short of the Hispanic American chief enthusiasm. After all, one does not really "die for dear old Rutgers" in the United States, but in Hispanic America many a student has given his life in his advocacy of political causes.

Nariño, who in a burst of patriotic enthusiasm translated it, printed thousands of copies in his own house, and gave them away so freely that his translation reached the most distant points of South America. Nariño's property was confiscated, his family proscribed, and Nariño himself condemned to ten years' imprisonment in Africa. He escaped when on the way to prison, and went to France and England, in each of which countries he tried in vain to get assistance for revolutionizing South America. Returning to New Granada, he was arrested, and sent to Spain, where this time he was securely locked up in a Madrid prison. Later, he got back to New Granada, and became one of the principal leaders in the early campaigns for independence.

Greatest of all the precursors of Spanish American independence, and probably entitled to rank with Bolívar and San Martín as one of the outstanding figures in the movement for separation from Spain, was Francisco de Miranda, sometimes called "The precursor." His father was a prosperous merchant of Caracas, a captain in a body of volunteer militia, and a friend of the captain-general. Born in 1756, Francisco was educated in the schools of his native city, but soon developed an especial fondness for the profession of arms. In 1772 he purchased a captaincy in the Spanish infantry in Spain, and served soon afterward in military campaigns in Morocco. Sent to the West Indies in 1781 with a Spanish force which was to operate against the English, in course of Spain's participation in the war of the American Revolution, Miranda took part in the successful campaigns against the British at Pensacola and in West Florida and the Bahama Islands, and was breveted a colonel. It was at this time that the idea seems definitely to have taken root in his mind of working for the independence of Spanish America. His own service in the Spanish army must have, in a measure, contributed to it, because he had found that as a creole his position involved him in much unpleasantness and many difficulties. While he was in Cuba he won the confidence and friendship of the captain-general, but other officers sent communications to Spain making serious charges against him, such as that he had had treasonable relations with the English and had engaged in smuggling transactions between Jamaica and Cuba. In 1782 a royal commissioner was sent out to enquire into his conduct, and in 1783 this official adjudged him guilty. Afterwards, the Council of the Indies exonerated Miranda, but its decision came too late. Miranda had already taken to flight, making his way to the United States. There he became acquainted with many of the most prominent men of the country, often discussing with them his plans for revolutionizing Spanish America. Among those deeply interested were Henry Knox and Alexander Hamilton. From 1785 to 1789 he spent much of his time in travel, going to England, Holland, Prussia, Austria, Italy, Turkey, Russia, Sweden, and possibly Egypt and Asia Minor. Everywhere, he got to know important people. While in Russia he was a close friend of Catherine the Great. He made the acquaintance of Spanish American creoles, hobnobbed with adventurers, and increased his own fund of knowledge by a study of the military and political methods of the lands he visited.

From 1790 to 1808 Miranda was actively engaged in efforts to interest the governments of England, France, and the United States in his projects for the freedom of Spanish America. Whenever relations were strained between Spain and some other country, Miranda might be expected to appear at the capital of the latter, asking support for his plans. He was wont to claim that the people would rise if he would appear at the head of an army, but that they were not able to cast off the Spanish yoke without assistance. Apparently a most persuasive talker, he also was always prepared to back up his arguments with a plethora of maps and charts, letters and provisional constitutions. Frequently he seemed on the point of getting aid, when something would happen to divert the promised help. Most of the time he spent in England, where he was encouraged by the British authorities, who frequently had him on the pay-roll, regarding him as a valuable threat to hold over the head of Spain, even when they did not act favorably upon his plans.

In 1790 he tried to avail himself of the Nootka Affair to gain the support of England, but when that dispute was peacefully adjusted Miranda went to France. There he made an impression upon some of the Girondist leaders, notably Brissot, who proposed to use him in promoting a revolution in Spanish America, but, early in 1793, when it seemed as if Spain might remain neutral in the war against France, the project was dropped. Meanwhile, Miranda had taken service in the French army, commanding a division and being promoted to the rank of brigadier-general. He distinguished himself by capturing Antwerp, but took part in the inglorious defeat of General Dumouriez at Neerwinden, although he did not join that officer in his treason to the French. Nevertheless, he was arrested, and remained in prison from July 1793 until early in 1795. Later that year he was again arrested, but was soon set free and ordered to leave France. He remained in the country in seclusion, however, until 1798.

In 1798 he was in England, once more endeavoring to get English support for the independence of Spanish America, and at the same time carried on negotiations for the aid of the United States. Prominent persons in each government were in favor of the enterprise, including Alexander Hamilton and the American minister to England, Rufus King, but the governments themselves held back. In 1800 and 1801 he was in France, hoping to interest General Bonaparte in his plans. All he got for his pains was a term in prison, without an opportunity to bring his project to the attention of the soon-to-be Emperor Napoleon. Returning to England, he at length, in 1805, embarked for the United States. He met President Jefferson and Secretary of State Madison, but they would not coöperate with him. So in 1806 he persuaded some two hundred Americans to join him in an attack on the Spanish colonies, though not revealing his real purpose to them until they were on the high seas, on the armed vessel "Leander." First impressions of him on the part of James Biggs, who recorded them in a letter dated February 9, 1806, were as follows:

"From the opportunity I have had to see and hear him, since my coming on board, I should suppose him to possess great talents. He excels all men that ever I have known, in colloquial eloquence and power of persuasion. He discovers a full mind, furnished with comprehensive and accurate information, improved by extensive reading, by travelling and observation. According to his own account he is in the fifty second year of his age. His appearance is that of sixty. Perhaps no man living can boast a more retentive memory. His manners and address are extremely pleasing. In the treatment of us, his volunteers, he is all affability and condescension. This may be his habit, or it may proceed from the interest he has at present in conciliating our esteem and good will. May his courteous demeanour continue when we shall have accepted our commissions, and have come under his power. He is very much disposed to conversation. With a fund of materials to render it instructive and amusing, he makes a judicious selection of topics; accordingly, to the young men, some of whom have just left college, he talks of literature, and recommends the study of the Spanish language and of mathematicks. Proficiency in these branches, he tells them, will ensure promotion in his army. The gentlemen more advanced in years are entertained with his ideas on the subjects of politicks and war. The general often cites a part of the history of his own life and travels, to illustrate the opinions which he seems anxious to inculcate. It is evident enough, that he aims to sow in the minds of his followers, the seeds of heroical deeds; of liberty, and revolution." [1]

At a later time, August 10, 1808, after the failure of the expedition, when Biggs was by no means predisposed in his favor, he wrote the following about him:

"He is about five feet ten inches high. His limbs are well proportioned; his whole frame is stout and active. His complexion is dark, florid and healthy. His eyes are hazel coloured, but not of the darkest hue. They are peircing [*sic*], quick and intelligent, expressing more of the severe than the mild feelings. He has good teeth, which he takes much care to keep clean. His nose is large and handsome, rather of the English than Roman cast. His chest is square and prominent. His hair is grey and he wears it tied long behind with powder. He has strong grey whiskers growing on the outer edges of his ears, as large as most Spaniards have on their cheeks. In the contour of his visage you plainly perceive an expression of pertinaciousness and suspicion. Upon the whole without saying he is an elegant, we may pronounce him a handsome man. He has a constant habit of picking his teeth. When sitting he is never perfectly still; his foot or hand must be moving to keep time with his mind which is always in exercise. He always sleeps a few moments after dinner, and then walks till bed time, which with

[1] Biggs, James, *The history of Don Francisco de Miranda's attempt to effect a revolution in South America* (2 ed. Boston, 1810), 8–10.

him is about midnight. He is an eminent example of temperance. A scanty or bad meal is never regarded by him as a subject of complaint. He uses no ardent spirits; seldom any wine. Sweetened water is his common beverage. Sweetness and warmth, says he, are the two greatest physical goods; and acid and cold are the greatest physical evils in the universe.

"He is a courtier and gentleman in his manners. Dignity and grace preside in his movements. Unless when angry, he has a great command of his feelings; and can assume what looks and tones he pleases. In general his demeanour is marked by hauteur and distance. When he is angry he loses discretion. He is impatient of contradiction. In discourse he is logical in the management of his thoughts. He appears conversant on all subjects. His iron memory prevents his ever being at a loss for names, dates and authorities.

"He used his mental resources and colloquial powers with great address to recommend himself to his followers. He assumed the manners of a father and instructor to the young men. He spoke of the prospect of success, and of the preparations made for him with great confidence. The glory and advantages of the enterprise were described in glowing colours. At another time he detailed his travels, his sufferings and escapes in a manner to interest both their admiration and sympathy. He appeared the master of languages, of science and literature. In his conversations he carried his hearers to the scenes of great actions and introduced them to the distinguished characters of every age. He took excursions to Troy, Babylon, Jerusalem, Rome, Athens and Syracuse. Men famed as statesmen, heroes, patriots, conquerors and tyrants, priests and scholars he produced, and weighed their merits and defects. Modern history and biography afforded him abundant topicks. He impressed an opinion of his comprehensive views, his inexhaustible fund of learning; his probity, his generosity and patriotism. After all, this man of renown, I fear, must be considered as having more learning than wisdom; more theoretical knowledge than practical talent; too sanguine and too opinionated to distinguish between the vigour of enterprise and the hardiness of infatuation." [1]

Miranda was willing to undertake the venture of the year 1806 with his handful of men, because he was convinced that the people would rise against the king of Spain the moment he set foot in the colonies. Gaining a slight reinforcement in the West Indies, he headed for Venezuela, but the Spanish authorities, forewarned of his coming, sent two ships of war which compelled him to take to flight. Getting additional help in the British West Indies, Miranda soon

[1] *Ibid.*, 288–291.

returned to the coast of Venezuela, and effected a landing at Coro. To his surprise, the people did not flock to his standard; rather, they ran away or displayed indifference, when they did not actively oppose him. So Miranda, unable to cope with the troops the Spaniards were sending against him, was obliged to reëmbark. Not one Venezuelan had joined him. Indeed, the creoles were unreservedly on the Spanish side, as they considered this to be an attack on behalf of England. Miranda had not taken into consideration the traditional hostility to foreigners, born of the days of the corsairs. The creoles might be preparing for separation from Spain, but very few of them were willing to risk a possible transfer to the dominion of another European country. Furthermore, they were probably not yet convinced that they themselves could defeat Spain, and, lacking any unusually favorable opportunity, they were unwilling to begin a conflict, the issue of which appeared to be so uncertain.

Did the lesson of Coro eventually come home to Miranda? Possibly, as many Spanish American writers assert, but not immediately. He returned to England, and renewed his efforts to obtain British aid, since England was at war with Spain. At one time he was on the point of succeeding. Sir Arthur Wellesley (the later Duke of Wellington) became deeply interested in his project, and at length a decision was reached for Wellesley to lead an expedition of ten thousand men, supported by a British fleet. Early in 1808 the army actually began to be assembled. At this juncture the news from Spain induced a change in British policy. Napoleon had seized the government of Spain, setting up his brother Joseph as king, and now found a national Spanish uprising against him. The British authorities decided to join with the representatives of the Spanish revolt against Napoleon, and so could not consistently sponsor an attack upon the colonies of a country which had become an ally. Wellesley was deputed to tell Miranda of the change in plans, and remarked many years later that he "never had a more difficult business" than this. As he put it:

> "I thought it best to walk out in the streets with him and tell him there, to prevent his bursting out. But even there he

was so loud and angry, that I told him I would walk on first a little that we might not attract the notice of everybody passing. When I joined him again he was cooler." [1]

Miranda did not again have an opportunity to interest outside governments in the Spanish American cause before the revolts of 1810 began, but he was not idle, as indeed he had not been for the past twenty-seven years, since 1783. He continued to address foreign governments, and *cabildos* and individuals in Spanish America (whenever it might be possible to get a letter through, which was difficult), and he talked with prominent Spanish Americans who came to Europe, as he had been doing for years. Bernardo O'Higgins and Simón Bolívar were perhaps to be the most famous of those he met, but there were many others. When the revolutions eventually took place, they broke out almost simultaneously in all parts of Spanish America. This has led many Spanish American writers to ascribe them to one directing force, of which Miranda was the head. According to them, he was the grand master of the American Lodge, whose principal aim was the overthrow of the Spanish régime. The meticulously accurate and uncompromisingly objective William Spence Robertson, who has examined almost every scrap of material extant about Miranda, says he can find no evidence of Miranda's leadership in this particular, and so rejects it. Substantially, however, it could be true, even if not through the medium of a formal organization; indeed, because of the secrecy of the methods employed there might have been such a society, and yet no papers in existence. With or without an actual grand mastership and plan for the insurrections, Miranda was the real chieftain of the movement at this time, and his influence, however casually exercised, must have been one of the principal factors in the background of the uprisings. When the wars began, Miranda quickly made his way to Venezuela, and took an outstanding part in the early stages of the conflict there.

So much for chronology with regard to the pre-revolutionary career of Miranda. It does not seem appropriate

[1] Stanhope, Philip Henry, *Notes of conversations with the Duke of Wellington. 1831–1851* (New York, 1888), 69.

to leave him, however, without some further discussion of his character and the meaning of his work. He has been called almost everything from the hero of heroes of the wars of independence to a mere vulgar adventurer, who plotted for England rather than Spanish America, and because of the lure of the mercenary's hire which England paid him. Something a little short of the former of these views is probably the most nearly correct, while anything approaching the baser characterization seems utterly unworthy of credence. Not only is there no worth while material to bolster up the latter opinion, but also there is so much in favor of the other that the writer accepts it as the more nearly proper interpretation, and would go much farther than his principal biographer in making him the "revolutionary god-father" of the principal sectional leaders in the outbreaks.[1] It is impossible to overlook his lifetime of effort for Spanish American independence. Nor may one disregard his failure to take advantage of opportunities which might have provided him with greater financial means, with an easy living; at times, he relinquished a British pension which he could have had simply by doing nothing, except to serve as a scarecrow for England in her relations with Spain. And the British were willing to pay him, for he was an unceasing threat of revolutionary propaganda in the colonies, if ever it should suit the purposes of the British government.

What manner of man was this Miranda? First of all, it may be admitted that he had his weaknesses. His relations with women were far from being above reproach, but this was a matter of no particular importance to Spanish Americans, then or since. An omnivorous reader, he collected valuable libraries of works, especially of books about military art and concerning Spanish America.[2] He knew something of English, French, Italian, German, Latin, and Greek, as well as Spanish, and became possibly

[1] The fact that Robertson accepts Miranda as in any respect worthy of being considered a hero is stronger evidence in favor of the Venezuelan precursor than the casual reader might imagine, for if ever there was a "canny Scot" who insisted on proof and had the minimum of an instinct for hero worship, William Spence Robertson is that man.

[2] His private archives contained sixty-three volumes of manuscripts, which are now in process of publication.

the best informed man of his day on many subjects, even if not the most capable exponent in practice of the ideas he had derived from his reading. It was natural that later he should have formed a low opinion of the military abilities of his compatriots in Venezuela, and natural, too, that he should not have been as competent as they to handle the situation there, since his mind ran to organized armies on European battle-fields, rather than to the guerrilla warfare which proved to be adapted to the conditions in Venezuela. Robertson makes a conscientious effort to point out all the defects of his "hero," such as his already mentioned deviations from the moral code, his vanity, his exaggerations and untruths when endeavoring to win support for his favorite project of revolutionizing Spanish America, and his failures to live up to the lofty ideals he himself pronounced, but it is impossible to read the remarkable Robertson biography without feeling an admiration for Miranda which Robertson himself does not express, presumably because it is "not in the documents." The following are excerpts from his great work which doubtless represent a correct picture of the distinguished Venezuelan:

> "To a casual acquaintance Miranda could appear jovial and cordial, yet to statesmen and publicists he ordinarily presented a dignified demeanor. This hauteur veiled an analytical mind which not infrequently detected hidden motives. Throughout life he was an ardent and discriminating student of men . . . Although Miranda's philosophy about the right of revolution was presumably influenced by the writings of Thomas Paine, yet some of his political ideas were in sharp contrast with those of the expatriated Englishman . . . It is not misleading to say that Francisco de Miranda was an aristocratic democrat. One of the most striking features about the mentality of Miranda is the catholicity of his interests. During his youth and early manhood, at least, his appetite for knowledge was insatiable. More than one well-informed person who came into contact with him during his remarkable travels commented upon the accuracy and the universality of his knowledge . . . An outstanding trait of Miranda was his persistence. It is not easy to find in the chronicles of filibusters or revolutionists a perseverance excelling that possessed by this Venezuelan patriot . . . To aid him to maintain a buoyant spirit in the midst of the frequent trials and bitter disappointments of his career Miranda was possessed of a vast fund of energy. His mind, if not his body,

seemed always in motion . . . Like Aaron Burr, Miranda was apt to become disgusted with men and with nations when they laid aside his schemes or postponed their execution . . . where he sanguinely expected to receive aid or coöperation. In view of his ruling passion, it is accordingly only just to Miranda to say that in reality he was not inconsistent. What he aimed to accomplish was the liberation of his native land: as an opportunist who wished above all else to promote this end, he was prepared to seek succor or encouragement from whatever nation held the best prospect of success. In this respect he resembles Christopher Columbus . . .

"Bolívar is the Spanish-American leader with whom Miranda may most aptly be compared. Each of these leaders got his initial impulse from a sojourn in strange lands. In early manhood both men dedicated themselves to the task of Spanish-American liberation. In mature life both became convinced that among world powers England was destined to establish the most significant relations with Spanish America. Unlike Miranda, however, Bolívar made no sustained effort to accomplish the emancipation of South America through the aid and support of foreign nations. Yet when the epoch of Spanish-American independence actually dawned, Bolívar had a great advantage over his aged compatriot, for he had remained in close touch with his fellow-countrymen; besides, his wide family connections gave him added influence and prestige. Though Miranda had dreamed of liberating the widely-scattered sections of South America, of establishing there a new family of states, and of giving them autonomous constitutions, yet the person who did most toward the accomplishment of that ideal was Bolívar . . . Still, among the founders of the Venezuelan Republic the great precursor of independence, Francisco de Miranda, occupies a niche which is not the least distinguished. As a promoter of revolutions, General Miranda holds a place in the history of Spanish America which is unique . . . Indeed the martyred Venezuelan may appropriately be styled the morning star of the Spanish-American revolution." [1]

Two things more had to join with the efforts of Miranda and the other precursors of the independence movement before Spanish America could be prevailed upon to rise against the mother country. It was necessary that the creoles should feel a reasonable confidence in their ability to defeat Spain, and the proper moment to strike had to be found. Over the years 1806–1807 something happened in the Plata region which at least in that important sector

[1] The excerpts brought together here are from the chapter entitled "The man and his rôle in history" in Robertson, *Life of Miranda*, II, 216–255.

of the colonies gave the creoles every right to feel that they could cope with the Spanish soldiery, and knowledge of the event must very greatly have increased the morale of Spanish Americans everywhere. In those years British armies which had been able to engage the troops of Napoleon were twice overwhelmingly defeated by the creoles when the former attempted to conquer Buenos Aires and the Plata country. On both occasions the Spaniards did little or nothing to help in the victory. So the idea was borne in upon the minds of the creoles that if they could win from British regulars in the face of Spanish failure, why certainly they might have a chance for success in a conflict with the Spaniards themselves. A three-century tradition of Spanish invincibility was difficult to overcome, but here was cause for believing there might be a loophole in it somewhere. The story is therefore worth the telling.

In 1805, when Holland was in the power of Napoleon, and Spain was fighting on the French side against England, a British expedition was sent to the Cape of Good Hope to seize the Dutch colonies in South Africa. With this objective attained, it was suggested by Sir Home Popham, commander of the fleet, that part of the forces be detached for the conquest of Buenos Aires and Montevideo, which were reported to be in a nearly defenceless state. Some time before, Popham had become acquainted with Miranda, and had been impressed by his plans, out of which had developed his own independent desire, however, to acquire the Plata region for the British Empire. He had no instructions to make the attempt, but he and his associates decided upon it on their own initiative. So, early in 1806, with six ships and an army of 1650 men under General Beresford, Popham crossed the ocean to Buenos Aires. In the face of their attack the viceroy, Rafael Sobremonte, displayed both incompetence and cowardice. He had sent most of his troops to Montevideo, leaving the capital city very scantily garrisoned, and when the British actually appeared he himself fled precipitately. The few Spanish soldiers were easily driven in, and Buenos Aires fell. Popham took possession of the funds in the royal treasury and sent them to England, where the "treasure of Buenos

Aires" was brought into London in an equipage which was decorated as if for a carnival or other gay affair. This was when the Popham enterprise seemed to be a success. The period of celebration was decidedly brief, however, and when the next mails were received from Buenos Aires, British discussions of the affair took on a new tone.

The commander of the Spanish fleet in the Plata was Santiago [1] de Liniers, a Frenchman who had been in the Spanish service since 1775. Learning that the creoles of Buenos Aires were conspiring against the English, he got into communication with them, and put himself at the head of the movement. He obtained some 1150 soldiers from Governor Huidobro of Montevideo, and attacked Beresford in Buenos Aires, being joined by the populace of the city, who also rose against the English. Beresford was compelled to surrender. Sobremonte now returned, but was received in a manner almost without precedent in the history of Spanish rule in America. A *cabildo abierto* was held which *deposed* him as viceroy and raised Liniers to that rank. This sovereign act of the people of Buenos Aires, who seem now to have become conscious of their power, was later accepted by the government in Spain, which confirmed Liniers in his position.

The British authorities had not authorized the Popham expedition, but a British army had *surrendered* to a more or less disorganized group of Spanish colonials, and this was an insult which had to be wiped out—to say nothing of the desirability of a Plata conquest, which had long attracted attention in British circles! An expedition of some ten thousand men was soon sent out under the command of General Whitelocke, a fortunate choice from the standpoint of Buenos Aires, as events were to prove, as this commander turned out to be incompetent. Early in 1807 the British captured Montevideo, after first defeating the unlucky Sobremonte, who had betaken himself to that post. When news of this reached Buenos Aires, the notables of the city gathered in extraordinary session, and enacted a decree that Sobremonte should be imprisoned and sent back to Spain.

[1] Or originally, in French style, Jacques.

Meanwhile, Liniers and his aides did wonderful work in preparing the scantily trained creoles for the attack, and so effectively that when the British appeared they had converted "every house into a castle and each soldier into a hero." In July 1807, Whitelocke advanced upon the city, and divided his army into fourteen columns to send them into the streets of Buenos Aires. Under the circumstances the British army hardly had a chance. The creoles fought them from street, window, and house-top. After two days of desperate battling, the British had lost three thousand men, and Whitelocke decided to surrender. He agreed to reëmbark his troops and evacuate the entire region of the Plata. So presently, once again defeated, the British army was withdrawn.

Coming such a short time before the outbreak of the wars of independence, it would seem that this incident should be accorded first-rank importance in its effect on the morale of the Spanish Americans in the approaching conflict. Of no inconsiderable importance, too, as affecting the inhabitants of the Plata, was the fact that they had obtained goods at unusually low prices during the brief period of the British occupancy, an experience which Havana had enjoyed in 1762–1763. The lesson was not lost on them. Decidedly the Plata country would not go back to the Spanish colonial system.[1]

Events in Spain now moved rapidly and spectacularly to provide the creole leaders in America with unique opportunities for promoting the revolutions, without even the initial disadvantage of pronouncing against the king of Spain. In 1807 Napoleon occupied Portugal, and followed this up by one of the most remarkable acts of treachery as against his ally, the king of Spain, which history records. French troops poured into Spain, and Charles IV (who had abdicated the throne early in 1808) and his son Ferdinand VII were persuaded to visit the French emperor at Bayonne, just beyond the Spanish border in France.

[1] The best account of the two British attempts to conquer Buenos Aires is Nowell, Charles Edward, *The British invasions of Río de la Plata* (Ms., University of California, Berkeley, 1932). This is a scholarly and well written Ph.D. thesis, some 450 pages long. It is in the Library of the University of California.

There they were taken prisoner, while French armies seized Madrid and other important points in Spain. On May 2, 1808, there was a general uprising in Madrid against the French. It was put down, but this was a prelude to the outbreak of war between the Spanish people and Napoleon, who soon placed his brother, Joseph Bonaparte, on the throne of Spain. Without a king or government of their own, the Spaniards organized themselves as best they could for the seemingly unequal conflict. All Spain rose, but each region acted independently. Juntas, or governing groups, were hastily formed in the various districts of the country, to carry on the war against the French, and Napoleon soon found that he had to cope with a nation in arms. His armies could march about almost at will, but could hold only the territory actually occupied. They had no front or rear, for the people rose everywhere around them, carrying on an incessant guerrilla warfare. Often beaten, the Spaniards were never destroyed, always reappearing to strike a blow where they were least expected. Meanwhile, the different local juntas began to unite, until at length, in September 1808, a supreme authority during the enforced absence of Ferdinand VII was agreed upon in a Central Junta, an unwieldy body of at first twenty-four and later thirty-five members. As Napoleon's armies overran most of the peninsula, the Junta took refuge in Cádiz, where in January 1810 it appointed a regency of five men, to arrange for the calling of a *Cortes*, or national legislative assembly, which was to be representative of Spain and the Americas. In September this body, the famous "*Cortes* of Cádiz," met for the first time, and for the next three years held forth as the *de facto* Spanish government of the country.

Very little was known at the time as to the exact status and powers of the various *Cortes* of earlier centuries, since the *Cortes* had met but once each in the reigns of Charles III and Charles IV, and then for comparatively unimportant reasons. Nothing was more certain, however, than that the *Cortes* of 1810 was like no other which had ever been held in the peninsula. It was a single-chamber body, designed to include elected deputies from the towns with a traditional right of representation, and also from the provincial juntas, other groups of fifty thousand in population, and the Americas. Since the Spanish American deputies could not arrive in time, and since a still greater number of Spanish deputies could not be chosen by the complicated electoral machinery provided, with most of the country in the possession of the French, their places were supplied by persons from those districts happening to be resident in Cádiz at the time. Thus the *Cortes* came to be made up of men who did not represent the conservative temperament of the interior of Spain, but who favored the radical views of Cádiz itself. Most of them dreamed of founding a governmental body which should possess the supposed virtues of the French Revolutionary Assembly and the British House of Commons, as well as those of the earlier *Cortes* of the peninsula. It was quite natural, therefore, that they should combine the ordinary conduct of government in the absence of the king with a thoroughgoing reform of the entire system. The great document of the *Cortes* of Cádiz was the constitution of 1812, which enthroned the people, through their representatives in the *Cortes*, as the ruling power in the state, relegating the heretofore absolute king to a decidedly secondary place. From the first, however, the reforms of the *Cortes* had tended in that direction, while many of its enactments directly concerned the Americas.

For years before the meeting of the *Cortes* of Cádiz the radical Spanish "Liberals" had been denouncing the Spanish colonial system, even pronouncing anathemas against it and writing literary effusions, such as the poems of Quintana, weeping for the sins of Spain in America. They had insisted that Spanish Americans should be given political equality with Spaniards, and the Central Junta went so far as to pass a decree to that effect in 1809. If actually carried out, that would have meant that Spanish America, with some thirteen millions or more in population as compared with about ten and a half millions in Spain, would control the destinies of the empire. On the other hand, the creoles were none too well satisfied with this measure, since it placed the Indians, negroes, *mestizos*, and mulattoes on the same plane with them. Radical reformers have been known quite frequently, however, to lose their idealistic enthusiasm when once they get to power and come face to face with facts. And so with the Spanish Liberals. They soon discovered that, after all, they were still Spaniards, and far from ready to turn over the country to the Spanish Americans. So they allowed Spanish America, not a majority of the deputies to the *Cortes*, but thirty in a total of 107. In like manner, they would not change the monopolistic, restrictive, economic methods of Spain in the colonies, despite their earlier announced objections to them. The ultimate effect was to promote the desire of leading Spanish Americans for a separation from Spain. They considered themselves deceived, and were disposed to complain that Spain was eager to receive funds from them for the war against Napoleon, but was not willing to give them their due representation in political affairs. According to them, they ought to be considered Spaniards, or else they ought to have their independence.

There were several outbreaks as early as 1809. On May 25 the inhabitants of Chuquisaca, the capital of the presidency of Charcas (Bolivia), deposed the Spanish authorities, and established a creole junta. In July, La Paz followed the example of Chuquisaca, declaring for the independence of the country, at the same time that it protested loyalty to Ferdinand VII. Royal troops were sent in from Lima and Buenos Aires, and the revolt was crushed. Pedro Murillo, the leader of the movement, was executed, but before he died is said to have exclaimed: "I die; but no one will be able to extinguish the torch which I have lighted." Later that same year, on August 10, a revolution in Quito overthrew the Spanish ruler in what is now Ecuador, setting up a creole junta instead, but "in the name of Ferdinand VII." Spanish troops from New Granada soon suppressed the new government. Revolutionary plans of 1809 in Bogotá, Caracas, and Valladolid (now Morelos, Mexico) were nipped in the bud. These events foreshadowed the more important happenings of 1810.

Public opinion in Spanish America was not yet ready for independence. So the creole leaders began the conflict on other scores. Despite the setbacks in Bolivia and Ecuador, they continued to claim the same right to set up juntas in Spanish America that the Spaniards had exercised in Spain, when the government was overthrown by Napoleon in 1808. When the *Cortes* attempted to retain the old Spanish régime in the colonies, they loudly proclaimed their loyalty to Ferdinand VII, against whose authority the *Cortes* was in fact carrying on a revolution. The uprisings of 1810 were *in the name of the king* against the *Cortes*, a battle of creoles against Spaniards, without any announced pretensions of independence. Some of the leaders meant that it should result in independence, but popular acceptance for the idea had to be the consequence of a gradual development. In this curious, roundabout manner, Spanish America came at length to the parting of the ways with Spain. The right moment had come. Spain was engaged in a life and death struggle with Napoleon. Yet a legal basis for the conflict in the Americas had been established, of a character which could not but appeal to many Spanish Americans who might otherwise have taken the opposite side. And the struggle was to be fought, not by England or some other country which might demand undue favors—even including vast cessions of territory—but by the creoles themselves, and wholly in their own behalf. The times were ripe. So the creole leaders, cheering vociferously for Ferdinand VII, struck out for independence!

CHAPTER XIII

THE WARS OF INDEPENDENCE: IN SPANISH NORTH AMERICA

FROM the first, Spanish America rejected Joseph Bonaparte and the French. On that score there was unanimity of opinion and action as between Spaniards and creoles. The acceptance of the various governmental agencies set up in the peninsula by the opponents of Napoleon was, however, a more doubtful issue. In the end, Spaniards and loyalists upheld the authority of whatever Spanish government might be in power in Spain, and the anti-Spanish creole element opposed it. In 1808 and 1809 there were a number of riots and tumults against the Spanish colonial officials, and in 1810 the wars broke out almost simultaneously in all parts of Spanish America. In general, the leaders were wealthy creoles who had been educated in Spain or had served in the Spanish armies. They already held positions in the *cabildos*, and appropriated them to their own purposes, using them as the machinery for the revolts. The revolutions thus began as municipal outbreaks, and became regional and national only by extension. One of the first acts of the leaders was to take over the old colonial militia, created to assist Spain as against foreign attack, and employ it for the objects of the revolutions.

One of the outstanding factors to be taken into consideration is that the wars were primarily social. In most parts of Spanish America they were a creole movement against the Spaniards, not a rising of the masses and not truly democratic. The Indians usually held aloof from the struggle, or even favored Spain, feeling that they had a better chance of preservation under the allegedly benevolent Spanish kings, with their humane laws of the Indies, than under the creoles, who were their near neighbors and lacked the glamour which comes from distance. Or perhaps it was mere force of habit or the conservatism of ignorance which kept them loyal to the old régime. Occasionally, they followed patriot leaders, either because they were attached to the leader, not the cause, or because they were forcibly recruited. The case of Mexico presents a certain distinction. There, down to 1821, the revolutionary armies were composed principally of Indians and *mestizos*, not creoles. The leaders in Mexico were separatists, but their followers, at least at the outset of the wars, thought they were fighting for God and Ferdinand VII; they were almost more royalist than the royalists themselves. But this was merely another phase of a social war, of the masses against the white aristocracy, with the creoles mainly on the Spanish side. Among the noteworthy commanders of the loyalists was that same Iturbide who in 1821 was to bring about the independence of Mexico from Spain. It is claimed that as early as 1814 he expressed himself in favor of the independence idea; "but first we must finish with these people," he said, referring to the soldiery of the revolutionary chieftains. When that had been accomplished, then Iturbide inaugurated the creole revolution of 1821, which was quickly successful.

Almost simultaneously, following the outbreaks of 1810, there was a declaration of a new social basis in all parts of Spanish America. The creole leaders were under the necessity of gaining adherents, at the same time that they wished to manifest their disapproval of the Spanish system. The laws for payment of tribute by the Indians were repealed, and the Indians were declared to have the same rights as others. And yet, as already stated, the Indians were not won over; it is said that on occasion they even objected to the release from their former tribute-paying status, to which habit had accustomed them, not knowing what new ill they might be compelled to suffer. Slavery was abolished —but the negroes were more often on the Spanish side in the ensuing wars.[1] As a gesture against Spanish social superiority, titles of nobility were suppressed—but many of the creoles tucked away their own titles for future use,

[1] As an instance of the pressure to obtain negro soldiers, a Buenos Aires law of May 5, 1817, may be cited. Privateers were instructed to bring all negro captives to Argentinian ports, and the government would pay fifty *pesos* for each one of them between the ages of twelve and forty capable of bearing arms. All others were to be "absolutely free." Article 16 of *Reglamento provisional del corso*, in Universidad de Buenos Aires, Centro de estudios de derecho internacional público, *Las presas marítimas en la República Argentina* (Buenos Aires, 1926), 191.

against the time when they could wear them once more in all their social splendor. There were many pronouncements against the church, which had been one of the most noteworthy props of Spanish social superiority over the creole and was in general pro-Spanish. The Inquisition was abolished, the clergy disfranchised, provisions made for the regulation of the various religious orders, and laws enacted calling for the rigorous subordination of church to state. As against the old economic and intellectual restrictions were such pronouncements as those favoring freedom of industry, freedom of commerce, freedom of the press, the repeal of burdensome taxes, the opening of the Spanish American territories to all the world, and invitations to foreigners of whatever race or religion to make their homes in Spanish America. There was perhaps more delay over settling the new forms of government than in any other phase of the revolutions, because the leaders themselves were divided as to whether they should have a monarchy or republic, with innumerable related questions, such as what prince might be invited to be the king, or whether a federal or centralized republic should be established. The one thing of which the creoles were certain was that they themselves were to replace the Spaniards in the different government jobs. To be sure, most of these enactments were not carried out in practice. Institutional nomenclature changed, but, as the story of the early republics shows, conditions remained in great part as they were. The colonial period lived on.

For a number of years after 1810 the principal problem of the creoles was the war against Spain. This divides naturally into two periods of time, before and after 1814. Down to 1814 the insurrections were carried on in the name of Ferdinand VII against the Spanish loyalists and the Spanish official class in Spanish America, with the latter representing the authority of the *Cortes*. In this period the patriots were everywhere defeated, except in the Plata country. In 1814 Ferdinand VII was restored to the Spanish throne. The moment was propitious for the reconciliation of Spanish America, if Spain had granted such liberal political and economic privileges as, for example, England had done in Canada. Ferdinand VII insisted, however, on a revival of the old absolutism and the outworn Spanish colonial system. This made reconciliation impossible. So, after 1814 the wars tended to become wars for independence, openly declared and in the name of the New World governments. Even so, the declarations were often delayed for several years.

As for the wars, they were indeed "wars," not one single great *War of Independence*. The different regions, for the most part, fought each for itself. Thus they might have been defeated in detail, if they had not been brought together to some extent by the plans of a great genius, José de San Martín. An Argentinian, he realized that his own country could never be assured of its independence while the Spaniards remained in strength anywhere in South America, despite the fact that the Argentian revolution against Spain had thus far maintained itself with comparative ease. So he planned to save Argentina by defeating the Spaniards in Chile and Peru. Successful in his campaigns, he was met on the borders of Peru by Simón Bolívar, the great hero of the north, who had defeated the Spaniards in Venezuela, Colombia, and Ecuador. The wars in South America, therefore, represented the converging upon Peru of a semicircle, whose extreme points began in Argentina and Venezuela. This was by far the greatest series of wars in the conflict with Spain. In Spanish North America they were on an independent footing. In Mexico there was a considerable war, but in Central America and the Caribbean islands there was virtually no fighting, although Central America became independent, and Spanish Haiti, or Española, was lost to Spain. It seems best to dispose of the lesser conflicts first, reserving for later discussion the great wars in South America which were to have their climax at Ayacucho in 1824.

The father of the revolution in Mexico was Miguel Hidalgo y Costilla. Born in the village of Pénjamo, in the province of Guanajuato, in 1753, Hidalgo was of old creole stock. He was educated for the priesthood, and at length became the curate in the village of Dolores, also in Guanajuato. Already fifty-seven years old when the outbreak of 1810 took place, he had had a somewhat peculiar career for a priest. In 1800, for example, he had been denounced before the Inquisition.

> "It was alleged that he studied the Holy Scriptures critically; that he spoke disdainfully of the Popes; that he showed little respect for the apostles and for Saint Teresa; that he doubted the virginity of the Mother of Christ; that he declared fornication to be no sin; and that he lived an immoral life, forgetting the obligations of priesthood and indulging in music, dances, and games. Several persons averred that the home of the curate . . . was known as 'little France.'"[1]

Hidalgo escaped serious punishment, but it would appear that the charges had a great deal of basis in fact, both then and in his later career at Dolores. With him at Dolores lived various members of his family, including two illegitimate daughters. His home was a centre for entertainment in the neighborhood, for discussion of the problems of the day, and for the reading of many books, whether of the legally forbidden type or not. It was at Dolores that he took his place as the leading conspirator against Spain in Mexico. Most prominent among his followers were two captains of a provincial regiment of dragoons, Ignacio Allende and Juan Aldama.

At length they set a date for the uprising, and placards were printed bearing the legend: "Americans, be alert, and do not be deceived. Today all the *Gachupines* are to be killed."[2] Before the day for the uprising, however, news was obtained by one of the conspirators that the plot had been discovered. Word was sent to Aldama at San Miguel el Grande on September 15, and he thereupon undertook a veritable Paul Revere ride through the night to Dolores, arriving there shortly after midnight, early on the 16th. A hurried consultation of Hidalgo, Aldama, Allende (who was sojourning there), and others followed, and it was decided to begin the outbreak at once. So, at two o'clock in the morning Hidalgo proceeded to the village jail and set

[1] Robertson, *Rise of the Spanish-American republics*, 77.

[2] Obviously the word "Americans" in this case meant Spanish Americans, more particularly those born in Mexico. The term "*Gachupines*" was a nickname for Spaniards in Mexico and elsewhere in Spanish North America. Among derivations suggested is the Portuguese word "*cachopo*," or child. Another is the Peruvian equivalent of *gachupín:* "*chapetón*," from the *chapeta*, or blush, of youth. In either case the slur as applied to the "tenderfoot" would seem to be indicated, attaining in time to a more vitriolic connotation.

The Idealized Hidalgo. The Spirit of 1810

free the prisoners. Afterward, the church bell was rung to call the villagers, not to mass, but to revolution. Hidalgo addressed them, and there arose from the crowd the *grito*, or cry, of Dolores, as it has since been called, signalizing the beginning of the long conflict with Spain. Around Hidalgo were gathered, as Robertson has expressed it,

> "priests, musicians, laborers, watchmen, and soldiers, who were armed with pistols, swords, lances, clubs, and stones. Some of Hidalgo's followers were on foot, while others were on horseback. With that small, undisciplined, and motley band Hidalgo audaciously dared to initiate a revolt against Spanish rule." [1]

With some six hundred followers, mostly Indians and *mestizos*, Hidalgo marched toward the neighboring town of San Miguel el Grande, proclaiming the revolution in the name of Ferdinand VII. Before he reached San Miguel another standard had been procured; at the chapel of Atotonilco a painting of the Virgin of Guadalupe, the Indian patron saint, was taken, and raised on a lance as a symbol of revolt on behalf of the natives of Mexico. The Virgin of Guadalupe had an extraordinary effect upon the Indian and *mestizo* masses of the country. Henceforth the favorite battle-cry was "Long live the Virgin of Guadalupe, and death to the *Gachupines!*" Men flocked to the banners of Hidalgo by the thousands. People of the upper classes held back, however, creoles as well as Spaniards, while the church fulminated against the revolution and its leaders. Advancing to Guanajuato, Hidalgo took that important city by storm, overwhelming it by force of numbers. The sequel was terrible to behold. The undisciplined hordes of Hidalgo could not be controlled, and the city was given over to pillage, violence, and murder. Barefooted Indians in a drunken frenzy killed their Spanish enemies, and then put on their great hats and uniforms; going about in them they appeared to be in a state of ecstacy, as if this contained an inner meaning of their own succession to the position formerly held by the hated *Gachupines*. And, indeed, the creole fared little better than the Spaniard in the orgy of blood at Guanajuato. It was a class war, of the Indian elements against the white.

[1] Robertson, *Rise of the Spanish-American republics*, 83

With now perhaps as many as a hundred thousand men, Hidalgo marched toward Mexico City. A Spanish force of two thousand engaged the Hidalgo hordes at the pass of Monte de las Cruces, only a few miles from the capital, and was defeated, leaving the road to the city clear. Allende favored an advance, but Hidalgo hesitated, and, instead, retired toward Querétaro. Ever since that time there have been arguments *pro* and *con*, as to whether he made the right decision. Could he have taken the city? Or was his vast army too weak in military quality? Or possibly did Hidalgo shrink from the experience of another Guanajuato, which in this case would have been even more terrible? At Aculco, near Querétaro, another tiny Spanish army, under the capable Félix Calleja, defeated Hidalgo. From this time forward, the cause of Hidalgo grew steadily worse. Many of his followers, having lost the first flare of their enthusiasm, deserted, and the leaders became divided as to the course of action to pursue. Hidalgo presently entered Guadalajara. Near that city, in January 1811, he fought a battle with Calleja at the Bridge of Calderón. With an army of perhaps less than ten thousand men, who were, however, trained soldiers, directed with courage and skill, Calleja utterly defeated Hidalgo, and scattered his men in all directions. The patriot leaders fled to the north, but were captured by Colonel Ignacio Elizondo, a one-time follower of Hidalgo who had secretly passed over to the other side. A trial was held, the result of which was a foregone conclusion. Eighteen officers were declared guilty of treason, and sentenced to be shot in the back. Allende and Aldama were among those who suffered death in this ignominious manner. The trial of Hidalgo himself took a somewhat longer time than that of the others. In the end he was required to put on priestly robes, and then was publicly unfrocked. Some days later, on July 30, 1811, he was executed by a firing squad. The heads of Hidalgo, Allende, Aldama, and Mariano Jiménez, another of the patriot generals, were cut off, and displayed in cages at the four corners of the public granary of Guanajuato. And there they remained for ten years!

The Mexican Revolution was by no means over, however—not even temporarily. Never again were there any vast agglomerations of patriots such as Hidalgo had commanded, but smaller and better trained groups began to wage a guerrilla warfare. The principal leader at the outset, after the fall of Hidalgo, was José María Morelos, also a priest. Born in 1765 at Valladolid (now Morelos), he was in his forty-fifth year when the *grito* of Dolores was raised. He immediately joined Hidalgo, and was commissioned to head the revolutionary movement in the coastal regions south of Mexico City. There he displayed a military ability which Hidalgo lacked, and presently had a great part of that territory under his control. Moreover, where Hidalgo's chief quality, perhaps, was as an inspirer of men, Morelos had other solid traits his one-time chief did not possess, including something of political capacity. Before a patriot congress which met in 1813 at the village of Chilpancingo, Morelos urged the formation of a Mexican government which should be independent of Spain. Accordingly, on November 6, 1813, the first declaration of Mexican independence was made. Morelos became the chief executive, as well as the commander of the forces in the field. Meanwhile, he had been carrying on a sanguinary conflict with the Spaniards, in which both sides neither gave nor asked for quarter. One of the greatest single successes of Morelos was the capture of Acapulco, but he wasted seven months in a siege of the city, and this allowed time for the ever dangerous Calleja to repair his forces. Late in 1815 Morelos was captured. Stripped of his priestly garments, as Hidalgo had been before him, Morelos was executed on December 22, 1815, being shot in the back.

For the next six years, the revolution went on in desultory style. From time to time, different guerrilla leaders stood forth prominently in opposition to Spain, notably Vicente Guerrero, but most of the country was always under Spanish control. One of the most attractive of the patriot generals in this era was Francisco Javier Mina, a Spanish Liberal whose hatred of the absolutism of Ferdinand VII induced him to join hands with the Mexicans against the crown of his native country. With a small force, recruited mainly in the United States, Mina landed at Soto la Marina in northern Mexico early in 1817, expecting the country to rise behind him. He did indeed obtain some followers, but not to the number he had hoped, and after a brilliant campaign he was captured, late that same year, and was shot. Some guerrilla leaders still held out in the southern part of the viceroyalty, but to all intents and purposes peace had been established by 1819. And yet the country was becoming more and more ripe for independence, awaiting only a leader with the right kind of political program in order to declare itself. Such a man was presently to appear in the person of Agustín de Iturbide.

The creoles might disapprove of Hidalgo and Morelos and their lower class following, and might hesitate to join the ranks of the Spanish foreigner Mina, but they were not satisfied with the existing Spanish rule. The Spanish *Cortes* had ordered its constitution of 1812 proclaimed in the colonies. When this was done in Mexico, advantage was taken of the freedom of the press to make revolutionary propaganda, and in such elections as were held the anti-Spanish element prevailed. Thereupon, the viceroy suspended the guarantees of the constitution in Mexico, thus giving a legal argument in favor of the revolutionists and causing dissatisfaction among the creoles. With the return of Ferdinand VII to the throne in 1814, the constitution of 1812 was in any event annulled. Early in 1820 occurred a very important event. A large army was gathered at Cádiz, with orders to proceed to Spanish America. Instead, under the leadership of Colonel Rafael Riego, it rose against the absolutism of Ferdinand VII, compelling him to accept a more liberal form of government, including the constitution of 1812. This produced something in the nature of a shock in Mexico. The ultra-conservative elements were disturbed by the effect that the radical, anti-clerical Spanish constitution might have upon the church in Mexico; even the royalists began to wonder whether they might not fare better under an independent Mexican rule. For their part, the creoles turned naturally to a discussion of the best type of government for Mexico. It was at this moment that Iturbide stepped into the spotlight on the stage of Mexican affairs.

Agustín de Iturbide

Iturbide was of part Indian blood, but passed for white; his father was a Spaniard. The family as a whole was devoutly Catholic and conservative. Born in 1783, Iturbide himself appears not to have taken kindly to education, except for his interest in military affairs. He was only twenty-seven years of age at the time of the *grito* of Dolores, being then a lieutenant in a regiment of colonial militia in Valladolid, his native city. Disapproving of the character of the movement, he rejected an offer of high military rank under Hidalgo. Instead, he took up arms on the Spanish side, and was rapidly promoted, distinguishing himself in the campaigns against Morelos. In 1816, however, he got into difficulties with his superiors over his administration of a military district under his command, and, though not convicted of the charges against him, was not employed in the field any more until the end of 1820, the year of the just mentioned revolution in Spain. The tumult of opinion existing in Mexico at the time has been well described by Iturbide himself, as follows:

"The new order of things, the ferment in which the Peninsula was placed, the machinations of the discontented, the want of moderation amongst the supporters of the new system, the vacillation of the authorities, and the conduct of the government and Cortes at Madrid, (who, from the decrees which they issued, and the speeches which some of the deputies pronounced, appeared to have determined on alienating the colonies,) filled the heart of every good patriot with the desire of independence, and excited amongst the Spaniards established in the country, the apprehension that all the horrors of the former insurrection were about to be repeated . . . Among the Europeans, and their adherents, some wished for the establishment of the Spanish constitution . . . Others there were who sighed after the old absolute government . . . The privileged and powerful classes fomented these different parties, attaching themselves to the one or the other . . . The Americans wished for independence, but they were not agreed as to the mode of effecting it, still less as to the form of government which they should prefer. With respect to the former object, many were of opinion that in the first place, all the Europeans should be exterminated, and their property given up to confiscation. The less sanguinary would have been contented with banishing them from the country, thus reducing thousands of families to a state of orphanage. The moderate party suggested only that they should be excluded from all public offices, and degraded to the condition in which they had kept the natives of the country for three centuries. As to the form of government, one party proposed a monarchy, tempered by the Spanish, or some other constitution; a second party wished for a federative republic; a third for a central republic; and the partisans of each system, full of enthusiasm, were impatient for the accomplishment of their different objects." [1]

Meanwhile, a guerrilla warfare was still going in the southern provinces of the viceroyalty, and, with no Calleja any longer available, the royalist forces were not meeting with success. In this situation the viceroy was prevailed upon to ask Iturbide to take command. The offer was accepted, and in November 1820 Iturbide marched south. He had very different objects in mind, however, from those of the viceroy. Instead of giving battle to the insurgent leader, Vicente Guerrero, Iturbide entered into negotiations with him, and reached an agreement providing for the independence of Mexico, in accord with a plan prepared by Iturbide. This, the so-called Plan of Iguala, named for the village where it was announced, on February 24, 1821, had as its main features what came to be known as the three guarantees: religion, independence, and union. The Roman Catholic religion was to be protected, and was to be the only faith tolerated in the country. Independence from Spain was declared, but Ferdinand VII was to be offered the crown, under a constitutional form of government; if he should not accept, some other European prince was to be selected. And the union of Spaniards and Mexicans, with equal rights, was proclaimed. A more skillful plea for the support of all groups in Mexico could hardly have been devised. Clergy and one-time royalists, as well as revolutionaries, were attracted to the standards of Iturbide, and he soon had an army with which the viceroy could not cope. A new viceroy, General Juan O'Donojú, last of the Spanish viceroys of Mexico, accepted the existing situation, and on August 24, 1821, signed the treaty of Córdoba with Iturbide, recognizing the Plan of Iguala. The Spanish *Cortes* repudiated the agreements

[1] Iturbide, Agustín de, *A statement of some of the principal events in the public life of Agustín de Iturbide* (London, 1824), 12–14.

entered into by O'Donojú, but was unable to support its objections with military force. There was, indeed, one significant change in the Plan, in that the people, through a national legislative body, were to be free to choose an emperor for themselves, even though he might not be a European prince—a step in the direction of the later enthronement of Iturbide. Thereupon, on September 27, the army of Iturbide entered Mexico City, and the war against Spain was virtually at an end. Early in 1822 the successful general of the revolution promoted a *coup d'état*, and became Mexican emperor under the name of Agustín I.

For a brief moment, the Mexican Empire reached far to the south to include Central America. In that region there had always been a close connection with the viceroyalty in Mexico, but it was recognized as a separate jurisdiction under the *audiencia* and the captain-generals of Guatemala, whose authority embraced what are now the five countries of Guatemala, Salvador, Honduras, Nicaragua, and Costa Rica. On the basis of propinquity and early association, Panama might well have decided to cast in her lot with Central America, despite the more recent connection with distant Bogotá, but circumstances ruled otherwise. The Spaniards at times employed the Isthmus as a base of operations against the patriots in Colombia, and the creoles in Panama quite naturally had their attention drawn to the issue of the conflict in that sector. Indeed, on several occasions they became involved directly in the fighting, as there were several brief campaigns in the Isthmus. At length, on November 28, 1821, a Panamanian *cabildo abierto* declared the independence of the country from Spain and its annexation to Colombia.

In what is now called Central America, there was no warfare against Spain worthy of the name. There was the same discontent as in the other colonies, and the same issue as between creoles and Spaniards, but the latter appeared to be too strongly entrenched for these sparsely settled communities to engage them in battle. There were, indeed, numerous plots and conspiracies, but none of them attained to any considerable dimensions. Perhaps the earliest in point of time was a movement in San Salvador, in November 1811, headed by Father José Matías Delgado, by some regarded as "the Bolívar" of Central America, but his activities were promptly suppressed. Most of the churchmen, however, were pro-Spanish, and their influence over the masses was sufficient to enable the authorities to maintain their control. Following the Spanish revolution of 1820, the people of Central America were called upon to elect provincial deputations, and in Guatemala the Spanish party prevailed. It thereupon deposed the weak, superannuated captain-general then in power, and replaced him with Gabino Gainza, a younger and more capable official.

The news from Mexico was more and more disconcerting to the royalists, however, especially after the treaty of Córdoba, recognizing the independence of Mexico. Chiapas, up until that time a part of Guatemala, announced its separation from Spain, and joined Mexico. Then on September 15, 1821, a popular assembly of the City of Guatemala declared the independence of all Central America, with the Spanish officials and the churchmen acquiescing in the decision. There was considerable doubt in Central America, however, as to the type of government which should be installed, and even as to the country to which they should belong. In the other districts of Central America, there was much jealousy of Guatemala, and much jealousy of the provincial capital in each region by itself. Thus early were the disjunctive tendencies of the Central American peoples manifesting themselves. As matters were, some communities favored joining Guatemala, others preferred a union with Mexico, while still others desired local autonomy. As the revolution, such as it was, had been carried on wholly by creole idealists—most of them radical republicans without practical experience in government—there was no spirit of compromise.

On the whole, the more conservative elements wished to join Mexico, distrusting the ability of their compatriots to make a satisfactory government by themselves. Iturbide, who was eager to annex Central America, wrote to Gainza late in 1821, expressing his opinion that the country "could not remain independent of Mexico." His letter was sent to the local governments of the different towns of Central

America, with a request that they manifest their opinion about it. Early in 1822, a majority of votes were received for annexation, and thereupon the creole "Consultive Committee" of Guatemala, which had been acting on behalf of the revolution, declared all Central America, except Panama, henceforth a part of Mexico.

It now became necessary to engage in the warfare which Central America had thus far avoided, since Costa Rica, most of Salvador,[1] and a number of towns in Honduras and Nicaragua refused to approve of the decision for the union with Mexico. Iturbide sent in General Vicente Filísola with an army to put down the opposition, and this he was able to accomplish, after defeating the patriot forces in Salvador. A little later, early in 1823, came the news that Iturbide had been deposed as emperor of Mexico. So Filísola, in order to avoid a civil war, called a congress of all the Central American provinces to meet in Guatemala. This time the delegates were, in the overwhelming majority, opposed to a continuance of the union with Mexico. On the first of July the independence of Central America "from Spain, Mexico, or any other power" was formally declared, and a republic of Central America was established. From 1823 to 1839 the republic maintained a precarious existence, breaking up at length into the five little countries which, with Panama, now dot the Isthmian belt.

To the north and east of what is now Mexico, on the North American mainland, the revolutions were involved with the factor of the nearness and the direct interest of the United States, complicated by United States fear lest England acquire some of those territories. When revolutionary activity broke out at Baton Rouge (Louisiana), in what was then West Florida, the United States seized the territory, to maintain order and to keep England from getting it. Meanwhile, also in order to forestall British action, pressure was brought to bear on Spain to sell East Florida, and by the treaty of 1819 (ratified by Spain in 1821) the Floridas were formally brought under the flag of the

[1] In December 1822 a congress of delegates in Salvador voted for annexation to the United States, hoping thus to avoid incorporation into Iturbide's empire. This interesting proposal met with no response from Washington.

United States. In Texas the armies of the revolution were made up mostly of Americans. In 1836 Texas won her independence from Mexico, and in 1845 joined the United States. During most of the wars of independence era, California continued to lead a somewhat idyllic life, tempered at times with hardships, because of the difficulty of getting needed supplies from Mexico, but never wavering in loyalty to Spain, and never doubting that Spain would win, hardly believing scattered items of news to the contrary or even that any serious warfare was going on. In 1818 California was rudely awakened when two Buenos Aires ships captured Monterey, but "the enemy" was "gloriously defeated," or at least left the country, and the province was not again disturbed.[1] In 1822 California joined Mexico, but in 1848, at the end of the Mexican War, was annexed to the United States. What are now New Mexico and Arizona were also added to the United States at the same time.

The case of Cuba was one of peculiar importance in the wars of independence era. As has already been set forth, Cuba is the key of the Caribbean and in a sense of the Western Hemisphere. This was clearly recognized in Washington. In 1809, for example, Thomas Jefferson, then president of the United States, said "We must have the Floridas and Cuba." The Floridas were soon acquired, but Cuba was a prime concern of the United States for many years, and in some respects still is. Cuba in the hands of Spain was not dangerous, because Spain was not dangerous, but the Washington government was unwilling for it to become a possession of some other power. England was particularly feared, and France in only less degree. For the same reason, the United States was opposed to the idea of an independent Cuba or a Cuban annexation to Colombia or Mexico, because in any of those cases the country might in fact be taken over by England or France. Indeed, the United States for a long time opposed annexation even to the United States,

[1] The "Argentina" and the "Santa Rosa" were the naval vessels involved in the California invasion, which was commanded by Hippolyte Bouchard, a Frenchman. Both boats carried a motley crew of all nations, but most of the officers were Americans. In the attack on Monterey, the second officer of the "Santa Rosa" was taken prisoner, and chose to remain in the province thereafter. This was the locally celebrated Joseph Chapman, often called the first American resident of California, though really the third.

lest England or France, with their superior navies, might conquer the island in time of war. The Washington government, therefore, despite its sympathy for the patriot cause elsewhere in the Americas, got squarely behind the retention of Cuba by Spain.

In Cuba, meanwhile, the issue of a possible separation from Spain presented itself, from the moment of the outbreak of the wars of independence on the mainland, but the majority of the Cubans were not yet ready to sever the ties with the mother country. A number of reasons account for this. Ever since the English occupation of 1762–1763 Cuba had been treated, on the whole, quite liberally by Spain, as gauged by the ideas of the period. So the Cubans did not have a serious grievance. And yet they probably would have joined their Spanish American brethren if it were not that Cuba is an island. A rebellion in Cuba had less chance of success than on the mainland. As the strategic key to Spain's possessions in the New World, too, Cuba was more strongly held than the other colonies, and the Spanish navy could prevent the island from receiving any substantial help. Other drawbacks developed, as the wars continued. Some of the ideas of the revolutionists did not appeal to great numbers of the Cuban people. In particular, they hesitated to accept the pronouncements for the freedom of the slaves. This was due only in part to economic considerations, but was based even more on the peculiar racial situation in the island. There were too many negroes in Cuba—indeed, over half the population, including the mulattoes—for the people to be willing to risk emancipation. The Cubans had almost before their eyes the gruesome scenes which had attended the winning of independence in the black republic of Haiti to the east. There the whites had been killed off or forced to flee, and many of the exiles had taken up their residence in Cuba. Cuba did not wish to become another Haiti.

Throughout the war period, however, there were many Cubans who sympathized with the revolutionists, and hoped to bring about a separation from Spain. Most of them were not in favor of independence, but wished to cast in their lot with Colombia, Mexico, or the United States. A number of secret societies were formed which advocated a revolt, the most famous of which was that of the Suns and Rays (*Soles y Rayos*) of Bolívar. After 1814 there were growing causes of grievance, too, as Ferdinand VII restored some of the worst features of the old colonial system. At length a revolt was planned, to break out on August 16, 1823. The Spanish authorities had kept well informed through their spies in the different organizations, and, when the day came, most of the leaders were arrested, while others saved themselves only by fleeing from the island. So the effort failed, but never again was the opposition to Spain to die away. Eventually, came the Cuban war of 1895 to 1898 against Spain, with the United States taking sides with Cuba in 1898. In consequence, Cuba was separated from Spain in 1898, and with the withdrawal of United States control in 1902 attained to her independence. The course of affairs in Puerto Rico had very closely paralleled that of Cuba, but in 1898 that island was taken away from Spain and annexed to the United States.

In the island of Haiti, the one-time Española,[1] a complicated series of events had been taking place. The French had possessed the western third of the island since 1697, and had developed a rich society of sugar planters, a bare minority in a country where the bulk of the population was made up of negro slaves. By all accounts, the former lived in a state of Sybaritic luxury, while the latter were cruelly oppressed. Into this atmosphere came the Declaration of the Rights of Man of the French Revolution of 1789, the effect of which was to abolish slavery in Haiti. The whites refused to accept the French decrees, and when the negroes rose against them in 1791 the revolutionary government in France supported the pro-republican black element. In course of the ensuing wars, some of the representatives of the planters invited the English government to annex the country, and British officialdom, nothing loth, took advantage of the request. For five years, 1793 to 1798, British troops and the native-born whites of Haiti fought the negro masses, and in the end, strange to relate, the latter

[1] For complications concerning the name of this island, cf. *supra*, 13, n. 1. The French ordinarily employed the term "Saint Domingue."

won. The black victory was due primarily to the emergence of a really great man among the Haitians, in the since justly celebrated Pierre Dominique Toussaint L'Ouverture.

Meanwhile, the Haitians had taken over the mandate of the French Republic, which had acquired the eastern part of the island from Spain in 1795, and had brought that territory under their control. In 1801 Toussaint L'Ouverture presented a plan for a constitution to a Haitian assembly, providing that Haiti was to be an autonomous province of the French Republic, with a governor who was to hold office for life and have the right to choose his successor. The constitution was duly promulgated, and Toussaint L'Ouverture became the governor. It was in that same year that Napoleon Bonaparte rose to be first consul of France, and he proceeded to reverse the policy of the republic in Haiti. An army was sent to the island which overthrew the Haitian government and restored slavery. Toussaint L'Ouverture was taken to France, made to suffer cruelly in prison, and died there in 1803 of hunger, cold, and a broken heart. The negroes of Haiti, however, were able to defeat the French, finding a most powerful ally in an epidemic of yellow fever, which nearly wiped out the opposing forces. In 1804 the independence of Haiti was declared, and to the accompaniment, indeed, of many viscissitudes was maintained from that time forth.

Spanish Haiti, as might be expected, was restive under black control, and in 1808 began a conflict which ended in the expulsion of the invaders from the west. Restored to Spain in 1814, this section of the island did not take any noteworthy part in the wars of independence until 1821, when a patriotic uprising brought a separation from the mother country. The name "Spanish Haiti" was adopted, and the country was declared to be a part of Colombia. Neither Colombia nor Spain took any effective action for or against this declaration, but the black republic to the west was not equally somnolent. Under their capable ruler Jean Pierre Boyer, the Haitians overran the new state, and early in 1822, after a brief life of nine weeks, it ceased to exist. In 1844 the people of this part of the island fought their real war of independence—against the black Haitians. They were successful, and in that same year began independent life under the name of the Dominican Republic. In difficulties from internal political anarchy and ever threatened by the more populous black Haiti to the west, this region permitted itself to be reannexed to Spain in 1861, but separated from her in 1865, and has maintained a somewhat precarious independent existence ever since.

In the end, therefore, Spain yielded all she had possessed in North America. And yet, amidst the welter of the Indian countries of the mainland and the black-blooded islands of the Caribbean, there remained much that was Spanish, and there it still is today.

José de San Martín

CHAPTER XIV

THE WARS OF INDEPENDENCE: SAN MARTÍN

THE great military genius of the wars was an Argentinian, José de San Martín. If anybody approached him in ability as a soldier it was, not Bolívar, but the latter's subordinate, Sucre. Sucre was to deliver the *coup de grâce* at Ayacucho in 1824, but the most important rôle in paving the way for final victory in the conflict with Spain was filled by San Martín. To assure the safety of his own country, he planned and achieved the independence of Peru. *En route* thereto, he overwhelmed the Spaniards in Chile. Directly or indirectly, five countries are indebted for their independence to San Martín: Argentina, Chile, Peru, Paraguay, and Uruguay. San Martín did not, indeed, intervene actively in the campaigns in Paraguay and Uruguay, but those countries in great measure owed their freedom from Spanish invasion to the diversion created by San Martín's operations, striking at the heart of the Spanish power in South America. Not impossibly, all the Spanish American mainland owes him gratitude on this account, too. When San Martín's work was done, Bolívar and Sucre came down from victorious campaigns in the north to put over the finishing touches in Peru and Bolivia. Even under the best of circumstances the achievements of San Martín would have been remarkable, but he had to undertake them under the handicap of the feeblest kind of support. It cost him more effort to get men, money, and ships from the patriot governments than it did to defeat the Spaniards. Indeed, a detailed story of the period shows that the fighting against the Spaniards was at times almost secondary to the issues of domestic strife, which occasionally reached the point of actual civil war. These are factors, however, which belong more properly in a history of the republican era. They have to be borne in mind in dealing with the wars of independence, but need not be fully discussed.

In 1808, the year of Napoleon's invasion of Spain, Santiago de Liniers was viceroy in Buenos Aires, and Francisco Javier Elío was the military commander at Montevideo. The latter persuaded the Spanish Central Junta to recognize his government as independent of that of Liniers, and in the following year, 1809, the popular Liniers was deposed in favor of Baltasar de Cisneros. The latter's situation was none too strong, especially since the troops available were made up wholly of the creole militia, under leaders who were already planning revolution. Early in May 1810, news came that the French had overrun most of Andalusia, the last of the Spanish provinces outstanding against them, and it seemed that Spain as an independent country was about to disappear. Meanwhile, groups of patriots, led by Manuel Belgrano, Cornelio Saavedra, Mariano Moreno, and Juan José Castelli, had been holding meetings to determine when the region of the viceroyalty should strike for the right of governing itself. Now the moment had come. The viceroy was informed that his power was no longer recognized, since the source of his authority in Spain had disappeared; he was virtually forced to call a *cabildo abierto*, to consider what steps should be taken under the circumstances.

The *cabildo abierto*, with some 250 present, voted the deposition of the viceroy, and placed the power temporarily in the hands of the regular *cabildo*, which was instructed to appoint a committee, or junta, to carry on the government. May 25 dawned rainy and cold, but all Buenos Aires was afire with patriotic enthusiasm that day. The *cabildo* was meeting in an attempt to select a junta, but its deliberations were interrupted by popular demonstrations. At length two young men, Domingo French and Antonio Luis Berutti, burst into the meeting, and demanded in the name of the people that the nine persons in a list which they were presenting should constitute the junta. Eight of the nine were creoles, including the four leaders mentioned above. The *cabildo* yielded, and the new government was sworn in, promising to preserve this part of the Americas "for our august sovereign Ferdinand VII." Thus, in a bloodless revolution, was the first great step taken in the creation of an independent country. Ferdinand VII had been indeed proclaimed, but the leaders were of one mind that never again would Spain dominate Argentina. They knew that they would have to fight the Spanish loyalists to maintain their position, and possibly the name of Ferdinand might have been dropped, if it had not been for the intimations received from the British minister to Brazil, Lord Strangford; he told them that the assistance of England (which Buenos Aires was actually, though surreptitiously, to receive over the next few years) could not be given to the revolutionary government if a "premature declaration of independence" should be made. As an ally of Spain against Napoleon, England could not take sides with an openly anti-Spanish movement in the Americas.

The fighting began almost immediately. Montevideo, Córdoba, Asunción, and the authorities in Upper Peru, or Bolivia, refused to acknowledge the junta, maintaining allegiance to the regency which had been created in Spain. Even in those provinces under patriot control, there were, of course, a number of loyalists. So the junta not only raised armies, but for a time also, under the influence of the fiery Moreno, proclaimed a reign of terror. The Cordoban royalists were soon defeated. One of their leaders was none other than Santiago de Liniers, but his record in the past was not sufficient to save him. Along with several others he was pitilessly executed. Continuing northward, the patriot army won a victory at Suipacha, and penetrated to the extreme limits of the viceroyalty in Upper Peru. The loyalists turned the tables on them at Huaqui, however, and the invaders from the Plata were driven back to Argentina. This campaign was typical of what went on in this sector throughout the wars. Patriot armies could advance into Bolivia, but could not hold their ground there. Then the loyalists would rush down into Argentina, and threaten to overwhelm the patriots, but in the nick of time there was always somebody to defeat them. Thus, Suipacha (1810) and Huaqui (1811) were followed by Belgrano's great victories of Tucumán (1812) and Salta (1813). Then came defeats in Upper Peru at Vilcapugio (1813) and Ayohuma (1813), and later at Sipe-Sipe (1815). In

1812 the government at Buenos Aires actually ordered Belgrano to retire to Córdoba, but fortunately he risked a battle instead. In 1814 San Martín checked the enemy after the defeats of the year before. In 1815, only the able campaigning of Martín Güemes, famous guerrilla chieftain of Salta, saved the river country from an invasion. After 1815, however, there were no major activities in this sector.

Meanwhile, there had been frequent changes of government at Buenos Aires. In 1811 the moderate counsels of Saavedra prevailed over the radical and extremist ideas of Moreno, whereupon the latter withdrew from the junta. Taking ship for England, he died *en route*. Thus passed the man whom some rate as the father of Argentinian independence. Presently, another issue appeared, which was to be the principal factor in the political life of the country for the next half-century. The ruling bodies in Buenos Aires generally favored centralization in a strong national government, or Unitarism, as it came to be called.[1] To the other provinces beyond Buenos Aires, this seemed to give too great a predominance to the region of the capital city, since the province of Buenos Aires alone had more in population and wealth than the rest of the country combined. The other provinces, therefore, favored the ideal of "Federalism," or a comparatively weak national government, under which each province would have rather thoroughgoing control of its own affairs, being bound to the nation as a whole by a somewhat loose tie. In addition to the issue between Federalism and Unitarism, there were always a number of others, such as the already mentioned struggle between the moderates and radicals, and for several years the battle between those who favored a monarchy, perhaps even with a Spanish prince, and those who wanted a republic. It was not until July 9, 1816, that independence from Spain was declared. And the later years of the "war of independence" in Argentina were much more nearly a

[1] The word in Spanish was "*unitarismo.*" Some have rendered this "Unitarianism" in English, and have called its proponents "Unitarians." These terms, obviously, are unsatisfactory. The writer has therefore preferred to coin the words "Unitarism" and "Unitarists," which cannot be confused with something else, and which have the virtue of retaining the root sound of the original.

series of domestic tumults than they were a conflict against Spain. This strife had far-reaching effects, preventing whatever possibility there might have been for the formation of one great country out of the jurisdiction of the former viceroyalty of the Plata, now represented by four republics. Whatever might have happened with respect to Bolivia, it would seem that the separate development of Paraguay and Uruguay had their origins in the objections of their leaders to the predominance of Buenos Aires.

Early in 1811 Belgrano marched into Paraguay with a small patriot army, but was soon defeated and captured by the superior forces of the Spanish governor; the latter had the backing of nearly the entire population, which looked on the invasion merely from the standpoint of the normal hatred it felt for Buenos Aires. The expedition was not without effect, however, as the seeds of revolution were sown among the Paraguayan leaders in their associations with the Argentinian prisoners of Belgrano's force; almost immediately they bore fruit in an outbreak against the existing government. The governor was overthrown, and was replaced by a patriot junta of three men, of whom the most important proved to be a certain Doctor José Gaspar Rodríguez Francia. This was in 1811. A note was at once despatched to Buenos Aires, saying that Paraguay would not enter into the government being formed there, unless in a confederation. Unable to enforce any stronger measure of control at the time, the junta at Buenos Aires recognized the government of Paraguay according to those terms. The Spaniards could not take any steps to overcome the Paraguayan revolution, as an attack by way of Bolivia was impracticable, and the patriot forces of the Plata were a barrier in the south. Thus there was an early end to the "war" in Paraguay; independence was declared in 1813. In 1814 Francia seized sole power, and in 1816 was formally declared to be supreme and perpetual dictator. Presently, he shut the country up from the world even more thoroughly than the Jesuits had done in colonial times. Until his death in 1840 he ruled as the *caudillo* of Paraguay. The story, however, belongs to the era of the republics.

The case of Uruguay was much more complicated, being involved with the whole stream of events in the affairs of the Plata country—with Argentina and Brazil, as well as the Banda Oriental (Eastern Shore—of the Uruguay), as Uruguay was then called. For nearly a year after the initial revolt in Buenos Aires, Uruguay remained quiet and, on the surface, loyal. But early in 1811, when Elío (now viceroy), who commanded at Montevideo, prepared to take the offensive against the patriots across the river, the entire Banda Oriental flamed into revolt under the leadership of José Gervasio Artigas. This vigorous personality, now generally regarded as the "Father" of Uruguay, was also one of the outstanding figures of the Plata region in those times. He has been characterized as follows:

> "Leading the people of his native province through the hectic decade from 1810 to 1820, he earned himself a permanent place in the history of the Plata basin. He it was who carried the torch of federalism through those early years, and, firm in his republican convictions, he steadily fought for absolute independence from the Spanish king and against the substitution of any other monarch in his place in America. Combatted by the Spaniards, by the unitarists of his own Plata region, and by the Portuguese, deserted at length by his own supporters, he finally went down before the onslaughts of his enemies. Nevertheless, his has been a lasting influence, and well has he earned his title of 'father of Uruguayan nationality.'" [1]

Allied with Buenos Aires troops, Artigas carried the war to the very walls of Montevideo, and from May to October the patriots besieged the great fortified city. Indeed, Elío managed to save it only by the very dangerous expedient of inviting Portuguese aid from Brazil. The Portuguese prince regent, John, later King John VI, and his wife Carlota Joaquina, elder sister of Ferdinand VII of Spain, made haste to comply with Elío's request. Carlota and John hated each other cordially, but in the matter of Uruguay they were in agreement. John wished to revive the traditional Portuguese claims in the Plata, but Carlota was concerned on her own account. She had for some time

[1] Bealer, Lewis Winkler, *Artigas and the beginnings of Uruguay, 1810–1820* (Ms., M.A. thesis, University of California, Berkeley, 1930), I–II. Bealer's thesis, probably the only extensive account of Artigas in English, is an exceptionally meritorious work.

hoped that she might receive a call to be queen of the Plata country, and had been actively conspiring to that end. When the Napoleonic armies were overrunning Spain, John invited the Buenos Aires and Montevideo governments to come under his protection, but they chose to remain "loyal to Ferdinand VII." The Elío request was joyfully received, and in July 1811, Portuguese troops began to pour into Uruguay. They dominated a large portion of the country. Elío himself, becoming alarmed lest the remedy prove more serious than the ailment, sought an understanding with the Buenos Aires government, which was on its part disturbed over reverses in Bolivia. The outcome was the treaty of October 20, 1811, by which the Buenos Aires government agreed to raise the siege and withdraw all its troops from the Banda, those of Artigas included, while the Portuguese agreed to do likewise. Nevertheless, the Portuguese stayed on until 1812, when, as a result of the influence of Lord Strangford, they were prevailed upon to leave. Until that time, the people of the Banda were left at the mercy of the Spaniards and the Portuguese, a condition which Artigas was unwilling to tolerate. He, therefore, began his evacuation in such a way as to traverse the entire province and take with him any and all who cared to accompany him.

Thus began the "exodus to Ayuí," an episode famed in the annals of Uruguay, as Artigas led his compatriots out of the country. So great was the faith of the people in Artigas that they followed him almost to a man—thirteen thousand people, what with men, women, and children, besides the three thousand soldiers Artigas had. A number of the children and old folks died from the hardships of the journey, but the great majority survived. When it is remembered that there were not more than sixty thousand inhabitants of Uruguay, of whom perhaps thirteen thousand were in Montevideo, the magnitude of this affair can be appreciated.[1]

[1] More than likely the population of Uruguay at that time was much less than sixty thousand. A United States official estimated the population as forty-five thousand in 1818. It would seem that, with few exceptions, the able-bodied men of the province accompanied Artigas. The Portuguese commander found only two aged Indians in the considerable town of Paysandú when he entered that place.

The treaty of 1811 was soon broken, and by the close of 1812 the siege of Montevideo had been resumed, but Artigas now stood solidly for the principle of Federalism as against the Unitarism of the Buenos Aires government. Consequently, serious friction arose when a constituent assembly, supposedly representing all parts of the old viceroyalty of the Plata, was called to meet at Buenos Aires in 1813. In sending the deputies representing the Banda Oriental, Artigas issued them the famed "Instructions of the Year XIII," which set forth in a masterly fashion the desires and aims of the Federalist element in the Plata region. These are of considerable interest, if only as an illustration of the influence of the Articles of Confederation and the Constitution of the United States.[1] Almost all of the Artigas demands were contrary to the ideas of the Unitarist delegates from Buenos Aires, who controlled the assembly. Therefore, on technical grounds, the Artigas deputies were denied seats in the assembly. This act brought several months of strained relations between Artigas and the central government, and finally, in January 1814, Artigas and his entire command withdrew from the siege of Montevideo. There followed a highly confused period of triangular warfare, with Uruguayans, Porteños (as citizens of Buenos Aires were, and still are, called), and Spaniards, each at war with the other two. Later in the year, Montevideo surrendered to the Buenos Aires general, Carlos de Alvear, and the Spanish dominion in the Plata terminated for all time.

The civil war continued. Artigas, backed by the upriver provinces, as well as by Uruguay, created a league, with himself at its head, as "Chief of the Orientals and Protector of Free Peoples." At the height of his power he was ruler over a territory embracing a third of a million square miles. Meanwhile, the Buenos Aires government had undergone many changes of form, as well as personnel and party complexion, as *coup d'états* and counter-revolutions had come and gone. After the fall of the Alvear government in 1815, peace with Artigas was effected

[1] Referring to a volume on the history of the United States, Artigas once said: "A copy of this should be in the hands of every Oriental child." By "Oriental," of course, he meant a citizen of the Banda.

by the mildly Federalist government of Ignacio Álvarez Thomas. There was no real reconciliation, however, particularly since the Spanish danger was no longer immediately threatening. So none of the Buenos Aires governments ever saw quite eye to eye with the unyielding chief of the Banda.

Artigas had, however, reached the zenith of his power; backed by a loosely knit organization whose essence was decentralization, and lacking readily realizable economic resources, he could not make the best use of his potential authority. In 1816, came a new danger, as the Portuguese to the north took advantage of the dissensions in the Plata, and again invaded Uruguay. Montevideo fell in 1817, but Artigas bitterly contested every inch of Uruguayan soil in a struggle which lasted over four years. Not satisfied with resistance within Uruguay, he even invaded Brazil, and commissioned privateers who harried Portuguese shipping in all parts of the Atlantic, even along the coasts of Portugal within sight of Lisbon itself. Yet the struggle was too unequal, and by 1820 his power was broken; his desperate and daring invasion of Brazil was checked, and he retired to Uruguay, where he was utterly defeated at Tacuarembó. Artigas fled the field with some three hundred men, leaving behind eight hundred dead and *fifteen* wounded! These figures are illustrative of the fierce and pitiless character of the conflict. Artigas withdrew to the province of Entre Ríos in Argentina, where he continued the struggle against the Unitarists. In September of that same year he fled to Paraguay, where Francia imprisoned him for a few months. Francia presently released him, and granted him a small farm and a pension. There in Paraguay, thirty years to the day after his entry, Artigas died, on September 13, 1850.

With the defeat of Artigas in 1820, there was no further resistance of moment to the Portuguese in Uruguay. In 1821 a Portuguese-controlled Uruguayan congress declared the country annexed to the United Kingdom of Portugal and Brazil as the Cisplatine Province. Following the winning of Brazilian independence in 1822 it was annexed to Brazil under the same name. The people of the country preferred the idea of a union with their Spanish-speaking brethren[1] of the Plata, and in 1825 a revolution broke out. Under the leadership of Juan Antonio Lavalleja and Fructuoso Rivera the Uruguayans drove the Brazilians from the country, and asked to be taken into the Argentinian government. The request was acceded to, and war between Argentina and Brazil followed. Argentina won most of the battles, but both sides were so exhausted financially and confronted by such serious internal troubles that they would have been willing to yield the matter in controversy, if it had not been for popular pressure against such action. Eventually, England intervened, on the ground of the damage being inflicted upon British commerce, and brought both countries together in a treaty of peace in 1828. The principal clauses of the document were those by which both Argentina and Brazil recognized the independence of Uruguay, which began its career as a republic forthwith.

On March 9, 1812, José de San Martín reached Buenos Aires, having made the voyage from Europe on a British ship. Nobody knew it at the time, and perhaps least of all the modest San Martín, but this meant the beginning of a new phase in the warfare against Spain. Who was this San Martín? He was the son of a Spanish father and a creole mother, whose paternal and maternal ancestors, however, were natives of Spain. The father had risen to be a captain of militia in Buenos Aires, but eventually became the secular administrator of Yapeyú, one of the former Jesuit missions of Paraguay. There, on February 25, 1778, José de San Martín was born. Whether he should be considered a Paraguayan or an Argentinian has been a mildly moot point, but at any rate the place where he was born was definitively acquired by Argentina in 1870, at the conclusion of the Paraguayan War. His father was transferred to a post in Spain in 1785, and four years later, *at the age of eleven*, José himself entered the Spanish army. From that time forward, he engaged in active service under the Spanish flag, taking part in campaigns in North Africa, Portugal, even on one occasion on board a frigate in the Mediterra-

[1] There was, nevertheless, a considerable Portuguese element at that time in Uruguay. Some Brazilian writers have claimed as many as fifty per cent.

nean Sea, and in the various wars of the revolutionary and Napoleonic era against France, rising to the rank of a lieutenant-colonel of cavalry. Between times, he became well read in geography, history, and military science. Hearing of the revolutions in South America, he decided to cast in his lot with his native land. Arrived in Buenos Aires, this young man of thirty-four, with twenty-two years of active military experience, offered his sword to the patriot authorities.

San Martín received a commission as a lieutenant-colonel, and at once set to work to introduce something of military discipline and a knowledge of military art among the soldiery and officers of his command. Sent to the front, he won a brilliant action early in 1813 against the Spaniards at San Lorenzo, and in January, 1814, he succeeded Belgrano as general-in-chief of the dispirited and defeated army of the north. As already mentioned, he checked the onrush of the victorious Spaniards, despite the poor quality of his army in a military sense; he employed guerrilla tactics, of which he had learned a great deal in Spain over the years 1808 to 1811, making use, among others, of that same Güemes who was again to play an important part in the campaign of 1815. In April, 1814, San Martín asked to be allowed to resign, on account of "ill-health," and to be made governor of Cuyo—the province, so it happened, which commanded the best passes over the Andes to Chile. A little later that same year, both requests were granted. Thus San Martín "retired," but what a retirement it proved to be! Whatever the state of his health, he had already devised his plan for the winning of the war, but, except in the case of a few friends whom he could trust, he kept his ideas to himself. As early as April, 1814, he wrote to one of his intimates that the war would not end in patriot victory until Lima should be captured, but to get there it would be necessary to go by way of Chile and the sea, as nothing but a defensive warfare could be waged in Upper Peru. He even mentioned the desirability of organizing a small, well-disciplined army at Mendoza, the capital of Cuyo, to be employed in passing the Andes and exterminating the royalists in Chile. For the greater part of the next three years he was making his preparations.

It is difficult to convey any idea in a few words of the immensity of his task. He had to assemble an army, and was obliged to supply it very largely out of such resources as he was able to develop in Cuyo. There he made cannon, powder, and uniforms for his army, and gathered provisions and equipment for his campaign. To supplement the little he could provide, it was necessary to get help from the impecunious and hesitant government of Buenos Aires, which also he had to win over to his views. Fortunately for San Martín, his friend Juan Martín de Pueyrredón became "supreme director" of the state early in 1816, and gave San Martín much needed support. The governor of Cuyo had also to keep in touch with the situation in Chile, joining hands with the patriots and deceiving the royalists; the latter might be incredulous about his project of crossing the Andes, but they could not be kept in entire ignorance of his plans. And perhaps greatest of all his problems was the passage of the "immense mountains" which barred his way.[1] Hannibal and Napoleon had led armies by well-known routes across the Alps, but San Martín would have to go some four thousand feet higher in the air, to an altitude of more than twelve thousand feet, in order to reach the passes by which he could proceed to Chile. And the passes were so narrow in places that only one mounted soldier could get through at a time. All in all, if San Martín were to accomplish his aims, he would have to surpass the military achievements of similar type of which human history had any record. Meanwhile, what had been going on in Chile?

Chile had been having an exclusive set of revolutions, counter-revolutions, and civil wars of her own. An agricultural country, the old captaincy-general had become a region of great landed proprietors, with the bulk of the popu-

[1] San Martín did not even have maps of the trails across the Andes, but obtained them in an ingenious way. He sent one of his staff, an expert engineer, to Chile by way of Los Patos Pass, the longer of the two routes he proposed to follow. Ostensibly the officer's trip was for the purpose of delivering to the Spanish commander a copy of the Argentinian declaration of independence of 1816, but in fact he was to make careful observations, so that he could draw a map upon his return. Once in Chile, as San Martín told him, he would either be hanged by the Spaniards, or sent back to Mendoza the quickest way—or by the Uspallata Pass, the other of the routes which San Martín planned to take. And so it worked out. The emissary went the long way, and was sent back the short—and San Martín obtained his maps.

lation living in a form of servitude under the aristocracy. The revolution, therefore, swept over the heads of the masses, who had very little to do with the conflict at any stage. It was in purest sense a creole war—of those who favored a separation from Spain against the few Spaniards and the other creoles who were loyal to the royalist cause. The "Father" of the revolution in Chile was Juan Martínez de Rozas, born at Mendoza in 1759 in the then Chilean province of Cuyo. A well-educated man, he had had broad experience in government, holding high positions in Chile. From Concepción as a centre, he began the organization of a patriot party. To combat this movement, the captain-general in Santiago arrested three of the patriot leaders on May 25, 1810, and prepared soon afterward to send them as prisoners to Peru. Thereupon, there was an excited meeting of the *cabildo* of Santiago, which promptly converted itself into a *cabildo abierto*, as numerous patriots joined in the deliberations. The pro-Spanish *audiencia* persuaded the captain-general to resign, and a meeting of government officials substituted a Chilean in his place, but this proved only a temporary solution. Word came that the uncompromising royalist Governor Elío of Montevideo had been appointed captain-general by the council of the regency in Spain, and the patriots of Chile were resolved at all hazards that he should never assume the position. The agitation was resumed, and it was decided to call a meeting of the leading citizens and functionaries of the capital to determine what to do. Creole patriots crowded the assembly hall. The Chilean occupying the captain-general's seat was persuaded to resign, and a governing junta was set up —needless to say, "in the name of Ferdinand VII." This took place on September 18, 1810, a day which is now celebrated as the principal Chilean national holiday.

This, however, was only a beginning of the patriot difficulties. A congress was soon elected by the principal citizens of the different districts of Chile, and by a maneuver which the radical opposition denounced as improper the conservative wing of the patriot leaders got control. This party desired as little change from the old régime as was consonant with the idea of a separation from Spain. The royalists, who had elected a few deputies, also voted with this particular group. Over against them were the radicals, of whom Rozas was the chief. They had much the same views as their contemporary, Mariano Moreno of Argentina, believing in independence and the formation of a republic, and favoring a program of inflexible and aggressive opposition to their opponents, after the pattern of the Jacobins of the French Revolution.

Another of the leaders of this party was Bernardo O'Higgins, who was to become the "George Washington" of Chilean history. His father, Ambrosio O'Higgins, was one of the most remarkable men in the last days of colonial times. An Irish peddler, he first attained to wealth in the old captaincy-general of Chile; presently he became captain-general himself, and later viceroy of Peru. His career has few if any parallels in the history of the colonies. Bernardo was an illegitimate son by a Chilean mother, born in Chillán, August 20, 1778. The period of his youth was one of great difficulties for him, as his father would not acknowledge him; indeed, it was many years before Bernardo knew who his father was. He was sent to England for an education, and in London he came under the influence of Miranda. Later, he went to Spain, where he associated with those who, like himself, were already looking forward to the revolution. All this time, he was obliged to live on a pension which was a mere pittance, and this was presently discontinued when his father learned of his anti-Spanish associations. In 1801 he returned to Chile, however, and as his father had now passed away, he inherited some rich estates which his hitherto somewhat hard-hearted parent had devised to him. A man of brilliant talents and high character, he was later to prove himself a brave soldier and a patriot of the finest quality.

The radicals soon withdrew from the Chilean congress, protesting beforehand against any measures the latter might undertake. In September, 1811, the congress was overthrown as a result of a military *coup d'état* led by the Carreras, José Miguel, Juan José, and Luis. Of these the leader was José Miguel, a wealthy aristocrat who had recently returned from a long sojourn in Spain; during his stay in that country he had participated in the Spanish uprising against Napoleon, becoming a sergeant in the Spanish army. A radical government was now installed, but Carrera, not satisfied with the position accorded him, upset this government as he had the one which preceded it; a little later, in December, 1811, he assumed dictatorial powers. In the ensuing strife Rozas was banished to Mendoza, where he died in 1813.

Meanwhile, in Peru there had been no revolutionary outbreaks of any consequence, and that country was serving as a royalist base for reconquests elsewhere. It was natural, therefore, that the viceroy should deem the times propitious for sending a Spanish expedition to Chile, since the patriots there seemed to be hopelessly divided. A small force was landed in southern Chile early in 1813, and it quickly overran the greater part of that section. In the military operations which followed, the Carreras proved to be incompetent, and were deposed, being supplanted by O'Higgins. Thereupon, the Carreras fomented another revolution. In the face of the Spanish threat, and unable to come to any agreement with José Miguel Carrera, O'Higgins yielded, like a true patriot, and allowed the former to take command. There followed the decisive battle of Rancagua, October 1 and 2, 1814. O'Higgins fought heroically and with great skill, but the Carreras failed once again, and the Chileans were routed. The Spanish forces entered Santiago, and took complete possession of the country. José Miguel Carrera and O'Higgins made their way across the Andes, and laid their rival claims before San Martín in Mendoza. And San Martín chose O'Higgins. That was the end of the intervention of the Carreras in Chilean affairs.

It was not until July 1, 1816, that the Argentinian government approved San Martín's plans for the invasion of Chile. A few days later, on July 9, 1816, the independence of the country was proclaimed, under the name of the United Provinces of the Plata.[1] At that moment the patriotic cause in all the Americas was at a low ebb. Ferdinand VII, restored to his throne in 1814, had shown by his uncompromising absolutism that the one-time colonies

[1] The name Argentina did not become official until 1853.

had nothing to hope for from him. And with the overthrow of Napoleon it had now become possible to send more Spanish troops across the seas. By 1816 the royalists were everywhere in control, except in the Plata region, and it was confidently expected that in a few more months the traditional peace of the Spanish Empire would be restored. All this was changed by San Martín's campaign of 1817.

With some difficulty, San Martín increased his forces from about 2500, which he had in September, 1816, to nearly four thousand four months later, making use of some seven hundred slaves under a promise of liberty, as well as of Argentinian soldiery and Chilean *emigrés*. Then in January, 1817, came the remarkable passage of the Andes. Trails there were, over the passes, two miles or more up in the air, but nothing deserving of the name of a road. And added to the normal effort of getting not only men but also cannon and other heavy equipment and baggage over the uneven ground, there was the problem of disease. In particular there was the *soroche*. Many human beings cannot avoid this dangerous illness, even when riding in trains at those altitudes, and others give way in the face of mild exertion, such as walking, but San Martín's men had to work, and work hard. Apart from these difficulties inherent in the immensity of the mountains themselves, there was the question of what to do in the face of the Spanish opposition. San Martín met this purely military situation in the most ingenious way, at one and the same time deceiving the Spaniards in Chile as to his intentions, and getting his own troops over the mountains with the main body of them in position to attack a weakened foe, scattered the length and breadth of inhabited Chile.[1] The op-

[1] San Martín adopted a cunning plan to deceive the Spaniards. To the Pehuenche Indians, who commanded the Planchón and Portillo passes, San Martín sent many gifts, and invited them to a conference near Mendoza. There he made a speech to their chiefs, saying that the Spaniards were foreigners who intended to steal their lands, their cattle, and their women and children; he told them he desired to pass through their country in order to fight the Spaniards. Permission was granted, after which the Indians gave themselves up to a drunken orgy lasting a week. Thus San Martín achieved his purpose—not that of obtaining a right to go unmolested through Pehuenche territory, but of making the Spaniards believe that he was going that way; he relied on the perfidy of the Indians for the information about his arrangement with them to be passed on to the Spaniards, and he was not mistaken!

erations were carried on over a front some 1200 miles in length. A small division started first in the far north on January 12, joining the Chileans then in rebellion in the Copiapó and Coquimbo district. On the 14th the far southern division began its march, coming eventually to Talca and the Maule River in the south. On the 18th and 19th the main forces of San Martín set out on routes over the Andes in the line of Santiago, going by way of the Uspallata and Los Patos passes. All these expeditions had been planned in great detail, and it may be said that they worked out "to the minute." Presently, San Martín found himself down the Chilean side of the Andes, and facing, not the bulk of the Spanish army, but a division of two thousand men. On February 12 he utterly defeated them in the battle of Chacabuco.

In a sense, Chacabuco marked the turning-point in the entire series of wars in the Americas. Such, for example, was the opinion of the then viceroy of Peru, Joaquín de la Pezuela, as he expressed it at a later time. Its immediate results were twofold. A threatened invasion of the Plata country by way of Upper Peru was given up. And the Spanish grip on Chile was all but pried loose. San Martín occupied Santiago the day after Chacabuco. A *cabildo abierto* wished to make him "supreme dictator," but he declined in favor of his companion-in-arms, O'Higgins, who was thereupon selected for the place. Some time later, a document purporting to be signed by O'Higgins on January 1, 1818, but to which he actually affixed his signature the following day, was formally announced on February 12, 1818, proclaiming the independence of Chile.

San Martín remained at the head of the army. There was still work to do. The Spaniards concentrated their forces in the naturally defensible city and port of Talcahuano, and could not be dislodged. Receiving a reinforcement of some 3500 men from Peru, they presently resumed the offensive. In a surprise attack they threw the troops of San Martín and O'Higgins into disorder, and defeated them at the battle of Cancha Rayada, March 19, 1818. If the Spaniards had advanced promptly, they might possibly have retaken Santiago, but they wasted several valuable days *en route*, giving San Martín time to reform his troops and bolster up their morale and that of the people of the capital. It was during this period, so it is said, that he delivered the only public speech of his career. In it he announced that there would soon be another battle, and that this time he would win. At length, the Spanish army reached the plains of Maipú, only a league to the south of Santiago. There, on April 5, San Martín gave them battle. The issue was for a time in doubt, but San Martín decided it by a charge in which he himself participated. The victory was complete. From this time forward, the Spaniards were never again a danger to the patriot government in Chile.

Chile had been recovered. The next stop was Lima! That meant a navy, as the intervening deserts and barren mountain ranges in the face of a numerically superior enemy were too much of an obstacle. The viceroy of Peru had some twenty-five thousand men in the field. At best, San Martín could not hope to have more than a fifth as many, and would have to depend on recruits in Peru to make up the balance needed. It was only with the greatest difficulty that he obtained any army or funds at all. O'Higgins gave him as much support as he could, but the distant Buenos Aires officials were more impressed by the direct importance of their own troubles in Argentina than they were by the indirect value of defeating the Spaniards in Peru. After Chacabuco in 1817, and again after Maipú in 1818, San Martín made journeys to Buenos Aires, and received some promises of help. Later, when his backer, Pueyrredón, had fallen from power, San Martín was ordered to lead his armies across the Andes, to assist the government in putting down the opposition. Rather than abandon his project, San Martín "resigned," referring his action, however, to his army, which continued him in command. "My destiny called me to Lima!" remarked San Martín later, in explaining his virtual disobedience of the Buenos Aires government. These events took place in 1820. Nevertheless, San Martín might not have been able to carry out his great plan, if it had not been for the Riego revolution in Spain in that same year. Until that time the Argentinian authorities felt that they had to be ready for a possible attack in their sector of the wars, not knowing the intended destination of the great Spanish army which was being prepared. The Riego uprising at least set free as many of the Argentinian troops as were already in Chile for the campaign in Peru.

Meanwhile, Chile had been developing a navy. Some merchant vessels were purchased, and converted into men-of-war. A few Spanish ships, also, were captured, including one frigate. And late in 1818 the services of a celebrated naval officer were contracted as commander of the fleet. This was Lord Thomas Alexander Cochrane, a one-time high ranking officer of the British navy, who had been dismissed in disgrace. Cochrane had many faults as a human being, including excessive pride and a quarrelsome disposition, but there was never any question about his personal courage or his qualities of leadership. The Chilean squadron soon controlled the seas, with the Spanish fleet taking refuge in Callao, the port of Lima. Twice in 1819 Cochrane made expeditions to Peru, trying to lure the Spanish ships from their anchorage, but in vain. Each time, however, he effected landings along the coast, and by so doing he at least promoted the cause of the patriots through the means of propaganda. The Spaniards still held some towns and the Island of Chiloé in southern Chile, but in 1820 in a surprise attack Cochrane wrested Valdivia from them. This was one of the most brilliant of the Cochrane feats of arms. Valdivia is on a navigable river, about fifteen miles from the sea, and both sides of the river were fortified; altogether, there were nine forts with 118 guns, and a garrison of over a thousand men. Cochrane's attacking force included the brig "O'Higgins," a schooner as a transport, and just 318 men. Yet, he took the forts, one after another, and finally the town itself.

On August 20, 1820, the great expedition to Peru left the harbor of Valparaíso. There were eight war-vessels and sixteen transports. In the army were 4430 men, slightly more than half of whom belonged to the Argentinian Army of the Andes, with most of the rest from the Army of Chile. Among the equipment carried were uniforms and arms for fifteen thousand men, in preparation for recruits to the patriot cause in Peru, for this was to be a campaign, not of military conquest, but of propagandism, to assist the Peruvians in winning their independence from Spain. Thus far, there had been very little anti-Spanish activity in Peru. An uprising in Cuzco in 1814 had, indeed, assumed great proportions, but it was a replica of the former revolution of Tupac Amarú and the more recent campaign of Hidalgo in Mexico. It was a war of Indians against white men, to the usual accompaniment of inhuman cruelties and atrocities. By the spring of 1815 the native hordes had been defeated. The rest of Peru, strongly held by Spain, seemed, on the whole, to be loyal to the mother country.

So it was going to be less important to defeat Spanish armies than it was to persuade the Peruvians to rise against the existing government—all the more so, since the Spanish troops in Peru vastly outnumbered those of San Martín; there were perhaps twenty thousand men in the Spanish forces. It was hoped that skilful propaganda would induce many of these to desert to the patriots. To his army San Martín once said: "Remember that you are come, not to conquer, but to liberate a people." To make Peruvian independence sure, he wanted to stir up the Peruvians to win their own independence. Later, at a time when it would have been easy for him to have captured Lima, he explained his seeming inaction, as follows:

> "People ask," said San Martín, "why I don't march to Lima at once; so I might, and instantly would, were it suitable to my views, which it is not. I want not military renown, I have no ambition to be the conqueror of Peru, I want solely to liberate the country from oppression. Of what use would Lima be to me if the inhabitants were hostile in political sentiment? . . . Far different are my views. I wish to have all men thinking with me, and do not choose to advance a step beyond the gradual march of public opinion." [1]

These were the words of a genius and a patriot far superior to the average statesman or military hero. They illustrate, also, the generous and self-effacing traits of the great Ar-

[1] This is the statement attributed to him by Basil Hall, an English interviewer. See Hall, Basil, *Extracts from a journal written on the coasts of Chili, Peru, and Mexico* (2v. Edinburgh, 1824), I, 212–213.

gentinian—one might fairly say the self-immolating character of the man, because it was inevitable, as later events showed, that such a policy would result in a decline in influence of its proponent. It was to be justified by success, but at the sacrifice of San Martín, the noblest figure of the American wars.

On September 8, 1820, a landing was made at Pisco, south of Callao. It is not necessary to recite in detail the ensuing campaigns. Some expeditions were made into the interior, which in a military way appeared to accomplish little or nothing, but they brought the country a step nearer to a declaration of independence from Spain. Most notable of these were the two headed by General José Ildefonso Álvarez de Arenales. Meanwhile, Cochrane, with the help of a small force commanded by Colonel William Miller, touched at port after port along the Peruvian coast, establishing an effective blockade. Earlier, Cochrane had been responsible for one of the most spectacular achievements of the war. Furtively entering the harbor of Callao one night, he seized the great Spanish frigate "Esmeralda," and towed it out of range of the fort's guns, before the Spaniards became aware of what was happening. Battles on the land were fought here and there, but neither San Martín nor the Spanish viceroys, at first Pezuela, and later José de La Serna, took full advantage of their opportunities to bring the military issue to a head. The greater success had been achieved by San Martín, however, for he had been able to undermine the morale of the Spanish forces, gaining many new recruits for his own army from those who had deserted from the enemy. The Spaniards were strongly entrenched in Callao, and continued to hold Lima for a time, but retained the bulk of their forces in the interior, up in the mountains.

With the success of the Spanish revolution of early 1820, the Liberals had been restored to power, and the constitution of 1812 was revived. In 1821 an agent of the Liberal government brought San Martín and La Serna together in an effort to obtain peace. It was known that San Martín, like many of the more conservative patriot chieftains, was inclined to favor a constitutional monarchy. When he first returned from Europe in 1812 he was as good a republican and democrat as anybody, but he was immediately impressed by the undisciplined character of the people and the lack of political training of their leaders. He realized, too, that there was more likelihood of European help for a monarchy than for a republic. Thereafter, he never failed to uphold the principle of strong government, of centralized authority against Federalism, and of the traditional monarchical idea as against a republic. From this distance it would appear that he was right, but in his own times the stand he took on political issues was included among the charges which brought about the undermining of his power. Nevertheless, the negotiations with La Serna fell through, because of San Martín's insistence upon the recognition of the independence of Peru, although he was willing, and even eager, to have a Spanish prince enthroned as king.

As the campaign wore on, more and more Peruvians came over to the patriot side. At times, Spanish forces, recruited in Peru, would change allegiance in a body. In July, 1821, La Serna, convinced of the inadvisability of further attempts to hold Lima, evacuated it, retiring into the interior. By so doing he saved the Spaniards from being defeated in 1821, thus prolonging the war for several years. Not even yet would San Martín enter the city, until he was invited to do so by the *cabildo*. And then he went in a very un-Hispanic way, not in pomp and glory at the head of his soldiers, with banners flying in a great noon-day parade, but almost alone and at night. Nevertheless, he seems to have been very amiably received. The following are the words of an Englishman who witnessed the event:

> "12*th July* 1821.—This day is memorable in the annals of Peru, from the entry of General San Martin into the capital. Whatever intermediate changes may take place in the fortunes of that country, its freedom must eventually be established; and it can never be forgotten, that the first impulse was due entirely to the genius of San Martin, who planned and executed the enterprise which stimulated the Peruvians to think and act for themselves. Instead of coming in state, as he was well entitled to have done, he waited till the evening, and then rode in

without guards, and accompanied by a single aid-de-camp . . . Instead of going straight to the palace, San Martin called at the Marquis of Montemire's on his way, and the circumstance of his arrival becoming known in a moment, the house, the court, and the street, were soon filled. I happened to be at a house in the neighbourhood, and reached the audience-room before the crowd became impassable. I was desirous of seeing how the General would behave through a scene of no ordinary difficulty; and he certainly acquitted himself very well. There was, as may be supposed, a large allowance of enthusiasm, and high-wrought expression, upon the occasion; and to a man innately modest, and naturally averse to show, or ostentation of any kind, it was not an easy matter to receive such praises without betraying impatience.

"At the time I entered the room, a middle-aged fine-looking woman was presenting herself to the General . . . He was next assailed by five ladies, all of whom wished to clasp his knees at once; but as this could not be managed, two of them fastened themselves round his neck, and all five clamoured so loudly to gain his attention, and weighed so heavily upon him, that he had some difficulty in supporting himself. He soon satisfied each of them with a kind word or two, and then seeing a little girl of ten or twelve years of age belonging to this party, but who had been afraid to come forward before, he lifted up the astonished child, and kissing her cheek, set her down again in such ecstasy, that the poor thing scarcely knew where she was . . .

"Old men, and old women, and young women, crowded fast upon him; to every one he had something kind and appropriate to say, always going beyond the expectation of each person he addressed. During this scene I was near enough to watch him closely, but I could not detect, either in his manner or in his expressions, the least affectation; there was nothing assumed, or got up; nothing which seemed to refer to self; I could not even discover the least trace of a self-approving smile. But his manner, at the same time, was the reverse of cold, for he was sufficiently animated, although his satisfaction seemed to be caused solely by the pleasure reflected from others. While I was thus watching him, he happened to recognize me, and drawing me to him, embraced me in the Spanish fashion. I made way for a beautiful young woman, who, by great efforts, had got through the crowd. She threw herself into the General's arms, and lay there full half a minute, without being able to utter more than 'Oh mi General! mi General!' She then tried to disengage herself, but San Martin, who had been struck with her enthusiasm and beauty, drew her gently and respectfully back, and holding his head a little on one side, said, with a smile, that he must be permitted to show his grateful sense of such good will by one affectionate salute. This completely bewildered the blushing beauty, who, turning round, sought support in the arms of an officer standing near the General, who asked her if she were now content: 'Contenta!' she cried, 'Oh Senor!'

"It is perhaps worthy of remark, that, during all this time, there were no tears shed, and that, even in the most theatrical parts, there was nothing carried so far as to look ridiculous. It is clear that the General would gladly have missed such a scene altogether, and had his own plan succeeded he would have avoided it; for he intended to have entered the city at four or five in the morning." [1]

This was soon followed by what San Martín had been striving for, all along: by a *Peruvian* declaration of independence. On July 28, 1821, a *cabildo abierto* of the notables of the city announced the severance of the tie which had for so long bound the country to Spain. With the Spaniards still in the field, however, and remembering the bickerings in his own Argentina over questions of government, San Martín thought it best, for the time being, to have a dictatorship; he therefore accepted the power when it was conferred upon him in August of that year by the *cabildo abierto*, under the title of Protector of Peru. Nevertheless, he announced that whenever Peru should freely decide upon the kind of institutions she desired, his own functions would cease, and he guaranteed that people would find no traces in his administration of the "venality, despotism, and corruption which have marked the administration of the Spanish government in America."

In September, 1821, Callao was taken, but thereafter the patriot cause made scant progress in a military sense. The Spaniards had discovered a capable soldier in General José Canterac, and San Martín would not even attempt to dislodge them from their mountain strongholds. Instead, he continued to subordinate military victories to propagandism on behalf of the independence idea. In furtherance of this policy he had employed Peruvians as much as possible in high commands, and on April 7, 1822, one of his Peruvian generals was badly defeated at the battle of Macacona. This may be said to have marked the turning-point in his fortunes, although the opposition to him had for some time

[1] Hall, Basil, *op. cit.*, I, 239–245.

been developing apace; as a dictator he was a shining target at which to aim the shafts of criticism. Whatever he did, he found opponents on the other side—opponents who were, in true Hispanic American fashion, too partisanly addicted to their own views to consider anything in the nature of a compromise. And at least one subject of Great Britain gave him as much trouble as anybody else. This was Lord Cochrane, who quarreled openly and scandalously with San Martín, and even went to the extreme, on his own authority, of taking the fleet away from Peru, depriving San Martín of his communications with Chile. Cochrane himself soon afterward resigned, and ever afterward attempted to belittle San Martín. Brave man and intrepid sailor that he was, however, Lord Cochrane was never anything but a common scold and an insignificant figure in comparison with the infinitely greater Argentinian hero. Perhaps the rudest of the blows San Martín had to endure was that his own soldiers of the armies of the Andes and Chile turned against him, for there was neither plunder nor military glory to be obtained under San Martín. It began to appear that he would not be able to finish his task without outside help. Just at this time, Bolívar came down from the north, and overran a great part of the former presidency of Quito, or modern Ecuador. San Martín had long been hoping to receive assistance from Bolívar, and he now arranged for a meeting with the "Liberator," as Bolívar was called, to take place at Guayaquil.

The meeting at Guayaquil is one of the most controversial topics in Hispanic American history. Historians still dispute, not only with respect to what actually took place in the interviews between the two, but also as to what each man thought. The two men themselves were striking figures. San Martín, then forty-four, was a man of distinguished appearance, with also the calm and patience of the statesman. Bolívar, just turned thirty-nine, was a man of slender figure, proud, restless, ambitious, and with piercing black eyes. The motives of San Martín stand out rather clearly in the light of what he did and such other evidences as have been adduced. The interpretations of Bolívar's conduct, however, range all the way from those calling for the severest condemnation to others in terms of the highest praise, the latter of which at least explain his actions in a way not unbecoming to himself. The main issue in discussion was that of the sending of troops by Bolívar to help overcome the last considerable nucleus of Spanish resistance on Spanish American soil, but there were a number of subordinate questions to be resolved. For one thing the title of Ecuador was in issue. San Martín desired it to go to Peru, but Bolívar felt that its possession was vital to the position of predominance he hoped to create for his republic of Great Colombia, and formally annexed it in July, 1822. When San Martín arrived in Guayaquil a few days later, on July 25, this point was no longer open for consideration. Bolívar welcomed San Martín "to Colombian soil."

In the next two days the two men held three meetings, one of an hour and a half, another of half an hour, and the third of four hours. All were private. Nevertheless, it is possible from many evidences to deduce much of what took place. Bolívar declined to give any substantial aid for the campaign in Peru, even when San Martín generously offered to yield the supreme command in his favor. The matter of the form of government for Peru seems also to have been mentioned. San Martín advocated monarchy under a European prince. The Bolívar explanation of the meetings made much of this, and especially of Bolívar's opposition to any European monarch in the Americas. And, to be sure, the Liberator probably had as great an obsession against any connection with a European prince as the Protector had for it. Bolívar said he had no objection to any country's adopting whatever form of government it might desire, but if there were to be a king he would prefer a man like General Iturbide of Mexico. His own preference, however, was for a republic, with a president to be elected for life—an idea which he later incorporated into his constitution for Bolivia. There are those who say that Bolívar hoped to be that president. And they are probably correct. At any rate, San Martín left Guayaquil, much disappointed in the results of the conferences and also, be it said, in Bolívar. To O'Higgins he wrote that Bolívar was "not the man we took him to be." Years afterward, a French traveler quoted San Martín about Bolívar in a statement which was both discerning and generous, as follows:

> "General Bolívar appeared to have considerable pride, which seemed to be inconsistent with his habit of never looking directly at the person with whom he was talking, unless it might be somebody far beneath him in station. I was able to convince myself of his lack of frankness in the conferences I had with him at Guayaquil, for he never responded in a positive manner to my proposals, but always in evasive terms. The tone he employed with his generals was extremely haughty, and little likely to win their affection. I perceived, and he himself told me, that the English officers who served in his army were the ones in whom he had most confidence. On the other hand, his manners were distinguished, and bore witness to the good education he had received. His language was sometimes a bit trivial,[1] but it seemed to me that this defect was not natural to him, and that he wished in that way to give himself more the air of the soldier. Public opinion accused him of an immeasurable ambition and an ardent thirst for command; he had occasion to prove the justice of this reproach completely. People have attributed to him a great disinterestedness, and that, too, with justice, for he died in poverty.
>
> "Bolívar was very popular with the common soldiers, to whom he permitted a license not authorized by the laws of war; but he had very little popularity with his officers, whom he often treated in the most humiliating fashion. As for the military feats of this general, one might say that they entitle him to be considered the most astonishing man South America has produced. That which characterizes him, above all, and forms in some fashion his special trait, is a constancy in every proof, which caused him to hold fast against difficulties, and never let himself be overwhelmed by them, however great might be the dangers into which his ardent spirit had cast him." [2]

The most important document with respect to the conferences, however, is a letter which San Martín himself wrote to Bolívar from Lima, one month later. It was not made known to the world until San Martín gave it out, years afterward, upon the death of Bolívar. Since the original was not found in Bolívar's papers, extreme partisans of the Liberator refuse to give credence to this bit of evidence,

[1] From what follows, it would appear that this means that Bolívar occasionally employed what might be called "strong language"—and in Spanish that means very strong language indeed!

[2] Lafond, Gabriel, *Voyages dans l'Amérique espagnole pendant les guerres de l'indépendance* (2v. Paris, 1843), II, 142–143.

but it is generally accepted as being what it purported to be. The following are some excerpts from it:

"The results of our interview have not been what I hoped for the prompt termination of the war. Unfortunately, I am fully convinced, either that you did not believe in the sincerity of my offer to serve under your orders with the forces at my command, or that my presence is embarrassing to you . . . Do not be under any illusions, general. The reports you have of the royalist forces are mistaken. They amount to more than nineteen thousand veterans in Lower and Upper Peru, and they can be assembled in the space of two months. The patriot army, decimated by sickness, will not be able to place more than 8500 men in line of battle, and of these a great part are recruits . . . Therefore, without the support of the army under your command, the operations which are being prepared . . . will be unable to obtain the advantages which should be expected . . . and thus the struggle will be prolonged for an indefinite time. I say indefinite, because I am firmly convinced, whatever may be the vicissitudes of the present war, that the independence of America is irrevocable. But I also am convinced that the prolongation of the war will cause the ruin of her people, and it is a sacred duty for the men to whom her destinies are confided to avoid the continuation of such an evil.

"Finally, general, my decision is irrevocably made. I have convened the first congress of Peru for the 20th of next month. The day after it is installed I shall embark for Chile, convinced that my presence is the only obstacle which hinders your coming to Peru with the army under your command. It would have been the crowning happiness for me to end the war of independence under the orders of a general to whom America owes her liberty. Destiny disposes otherwise, and it is necessary for me to conform to it . . .

"I have spoken to you with frankness, general, but the sentiments which this letter expresses will remain buried in the most profound silence; if they were to become known, the enemies of our liberty might avail themselves of the information to prejudice our cause, and intriguers and ambitious persons might employ it to foment discord . . . With these sentiments and my wish solely that you may be the one to have the glory of terminating the war of independence in South America, I remain your very affectionate servant." [1]

[1] San Martín to Bolívar, Aug. 29, 1822, in Mitre, IV, 615–617. The moral superiority of San Martín in this affair and, conversely, the blot it would have made on the reputation of Bolívar, if the full story became known, might very easily account for the failure of this letter to appear in the Bolívar archives. Presumably, the letter, if received, was promptly destroyed.

This letter foreshadowed the action taken by San Martín in the ensuing weeks. Returning to Lima from Guayaquil, San Martín had found that there had been a revolution in that city during his absence, and his representative, Bernardo Monteagudo, had been overthrown. San Martín himself was outwardly well received, but he knew that Peruvian public opinion was in fact no longer on his side. A sick man and almost overwhelmed by the accumulating difficulties of his position, knowing also that no help could be expected from Bolívar while he himself was in Peru, San Martín rapidly reached the decision to surrender his authority and leave the country; this action, he hoped, might persuade Bolívar to enter Peru and put the finishing touches on the work which San Martín had in the main accomplished. He wrote to O'Higgins that he was tired of being called a tyrant and of being accused of aiming to become a king or an emperor. So he had sanctioned the calling of a Peruvian congress. When it assembled, in September, 1822, he resigned his title of Protector. In an admirable farewell address, he expressed himself as follows:

> "I have witnessed the proclamation (*declaración*) of the states of Chile and Peru; the standard which Pizarro brought to enslave the empire of the Incas is in my possession, and I have ceased to be a public man; thus am I recompensed with usury for my ten years of revolution and warfare. My promises to the peoples in whose countries I have fought are fulfilled: to achieve independence and leave the selection of their governments to their own will. The presence of a fortunate soldier, however disinterested he may be, is dangerous to those states which are newly established. For another thing, I am weary of hearing people say I wish to make myself a king. Nevertheless, I shall always be disposed to undergo the ultimate sacrifice for the liberty of the country, but in the category of a mere individual, and nothing more. As for my conduct in office, my compatriots, as in most affairs, will be divided in opinion; their children will render the correct verdict. Peruvians, I leave you with an established national representation. If you give it your entire confidence, then your songs will be those of triumph; if not, anarchy will devour you. May Heaven preside over your destinies, and may these heap up your measure of happiness and peace." [1]

[1] Quoted in Mitre, III, 665–666.

Congress offered him the position of commander-in-chief of the army, and urged him to remain in power, but San Martín would not accede to its requests. With surprising suddenness, he left the country, bound for Chile. Before going, however, he confided to his friend, Tomás Guido, the real reasons for his withdrawal. Guido tried to dissuade him, but without success. According to Guido, San Martín expressed himself as follows:

> " 'I have meditated thoroughly over all that you say,' answered the general, visibly moved. 'I am not unaware, either, of the interests of America or of my imperious duties, and I am consumed with grief in abandoning comrades whom I love like children and the generous patriots who have aided me in my tasks. But I could not stay a single day without complicating my situation. I am going. No one, my friend, can dissuade me from the conviction I hold that my presence in Peru would occasion worse disasters than my departure. That is the message I get from the judgment I have formed of what is going on within and without this country. Rest assured that for many reasons I can no longer maintain myself in my post, except under conditions which are decidedly contrary to my sentiments and my firmest convictions. I am going to tell you: one of them is the unavoidable necessity to which circumstances have constrained me, if I am to sustain the honor and discipline of the army, of shooting some officers; and I lack the courage to do so to companions-in-arms who have followed me in prosperous days and in adversity.' "

At this point Guido remonstrated, insisting on the real loyalty of the army to San Martín, despite the evil influence of a few officers.

> " 'Well,' proceeded the general, 'I appreciate the sentiments which move you so warmly—but in reality there is a greater difficulty, which I could not overcome except at the expense of the fate of the country and of my own credit, and I cannot face such an eventuality. I am going to tell you without beating about the bush (*sin doblez*). Peru is not big enough to hold Bolívar and me. I have seen through his venturesome designs; I have grasped the annoyance he would feel over the glory which might fall to my lot in the prosecution of the campaign. He would not fail to find an excuse, however bold, to enter this republic, followed by his troops; and then perhaps I would not be able to avoid a conflict to which an unhappy fate might impel us, thus offering a humiliating scandal to the world. The spoils of triumph, to whichever of us two fortune might incline itself,

would be gathered in by the "tenderfeet" (*maturrangos* [1]), our implacable enemies, and we would appear to have converted ourselves into instruments of base passions. I shall not be the one, my friend, to leave such a legacy to my country, and I would prefer to die before making a boast of the laurels gathered in at such a price—by no means that! Let General Bolívar enter the country if he can, taking advantage of my absence; if he should be able in Peru to make sure of what we have won, and something more, I shall be satisfied; at all events his victory would be a victory for America.'"

Following some further argument of Guido against his plan, San Martín concluded as follows:

"'No, San Martín will not be the one to contribute a single day by his conduct to the merry-making of the enemy, by assisting in affording them an opportunity for satisfying their desire for vengeance.'" [2]

In Chile, San Martín found his own name execrated and the government of his friend O'Higgins in a precarious position. Very sick himself, he would also have been penniless, if it had not been that the government of Peru sent him a small sum of money. He made his way to Mendoza, and remained there a few months in obscurity. There he received news of the death of his beloved wife. And, early in 1823, word came that O'Higgins had fallen. Going to Buenos Aires, he was treated with neglect, and in 1824 he left that city with his little daughter for Europe. Whatever means of support he had were lost by a friend of his in disastrous speculations. In this juncture he was saved by a former companion-in-arms in the Spanish army, a Spanish banker named Alejandro Aguado, who gave him a home just outside of Paris. All honor to this Spaniard who thus so generously overlooked the achievements of a man who had been among the foremost in costing his country an empire! In 1829 San Martín sailed for Argentina, hoping to live in retirement at Mendoza. This was a time of excited political partisanship between the Federalists, then in power in Buenos Aires, and the Unitarists, to which

[1] "*Maturrangos*" is a Spanish American colloquial term, meaning a poor horseman or a clumsy, rough person. It was used, obviously, in the same disparaging sense as was ordinarily implied in such words as "*gachupín*" and "*chapetón.*" Cf. *supra*, 242, n. 2.

[2] Guido, 240–243.

group San Martín might have been expected to belong. So he was greeted with slander and insult, even before he got off the ship. Not wishing to become involved in factional strife, he immediately returned to Europe, never again setting foot in his own country. In 1848, on account of the bad state of his health, he moved to Boulogne, and there, on August 17, 1850, he passed away.

And it fell out as he had judged. Bolívar entered Peru, and reaped the glory which more properly belonged to San Martín. But there again San Martín was right. Posterity, as the great Argentinian predicted, saw matters in truer perspective. And posterity has recognized the high place of San Martín, not only as the outstanding military genius of the wars of independence, but also as a man who in traits of character deserves to rank with Washington, Lincoln, and others among the noblest figures the world has known.

Simón Bolívar

CHAPTER XV

THE WARS OF INDEPENDENCE: BOLÍVAR

San Martín was an outstandingly great figure of the wars of independence era, with Miranda only a little less noteworthy. After them come O'Higgins, Sucre, Belgrano, Moreno, Artigas, Hidalgo, Morelos, and Iturbide. Over in Brazil the young Dom Pedro is deserving of favorable mention. And there were a host of others, generals and statesmen, who rank far up in the list of patriot heroes, perhaps with a rating as good as or even better than some of those mentioned above. Perhaps at the very top, however, is one other leader, an extraordinary individual and the most famous Spanish American of his times: the Venezuelan Simón Bolívar. He was a great man in Spanish American history from at least two standpoints. There was in the first place his share in producing the victory over Spain. In that respect, perhaps, he was second, if to anybody, only to San Martín. But Bolívar also merits consideration as probably the leading political thinker and statesman Hispanic America has produced; if some others may be said to have possessed more considerable attainments in these respects, there were none who equaled him in influence. His real greatness lies more in the field of politics than in that of war. He announced the ideals in government toward which Hispanic America has been evolving ever since. This is a part of his work which cannot be discussed in any detail here, as it belongs to the era of the republics, but it is enough to entitle him to be considered perhaps the greatest Hispanic American who has yet appeared—a greater even than San Martín, if also in many respects a less admirable figure.

It is easy to like San Martín. He was at one and the same time a man of broad vision and one who almost unfailingly did the right thing. In Anglo-American countries he would have been a greater success than Bolívar. Bolívar, however, more truly fitted the atmosphere of Hispanic America, even in his failings. And of failings he had almost as many as virtues, and his detractors vie in numbers with his panegyrists.

Something has been said already about his comparatively selfish rôle in the negotiations with San Martín at Guayaquil. Other instances of his selfishness, disobedience, and cruelty are referred to hereinafter, and they could be multiplied almost without limit. He had a pronounced case of "megalomania," justified beyond a doubt, but a trait which does not excuse itself to the Anglo-American mind. During a banquet following the conferences of San Martín and Bolívar at Guayaquil, the two men were called upon to propose a toast. San Martín gave a properly patriotic, but conventional response: "For the speedy termination of the war, the organization of the different republics of the continent, and the health of the Liberator of Colombia." And what was the Bolivarian toast? Here it is: "To the two greatest men of South America: General San Martín and myself!" It must be admitted that this was frank and decidedly colorful, and it was characteristic of the man. He was fond of resounding titles. Not only was he the "Liberator," but also the "Illustrious Pacificator." Often when he was actual or virtual dictator, and sure of his grip, he would "resign," knowing well that his resignation would not be accepted. This occurred on at least eight different occasions. He was perfectly open, and went to great excess, in flaunting the moral code, so much so that even his closest admirers in Hispanic America (who would not ordinarily concern themselves over the illicit love affairs of their hero) feel under some mild necessity of apologizing for him. Most famous among his mistresses was Manuela Sáenz; she was the wife of an Englishman named Thorne, but is more generally known by her maiden name. Thorne, however, was much too tame for Manuela, and she left him to become the companion, openly so, of Bolívar in his later years. Unquestionably, Bolívar was personally ambitious. He hoped to vie in fame with his idol, Napoleon. Never would he have yielded the field to a San Martín, as the latter did to him in Peru; Bolívar's conduct toward San Martín was similar to what he displayed toward many another in Venezuela and Colombia in the years before the meeting of Guayaquil. And great as he was in statecraft and war, it has often been asserted that he was not a practical statesman and had many shortcomings as a military leader.

When all these charges have been made, however, passing over ultra-partisan screeds against him, everything else is in favor of Bolívar. Fiery and impetuous, he was also absolutely fearless, one of the few men of whom it may truly be said that he loved danger. That, indeed, was one of his defects as a general, since Bolívar himself liked to mingle in the fray, instead of remaining safely in the rear to direct it. He was a veritable human dynamo for energy and capacity for work. When his own position was not involved, he was great in his generosities. He could endure misfortune. And, despite his personal failings, he was a real patriot and a genuine lover of freedom. He was a man of wonderful enthusiasms, a born leader of revolutions, an inspiring and stimulating figure, a stirring orator in time of need. He was a great genius—a dreamer—an idealist in many ways—capable of looking ahead, far beyond his time. And he did not have one all too frequent weakness of Hispanic American politicians: he had no ambition for private wealth. Riches he possessed at the beginning of his career, and easily threw them into the scales as part of the risks involved in his chosen course. In financial affairs he was a man of meticulous integrity, as incorruptible as Washington.

The northern half of the semicircle which depicts the war in South America can be accounted for in no better way than by following the career of Bolívar. Simón de Bolívar was born at Caracas on July 24, 1783, the son of parents who were wealthy and influential. His ancestry included numerous families of high noble rank—if also, as might be said of most of his contemporaries, very probably a few who were Indian. His father died when he was three years of age, and his mother when he was nine, wherefore he was brought up by some of his relatives. Among his teachers was Andrés Bello, who at a later time in Chile was to become one of the outstanding figures among the learned men—some say the greatest—Hispanic America has produced. Bolívar preferred one of his other teachers, however, an odd visionary by the name of Simón Rodríguez, who has been called a "living caricature of Rousseau," eternally unadapted to the world about him. Nevertheless, this man was the principal companion and confidant of Bolívar's youth, and Bolívar always claimed he owed a great deal to his influence.

Early in 1799, when Bolívar was not yet sixteen, he was sent to Europe, going by way of Mexico to Spain. There, because of his high connections, he frequented the loose court of Charles IV, and presently fell in love with the niece of the Marquis of Toro. Despite the youth of the principals, they were married in 1802, when Bolívar was not yet nineteen. Meanwhile, he had visited Paris, where he was deeply impressed by the achievements of his hero, Napoleon Bonaparte. Returning to Venezuela in 1802, Bolívar had the misfortune to lose his young wife, who died early in 1803. Bolívar never married again. To assuage his grief, he chose the route of dissipation. For several years, he lived the life of a libertine in Paris, but also traveled in England, Spain, Italy, and Austria. Part of the time he was accompanied by his old tutor, Rodríguez. Learning that he had inherited a fortune of some four million *pesos*—probably worth far more than the equivalent of four million dollars today—he proceeded to scatter his money with the extravagance of a prince. He himself says he spent 150,000 francs in London in three months, and it would be safe to say that this amounted to at least as much as thirty thousand dollars—possibly twice as much. Going by way of the United States, he returned to Venezuela in 1807. There he seems to have associated with those creole members of the aristocracy who were already plotting against Spain.

The disasters of 1810 in the Spanish peninsula were, in Venezuela as elsewhere, the occasion for the patriot uprising. On April 18, 1810, the *cabildo* of Caracas called for what amounted to a *cabildo abierto* to meet next day to determine what to do. On the 19th, in an excited session, the resignation of the captain-general was demanded.

Threatened by a throng of creole revolutionaries, the captain-general had no choice but to renounce his command, and a new government was formed, entitled the "Supreme committee for the preservation of the rights of Ferdinand VII." This, of course, was nothing more than the same device employed elsewhere in the colonies to give the color of legality to a move which was in fact intended for a separation from Spain. Most of the provinces of the country followed the lead of Caracas, and steps were taken immediately to meet the inevitable Spanish attack. It was necessary to procure arms and munitions abroad, and a number of missions were sent out to get as much assistance as possible. Bolívar was one of three who went to England. They were well received by officials of the British government, which was playing a cautious double game with respect to the outbreaks in Spanish America. On the one hand, England was the ally of Spain against Napoleon, and would not openly take any action which might offend the authorities in the peninsula. On the other hand, no government of those times was more completely dominated by the mercantile classes than England, and the merchants wanted to be assured of freedom of trade with the heretofore forbidden regions of Spanish America. So a great deal of help was in fact given surreptitiously, though much more in later years, after the wars with Napoleon were over. As another part of their mission the three Venezuelans persuaded Miranda to return to their country, to put himself at the head of the revolution. This was in itself equivalent to a declaration of war against the government in Spain. Late in 1810 both Bolívar and Miranda were again in Venezuela.

There had already been some desultory fighting with Spanish loyalists, but the most important action over the next few months was a declaration of independence by a Venezuelan congress on July 5, 1811. This time the "rights of Ferdinand VII" were thrown into the discard. In ensuing deliberations the idealistic conceptions of the French philosophers and of United States Federalism were adopted, over the objections of Miranda and Bolívar; so the quarrels of Federalists and Unitarists began in Venezuela, as had happened these same years in the territories of the Plata. Thus the royalists were able to strengthen their position. Furthermore, the revolution had been a purely creole affair, and the colored elements—*mestizos*, mulattoes, and negroes, who hated the colonial aristocrats—were hostile to the new régime.

Affairs were in none too satisfactory a state for the patriots, when on March 26, 1812, during Holy Week, there occurred a terrible earthquake which destroyed Caracas and several other cities in patriot hands, with a loss of some twenty thousand lives, while the leading royalist towns suffered comparatively little. Thereupon, a number of priests in sympathy with the royalists, headed by the archbishop of Caracas, preached that the calamity was a divine punishment upon those innovators who had denied "the anointed of God, Ferdinand VII." It proved a tremendous advantage to the royalists, whose ranks were swollen by enlistments on the part of those who wished to incur favor with the Almighty, who had chosen, as they thought, to support the cause of Spain. Moreover, many of the patriot soldiery deserted to the other side. Congress endeavored to meet the situation by dropping quarrels over political principles and making Miranda commander-in-chief of the army and dictator, but it proved to be too late to check the advance of the royalists. Already displaying his jealousy of anybody in authority over him, Bolívar opposed the dictator, and unwillingly accepted the post of commandant of the important city of Puerto Cabello. Lack of discipline, indeed, was general in the patriot ranks, and many of the Venezuelan officers were hostile to the veteran leader, because he preferred the counsels of the more experienced military men among the foreign adventurers of his staff to those of the ill-trained Venezuelans. Nevertheless, he was operating with reasonable success against the Spanish leader Domingo de Monteverde, when a crushing blow was dealt to the patriot cause. Puerto Cabello, the strongest fortified city of Venezuela, the "bulwark of liberty," in which great quantities of munitions were held in reserve for the patriots, was betrayed to the royalists by Francisco Fernández Vinoni. Bolívar did what he could to save the city, but most of his soldiers went over to the enemy, and he was obliged to retire.

The surrender of Puerto Cabello broke Miranda's spirit. At one stroke the overwhelming advantage in the campaign had passed to the royalist side. Numerically his army was still superior to Monteverde's, but its morale was weak, and desertions and the hostility of the masses were certain, very soon, to give the situation a turn for the worse. Furthermore, the royalists now had ample munitions, as against an under-supply for the patriots. In this juncture the English government offered mediation between Spain and her colonies, on the basis of freedom of trade with them for English ships. This influenced Miranda to take steps for an adjustment with the enemy. What followed is a matter of vitriolic controversy, as it was to involve the betrayal of Miranda to the Spaniards by Bolívar. To justify this act the admirers of the latter have had to besmirch the name of Miranda. Charges have been brought to the effect that Miranda was a traitor, or that he sold out for a paltry sum of gold, or that he was acting in the interests of England instead of Venezuela. Perhaps the mildest of the objections to his conduct are that he had grown old and was no longer competent to handle such an affair as the Venezuelan revolution. There may have been an element of truth in this, but in the light of Miranda's lifelong career and his sad fate all the other allegations are no better than a defensive *tu quoque* on behalf of Bolívar. In point of fact, it is probable that no other patriot commander could have done any better at the time. On several occasions in later years Bolívar abandoned Venezuela or Colombia when conditions were certainly no more unfavorable than they were under Miranda in 1812. The latter went a step farther than in the Bolívar campaigns of the future in that he made a capitulation, hoping to protect the lives and property of his followers. The result of his effort proved that no good result could be anticipated if the experiment were tried again.

What happened? Miranda proposed an armistice, and eventually the so-called "capitulation of San Mateo" was arranged. The main features of the document were that the patriots, who now held little more than the territory around Caracas and its port of La Guaira, were to lay down their arms, on the promise of the Spanish commander, however, of an amnesty which would completely wipe out the offences against the mother country involved in the revolution. With the definitive treaty not yet signed, Miranda left it to one of his officers to surrender the city of Caracas, and himself proceeded to La Guaira. There he was offered an asylum on a British boat, but decided to stay one more night on Venezuelan soil. It proved to be a fatal choice. That night a number of his Venezuelan officers, instigated by a man named Casas, the governor of the port, and led by Bolívar, seized Miranda, threw him into prison, and informed Monteverde of what they had done. Furthermore, Casas prevented any patriot vessels from leaving the harbor. Monteverde reported the affair to his own government as follows:

> "As soon as I reached Caracas I gave the most peremptory orders for the detention of the rebel leaders who were at La Guaira, but fortunately by the time that I reached that port . . . Casas had with the advice of Pena and by the aid of Bolívar thrust Miranda into a prison and also detained all of his companions who were in that port. In this transaction Casas risked his life . . . Peña and Bolívar ran a similar risk . . . I cannot forget the interesting services of Casas, nor those of Bolívar and Peña; because of these services I have not touched their persons, simply conceding to Bolívar passports for foreign countries; for his influence and connections here might be dangerous in the present circumstances." [1]

Bolívar, indeed, received his passport, "in recompense for the service which you have rendered to the king," said Monteverde, "in the imprisonment of Miranda." As for Miranda, at the time of his arrest he cried out haughtily and, no doubt, somewhat contemptuously: "A tumult! A tumult! Such men as you are capable only of tumults!" History does not record that he ever again made any complaint. Meanwhile, Monteverde had failed to live up to the terms of the capitulation, punishing the patriots who fell into his hands. And Miranda was no exception. He

[1] Quoted in Robertson, *Life of Miranda*, II, 183.

was taken to Spain, thrown into prison in Cádiz, and died there, July 14, 1816.

What must be the judgment with respect to the Bolívar-Miranda episode? As for Miranda, it is safe to adopt the conclusions of the ultra-objective historian, William Spence Robertson, who says:

> "To the writer it seems that in agreeing to the Capitulation of San Mateo, the first Dictator of Venezuela was influenced by the idea that such a course was the best policy which he could adopt for the welfare of his native land . . . After the fall of Puerto Cabello, in view of the desertions from the patriot army and the increase of Monteverde's forces, the prospect of victory for the Venezuelans steadily declined. Miranda's judgment may be questioned but not his patriotism . . . Not the least of Miranda's mistakes,—at least in the eyes of his countrymen who knew little or nothing of his long duel with the ubiquitous agents of Spain,—was his inexplicable decision to await neither at his military headquarters nor in the capital city the termination of the definitive negotiations for peace. The epic of his life supports the interpretation that, animated by a keen desire to avoid falling into the merciless clutches of those inveterate foes who had persecuted and hunted him since 1783, he had resolved to leave his post." [1]

And again:

> "For the fateful surrender at San Mateo the generalissimo was denounced and betrayed by his own compatriots. Nevertheless a careful study of this event in the light of his personal experiences with agents of the Spanish Government discredits the view that he was a traitor to the cause of Venezuelan independence. The fairest interpretation of his actions which can be made is that he wished to evade his implacable enemies and later to resume the struggle for independence." [2]

These are the views the writer would adopt. The charge of treason appears nothing short of ridiculous, and it goes without saying that it was amply disproved by the fate of Miranda. The conclusion is almost inescapable that he hoped to do just what Bolívar himself did on later occasions: retire for the moment, with the idea of striking again, when the situation might be more favorable.

And Bolívar? The most generous interpretation is that

[1] Robertson, *Life of Miranda*, II, 194.
[2] *Ibid.*, II, 248.

he really considered Miranda a traitor. When Monteverde complimented him for his part in the imprisonment of Miranda, he replied, so it is alleged, that he had seized him "in order to punish a traitor to his country, not to serve the king." It is difficult to escape the belief, however, that some of the defects of Bolívar were in the background of what he did on that famous occasion. It is clear from the evidence that his associates, Casas and Peña, had already turned traitor to the patriot cause. Such a charge can hardly be brought against Bolívar, but there is no doubt that he and many others of the Venezuelan officers had long felt a certain resentment against the somewhat domineering leadership of Miranda, who did not conceal his disgust over their lack of military attainments. Furthermore, it is more than probable, as has often been asserted, that Bolívar's jealousy of anybody who outranked him and his own ambition for the place of power had something to do with his action toward Miranda. By betraying him, Bolívar ensured his own safety, as it turned out, and made it probable that he himself might eventually take command in a later revolution. Certainly that is what happened. With Miranda out of the way, Bolívar was henceforth the outstanding leader in the campaigns of the north. Only the most ardent Bolivarian partisan can excuse the conduct of the eventual Liberator in the Miranda affair.

Bolívar made his way to the Dutch island of Curaçao, off the Venezuelan coast. Later that same year, 1812, he went to Cartagena, to ally himself with the patriots of New Granada, or Colombia. The revolutions in this country had followed a very complicated course, responding to the rough and mountainous character of the land and the confusing varieties of population, with the whites mostly in the cities, Indians and *mestizos* of widely differing types and capacities in the rural districts, and negroid peoples along the coasts. Sectionalism was perhaps more truly at home in New Granada than in any other part of the Americas. On July 20, 1810, with news at hand of the uprisings in Venezuela and the presidency of Quito, or Ecuador, as well as information of Napoleon's successes in Spain, some creole leaders of Bogotá, with the support of the *cabildo*, compelled the viceroy to call a *cabildo abierto*. Out of this came a government headed by a junta, which at first recognized the superior authority of the Council of the Regency in Spain. Presently, it dropped the idea of subjection to those in power in the Spanish peninsula, ruling in the name of the captive king, Ferdinand VII. Unlike what happened elsewhere in the colonies, the revolution in the capital city was not adopted by the other regions of the country; rather, it was imitated in separate revolutions, which set up juntas of their own. To make the situation more complex, there were divisions along a number of other lines, both in New Granada as a whole, and the different districts. The most prominent of these was the conflict between Federalists and Unitarists. Notable among these governments was that of Cartagena, which on November 11, 1811, declared its independence from Spain. During that same year, meetings were held in Bogotá which proclaimed governments for Cundinamarca (the central province of the country, including Bogotá) and for all New Granada; that of Cundinamarca declared its independence on July 16, 1813.

For two years, Cundinamarca was busy with a civil war between Federalists and Unitarists, with the latter, under Nariño, the revolutionary precursor of other days, having the better of the conflict. In 1813 the Nariño government had to meet a Spanish invasion from Ecuador. In the latter country, after the suppression of the revolutionary movement of 1809, there was another uprising in 1811, to the accompaniment of a declaration of independence in December. By the following December the Spanish power had again been established. It was as a continuation of this campaign that the loyalist troops marched north in 1813. A year later, the patriot army of Cundinamarca was badly defeated, and Nariño himself was sent as a prisoner to Spain.

The government of Cartagena confirmed Bolívar in his rank of colonel, which he had held in Venezuela, and he was placed in command of a post along the Magdalena River. He now issued a *manifiesto*, or public declaration, to the inhabitants of New Granada, the first outstandingly prominent document emanating from him in a long series of proclamations and pronouncements which reveal Bolívar at his best. In this he argued convincingly for the necessity of freeing Venezuela from the Spaniards, if the people of New Granada were to avoid a Spanish reconquest. His ideas gained many followers, and from this time forward there was in fact a close connection between the revolutions in the two countries. Early in 1813, disregarding the orders of his superior officer, Bolívar engaged in a brilliant campaign along the lower Magdalena, clearing that region of the royalists. Proceeding eastward, over the cordillera, he won a fine victory at Cúcuta. He was now authorized to undertake his plan for the recovery of Venezuela.

In Venezuela the Spanish authorities had gone to excess in persecuting the defeated patriots, and their abuses contributed to the outbreak of a second revolution early in 1813. Santiago Mariño emerged as the principal leader, and was soon in control of eastern Venezuela around Cumaná. It was at this juncture that Bolívar began his invasion from the west. All the way from Cúcuta to Caracas he went from one victory to another. Moreover, he issued a famous proclamation calling for a "war to the death" with all Spaniards, in which even Spanish neutrals were to be killed, unless they should work actively for the patriot cause. For the next several years, this policy and the retaliations of the royalists plunged Venezuela into a bloody shambles, comparable to the period of the Hidalgo revolt in Mexico. In August, 1813, Bolívar entered Caracas. This was no quiet entry, such as a San Martín would have made, but a theatrically triumphant one, with his carriage being drawn by a bevy of beautiful maidens. Shortly after this, he was proclaimed by the title, which ever afterward he prized so much, of the Liberator of Venezuela. He now became the virtual dictator of the country, and cleverly associated Mariño with him by declaring that the latter ought to become the chief executive, as soon as the war should be over.

The Spaniards had not been expelled from the country, however. They held Puerto Cabello and several other towns in the west. Late in 1813, receiving reinforcements, they took the offensive again. Soon afterward, Monteverde, who had been wounded, was succeeded by José Tomás

Boves, a bloodthirsty Spaniard, whom Bolívar's "war to the death" policy fitted like a glove.[1] He was able to recruit the half-savage *llaneros*, or plainsmen, of Venezuela, who hated the creole aristocrats. Mulattoes and *mestizos*, they much more easily understood such words as "pillage" and "slaughter" than they did the "liberty" proclaimed from Caracas. Hoping to hold them in check, Bolívar invoked the terror, after the pattern of the French Revolution, and on one occasion caused over eight hundred royalist prisoners to be put to the sword. The only fruit of this barbarous act were other barbarisms on the part of the enemy. In June, 1814, Boves crushingly defeated Bolívar and Mariño at La Puerta, whereupon Bolívar abandoned the capital. The populace, in fear of Boves and his *llaneros*, followed him in a tragic exodus to the east. Whole families perished along the way. Boves sent Francisco Tomás Morales, his second in command, in pursuit, and the latter defeated Bolívar again, at Aragua, in August. Once more the patriot cause was lost. Some of the leaders demoted Bolívar and Mariño from their commands, and even discussed whether they should not condemn them to the same fate which Bolívar had inflicted upon Miranda, two years before. At length, they allowed them to embark for Cartagena. All Venezuela was now in royalist hands except the Island of Margarita, where the patriot leader Juan Bautista Arismendi held forth.

Back in Cartagena in September, 1814, Bolívar was commissioned to reduce Cundinamarca and compel it to join the confederation. Upset by the defeat of Antonio Nariño at the hands of the royalists in the south, Cundinamarca was unable to put up an effective resistance. Bolívar laid siege to Bogotá, which was compelled to surrender, and Cundinamarca joined the confederation. Returning north, Bolívar was sent, early in 1815, on a fresh campaign against the royalists of the Santa Marta district. These were days which found Bolívar at his worst. Far from energetically prosecuting the attack upon the enemy, he indulged him-

[1] The real name of Boves was Rodríguez. A native of Asturias, he had been condemned to eight years' imprisonment at Puerto Cabello. On being pardoned, he took the name Boves out of gratitude to one of his benefactors.

self in banqueting and petty vanities, and also gave free rein to a quarrel with a rival commander, Colonel Manuel del Castillo. He went so far as to besiege Castillo in Cartagena, at a time when it was known that a Spanish fleet was approaching with the greatest army yet sent to those shores, some ten thousand men under General Pablo Morillo. Morillo had by this time taken the Island of Margarita in Venezuela. As there was no other effective resistance in that country, it was a certainty that he would soon appear before Cartagena. Bolívar solved his own personal situation at this time by taking ship for Jamaica, in May, 1815.

At this point the word *finis* might have been written to the career of most men in Bolívar's position, but he was never so admirable as at a moment like this, and especially through the medium of the pen rather than the sword. The cause of the patriots in Spanish America seemed hopeless. New Granada appeared to be certain to fall into the hands of the Spaniards; in point of fact Cartagena was taken soon afterward, in December, 1815, and early in 1816 Bogotá and the rest of the country submitted. Only the Plata region was still under patriot control. Yet, in September, 1815, Bolívar published one of his greatest documents. Over the years from the outbreak of the wars to the death of the Liberator, Bolívar was to write many an important *manifiesto* or *pronunciamento*, such for example as the already mentioned address to the people of New Granada, but there are three of his papers which have been regarded as outstanding in their influence beyond all others. The first of them was the one now being referred to, in the form of a letter to a friend, but really intended to influence public opinion in Europe and the United States. The other two were his address to the Congress of Angostura in 1819 and the constitution which he prepared for Bolivia in 1826. Like the two last-named documents, Bolívar's letter of 1815 is noteworthy mainly for its political significance, wherefore it belongs more properly in the story of the republican era, but it may be observed here that not for a moment did he contemplate the possibility of Spanish victory. Most of his letter was concerned with prophecy as to what the Spanish American countries would be, after their independence had been won. Perhaps the normal view at that time would have been that if the colonies had shown an inability to cope with Spain when the latter was busy with the wars against Napoleon, they had slight chance of success now that she was free to send her armies overseas. But Bolívar had no doubt of the issue. Nor was this bluster. Few of his documents discussing conditions are in a calmer tone. Bolívar was still undaunted and unconquered, and ready to renew the conflict at the first opportunity.

In 1816 Bolívar began another campaign, which proved notable only for its disasters. Going to Haiti, he received aid from President Alexandre Pétion and several foreign merchants, and with a small force headed for Margarita Island, where Arismendi had again raised the standard of revolt. Arriving there in May, Bolívar was recognized as the commander-in-chief, with Mariño second in command. Soon afterward, he issued a proclamation freeing the slaves, as he had promised Pétion he would do, and also announced the abolition of his former "war to the death" policy against the Spaniards. There followed a brief series of movements on the mainland, in which Morales, the Spanish general, defeated Bolívar. Once more he was blamed for the failure, and threatened with death by his companions, Mariño and Juan Bermúdez, but finally was obliged by them to reëmbark for Haiti. Various patriot bands made their way into the far interior, to the plains of Venezuela. There, although they were able to maintain themselves, they soon recognized the need of a leader who might be the supreme commander. Hence, Bolívar was invited to return. The Liberator required no very great urging. In December he landed at Barcelona in the east, and presently advanced toward Caracas. In January, 1817, he encountered a royalist force, and was again defeated.

From this unhappy experience Bolívar derived much profit, because he now became convinced that his direct attempts to recover Caracas must prove unavailing. He therefore decided upon a plan which was eventually to bring victory. In the interior, in the basin of the Orinoco, the Spaniards would be at a great disadvantage if they endeavored to attack him. So he proposed to operate there.

At this time, too, the patriot leaders were beginning to recruit troops among the *llaneros*, who had been of such assistance to the royalists in the terrible Boves days. The Spaniards were soon driven out of the province of Guayana, following the occupation of Angostura (now Ciudad Bolívar) in July, 1817.

Bolívar now had to contend with a much more serious enemy than the Spaniards, in the form of dissension within the patriot ranks. Mariño at one time set up a new Federalist government, with himself as commander-in-chief of the army, but was chastened by defeat, when the Spaniards attacked him, and outwardly made peace with Bolívar. More difficult to deal with were the jealousies of the whites engendered among the mulattoes and *mestizos*. Several of the guerrilla chieftains in the patriot forces were responsible for this feeling. Most noteworthy among them was General Manuel Piar, a violent and cruel man, who nevertheless had won some spectacular victories. Piar, joining with Mariño, was soon in open rebellion. After several months of maneuvering, Piar was surprised and captured. Tried by a council of war, he was condemned to death as a deserter and mutineer, and was shot in the presence of the whole army. Meanwhile, Mariño saw fit to retire to Margarita Island, and he was not again prominent during the war. The execution of Piar accomplished a very necessary thing. It firmly established the authority of Bolívar, heretofore rather insecure, at the same time introducing something of morale and discipline into the patriot forces.

At about this time a man was coming to the fore in western Venezuela who was to be one of the most notable of the patriot leaders, José Antonio Páez. He soon became the idol of the half-savage *llaneros*. During the remainder of the war Páez was responsible for some astonishing feats of arms. On one occasion he promised to have boats ready to enable Bolívar's army to cross the Apure River. When Bolívar arrived, the only boats in sight were those belonging to the enemy on the other side. "Where are your boats?" Bolívar asked. "There they are," replied Páez, pointing to those of the Spaniards. Then getting together a group of fifty *llanero* horsemen he called out to them "To the water, my boys! Follow your uncle!" With that, in the face of the Spanish fire, Páez led a cavalry charge *through the river*, and captured the fourteen boats on the opposite shore. This must have been one of very few instances in history when what might be called a naval battle was won by a charge of cavalry! Nevertheless, when Morillo returned to Venezuela from New Granada in 1816, Páez had been obliged to retire from the positions he had conquered in the west and join Bolívar. Bolívar also was unsuccessful in his campaigns against Morillo in the direction of Cumaná, late in 1817 and early in 1818, and had to retreat to Angostura. Once more the patriot cause seemed lost, but Bolívar, far from being cast down, announced plans for calling a congress and establishing a regular government, and also for crossing the Andes to liberate New Granada!

Important events were now going on abroad which were to have a great influence upon the course of the wars. Spain herself was leaving Morillo to fight her battles, without further reinforcements of any account to help him, but there were hopes that the powers of the Holy Alliance might assist Spain in regaining her colonies. It was clear, however, that England and the United States would oppose any such plan, which made it fairly certain that the effort would not be made. Meanwhile, the United States recognized the belligerency of the Venezuelan patriots in December, 1817, and individual Americans and Englishmen enlisted in the patriot service by the thousands. The Americans were more prominent in the privateers, which almost swept Spanish shipping from the seas. The English were much more to the fore, however, in the Venezuelan sector of the wars. Despite the complaints of the Spanish minister to London, the Venezuelan diplomatic agent, Luis López Méndez, carried on activities in England which were as significant as those of Bolívar in the field. He was able to obtain more than a million pounds sterling from English merchants, hungry for trade, and to buy munitions and other equipment in great quantities. Moreover, soldiers were recruited, mostly in England and to some extent in Germany, to reinforce the army of the Liberator. During the years 1817 to 1820 over five thousand men sailed from

British ports for Venezuela, well trained and fully armed. Most of these were incorporated in what came to be called the "British Legion." They upset the advantage which hitherto had lain with Morillo, and eventually gave the patriots a chance to take the offensive.

On February 15, 1819, the new congress met at Angostura, and it was at this time that Bolívar delivered his previously mentioned famous address. Congress elected Bolívar president of the republic, and made him dictator in the war areas. Bolívar went ahead with his long dreamed of plans for the liberation of New Granada, which he now regarded as forming a part, with Venezuela, of a republic of Colombia—another of his dreams. During June and July, leaving his cavalry in Venezuela, and coöperating with Francisco de Paula Santander, a prominent New Granada leader, Bolívar took his infantry, and set out for the passage of the Andes at one of its highest and most difficult points. The idea was to strike close to Bogotá at a place and under circumstances which would make it less easy for the enemy to defend themselves against him. With some two thousand men, including the British Legion, Bolívar achieved the great exploit of crossing the cordillera in a desert region and at an altitude of thirteen thousand feet. Many perished from cold or other hardship, but the main body of the troops got through. On August 7, 1819, the royalist army was destroyed in the battle of Boyacá, and three days later Bolívar entered Bogotá. Boyacá was to New Granada what Chacabuco and Maipú had been, shortly before, for Chile. It broke the Spanish power in New Granada, and with the failure of Ferdinand VII to send any more military aid from the peninsula the royalist supremacy was never again revived.

Bolívar quickly returned to Venezuela amidst the ovations of his countrymen, and in December proposed a constitution for the republic of Colombia, which was to include Venezuela, Cundinamarca, and Quito, or, in terms of modern countries, Venezuela, Colombia, and Ecuador. Congress enacted his suggestion into law, and Cúcuta (in New Granada near the Venezuelan border) was selected as the capital until such time as a city of "Bolívar" could be

Antonio José de Sucre

founded. In 1820 there occurred the already often-mentioned Riego revolt in Spain, which not only prevented the sending of a large Spanish army to the Americas, but also restored the Liberal party to power. There followed negotiations between Bolívar and the Spanish generals, with an armistice for a time, but it was impossible to agree on terms of peace. It was during this period that Morillo, whose efforts on behalf of Spain had deserved a better lot than fate accorded him, was given permission to return to Europe, being succeeded by General Miguel de La Torre. By now, the Spaniards held little more than the region between Caracas and Cumaná. On June 24, 1821, Bolívar decisively defeated La Torre at the battle of Carabobo, and five days later reëntered his native city of Caracas. Just as Boyacá had been in New Granada, so was Carabobo in Venezuela. The war in that sector was virtually over.

It was now decided to reduce Quito, or Ecuador, which had remained in royalist hands since the abortive revolutions of 1809 and 1811. Bolívar wanted not only to defeat the Spaniards, but also to prevent this territory from being taken over by San Martín's government of Peru. Once again in 1820 the patriots of Ecuador had risen against the Spaniards, proclaiming their independence, and appealing to Bolívar for assistance. Bolívar sent one of his best officers, Antonio José de Sucre, with about a thousand men. From this time forth Sucre was to prove himself one of the greatest military geniuses of the wars.

Born on February 3, 1795, at Cumaná, Sucre was only fifteen years of age at the outbreak of hostilities in 1810. Nevertheless, he enlisted in the patriot armies almost immediately. Curiously enough, he did not meet Bolívar until the latter was returning to Venezuela, after the battle of Boyacá. They quickly became the warmest of friends, the "Achilles and Patroclus of the American Iliad," they have been called. Perhaps as good a description as any of this splendid character is one attributed to Bolívar, as follows:

> "Sucre has the best intellect in all Colombia. He is methodical, and capable of the most lofty conceptions. He is the best general of the republic, and its leading statesman. His principles are

excellent and firmly rooted, and his morality is exemplary. He has a great, strong soul. He knows how to persuade men and to lead them. And he knows how to judge them . . . He is the bravest of the brave, the most loyal of the loyal, the friend of law and not of despotism, partisan of good order, the enemy of anarchy. And finally he is a true liberal." [1]

San Martín did not know Sucre personally, but he had corresponded with him, and had a high opinion of him. To a Frenchman who asked him for an expression of his views, he had this to say:

"Brave and active, he joined with these qualities to a high degree a great prudence; and he was a most excellent administrator, as is proved by the good order and satisfactory economic situation of the provinces where he was in command. The troops under his orders observed a severe discipline, which contributed to make him beloved by the people, whose interests he respected, thus diminishing the inevitable evils of war. General Sucre was exceedingly well informed; he also possessed a knowledge of military affairs which was more extensive than that of Bolívar. If to these traits are added those of great moderation and much modesty, one will be convinced that he was one of the most meritorious men of the republic of Colombia." [2]

Embarking at Buenaventura, Sucre's little army reached Guayaquil in May, 1821. In the ensuing operations, yielding to the requests of his subordinates and against his better judgment, Sucre engaged the enemy in the battle of Ambato, and was defeated. This had at least one important result. Sucre asked San Martín for a reinforcement from Peru, and the generous Argentinian sent him between 1300 and 1400 men. Later, when it became evident that Bolívar intended to utilize them in a conquest for Colombia, with San Martín claiming Ecuador for Peru, orders were sent for their return. Nevertheless, Sucre was able to persuade them to remain for the battle which proved to be decisive in this section. Meanwhile, Bolívar hastened southward from Bogotá with an army, intending to march overland to Quito. Meeting a royalist force near the borders of Colombia and Ecuador, he won what has been called

[1] Quoted in Mitre, III, 546–547.

[2] Lafond, Gabriel, *Voyages dans l'Amérique espagnole pendant les guerres de l'indépendance* (2v. Paris, 1843), II, 144.

the "Pyrrhic victory" of Bomboná, in which he lost nearly three times as many men as his opponents, and was stopped in his tracks, unable to advance, and, indeed, in difficult straits in the extraordinarily wild mountain country of that region.[1] Fortunately for him, it was just at this time that Sucre, maneuvering with remarkable skill, was able at last to inflict a crushing defeat upon the Spaniards. He posted his troops on Mount Pichincha, a volcano which towers above the city of Quito, itself a mile above sea level. The battle took place on May 24, 1822, and the following day Sucre entered Quito. Both there and in the north where Bolívar was operating, the royalists surrendered, and Bolívar himself soon made his way to Quito.

The story has already been told of the meeting of Bolívar and San Martín, and of the withdrawal of the latter from Peru. The various Peruvian governments which followed met with nothing but disaster in their campaigns against the Spaniards. In 1823 the patriot armies were badly defeated at Torata, Moquegua, and Zepita, and Lima once more fell into the enemy's possession. Requests were meanwhile being made of Bolívar for assistance. He sent several thousand men, and early in September, 1823, he himself disembarked in Callao. At once he was given supreme military and political command.

The situation was extremely difficult. The viceroy, La Serna, who had some eighteen thousand men under arms, soon retook Callao. Bolívar had about ten thousand men at his disposal, but fortunately obtained a great advantage through dissension in the ranks of the royalists. There had been another revolution in Spain, in 1823, and this time the reactionary Conservatives came back to power. The loyalists in Peru were divided as between Liberal and Conservative policies, and had a civil war among themselves which diverted nearly half their forces from the campaign against Bolívar. Climbing the highest part of the Peruvian Andes,

[1] For a vivid description of the rough character of the territory through which Bolívar attempted to march, see Franck, Harry Alverson, *Vagabonding down the Andes* (New York, 1920), 85–126. The Franck account has much casual social comment, but makes it clear, nevertheless, that it is task enough for one man to get through that country in time of peace, let alone an army in the face of an enemy.

Bolívar at length assembled some nine thousand men in a plateau region twelve thousand feet above sea level. On August 6, 1824, he defeated General Canterac in the battle of Junín. Canterac retired in disorder toward Cuzco, losing over a third of his army in desertions along the way. Shortly afterward, Bolívar took leave of his troops, placing Sucre in command. La Serna now made a supreme effort, and got together some ten thousand men, although all but about five hundred Spaniards were natives of Spanish America, and their morale was none too strong. In their rear, too, the rebellious Liberalists were still carrying on a civil war. There followed a campaign worthy of close study by those interested in military history. At length, on December 9, 1824, the two armies came to grips. Sucre had only some six thousand men against nine thousand, but he had maneuvered into a position in the Valley of Ayacucho where he might have a chance of success. And success he had! The royalist army was utterly destroyed. La Serna was wounded and taken prisoner. Canterac, with the option of falling into the hands of either the patriots or the hostile Spanish Liberalists, chose the former, and surrendered the remnant of the beaten army that same day to Sucre.

The battle of Ayacucho is generally accepted as marking the real end of the wars of independence. There was some more desultory fighting in Bolivia; and the Spaniards held out in southern Chile, in the Island of Chiloé, until January 19, 1826, and in Peru at Callao until January 22, 1826. The surrender of Callao may be said to have been the last formal act of the wars. It was a number of years, however, before Spain recognized the independence of any of the New World republics.[1] Nevertheless, all that happened in a military sense after Ayacucho amounted to little more than mopping up the fragments of Spanish resistance. It would appear to be quite appropriate that at that celebrated battle participated soldiers who had fought in the Argentinian, Chilean, Peruvian, Ecuadorian, Colombian,

[1] Spain recognized the independence of Mexico in 1836. In course of time the other republics were also recognized, some of them not until several decades after 1836, however.

and Venezuelan theatres of the wars, as well as a few foreigners, some of whom had taken part in the great campaigns of the Napoleonic era in Europe. It brought enduring fame to the noble Sucre, who otherwise might have been relegated in reputation to a position no better than that of a score of the lesser generals. To Bolívar the victory of Ayacucho could have given no greater honors than he already possessed. To Sucre it lent a distinction which could hardly have found a more worthy subject.

The rest of the story concerning Bolívar and his great lieutenant, Sucre, may quickly be told at this point, reserving further discussion of their remaining achievements for the history of the republics. On August 6, 1825, the independence of Upper Peru was proclaimed by a congress of delegates at Chuquisaca (now Sucre), and a few days later the name of Bolívar, hence modern Bolivia, was formally adopted for the country. Bolívar was announced as the president of the new republic, with Sucre the supreme ruler in the absence of Bolívar. Early in 1826, Bolívar wrote his famous constitution for Bolivia, and shortly afterward transferred his own executive power to Sucre. With some modifications the constitution was adopted, though later cast into the discard. Sucre was elected president in October, 1826, but resigned, after an honorable but stormy rule, in August, 1828. Going to Quito, he joined his wife, to whom he had recently been married by proxy. There, in 1829, he was required to take the field again to meet a Peruvian invasion. The Peruvians found Sucre more than a match for them, and were driven from the country. In 1830, Sucre was in Colombia as a member of a commission which sought unsuccessfully to prevent the secession of Venezuela from Colombia. On his way back to Quito, while in southern Colombia, he was murdered on June 4 of that year, probably at the behest of the military commander of that district. Thus, at the early age of thirty-five, passed one of Hispanic America's favorite heroes. The man who might best have taken the place of Bolívar was summarily removed from the scene.

And what of Bolívar? Despairing at length of getting Bolivia and Peru to join in with his projects for Great

Colombia, and hearing of disorders in the north, he returned in 1826 to Bogotá. Thenceforth, his life was one running series of difficulties, including several attempts to assassinate him. On one occasion he was caught with his mistress, Manuela Sáenz, but while she held off the conspirators with adroit parleying, Bolívar jumped through a window and hid himself under a bridge. Great Colombia *independent* became a country rent asunder with private ambition and political dissension. Early in 1830 came Bolívar's last resignation, but this time it was requested of him, and there was no escape. Deeply disappointed in the result of his work and in failing health, he penned his farewell message to the Colombian Congress, remarking that "Independence is the only blessing which we have acquired, at the expense of everything else."

He resolved to leave the country, nevermore to return, and he was embittered yet more when he learned, a little later, of the assassination of Sucre. He even declared that he regretted the revolutions he had led, and refused medicines to restore his health, saying that he preferred to die. Upon his arrival at Cartagena he was asked to head a movement which would again have made him the supreme ruler of the republic, but, a mere shadow of his former self, he refused. "It is impossible for me to resume power," he wrote to a friend. "How can I help this nation when I no longer have even the strength to stand upright?" Early in December he came to Santa Marta, where, unable to walk, and sick unto death, he was persuaded to accept the services of a French physician. He suffered terribly, but never complained, though heart-broken over the ingratitude of his compatriots, and pessimistic over the future of the country. One day he asked the doctor what he had sought in coming to this part of the world.

"Freedom!" came the reply.

"You found it?" asked Bolívar.

"Yes, general," said the doctor.

"Well then," remarked Bolívar, "you are more fortunate than I. Go back to France, where I should like to accompany you. There is too much of a rabble here."

By this time the five regions to whose independence he

had contributed were no longer the one great country he had dreamed of, but the five countries they are today: Venezuela, Colombia, Ecuador, Peru, and Bolivia. And the two which owed him the most were uncompromisingly hostile in sentiment to him, especially his native Venezuela, where his old friend Páez had placed himself at the head of a separatist movement. Sinking rapidly, he at length received the last sacraments, after which his farewell proclamation to his countrymen was read. At one point it ran: "I have been the victim of my persecutors, and they have brought me to the gates of the tomb." Here Bolívar interrupted hoarsely: "Yes, to the gates of the tomb . . . that is where my fellow-citizens have consigned me . . . but I forgive them . . . Oh, that I might carry with me the consolation of knowing they will remain united!" On December 17, 1830, he died. His one-time great fortune gone, it is said that it was necessary to borrow money from the neighbors to meet the expenses of the funeral. Thus passed Bolívar—for all his faults, the greatest man of the period. He died bitterly disappointed—but his work lived on! And twelve years later a repentant Venezuela consented to receive his remains.

Bolívar and San Martín! San Martín and Bolívar! As Mitre says:

> "Both were great according to the measure of their opportunities (*en su medida*), the greatest men, after Washington, that America has produced, worthy of figuring in the universal pantheon as collaborators in human progress. Both fulfilled their redemptory mission in the order of events, the one giving the first signal for the continental war, the plan for which he conceived, and the other terminating it gloriously. Without San Martín in the south of the continent, and without Bolívar in the north, it is difficult to understand how that combination of revolutionary forces could have been effected which gave the final triumph, nor how the one without the other might have been able to complete the task of liberation." [1]

[1] Mitre, IV, 159–160.

CHAPTER XVI

THE WARS OF INDEPENDENCE: RELATIONS OF ENGLAND AND THE UNITED STATES

It does not need to be said that Spanish America and Spain did not fight their long series of wars in an air-tight compartment by themselves, unaffected by events elsewhere. Such a deviation from normal course as the conflicts represented was bound to, and did, have repercussions in Europe and the United States, and in a degree these affected the issue of the warfare itself. So, at least a few words must be said about this factor, before bringing the subject to a close. In general, continental Europe sympathized with Spain, and might have come to her assistance if it had not been for the opposition of England and the United States, especially of England, whose navy had proved itself to be an almost insuperable bar to any campaigning overseas. Public opinion in England and the United States favored the patriot cause, and it was possible for the people and the governments of these countries to render services of almost incalculable value in bringing about or preserving Spanish American independence. The question is sometimes raised as to which nation, through the medium of diplomacy or the assistance of individuals, gave the greater help, and anti-United States opinion in the southern republics has not infrequently tended to belittle that of the United States in comparison with England. To attempt even an approximate evaluation would be futile. It is probably true, however, that the then greater power of England, with the British navy, would tip the scales in her favor, even though there was a more genuinely widespread enthusiasm for Spanish American liberty in the United States, along with a great plenty in the way of substantial assistance.

In Great Britain the Spanish American wars were not taken up on their own merits, but were complicated with other factors. For many years, periodically between 1776 and 1808, the British authorities had given reason to Spanish America to expect help if any movement for independence should begin. Especially from 1790 onward, Great Britain frequently considered plans for revolutionizing the Spanish colonies. This explains the consideration shown to Miranda at the British court, which was usually hostile to Spain, when not openly at war, down to 1808. The mercantile classes were always conscious of the wealth which might be obtained through the medium of Spanish American trade, and did not fail to impress their views upon those in power. On the other hand, the government had to consider the general situation in Europe. From 1808 to 1814 England was an ally of Spain against Napoleon. After that, England cooled toward the absolute Ferdinand VII, who proposed to restore the restrictive colonial system, which would have shut out British trade, but an open break with Spain might have resulted in complications with England's other allies in Europe.

So England gave no direct assistance to Spanish America until 1823, endeavoring to play the double game of maintaining friendly relations with Spain and yet of participating in Spanish American commerce as much as possible. The two things were incompatible, and involved the government in much left-handed aid to Spanish America, although it was not openly admitted; indeed, a sincere effort appears to have been made to preserve British neutrality, with laws being enacted to prevent the sales of munitions to the patriots or the enlistment of soldiers for their armies. It proved impossible to enforce these laws, however. Even the recognition of the new governments was delayed until the clamor of the merchants compelled the authorities to take action. In fact, there was very little sympathy *as such* in England for the patriot cause. The prince-regent, later to become George IV in 1820, was bitter over the separation of the United States from England, and this and his narrowly aristocratic, undemocratic instincts made him favor Spain over any Spanish American *republics*. The Conservatives were in power, and the "best people" often followed the king, but commercial interest, as opposed to mere sentiment, was enough to influence the government in its decisions. Eventually, the military achievements of some of the noteworthy British leaders fighting on the patriot side attracted attention, and their services have been cordially remembered in Spanish America ever since. Lord Cochrane, who incidentally was Scotch, and Admiral William Brown and General William Miller, who happen to have been Irish,[1] were the most famous of these, but there were a number of others. Furthermore, as already pointed out, thousands of unemployed veterans of the Napoleonic wars were enlisted in the patriot service, especially under the standards of Bolívar.

Down to 1820, the British authorities were not even avowed opponents of intervention by other European countries on behalf of Spain, although Viscount Castlereagh, the British prime minister, appears to have given some hints as early as 1817 that there should be no armed interference by continental Europe in Spanish America, except on such terms as England might dictate. Russia at one time seemed willing to help Spain, but would not do it alone. The post-Napoleonic French monarchy sympathized with Spain, but France had no commercial interest in Spanish America, and so would not incur the expense of entering the war. The turning-point in British policy came at the time of the Spanish Liberalist revolution of 1820, when Ferdinand VII appealed to other European monarchs for assistance in the name of the suppression of democratic movements. Castlereagh did not like the idea of Spanish American *republics*, but he was equally opposed to the establishment of monarchies under the protection of France, and by this time he and his colleagues were firmly resolved that there should be no restoration of the Spanish colonial system.

By 1822 the virtual independence of Spanish America and the United States recognition of some of the new governments stirred the British merchants to renewed efforts on behalf of a British recognition. In 1823, France sent an army into Spain which restored the absolutism of Ferdinand VII, and this at least awakened the British ministry to a policy of insistence that the French intervention must not be carried overseas; in a conference of October 9, 1823,

[1] Miller was born in England, but is often referred to as "the Irishman."

George Canning (the successor of Castlereagh) told Polignac, the French minister, that foreign interference in the affairs of the Spanish colonies would be the signal for an immediate British recognition of independence; the possibility that this might be accompanied by direct military support must have been borne in upon the minds of Spain's friends in continental Europe. British consuls now began to be sent to Spanish America; commercial recognition had been extended as early as June, 1822, although without any political recognition of the new governments. Canning had some discussions with Richard Rush, the United States minister, to see if England might count on the United States, if France should attempt to aid Spain in America. It was clear that the United States would strongly oppose any such European action. At length, in 1825, the government of the United Provinces of the Plata was recognized, in part in deference to British commercial propaganda, but also in retaliation for the French occupation of Spain. The French troops had overstayed their time in the peninsula, and there was a considerable criticism of the British government for having allowed them to go in there at all. It was by way of meeting this attack, and not with reference to his alleged suggestion of the Monroe Doctrine, that Canning made his famous boast in 1826:

> "I looked another way—I sought compensation in another hemisphere . . . I resolved that, if France had Spain, it should not be Spain *with the Indies*. I called the New World into existence to redress the balance of the Old."

Based, as this was, on the mere fact of British recognition, the boast falls somewhat flat. Spanish America had won her own independence, and she had been recognized by the United States nearly three years before the English recognition. Furthermore, there had been no public British pronouncement even remotely approximating that of the United States in the Monroe Doctrine. Nevertheless, there was always the British navy in the background, accompanying the known opposition of England to any European intervention in Spanish America—as evidenced, for example, in Canning's statement to Polignac. The British recognition of 1825 was protested by Spain, Austria, Prussia, and Russia, but no further action was taken. All in all, British assistance to Spanish America in the era of the wars was great, whatever may have been the guiding motives.

In the United States the attitude of the *people*, as distinct from the government, was, from the first, one of profound satisfaction and sympathy with respect to the patriot cause. The terms "liberty" and "independence" were words to conjure with in those days in the United States, and the analogy of the American Revolution against England suggested itself very readily. Furthermore, Spain was exceedingly unpopular. People hated her absolutism, and there were constantly recurring disputes over the opening of the Mississippi and over Florida to inflame popular opinion. The enthusiasm on behalf of the revolutionists was almost wholly altruistic, since the United States trade with Spanish America was then, and for many years after the founding of the republics, a thing of small account, and United States investment was almost nil. American sympathy expressed itself in various ways. Articles in newspapers and other writings kept the subject constantly before the minds of the people. Presently it crept into politics, and became a live issue, especially after 1815, when the war of the United States and England had come to an end and the era of Spanish American declarations of independence had begun. Henry Clay, one of the leading political figures of those times, espoused the Spanish American cause, and employed it as one of his favorite weapons in debate. Government officials generally, including the presidents, felt sympathy for Spanish America as individuals, even though in their public capacity they drew back. Furthermore, thousands of Americans enlisted under patriot banners, as is hereinafter pointed out.

There has been a disposition in recent years among anti-United States elements in Spanish America to deny that the people or government of the United States gave any help toward the winning of Spanish American independence.[1]

[1] A good illustration of this Spanish American practice is to be found in the controversy between the historian Matías Romero, then Mexican minister to the United States, and Senator Money, appearing in several numbers of the *North American review* for the year 1897.

Not to mention statements which are untrue, there are writings of Spanish Americans in which the facts are selected in such a way as to make out a case against the United States *government;* they imply that it was at fault when it was only observing its duty under international law, omitting material which might warrant a more favorable view, and especially failing to give due weight to the real sympathy and aid of the American *people.* As for the action of the government, the uncertainty of affairs in Spanish America must be borne in mind. In the first place, it was a long time before the different regions declared their independence, and then there arose many subsidiary questions. What nation did they represent, and what were the national boundaries? And, in the midst of the dissensions and revolutions within the revolutions themselves—those between the Unitarists and Federalists of the Plata, for example—which faction was the one to be recognized? [1] It would not have been fair to Spain to accord recognition before independence had been won, and in an age which had no steamboats, railways, cables, telephones, telegraphs, wireless, or radio it was difficult to obtain early or reliable information. Yet, the United States was the first important outside country to recognize the independence of the new republics, and the Monroe Doctrine was a material help in assuring the victory which Spanish America had already won. There is nothing that can be said against the United States which cannot be said with even greater reason against England, with vastly more reason than that against France, and with overwhelmingly more reason against the rest of continental Europe. Unfortunately, however, all of the attacks are against the United States, and they represent the *feeling* of a considerable body of opinion in Spanish America. It is therefore worth a little space here in a measure to demonstrate the injustice of this view.

When word first came of the outbreaks in Spanish America, the government of the United States took steps to keep itself informed of the progress of the movements, sending

[1] In a speech of March 28, 1818, Representative Smith of Maryland argued against a recognition of the Buenos Aires government, since it would inflict an injury on the "gallant and brave Republican, General Artigas." Bealer, *op. cit.*, 147.

agents to the regions where the revolutions had broken out. The first of these was Joel Roberts Poinsett of South Carolina, something of a gentleman adventurer, a wealthy man who had traveled widely in Europe, and who had had the opportunity of declining a post in the service of the Russian czar. At a later time, in the post-independence period, he was to be quite prominent in connection with United States relations with Mexico, and still later was minister of war in President Van Buren's cabinet. Instructions were issued to him on June 28, 1810, to go to Buenos Aires, and possibly to Chile and Peru if circumstances should make it seem desirable, and to keep the Washington authorities advised as to the course of events. He was reminded of the possibility of the Spanish American provinces severing the ties which bound them to Europe, and was to communicate an impression of the good will of the United States, whatever governments or relations with Europe they might have; if they should separate from Spain and establish their independence, he was to let them know that the United States would want to promote the most friendly relations with them. Poinsett was in South America for more than four years, and acted as if he were the consul and minister for the United States, though not officially so called, lest that might imply recognition of the patriot governments even before they had declared their independence. Indeed, he interpreted his duties so liberally that at one time while he was in Chile in the Carrera period he actually held a military command in the patriot forces. In this he exceeded his instructions, of course, but he was not censured for his action.[1]

[1] Stillé, Charles Janeway, "The life and services of Joel R. Poinsett," in *Pennsylvania magazine of history and biography*, XII (129–164, 257–303; July and Oct., 1888), 154–155, tells the following interesting story of Poinsett's military experiences in Chile:

"To complete his mission it was necessary for him to cross the Andes and negotiate a treaty with the authorities of Chili. This province was then governed by the popular Junta, while Peru was still under the authority of the Spanish Viceroy. The two provinces were engaged in war with each other, so that until the war ended it was impossible to tell whether it would be practicable to conclude such a treaty as Mr. Poinsett was instructed to make. There seemed, indeed, little probability that hostilities would soon be brought to a close. Mr. Poinsett became irritated by the helpless inactivity which he was obliged to maintain. Fired by the example of Carera [*sic*], the leader of the Chilian army, and yielding to his influence, he was induced by him to

Numerous other agents were sent to Buenos Aires and other parts of Spanish America, and they were constantly reminded of the secret interest of the higher officials of the United States in the possibility of independence. For example, in a letter to Poinsett from James Monroe, then secretary of state, dated April 30, 1811, it was remarked that the disposition of the Spanish provinces to separate from Spain and establish independent countries "excites great interest here." Monroe went on to assert that our relations would then be much more intimate and our friendship stronger than if they were colonies subject to a European power. And this was in the days when Spanish America was still in the early stages of battling "in the name of Ferdinand VII!" This Monroe letter and many similar communications sounded very much like a hint to the Spanish American governments to declare their independence. It is clear that the United States was waiting only for the right moment to come when recognition might be accorded, and the "right moment" would be when the colonies had declared their independence and were assured of victory in the war with Spain.

The United States Congress early showed a tendency in the direction of recognition. When news came of the Venezuelan declaration of independence in 1811, a special committee of Congress reported a resolution expressing "friendly solicitude" and a readiness, whenever the Spanish American governments should "by a just exercise of their rights"

accept the command of a division of his army. He could, it is true, find nothing in his instructions as *Chargé d'Affaires* to justify such an act, but he never was idle or inactive when the interests of his country required him to confront personal danger, and he did not hesitate to take the responsibility. Shortly after he had assumed command, he learned, through an intercepted letter to the Viceroy of Peru, that the commandant at Talcahuano, on the bay of Concepcion, had seized eleven American whalers which had touched there for supplies, and that the crews of these vessels would be sent to Callao as prisoners as soon as a 'set of irons could be completed for the purpose of securing the men.' He immediately put his army in motion for Talcahuano and completely surprised the Peruvian detachment in charge of the vessels. He then posted his artillery in a commanding position and demanded its unconditional surrender to the Junta of Chili. His demand was at once complied with, the Peruvian commander who 'was completing the irons' was made prisoner and the vessels were released. It is not easy, of course, to describe the surprise and gratification of the American captains when they found that their liberator was one of their own countrymen, exercising his functions as *Chargé d'Affaires* in this novel and efficient way."

become nations, to unite with the president to establish relations with them. Almost from the beginning the patriot governments were accorded the rights of belligerents, which, among other things, permitted their ships to make use of United States ports. It was several years, however, before anything could be done about recognition, not only because most of the Spanish American colonies had not yet declared their independence, but also because in the earlier campaigns the Spanish arms were successful. By 1817 a changed situation had developed. The provinces of the Plata had declared for independence in the previous year, and San Martín had won the important battle of Chacabuco in Chile in the spring of 1817. It was decided to send a commission to South America to learn what was really going on, so that the United States might be ready for eventualities. When the members of this commission returned, late in 1818, no two of them could agree. One of them wrote a glowing report. A second member would not sign it. And the third, who had been an enthusiast for independence when he left for South America, had no confidence in the patriots at all when he returned. As an official commission they had been very well received, but had found it difficult to get at the facts. Nevertheless, they had been able to observe the political instability and civil conflicts in the countries they had visited, and had information that the Spanish forces were still strong in Peru and Upper Peru. As a result, Monroe, now president, was obliged to continue a neutral course, although his impulse had been in favor of independence; indeed, but for his clear-visioned secretary of state, John Quincy Adams, he might have risked recognition anyway, but Adams convinced him that it was not yet the proper time.

Henry Clay had long been an ardent supporter of the patriot cause, but from 1817 on, as a member of the House, he was especially active on behalf of independence. A brilliant and romantic orator, he delivered speeches which had a wide effect throughout the Western Hemisphere; many of them were translated into Spanish and read to the patriot armies in the field, and his name was a household word in Spanish America. Clay was not alone; on several occasions congressmen arose even from sick-beds to speak in advocacy of the measures which Clay recommended. But, for the time being, the majority, although their hearts were with Clay, preferred to follow the dictates of propriety and expediency, influenced in part by a fear that precipitate action might hinder the negotiations for the purchase of Florida from Spain. With this last-named issue approaching solution over the years 1819 to 1821, Congress moved rapidly in the direction of recognition, having also the more reason because of the trend toward patriot success. Early in 1821 Clay got two resolutions through the House. The first was to the effect that the House joined with the people of the United States in sympathy for the South American peoples in their war with Spain. This passed, 134 to twelve. In the second, the House announced that it was ready to support the president whenever he might think it expedient to recognize the South American governments. The vote for this was eighty-six to sixty-eight. This marked the climax of Clay's official efforts, as he retired from the House in that same year. It has been claimed that his many years of pleading on behalf of Spanish America did not bring recognition a day nearer, but he certainly did a great deal to crystallize American public opinion in favor of Spanish America and against European intervention; in so doing he had his share in producing the Monroe Doctrine, besides influencing those thousands of his fellow-citizens who took an active part in the conflict.

The real man in the driver's seat at the White House in Spanish American questions after 1817 was, not Monroe, but Adams. He had to contend with, not only popular clamor, the attacks of Clay and Congress, and the disposition of Monroe to yield, but also his own feelings as an individual. Clay himself was not more convinced of the justice of the Spanish American cause or more desirous of independence, but Adams, with a clear-headed perception of the facts, wanted to be sure he was right before he committed the government of the United States. He had troubles with the Spanish ministers, who complained over the departure of Spanish American privateers from United States ports, and threatened not to ratify the Florida purchase treaty. He was pestered by the Spanish American agents, demanding recognition, even before they had been instructed to ask for it, giving licenses for and equipping the privateers in the ports of the country, and generally acting in an annoying and undiplomatic fashion. He was bothered by the too generous zeal of the American agents in South America, as for example the one who, "swelling upon his agency into a self-accredited Plenipotentiary," as Adams put it, made a treaty of commerce with Buenos Aires, which would have implied recognition.[1] He even had difficulty in holding back his colleagues in the Cabinet. Yet, all the time, his letters to the United States ministers in Europe stressed the opposition of the United States "to a third-party intervention of any sort," and asked that the European governments should consider the question of a recognition of the Spanish American republics.

At last, in 1821, it seemed as if the proper moment had come. A stable government was set up in Buenos Aires which began paying its debts in gold and recalled the privateers, revoking their commissions; San Martín had captured Lima; Bolívar had won the great battle of Carabobo; and Iturbide had overthrown the Spanish power in Mexico. In other words, independence had been achieved. Furthermore, the Florida purchase treaty of 1819 had at length been ratified by Spain in 1821. The United States now rapidly approached recognition. Monroe's annual message of December, 1821, foreshadowed the definitive announcement of the new policy. On March 8, 1822, Monroe sent a message to Congress, recommending the recognition of

[1] According to Paxson, 153: "His own agents caused him the greatest trouble. In one of the revolts in Buenos Ayres, Devereux guaranteed a loan that saved the life of the existing government. For this he was dismissed in 1817 by the predecessor of Mr. Adams. His successors, Worthington and Halsey, did little better. The former, 'swelling upon his agency' until he broke out 'into a self-accredited Plenipotentiary,' negotiated a commercial treaty on his own responsibility. The latter entered into privateering schemes and sent blank commissions to the United States. He was summarily removed."

Another writer says that John Devereux made the loan, and that Thomas Lloyd Halsey, then United States consul at Buenos Aires, guaranteed it, being disavowed later by the Washington authorities. This same Halsey had several times before urged his government to lend money and supply arms to the insurgents of Argentina—or the United Provinces of the Río de la Plata, as the country was known officially in those days. Devereux presently received an appointment as a general in the armies of the Plata. Cf. Chandler, 92–99.

the South American republics. The appropriate bills were soon prepared and passed, and on June 19, 1822, Manuel Torres was presented to Monroe by Adams as the representative of Colombia. This was the first formal act by any important country, outside of Hispanic America itself, in recognition of a Spanish American government. Over the course of the next few years, the other prominent countries of Spanish America were recognized by the United States.

A more important action was to come with the Monroe Doctrine pronouncement of 1823. Canning and the United States minister, Richard Rush, held a number of conferences which made it clear that the attitude of England and the United States would be the same in opposing European intervention, but Rush told Canning he had no authority to agree to a joint action of the United States with England. At the same time, he urged British recognition of the Spanish American governments, to which the British authorities were at that moment distinctly opposed. Nevertheless, the United States could now feel assured of the support of England in any policy as against European assistance to Spain. So, at Adams's suggestion, the United States decided to act independently of England, and the Adams-written "Monroe Doctrine" was the result. It appeared in two widely separated paragraphs of Monroe's annual message, December 2, 1823. The first of the pertinent statements grew out of a mention of the Russian aggressions in the Pacific northwest, and went on to remark that the American continents were "henceforth not to be considered as subjects for future colonization" by *any* European powers. The second made specific reference to the Spanish American countries, which had established their independence, and to recent activities of the continental European powers in helping other members of their group to recover territory or authority they had lost. With these European monarchies in mind, the message asserted that "We should consider any attempt on their part to extend their system to any portion of this hemisphere as dangerous to our peace and safety." Elsewhere the message disclaimed any intention of interfering with the existing colonies or dependencies of European powers in the Americas.

As might have been expected, the Monroe Doctrine was roundly berated in continental Europe. In England the pro-recognition elements, noticing only the second part of the pronouncement, received it with enthusiasm, but Canning was far from pleased. He saw the bearing of the first clause, and that it hit England as well as continental Europe.[1] In South America the Doctrine was acclaimed by governments, press, and public. Santander, the vice-president of Colombia and acting president in Bolívar's absence, referred to it in a message to the Colombian Congress as "Eminently just,—an act worthy of the classic land of liberty." Bolívar himself is said to have mentioned it favorably. The Buenos Aires government, in its report of December, 1824, to the Congress of the Plata provinces, spoke of the United States as having "constituted itself guardian of the field of battle, in order to prevent any foreign assistance being introduced in the aid of our rival." These are fair statements as to the importance of the Monroe Doctrine in the background of the maintenance of Spanish American independence. Spanish America had won it, but England and the United States made sure that the effort would not have been in vain.[2]

The recognition of the new republics by the United States, the Monroe Doctrine, and the later efforts of the United States to get Spain and other countries to recognize the independence of Spanish America constitute probably the greatest assistance on the part of the United States to the patriot cause. Interesting and important services were, nevertheless, rendered by individual Americans. There was no organized American group such as the "British Legion," but many citizens of the northern republic fought in the patriot armies, although perhaps more often in the Mexican sector of the field than elsewhere. A number of

[1] "Canning, however, saw the bearing of it and objected to the principle it set forth . . . He was evidently a little taken aback at the turn his proposal had taken." Latané, John Holladay, *The United States and Latin America* (New York, 1920), 78. The proposal referred to was Canning's suggestion to Rush that Great Britain and the United States should make a joint declaration of policy concerning Spanish American affairs.

[2] This is not the place to discuss the Monroe Doctrine from the standpoint of its later very important bearing on the relations of the United States with Hispanic America. Obviously, that story belongs to the era of the republics.

veterans of the War of 1812 enlisted later in the organized navies of Argentina, Chile, and Colombia, and some of them rose to high rank. Thousands sailed on the Spanish American privateers, most of which were fitted out in United States ports, especially Baltimore.

Adams himself admitted to the Spanish minister that the privateers were manned primarily by Americans. They rendered great services against Spain. The Spanish ships were as unsafe upon the high seas as they had been against the buccaneers of the seventeenth century, unless convoyed by a battle fleet—and Spain now had few men-of-war. To be sure, the privateers were not too careful whom they attacked, and at times differed very little from the category of pirates. Some went to a Spanish American port before going out as a privateer, but others never saw Spanish America at all, although provided with a license from a Spanish American agent. Out of thirty-six privateers which were the most successful of those operating in the Atlantic under the flag of the United Provinces of the Plata, or Argentina, from 1815 to 1821, thirty-one were fitted out in United States ports; one of the others was equipped in Buenos Aires, but the captain and a majority of the crew were citizens of the United States.[1] Prizes were taken in sight of the Spanish city of Cádiz, but the favorite field of operations was the West Indies; the nearness of the United States ports in which the captive boats and their cargoes could be disposed of was a prime factor in the choice of the West Indies as a cruising ground.[2] The Swedish island of St. Bartholomew (now French) was one of the principal bases, possibly the most important, of the Buenos Aires privateers in the West Indies. The United States government was sincerely opposed to the privateers, and made every effort to check their activity, hunting them down, restoring prizes they captured, and discharging public officials who gave them their support. On the whole, however, this action was ineffective, for whenever a case came before a jury it was impossible to secure a conviction; this was es-

[1] Currier, Theodore Shirley, *Los corsarios del Río de la Plata* (Buenos Aires, 1929), 20.

[2] Cf. *ibid.*, 21–22.

pecially true in Baltimore. The practical result was that the ports of the United States, Baltimore preferred, became perhaps the principal base for privateering operations against Spain.[1]

The services of the United States citizens in the regular military or naval units of the patriot governments were not so spectacular and not so combined in large groups as were the English. To be sure, it was mainly Americans who accompanied Miranda in his early descents upon Venezuela, and considerable bodies of them fought together in Texas, then under Mexico, and under some of the patriot leaders in northern Mexico. In the South American field, except as concerns the privateers, the American participation was more a haphazard individual matter. Much study is necessary before the full story can be told. Nevertheless, the records of a number of Americans are available, at least in part, and it is perhaps worth while to say something about a few of them, by way of illustration.

Perhaps the most distinguished American in the wars was Charles Whiting Wooster, who rose to become a rear-admiral and the commander-in-chief of the Chilean navy. A grandson of David Wooster, one of the eight brigadier-generals named by the United States in 1776, he was born at New Haven, Connecticut, in 1780. He went to sea when only eleven years of age, and at twenty-one was captain of an American merchantman. In the War of 1812, he was commander of the privateer "Saratoga," capturing twenty-two British vessels, including the privateer "Rachael," which he took after a battle off the port of La Guaira. He is believed to have met José Miguel Carrera, one of the famous Carrera brothers of Chile, when that individual was in the United States in 1816. Certainly Carrera induced many Americans to go to South America at that time. Wooster was ready for adventure, as his wife had just died and he had no ties to hold him back; accordingly, he took command of the armed bark "Columbus," which left New York late in 1817. Ostensibly the "Columbus" was to engage in the well-known three-cornered trade of those

[1] A study of the American privateers serving the governments of the Plata is now in course of preparation by Lewis Winkler Bealer.

days, going to the northwest coast for furs, thence to China for silk, and back to the United States. In fact, underneath his peaceful cargo, Wooster carried guns, artillery grenades, powder, and cannon-balls, destined for Buenos Aires, where he arrived early in 1818. From there he went to Valparaíso, and sold the "Columbus" to the Chilean government. It was renamed the "Araucano," and Wooster himself was placed in command, with a commission as captain. At that time there were only two other captains in the Chilean navy and one admiral. So Wooster was one of the founders of this branch in the Chilean service. He soon became captain of the frigate "Lautaro," while another American, Raymond Morris, took command of the "Araucano." The Spaniards still held the strongly defensible port of Talcahuano, and Wooster distinguished himself in the campaigns there. On October 27, 1818, he made a brilliant capture of a Spanish frigate, he himself being the first to board her. For this exploit he was highly commended by the Chilean government.

Late in 1818 Lord Cochrane reached Chile, to take command of the navy. Cochrane had fought in the War of 1812, and felt the customary dislike of British navy men of that period for Americans. It is certainly no reflection upon Wooster that Cochrane almost immediately began to display an animus against him; this same Cochrane quarreled indiscriminately with many persons in whatever part of the world he happened to be—in England, Peru, Brazil, and Greece, as well as Chile; indeed, his favorite enemy in the Chilean service was San Martín. One of Cochrane's first acts was to suspend Morris. Shortly afterward, early in 1819, Cochrane ordered Wooster to sail for Callao. Wooster informed him that his crew had not been paid or clothed and were discontented and that his ship was not ready to go, whereupon Cochrane sent him an insulting letter, commanding him to sail that very night. Wooster resigned instead. For the next three years he was engaged principally in the whaling industry, but reëntered the navy in 1822 when Cochrane was about to retire. Over the next few years he took part in several expeditions against the Spaniards in the Island of Chiloé, commanding the naval forces and showing great personal courage. According to President Vicuña of Chile it was principally due to him that Chiloé was eventually taken in 1826. When he left the navy in 1829 he was rear-admiral and commander-in-chief. He remained in Chile until 1835, when he returned to the United States, where he died in poverty in 1848.

Many other Americans served in the Chilean navy. There was Freeman Oxley, a man of tremendous bravery. He was officially commended for his valor in a battle between a Chilean and Spanish ship in 1823. As an officer in Wooster's fleet before Chiloé in 1826, he was a little too brave, and was killed as he attempted to board an enemy launch. He was highly praised by the Chilean historian Barros Arana for his intrepidity at all costs. There was a Lieutenant Charles Eldridge, formerly of the United States navy. He went to Buenos Aires in 1817 in a Baltimore ship, and thence to Chile, where he entered the navy. In that same year he was killed in course of an attack on Talcahuano. Daniel Carson, who had been a lieutenant in the United States navy, came out with Eldridge, and was wounded the same day the latter was killed. He took part in Cochrane's expedition to the north in 1819. Paul and William Delano [1] were from Massachusetts, and both joined the Chilean navy in 1819. William was in command of the transports in the San Martín expedition to Peru of 1820, and was in the Peruvian campaigns of that year and the next. Both of the Delanos remained in Chile, and married into the aristocracy. Their descendants have been prominent in Chilean history, and today, after the Spanish fashion, they write their name with an accent over the "e"! Samuel Johnston reached Chile in 1811, and served the country in various ways. He was a first lieutenant in the navy on the "Colt," an armed brig from the United States, which was bought by Chile in 1813. There were sixteen Americans on the "Colt," of whom seven were officers of high or low rank. The boat was taken by the Spaniards that same year, and the men were kept in a dungeon in Callao for four months. At length,

[1] One wonders if there may be any connection between the Chilean Délanos and President Franklin *Delano* Roosevelt of the United States. Cf. *infra*, 332, n. 2.

both the men and the boat were released. Undoubtedly the most important service on the part of Johnston was his founding of the first newspaper in Chile, the predecessor of the "Mercurio," which is the leading Chilean journal today. Returning to the United States, he published (at Erie, Pennsylvania, in 1816) a volume concerning his experiences, the first book about Chile to be printed in the United States.

Among those who took service in Argentina were Doctor Franklin Rawson of Massachusetts and John Anthony King of New York City. Rawson's son Guillermo later became a prominent political figure in the country, being a member of the cabinet of President Mitre, and having the town of Rawson in Patagonia named after him. King was only fourteen when he reached Buenos Aires in 1817, coming in a Baltimore ship. Entering the army as a flag-bearer, he fought in the campaigns of Upper Peru and Peru, serving many years and advancing to the rank of colonel. Returning to the United States, he published a book entitled *Twenty-four years in Argentina*. The services of the American privateersmen under the flag of the United Provinces have already been mentioned; they contribute a long list of names to that of the Americans who took an active part in the wars of independence.[1]

Alexander Macauley, Felix Jastran, and John Daniel Daniels [2] may be mentioned among those who fought for Colombia. Macauley was from Baltimore, although born in New York City. He served at least two years in the Colombian army, becoming a colonel. On April 27, 1811, he won a brilliant victory at Popayán, which has been widely heralded in the annals of the republic. Other victories accredited to him were those of Juanambú, Buesaco, and Calambuco. He was at length taken prisoner by the Spaniards, and shot at Pasto, Colombia, in January, 1813. Jas-

[1] Currier, *op. cit.*, appendix 1, lists thirty-six Argentinian privateers, nearly all of which were commanded by Americans and had American crews (cf. *supra*, 327). The names of the commanders and a brief note on the operations of each boat are also given. Nine of these vessels had been American privateers in the War of 1812 with England.

[2] Hasbrouck, 347–348, spells the name Danells. In addition to Daniels, or Danells, Hasbrouck mentions nine other Americans who were officers in the Colombian navy. *Ibid.*, 348–349.

tran "began his long military career in 1813, received a commission as colonel, and saw hard fighting in the early engagements as well as at both battles of Carabobo and Ayacucho." [1] Daniels, born in 1786, was from Baltimore, and turns up as a captain of the Colombian navy in 1818. In 1822, as an agent for the Colombian government, he bought the "Hercules" in the United States, presenting it as a gift to the republic of Colombia. Renamed the "Bolívar," this boat had a crew of 220, most of whom had formerly served on the United States frigate "Macedonian"! Doubtless, this is a hint as to what became of many of the naval veterans of the War of 1812.[2]

Certainly it would seem that the United States and the citizens of the northern republic played an interesting and not unimportant part in the Spanish American wars of independence.

[1] Hasbrouck, 350.

[2] The names of American officers given here are only a few out of many. Others are mentioned in Chandler, 114–138. But there were many more.

A curious case which came to the writer's attention was that of the Thayers of Chile. When the writer was in Chile, he became acquainted with Tomás Thayer, who was in charge of the manuscript division of the Biblioteca Nacional, or National Library, of Chile. At the same time, William Roscoe Thayer was head of the library of the Massachusetts Historical Society. Both men were fine scholars; the Massachusetts man was once president of the American Historical Association. Neither had ever heard of the other. Eventually it developed that they were related. The great-grandfather of Tomás Thayer had been captain of a Boston ship of the independence era on a voyage to the Pacific northwest. The boat was wrecked off the coast of Chile, and the crew were obliged to take refuge in that country. One of them was the son of the captain, Thayer's grandfather, a mere youth at the time. He found Chile very much to his liking, married a *señorita* of good family, and settled there permanently. It is at least an odd coincidence that several generations later two members of such widely separated branches of the Thayer family should be engaged in the same type of a highly specialized form of work.

CHAPTER XVII

THE MATURITY AND INDEPENDENCE OF COLONIAL BRAZIL

In dates at least and in underlying conditions the history of colonial Brazil parallels that of the Spanish American colonies. The Portuguese system was after the same pattern as that of Spain, and the movement for independence received its first important impulse from a Napoleonic invasion of the Iberian Peninsula, with a separation from the mother country following, in the same period as the Spanish American wars with Spain. Only the incidents vary, although the outcome in Brazil, after a brief war with Portugal, was to be the establishment of an empire instead of a republic.

There was not enough difference between the Portuguese and Spanish colonial systems to justify a detailed description of the former, and the likeness between them was all the more marked as a result of the union of the two crowns from 1580 to 1640. Brazil was governed "of, by, and for," not the Brazilian people, but the Portuguese monarchy. All the functions of government were exercised by the viceroy, who was directly subject to the king of Portugal. Most of the important government jobs were held by Portuguese subjects from Portugal, not Brazil; even so, a Brazilian might hold high place, provided he were a graduate of the University of Coimbra, Portugal. Economically, the same sorts of restrictions and prohibitions obtained as in the Spanish colonies, although perhaps less strictly enforced. Trade was confined to the traffic with the Portuguese ports of Lisbon and Oporto; even a commerce between *capitaneas* was forbidden.[1] Only Portuguese ships could be employed in carrying goods, and there were the usual almost innumerable

[1] Owing to the close connection between England and Portugal, the English were able to establish themselves in the commerce of Brazil much more freely than they could in the Spanish colonies. So, Brazil very early became accustomed to British goods, although they obtained them by way of Portuguese ports. British subjects were allowed to establish mercantile houses in Brazilian cities, however. Some other foreigners in Brazil also participated directly in the business of the country.

regulations favoring Portugal and the crown at the expense of Brazil, such for example as the oppressive royal monopolies. Diamonds and brazil wood were among the many monopolized items. Other important sources of revenue were the customs duties and the royal fifth of all precious metals mined. Brazil was so much larger and potentially so much richer than Portugal and the other Portuguese colonies, however, that it at length became the most noteworthy field of Portuguese colonization and exploitation. Many Portuguese made their fortunes in Brazil, and carried them back with them to Portugal. Others retained their estates in Brazil, but resided in Portugal, spending their profits there. In course of time, there developed an economic interdependence which survived the separation from the mother country and is a factor in the economic life of the two countries even at the present time. A financial crisis in Portugal would result in a calling in of funds from Brazil, while business troubles in Brazil very nearly meant catastrophe in Portugal.

While the social structure was much the same as in Spanish America, there were certain features growing out of the peculiar conditions of Brazilian life which distinguished it from the norm of Spanish America. The striking fact was that of the intermixture of the white, red, and especially the black races in a country which was in the tropical and sub-tropical belts. As in Spanish America, the whites were few in numbers, but were the dominating people. There were very few white women in Brazil, wherefore the white men formed unions with the reds and blacks; they perhaps felt less repugnance against such unions than other white peoples, because the Portuguese in Europe, as the leading importers of African slaves, had already become accustomed to them, modifying their own racial character through the introduction of negro blood. There were perhaps a few advantages from this tendency toward miscegenation. The Indians and negroes added something of bodily strength and physical endurance. The "Mamelukes," resulting from an intermixture of whites and reds, were an especially competent and active class, often superior to the whites themselves, but they were eventually swallowed up in that intermingling of the races which followed the arrival of the blacks.

Unquestionably the disadvantages of miscegenation far outweighed whatever advantages there were. The Portuguese colonists themselves were generally very inferior intellectually and morally, and did not raise the level of the mixed races in these respects. In fact, immorality was enhanced, as most of the unions were illegitimate, and the family failed to establish itself on a sound basis. The government made no attempt to correct this situation, feeling that its own rule depended to a great extent on the ignorance and degradation of the colonists. The church endeavored to combat the evil of immorality, but its efforts were ineffectual; the state of sacerdotal celibacy itself was none too rigidly observed. Nevertheless, the intermixture of whites and reds might have worked out acceptably, as it did in Chile, but the addition of the negroes had tragic consequences.

Beginning in 1574, vast numbers of negroes were imported into Brazil, and there followed the inevitable intermingling of races, not only of black with white, but also of black with red; indeed, the latter was at first the more prominent of the two, since there was a desire for the black slaves to reproduce, to provide more slaves, and comparatively few black women were brought from Africa. There was, of course, the tendency to breed out, in accord with the law of Mendelism. Before the negroes came, the progeny of "Caramurú" were evolving to become white or red again, for the Mamelukes were not a fixed racial group, although always being recruited anew. But the blacks changed the situation. Except as they retained their purity of race in the far back country of Brazil, the Indians were absorbed and disappeared. The whites certainly did no better than hold their own, and they did not even do that in the northern districts, around Bahia and beyond. There, black became the prevailing color, with only a few persons reasonably entitled to call themselves white. In the south, which was less adapted to plantation life, there were not so many negroes, and therefore a better defence against the inroads of the blacks. It takes a very generous interpretation, however, to say that this part of Brazil is white, as is sometimes done. It early became, and has remained, very largely black. There are probably very few old Brazilian families which have no Indian or negro ancestors, and many of them would not have to go very far back into the past to find clear evidence of the latter color. In 1818, at the close of the colonial era, the population of the country (apart from the unconquered interior) was estimated to be a little more than three millions,[1] of whom a fourth were white. Negro blood predominated in the other three-fourths of the people, and was probably present in no slight degree among those considered white. Among subsidiary effects of the Brazilian miscegenation on a nation-wide scale was the development of disease. A too great tendency toward promiscuity weakened the fibre of the race physically, especially as the result of venereal ills. The figures authoritatively offered for those afflicted in this fashion, even in recent times, are appalling and almost unbelievable. Other forms of sickness contributed to the breakdown in the health of the Brazilian people. For example, yellow fever made its appearance in 1686, and became almost chronic, until wiped out by the discoveries of the early twentieth century.

One result of the racial situation was that eventually the comparatively white south outstripped the originally more important north. The modern history of Brazil is the history of the south, of a southern white aristocracy, of the Paulistas. With the development of prosperity, especially following the gold discoveries, more whites came in, mostly Portuguese, but also a few others. With them came some white women. In 1763, Rio de Janeiro replaced Bahia as the capital, thus recognizing the greater prominence of the south. To be sure, Rio de Janeiro was chosen in part because of its much better location with respect to any possible trouble with the Spaniards of the Plata, but that had been equally true for more than two hundred years; indeed, it is odd that this wonderful harbor was so long neglected

[1] In 1820 the four largest cities were Rio de Janeiro, Bahia, Pernambuco, and São Paulo, with populations of about a hundred thousand, seventy thousand, twenty-five thousand, and between fifteen and twenty thousand respectively.

by the Portuguese, for no permanent Portuguese settlement was founded there until after the expulsion of the French in the middle of the sixteenth century. After 1763, Rio de Janeiro became a cultivated Portuguese city, very largely white.

There never was, and is not yet, such a thing as a Brazilian race, but the effects of history have developed the racial conglomerate into what might be called a Brazilian people. Such achievements as the defeat of the Dutch and pride in the wealth and greatness of Brazil joined with a growing disapproval of Portugal in its weakness, comparative impotence, and decadence to make them feel Brazilian, if indeed somewhat hazily in the nationalistic sense. And yet, it was many years before there was even a thought of independence. The delay certainly could not be ascribed to the good treatment they received, because they did not receive it. The Portuguese system in itself was bad, though of the generally accepted type in those days. It is an open question whether or not it was even worse in operation than that of the Spaniards. One writer has called it "the most oppressive régime of which there is an example in modern history," as of the time of the Marquis of Pombal, famous Portuguese minister of the eighteenth century. Yet, Pombal introduced many important reforms. And most writers appear to consider the Portuguese rule in the colonies milder than the Spanish, if only because of the comparative weakness of Portugal and her neglect in the administration of Brazil. Nevertheless, the Portuguese officials were perhaps more than usually arbitrary, grasping, and dishonest, throughout the colonial period, even fighting one another over the spoils. The subordinate officials were notoriously ignorant. Those who were recruited from among the Brazilians had little or no education, as there were no universities and only a few less advanced schools in the country,[1] and the circulation of printed works was forbidden. This, it will be recognized, was a worse situation than in the Spanish colonies.

Nevertheless, although the system itself had few, if any,

[1] The children of the wealthy ordinarily were sent to Portugal for an education, especially to the University of Coimbra.

redeeming features, the full weight of its evils fell only upon the considerable towns, as the government was weak. In the rural districts there was a great deal of independence in fact, although upon a somewhat wretched basis, and the whites in the cities were bound by traditions of loyalty; since they were not subjected to physical cruelties, they perhaps did not feel that they had any particular grievance. They did not like the system, generally accepted though it was, but they were too apathetic and submissive, too little enlightened, and too indolent, to claim any political rights or to resist the Portuguese in their reservation of the chief benefits for themselves.

In the long reign of John V (1707–1750) the evils in the Portuguese government of Brazil from the standpoint of venality and corruption reached their height, even surpassing the record of the Spanish colonial officials during the weak reigns of the seventeenth century. After 1750, however, a new turn was given to Portuguese administration by the Marquis of Pombal, Portugal's most famous contribution to the ministers of the "enlightened despotism," and the virtual dictator of Portuguese policies for a period of twenty-seven years. Government in the colonies was more carefully supervised, and many improvements were introduced, but the general tenor of all the changes was in the direction of increasing the advantages of the crown. New forms of taxation were devised. Industries which might compete with Portugal were more strictly forbidden. And the Jesuits, as an alleged rival of the monarchy, were expelled. Even after Pombal's time, there were such decrees as one of 1785, which ordered the closing of all the factories in Brazil and prohibited manufacturing of any sort.

Nevertheless, along with the "despotism" of the eighteenth century, there was also the "enlightenment," as represented, for example, by the French philosophers and encyclopaedists. Something of this phase of the era percolated into Brazil, especially through the medium of those Brazilians whose parents were wealthy enough to send them to Europe for an education. In 1786, José Joaquim da Maia, a Brazilian student at Montpellier, France, wrote to Thomas

Jefferson, who was then in Paris, soliciting the aid of the United States in freeing Brazil from the Portuguese yoke. Jefferson, as an individual, expressed an interest in these views, and even granted an interview to Maia in 1787, but, of course, refused to promise any help.[1] Maia was not alone in his hostility to Portuguese rule. Many others felt the same way, especially in Minas Geraes, where a plot against the government was fomented in 1789. The leader in the enterprise was a certain Joaquim da Silva Xavier, whose nick-name, "Tiradentes" (the Tooth-puller), is usually applied to this affair. There was treason within the ranks, and the conspirators were captured. Tiradentes was executed in 1792, and the others were deported to prisons in Africa.

In 1807 Napoleon sent Marshal Junot into Portugal with a French army to conquer the country. Under the necessity of making a quick decision, the Regent John (the later John VI) emigrated to Brazil, with all his court, under the convoy of a British fleet. The Portuguese royal family made a hurried flight, not however before the kind-hearted John had ordered supper and a bed to be prepared for the rapidly approaching French marshal. Altogether, there were eight ships of war and forty merchant vessels in the fleet which went to Brazil, and what with the royal family, the government officials, and most of the Portuguese nobility there were about fifteen thousand persons on board. The voyage was a difficult one—all the more so, since insufficient preparation had been made. Soon, so it is said, there was a shortage of clothing in the royal family, with the result that the infant Prince Pedro and several others had to be provided with bed-sheet suits. In January, 1808, John landed at Bahia. There had been some doubt as to the welcome the royal party might receive, owing to the unpopularity of the Portuguese colonial system, but John promptly showed that the Portuguese government *in Brazil* was a very different thing from the Portuguese govern-

[1] A number of different dates and different versions of this event are given in the books which mention it. It is amply discussed in Jefferson's correspondence, of which Custer, Ferdinand Varella, *Republican sentiment in Brazil in the eighteenth century* (Ms., M.A. thesis, University of California, Berkeley), 79–89, avails itself for an interesting and probably correct account.

ment *in Portugal.* On touching at Bahia he announced that the ports of Brazil were to be open to the world and to the ships of any friendly nation. Furthermore, he abolished or lessened the burden of some of the royal monopolies, and reduced the import duties. In a sense, his arrival marks the beginning of real Brazilian independence, paralleling the outbreak of the revolutions in Spanish America. As for the immediate question of the reception of John and his party, the decree settled that. Both at Bahia and Rio de Janeiro they were hailed with great acclaim.

A number of other beneficent acts were promptly undertaken. The laws prohibiting industry and handicapping agriculture were annulled. And what might be called the machinery of civilization made its appearance for the first time. A mere mention of the innovations makes clear how backward Brazil had been under Portuguese rule before. Printing-presses were set up, and the prohibitions against books were lessened. A national library was founded in 1814. A mint, a powder-factory, a bank, a school of medicine, and a quarantine station were established. It is said that vaccination was introduced into Brazil in these years. The story is told that the Marquis of Barbacena (an outstanding figure in this period), wishing to prove its virtues to the sceptical Brazilians, vaccinated his own son. Then there was a period of excited waiting, to see whether the youth would die. As the tale goes, he *did* die—but not until many years afterward, at an age of 104!

In retaliation against Napoleon, an Anglo-Portuguese expedition was sent to French Guiana which conquered that territory in 1809. By the European treaties of 1815 it was restored to France, but in a roundabout way the campaign contributed to the improvement of Brazilian agriculture. Many new plants were imported from French Guiana, and replanted in Brazil. Out of this incident there developed the new Portuguese policy of introducing agricultural variety into Brazil. Formerly, Portugal had discouraged all-round agriculture, confining Brazil in the main to sugar. Now a botanical garden was established at Rio de Janeiro, and the seeds or cuttings of the new products were distributed from there. Learned men were invited to visit the country, and immigration was encouraged at government expense. Rio de Janeiro was enlarged and rebuilt, with a number of parks added, to beautify the city. And the genteel blood of the court, including women of quality, made for a cultivated society such as Brazil had never known. All in all, a Portuguese government was created, just as it had existed in Portugal, but now with Brazil as the centre.

All was not as it should be, however, for there was an evil side to the new state. The maintenance of the court necessitated a vast expense, and Brazil had to provide it. Furthermore, the courtiers, with their natural superiority complex, felt that they must be taken care of, whatever might become of the natives of the country, and preëmpted the best houses of the capital for themselves. The ousted Brazilian families were not alone in regarding this as an unwelcome intrusion. Unwise financial measures were adopted which got the treasury into difficulties.

Nevertheless, the glamour of the royal presence and the military successes of the monarchy were sufficient for a time to hold in check the dissatisfaction of the people. In 1815, Brazil was declared a kingdom under the Portuguese monarch, a pronounced step in the direction of independence. The following year the queen died, and the regent became king in his own name as John VI. It was now some time since Portugal had been recovered from the French, but it was a source of satisfaction to the Brazilians that the royal family had not seen fit to return to Lisbon. Meanwhile, the preliminary steps had been taken which were to lead to the conquest of Uruguay. As hereinbefore set forth, Brazilian forces invaded the country in 1811 and again in 1816, and in 1821 it formally became a possession of the Portuguese crown.

Brazil was now a much more important country, obviously, than Portugal, but the government was still in the hands of the Portuguese. Many of their measures proved to be exceedingly unpopular. By way of illustration, mention may be made of a tax which was to be in operation for forty years in Brazil for the benefit of the Portuguese nobles who had suffered as a result of the war with France.

This provoked deep resentment. Furthermore, the republican elements, encouraged by the tendencies in Spanish America and by the example of the United States, grew more and more eager to put their own governmental principles into practice. Early in 1817 there was an outbreak in the province of Pernambuco. The Portuguese governor was obliged to capitulate, the Portuguese flag was torn down, and an independent republic was announced. Requests for support were sent to the other provinces, and soon much of the north had joined with Pernambuco. In Parahyba, Rio Grande do Norte, and Alagóas the republic was proclaimed, but Ceará and Bahia would not rise. The rest of the country did not respond. A fleet and an army of five thousand men were despatched to put down the movement, and the isolated and insufficiently armed republicans were forced to surrender, but not until after three months of hard fighting. The principal leaders were executed, and a number of the others were thrown into prison. Peace was restored, but the rivalries of Portuguese and Brazilians continued. It was certain to result in another and greater civil conflict whenever a favorable opportunity for the Brazilians should present itself.

The Riego revolution in Spain was soon imitated in Portugal, where a Liberal outbreak, early in 1820, was successful. A demand was instituted for a constitution like the radical Spanish constitution of 1812, and a provisional junta was set up which issued a call for a *Cortes*, to serve also as a constitutional convention. In Brazil as well as Portugal, the soldiers were in favor of the new government, and in February, 1821, John was compelled by a mutiny of the troops to accept it. John, whose presence in Portugal had been insistently demanded by the authorities there, now decided he had better go, if he were to save Portugal for the dynasty. When he left, he was followed by more than three thousand Portuguese nobles. Before departing he is said to have addressed his son, whom he left in charge of the government: "Pedro, if Brazil has to be separated from Portugal, as appears likely, you take the crown for yourself, before somebody else can gather it in." [1] The situation fa-

[1] This is one of many versions of this celebrated bit of advice.

vored the chances of the young Dom Pedro. He had just turned twenty-one, had more than average intelligence and ability, and was exceptionally courageous. Furthermore, he had been brought up to foresee the separation of Brazil from Portugal, and had become the leader of the Brazilian liberalist party at court.

The people of Brazil were exceedingly displeased over the departure of John VI, because it was well known that the Portuguese *Cortes* wished to restore the colonial system, and it was feared that the weak, easily-influenced John might be persuaded to agree with this policy. Surely enough, the activities of the *Cortes* soon gave ample cause for discontent in Brazil. Brazilian deputies to the *Cortes* had been elected, but the *Cortes* began to frame a constitution before they arrived. This led to angry feelings, as the Brazilians did not propose to be treated any longer as secondary. Provision was made in the new constitution for the government of Brazil by a junta, to be responsible to the *Cortes;* no Brazilian laws or commercial measures were to go into effect until they had received the sanction of the *Cortes;* the old *capitanea* districts were revived, and a number of them ordered detached from Brazil, to be governed directly from Lisbon; and the Portuguese commercial monopoly was reëstablished. Furthermore, an insulting decree ordered the return of Dom Pedro to Portugal. These enactments came at a time when Brazilian opinion was already highly incensed over the extravagance of the Portuguese courtiers; those who had gone back to Portugal with John VI had engaged in a sordid scramble to obtain sudden wealth, to enable them to cross the seas in comfortable circumstances, and those who still remained were imitating their example. The natural result of these events was to produce indignation and alarm. There were various outbreaks. Success appeared to turn upon the attitude of Dom Pedro. Pressure was brought to bear upon him to induce him to stay, or even to declare the independence of Brazil. Chief among those who influenced him was José Bonifacio de Andrada e Silva, since called the "Patriarch of Independence." A distinguished savant and man of letters, formerly a professor at Coimbra, he presently became minister of the interior and foreign affairs in Pedro's cabinet. By this time, Pedro had already announced that under no circumstances would he return to Portugal.

For a while, Pedro endeavored to bring about an adjustment with Portugal, maintaining the union, but with a separate government for Brazil, which should have her own legislative body. Pending discussions of his plan, he decreed that no Portuguese law was to be enforced in Brazil without his consent, and declared that he would resist the landing of Portuguese troops. These decisions he justified by asserting that John VI was virtually a prisoner in Portugal and that any acts in his name should be without effect. When he sent delegates to Portugal to seek approval for his proposals, they were insulted by the *Cortes*, which reiterated its demands for Pedro's return. Efforts at compromise had now been exhausted, and independence was the only recourse. On September 7, 1822, Pedro was at the Ypiranga River in the province of São Paulo, when word came that the Portuguese *Cortes* had annulled his acts and condemned his councilors as guilty of high treason. This was the last straw. That very day, in the presence of a large assemblage, Pedro gave the "cry" (*grito*) of Ypiranga, declaring the independence of Brazil. Returning to Rio de Janeiro, he was enthusiastically acclaimed, and on October 12, 1822, was recognized as the constitutional emperor of Brazil.

Portugal was by no means ready to accept the new turn of affairs, and war soon broke out. The Portuguese forces were concentrated in Bahia, and early in 1823 defeated a Brazilian expedition sent against them. At this juncture the ubiquitous Lord Cochrane arrived in Brazil, and was placed in command of the fleet. In the ensuing campaign he displayed his customary brilliancy, and later that same year compelled the Portuguese to evacuate Brazilian territory and sail for Portugal. The Portuguese were expelled from other parts of the country, too, including Uruguay, which was formally annexed to Brazil. By the close of 1823 the authority of Pedro was undisputed, and two years later the independence of Brazil was recognized by Portugal.

Thus was the separation of Brazil from the mother country achieved. Unlike the Spanish American colonies, she chose to set up an empire instead of a republic. Many Brazilians would have preferred the latter, but the fact that a prince of the royal family had taken the lead in the movement made it inevitable that the republican experiment should be put off, just as it probably would have been in Spanish America if the circumstances had been the same. Not until 1889 did Brazil become a republic. However, in the light of Spanish American experience in the meantime, the long Brazilian peace of Pedro II (1831–1889),[1] and events in Brazil since 1889, it is doubtful whether the postponement should be viewed as a mishap. It may well have been responsible for the extraordinary development of that country and for the maintenance of its territorial integrity.

[1] Pedro II did not enter upon his imperial duties until he became of age in 1840. Down to 1844 the nation was torn with civil war. Afterward, Brazil took part in the conflict which resulted in the overthrow of Rosas of Argentina in 1852, and also in the Paraguayan War of 1865 to 1870. Chile is the only other Hispanic American country able to rival Brazil in abstention from war in these years, but, of the two, Brazil perhaps had more of the atmosphere of an underlying peace.

ESSAY ON AUTHORITIES

ESSAY ON AUTHORITIES

There is, of course, an almost incalculable amount of material available for a study of the colonial period of Hispanic American history. If only the important printed items were included, a list could be prepared, with not more than two lines to an item, which would much more than fill this volume. Obviously, only a small fraction of these works can be mentioned here, but, with the aids herein provided, the scholar should also be able to find most of the other materials among those which are generally known. Nevertheless, the scholar, or historian, is not the person to whom this essay is primarily directed; it is more particularly for the use of the general reader or for the student who has not yet become an expert in the field. On that account the principal section here is the one named Books, with very few entries in the groups (so important for the scholar) called Bibliographical Aids, Printed Documents, Periodicals, and Manuscripts. Furthermore, a preference is given in the Book part to volumes in English. Exceptionally noteworthy items in other languages do appear, but not nearly in proportion to their importance. Even the works in English are in the main limited to those which have a direct bearing upon considerable portions of the entire field. Thus, scores of important monographs are omitted, although indications are given as to how such treatises may be found. Indeed, some volumes have been included rather than others, equally meritorious, merely because they have been cited in the text. The following chart shows how the material has been classified for presentation.

I. PRINTED MATERIAL

BIBLIOGRAPHICAL AIDS
- A. *Bibliographies*
- B. *Syllabuses*

DOCUMENTS

PERIODICALS

BOOKS
- A. *General works*
  - a. On colonial Hispanic America
  - b. On colonial and republican Hispanic America
- B. *The Spanish colonies to 1810*
  - a. Contemporary accounts
  - b. Later works
- C. *The Spanish American wars of independence*
  - a. Contemporary accounts
  - b. Later works
- D. *Portuguese Brazil*

II. MANUSCRIPTS

ARCHIVE GUIDES

UNPUBLISHED THESES

Because of these various groupings, a finding list (by authors' names and item numbers) is herewith provided:

I. PRINTED MATERIAL

BIBLIOGRAPHICAL AIDS

A. *Bibliographies*

There are many volumes of bibliography dealing directly with the colonial era in Hispanic America, and very many more which include that, or a part of it, in a larger or somewhat different field. Furthermore, most of the items in the group entitled Books have lists of materials in them, and learned periodicals have bibliographical sections and book reviews which enable one to keep up to date. A number of bibliographical works in English on Hispanic America will readily present themselves to the mind of the student of this field.[1] Of more importance are the general bibliographies of America, such, for example, as those of Harrisse and Sabin. Nevertheless, only six items are listed below, and these not necessarily because they are the most noteworthy—although most of them may well challenge comparison—but because they are representative of the field.

1. Jones, Cecil Knight. *Hispanic American bibliographies, including collective biographies, histories of literature and selected general works . . . with critical notes on sources by José Toribio Medina.* Baltimore, 1922.

   Published originally in six numbers of the *Hispanic American historical review* (August and November, 1921, and the four issues of 1922), this is now in book form. It is one of the fundamentally essential tools of the Hispanic American field, of the republican as well as the colonial era. A bibliography of bibliographies, it lists no fewer than 1281 works of bibliography. 190 of these are in a "General and Miscellaneous" group. The others are entered according to the present-day countries of Hispanic America. The author has for many years been the bibliographer of the *Hispanic American historical review,* and has also been connected with George

[1] A partial list in Wilgus, Alva Curtis, *A history of Hispanic America* (Washington, 1931), 673–677, shows ninety-three bibliographies of Hispanic American history, all in English. Also, note comment in items 1 and 6. An undoubtedly important additional item—not yet at hand as this volume goes to press—is Pan-American union, *Bibliography of the liberator Simón Bolívar* (2 ed. Washington, 1933). This lists 1424 titles. A 1930 edition, in mimeographed form, listed only 336 titles. I am informed that the new edition "is an excellent piece of work and right up to date" and that "there is nothing else comparable to it." If I had had a chance to see this work, I might have decided to give it formal entry, since a full bibliography of Bolívar goes a long way toward being a bibliography of the wars of independence in South America. This volume is also being issued in Spanish.

Washington University and the Library of Congress. Additions to the Jones list have appeared from time to time in the *Hispanic American historical review*.

2. Keniston, Ralph Hayward. *List of works for the study of Hispanic American history*. New York, 1920.

Not intended to be an exhaustive work of bibliography, this is entered merely as one of the best examples of numerous smaller volumes of this type in English devoted to Hispanic America. It aims to help the scholar, including bibliographies, documents, and periodical literature, as well as books. Most of the items are in Spanish, but little or no description is given. The arrangement is for Hispanic America in general and then by countries. A considerable proportion of the material is for the colonial period. The author, at present a professor of Spanish in the University of Chicago, was amply competent to undertake the task he set for himself. The volume was issued under the auspices of the Hispanic Society of America.

3. Medina, José Toribio. *Biblioteca hispano-americana (1493–1810)*. 7v. Santiago, Chile, 1898–1907.

The greatest bibliographer of modern times, Medina in this work furnishes the best example of the hundreds of bibliographical volumes he compiled, to say nothing of the numerous books of history by this remarkable Chilean.[1] Indeed, many of his "*Imprentas*," or bibliographies, were in the nature of preliminary studies for this masterpiece. Entirely concerned with the colonial period, it lists 8481 items, arranged chronologically by date of publication, with the briefer volume VII devoted to additions and amplifications. Medina includes not only all works printed in Spanish America prior to 1810, but also all works published elsewhere by Spaniards who had lived in Spanish America or by Spanish Americans, no matter what the subject of their writings. The works of Spaniards and foreigners about Spanish America are also given entry. A careful study of each item appears, covering such technical features as editions and descriptions of contents. An index in each of the volumes is a serviceable feature. The general reader may never have occasion

[1] For a brief account of the life, character, and astounding achievements of this extraordinary man, see Chapman, Charles Edward, "A recuerdo of José Toribio Medina," in *Hispanic American historical review*, XI, 524–529; Nov., 1931.

even to glance at this great Medina work, but he ought to know it exists.

4. Moses, Bernard. *Spanish colonial literature in South America.* London and New York, 1922.

The author of this volume had a distinguished career in the service of the United States government in the Philippine Islands and elsewhere and as a university professor, being a member of the faculty of the University of California for many years. There he gave the first course in Hispanic American history ever offered in a university of the United States. He also is entitled to be called the pioneer United States historian in the recent development of the Hispanic American field, which since his day has assumed such important proportions. Cf. item 40. It is fitting that Moses should have written the *Colonial literature* volume, since he knew the printed works on colonial Hispanic America possibly better than any Anglo-American student of his times. In his own writing he used, in the main, printed materials, the possibilities of which are even yet far from being exhausted. Students who have more recently been exploring the great archival repositories have turned up new materials, but the books of Moses (several of which are entered here) still stand as among the most valuable in the field. The *Colonial literature* is organized by chapters according to different events, regions, and periods of time, and covers the entire colonial era prior to 1810. It aims "to introduce the reader to the men of letters in the colonies who wrote under the inspiration of their experience in the New World, whether their contributions were in the realm of poetry, history, geographical description, or ecclesiastical discussion." By no means a mere list of writers and their works, it gives a rather detailed account of both, and is probably the best volume in English for information of this type. There is, indeed, an index by authors' names of the books mentioned in his text, and also a general index. Like item 2 and several others of the Moses books, this is a publication of the Hispanic Society of America.

5. University of California. *Spain and Spanish America in the libraries of the University of California: a catalogue of books.* 2v. Berkeley, Calif., 1928–1930.

A number of libraries or other institutions have published lists of the books they possess on Hispanic

America. The item entered here is merely one such publication, although it represents one of the best single collections in the United States. While Spain and republican Spanish America are included, the colonial period in Spanish America accounts for a large proportion of the entries. Especially is this true of volume II, devoted to the widely known Bancroft Library, the great bulk of whose materials are for the colonial period. Nevertheless, volume I, for the general and departmental libraries of the University, also contains much material. The arrangement in each volume is alphabetical by authors' names, and there are valuable subject indexes. These volumes are popularly called "the Cebrián Catalogue," because their publication was made possible through the contributions of Juan C. Cebrián, a Spaniard long resident in San Francisco. Naturally, the volumes are already in part out of date, as many purchases have been made and gifts received since they were published.[1] They nevertheless provide an exceedingly useful bibliography, just as they stand.

6. Wilgus, Alva Curtis. *The histories of Hispanic America*, in Pan American Union, *Bibliographical series*, no. 9. Washington, 1932.

Strictly speaking, this is not a "printed work," since it has so far appeared only in mimeographed form. In five chapters, each devoted to a century, from the sixteenth to the twentieth inclusive, Wilgus discusses the more noteworthy general books and the special volumes on each region, giving authors' names, titles of their writings, something about editions, and a little concerning the authors themselves and the value of their works. For supplementary information, one is referred to a "Selected list of bibliographical collections," in which fifty-six items are named, only a few of which are in English.[2] The Wilgus *Histories* in its present form must be used with discretion, because of numerous errors in detail. When these are corrected, it is likely to be the familiar handbook of many graduate students. For the general reader, a half hour with it would help him to realize the vast amount of material available

[1] Cf. Bealer, Lewis Winkler, "Some recent additions to the South American collection in the University of California libraries," in *Hispanic American historical review*, XII, 103–106; Feb., 1932.

[2] Cf. item 1, *supra*, and 350, n. 1.

for the history of colonial Hispanic America. It must be borne in mind, however, that the volume is as yet merely a tentative presentation. Not until needed changes are made will its full usefulness be realized.

B. *Syllabuses*

The syllabus, of course, does not compare with bibliographies in importance for the scholar, but it is very helpful to the general reader and to the neophyte in the field, containing not only lists of material, but also outlines of lectures. Because of the latter feature, it might well be included in the Books section, but it seemed more properly to belong here. Only two items are listed, but others have appeared from time to time in the *Hispanic American historical review*, and several more have had separate publication.[1]

7. Bolton, Herbert Eugene. *History of the Americas: a syllabus with maps*. Boston, 1928.

Prepared to accompany his great History 8 (History of the Americas) course at the University of California [2] and similar classes at other institutions, this is the work of one of the greatest historians in the United States, a former president of the American Historical Association, and a recognized expert in the Western United States and Hispanic American fields.[3] If Moses is entitled to be called the pioneer of the twentieth century movement in the development of the latter, Bolton is also a pioneer from several standpoints: in the employment of hitherto unused manuscript material, emphasizing this, also, in the work of his students; in the study of regions hitherto supposed to be "without a history," but which have proved to be decidedly worth knowing; and in his point of view as to the unity of the history of the Western Hemisphere. See item 12. His *Syllabus* is one expression of that point of view, dealing with the Western Hemisphere, the Americas, as a whole. No fewer than twenty-four of the sixty lecture outlines it contains relate directly to colonial Hispanic America. Lists of readings accompany

[1] Wilgus, *Op. cit.*, 672, lists fifteen syllabuses.

[2] This well known class has enrolled as many as 1258 pupils, probably the largest university class in history this country has ever seen.

[3] A list of Bolton's writings up to 1932, including twenty books, seventy-three articles, and twenty-three maps, is to be found in *New Spain and the Anglo-American west* (2v. Lancaster, Pa., and Los Angeles, 1932), v. II, 245–252.

each lecture outline, and there is a total of ninety-two maps in the volume. Arrived at independently, my own view of Hispanic American history, as presented in this volume, coincides with that of the Bolton *Syllabus*, fitting in with it in chapter headings and arrangement. The two may therefore be used together, at least in so far as colonial Hispanic American material is concerned.

8. Pierson, William Whatley. *Hispanic-American history: a syllabus*. Chapel Hill, N. C., 1916 (w. diff. title); 3 ed. 1926.

   The work of a leading scholar in the Hispanic American field, this volume devotes five of its ten chapters to the colonial period in topical outlines and useful reading lists.

DOCUMENTS

Published letters, diaries, reports, statements, handbills, or other printed materials which were not designed originally as formulated accounts for presentation to the public as periodical articles or books are sometimes referred to as printed documents. This type of evidence is, of course, of tremendous value to the scholar, but is of interest to other readers only as selections (in translation, if originally in another language than English) are deemed worthy of reissue in volumes or magazines for the general public. Government documents constitute the great bulk of the material of this sort available, since private communications much more rarely find their way into print. An entire volume would be none too great a space for an adequate discussion of this group of writings. Among the better known items are the three collections of inedited documents of forty-two, twenty-five, and twelve (to date) volumes respectively about colonial Spanish America, not to mention the 112-volume set for the history of Spain, which in fact contains a great deal about the colonies; the title of each of these sets begins with the words *Colección de documentos inéditos*. Equally famous and perhaps even more useful is the *Recopilación*, or compilation, of the laws of the Indies. Appearing in many editions, this is usually in the form of a four-volume set. The thirty-two-volume *Memorias del general O'Leary* (about Bolívar) is a famous item for the wars of independence era, among thousands which could be named. The parallel materials for Brazil are much less widely known. The items listed below—an infinitesimal few out of the many which the scholar might consider indispensable—are examples of republications for popular consumption. Many others of the same type might be added.

9. *Biblioteca Ayacucho.* 63v. to date. Madrid, 1915–

Named in honor of the decisive battle of the wars of independence in South America, this set is primarily concerned with that period, although an occasional item outside that field is included in the set (e.g. item 22). About sixty per cent of the volumes are made up of recollections, letters, diaries, or other records of participants in the wars, such as Cochrane, Miller, O'Leary, Páez, Paz, and Sucre, to name only a few of the better known individuals among them. The other forty per cent of the volumes are monographs about some phase of the wars, with a stray item, now and then, on some other subject. This set might therefore be entered with the group called Books, as well as here under Documents. Although some of the recollections included were written originally in English, these volumes are all in Spanish. They are an exceedingly important source of information for the student of this period.

10. Bolton, Herbert Eugene, *ed. Spanish exploration in the Southwest, 1542–1706.* New York, 1916.[1]

The editor of this collection (cf. item 7) is especially well known for his studies of the frontier regions of the Spanish and English spheres of influence in North America, and particularly for that part of the United States often designated broadly as the Southwest, but including the Pacific coast, as well as the mainland border areas of Mexico and the United States. That is the field of this volume. Some of the more noteworthy first-hand accounts of the Spaniards who explored these territories are here carefully translated and annotated.

11. Cleven, Nels Andrew Nelson, *ed. Readings in Hispanic American history.* Boston and New York, 1927.

This is a compilation by a capable scholar of a set of materials designed to illustrate the whole field of Hispanic American history, through an orderly presentation of writings, almost all of which were contemporary with the periods under which they are listed. All items not originally in English, which means all but a very few, have been translated. Considerably over half of the book is devoted to the period from colonial beginnings to the battle of Ayacucho in 1824, containing seventy-three documentary selections in 458 pages.

[1] Charles Scribner and Sons, publishers.

PERIODICALS

Articles in periodicals differ technically from books only in the type of publication where they are found, in that they are but one item out of a number, in a magazine of more or less regularly recurring issue. Usually, books are longer than articles, but not necessarily so; indeed, a periodical article, when published separately, becomes a book—or, if some distinction because of size appears desirable, a pamphlet. The importance of this type of material is determined by the same standards one would apply in judging a book, but there is undoubtedly a higher percentage of slipshod, superficial work in periodical literature than there is in books. With few exceptions, the most noteworthy discussions of at least the broader phases of Hispanic American colonial history will be found in those materials classed as books, rather than in periodical articles. The general reader may therefore pay comparatively little attention to this form of literature, although he may well find much of interest and importance, if he cares to give free rein to his curiosity. There is an astonishing amount of periodical material available,[1] although (since magazines and newspapers in great numbers are a comparatively recent affair) much less for the colonial era than for later times. Except for articles in periodicals which were contemporary with the Hispanic American colonial past, not many in this field are really noteworthy, unless they appear in the magazines for the scholar. Several periodicals of this type might be mentioned, but only one of them is essential for the general student of the field, the one given in item 13 below. As for important articles, it would not be difficult to compile a list of a thousand. Only one is given here, however.

12. Bolton, Herbert Eugene. "The epic of Greater America," in *American historical review*, XXXVIII, 448–474; April, 1933.

    This is Bolton's presidential address at the meetings of the American Historical Association, held at Toronto in December 1932. In it he brings out a new view of American history, on the basis of the unity of the Western Hemisphere, the same view which has been the foundation stone of his teaching at the University of California for many years. Cf. item 7. He demonstrates, with a wealth of illustration, that Hispanic America and the United States

[1] A survey of *Poole's index* and the *Readers' guide* for the years 1902 to 1925 revealed approximately two thousand articles about Cuba alone, to which must be added those in magazines not listed in the above-named volumes and others in newspapers.

are not two separate fields, but parts of the same field, wherefore the broad historian of either must inevitably know the history of both. Historiographically, this article may prove to occupy a place comparable to that of the celebrated Turner article entitled "The significance of the frontier in American history," published in 1894. Like that article, it offers a new point of view, calling for an expansion of the scope and the working field of American history.

13. *Hispanic American historical review.* 13v. to date. Baltimore, 1918–1922; Durham, N. C., 1926– .

Founded with the sanction and approval of the American Historical Association in its meetings at Columbus, Ohio, in December 1916, this has become the indispensable organ of the Hispanic American scholars in the United States. Under the able guidance of James Alexander Robertson, who has been the managing editor since it was first published, it ranks second only to the *American historical review* as a magazine of history in the United States, and is almost a *sine qua non* of the specialists in Hispanic American history. It is after the usual pattern of the historical periodical. A portion of the space is given to articles, varying in type from the broad exposition of points of view by mature experts to the detailed accounts of trained scholars making contributions to the history of the field. In addition to the news and comments concerning members of the profession and the publication of noteworthy documents, it also publishes reviews of the new books about Hispanic America and has other valuable bibliographical material. The readers of this periodical are enabled to keep abreast with the work being done in the field. They may also, through the facilities it affords, make their way to the materials for any part of Hispanic American history in which they may be interested. This valuable publication deserves the support of all students of Hispanic America. Even the general reader should find it interesting and useful, and certainly he ought to know of its existence.

BOOKS

All printed materials not included in the categories already discussed may be classed technically as books. To put it in another way, books are formulated accounts, published apart from other materials, for a general public. Usually of considerable length, they need not attain to any great number of pages, although the shorter accounts are sometimes called pamphlets, instead of books. The problem of the selection of items for entry, even under the limits provided for in this essay, is very great, since on any basis there are hundreds of volumes with strong claims to consideration. It goes without saying that the various encyclopaedias contain useful information, especially for a preliminary survey, but they do not call for entry. Many books on other subjects have valuable chapters on colonial Hispanic America; such, for example, are the volumes of the *Cambridge modern history*, notable especially for their bibliographical aid. Nevertheless, if the reader of the present work has curiosity enough to wish to find such books, it is best for him to avail himself of the guides already referred to, in order to get to them. Except for books of unusual value, such as the Altamira item (26 below), that class of material is omitted here. So also many books dealing with Hispanic America, which, however, are primarily concerned with the republican era, with comparatively little of note about the colonies. And to avoid confusion, many works of merit on the field itself are either omitted or given brief mention in broad descriptive paragraphs or in footnotes, so as to save formal entry and detailed characterization for those authors and their volumes which are especially representative and deserving of attention.

A. *General works*

There are no important works in English over the entire field covered here, except as it is included as a portion of the material in books over a still broader field, such as those in section "b" below.

a. On colonial Hispanic America

14. Barros Arana, Diego. *Compendio de historia de América.* 2v. Santiago, Chile, 1865.

The country which produced the great historian and bibliographer Medina (see item 3) has also given us such famous historians as Vicuña Mackenna and the author of the item entered here, both of whom are especially well known for their important many-volume histories of Chile. Yet, in his comparatively obscure *Compendio*, Barros Arana virtually announced what may now be called the Bolton thesis of the unity of the Western Hemisphere. His two volumes cover the subjects of indigenous America, the discovery, the conquest, the colonial period, and the revolutions. While primarily concerned with Spanish America, Barros Arana has a number of chapters, also, on Brazil and the United States. Not the best example of his work, these volumes have been superseded, perhaps, by those of Navarro y Lamarca (item 15 below), but they have their place in any consideration of Hispanic American historiography.

15. Navarro y Lamarca, Carlos. *Compendio de la historia general de América.* 2v. Buenos Aires, 1910–1913.

Except for the just mentioned Barros Arana *Compendio*, no other work so nearly fits the field of colonial Hispanic America as this, which covers the history of Spanish America, Brazil, and the United States from the earliest times to the attainment of independence. Thus it agrees with the Bolton thesis of the unity of American history. These volumes are in most attractive form, with illustrations on almost every page, and with the story in an interesting flowing style. They are, nevertheless, the work of a scholar, who has provided ample bibliographical data, and who is careful in the presentation of his facts. To be sure, there are some errors, as is inevitable in a history of such a broad field. Such few indications of bias as appear (pro-church, anti-Spanish, pro-Argentinian) are so mild and slight that they cannot be said to mar the volumes in any great degree. Unquestionably, this is one of the fundamental works in the field—so much so, that even the Anglo-American reader who does not understand Spanish should at least have heard of it.

b. On colonial and republican Hispanic America

Most noteworthy of the books in this group in English are the one-volume texts, most of them by historians who are recognized as leaders in the Hispanic American field. Their writings are worthy of the attention of the general reader for point of view, their estimate of men and events, and for bibliographical help. The majority of them have given comparatively little space to the colonial period, however. The following are the names of these authors, arranged in order of number of pages devoted to colonial Hispanic America as covered in the present volume (omitting pre-discovery material): Mary Wilhelmine Williams, 243 pages in 696 (797–101), about a third; Alva Curtis Wilgus, 218 pages in 609 (664–54), also about a third; William Warren Sweet, 154 pages in 342 (383–41), nearly half; James Fred Rippy, 143 pages in 493 (540–47), less than a third; William Spence Robertson, 131 pages in 510 (569–59), about a fourth; Herman Gerlach James and Percy Alvin Martin, 91 pages in 467 (493–26), about a fifth; Hutton Webster, 78 pages in 177 (228–51), nearly half; William Robert Shepherd, 55 pages in 237 (237–0), about a fourth. Comparable to these are the *Latin America: its rise and progress* (Fr. ed., w. diff. title, Paris, 1912; Eng. ed., New York, 1913) of Francisco García Calderón, almost wholly concerned with the republican era, and the item entered below.

16. Dawson, Thomas Cleland. *The South American republics.* 2v. New York and London, 1903–1904.[1] Various reissues.

    Dealing only with the eleven republics of South America in eleven separate sections, this is primarily concerned with the pre-republican era (some seven hundred pages in 1001). The author was an official in the United States foreign service for many years, being a secretary of legation in Brazil, minister to the Dominican Republic and Colombia, and chief of the Division of Latin American Affairs in the State Department, besides holding other posts connected with Hispanic America. These volumes are written in popular style, without bibliographical aids or citations to authorities, but present a good running account. They are an interesting and useful preliminary survey for the countries covered.

B. *The Spanish colonies to 1810*

a. Contemporary accounts

For the scholar, this type of material vies with printed documents and manuscripts as the richest field for investigation, and even the general reader should have some idea of the wealth of evidence it contains and of the extraordinary interest of these publications in themselves. Most of them appeared originally in Spanish or, at any rate, in a language other than English, but many have since been translated, appearing either separately by themselves or else in some of the great sets of republications of original narratives. There was an astonishingly great number of such writers. The Moses *Colonial literature* (item 4) and the Wilgus *Histories* (item 6) name several hundred without exhausting the list.[2] Only a few are entered here, including those whose works

[1] G. P. Putnam's Sons, publishers.

[2] Cf. *supra*, 198, n. 1, for the long list merely of those whose names figure as writers with reference to the Spanish approaches to California.

have been directly quoted in this volume, together with several others—but just a few out of scores!—which are available in English. After the reader has obtained a good foundation through the medium of the best accounts of recent publication, he should go to some one or other of the volumes in this group, which are likely to give him a bit of the atmosphere of the past and much pleasure and profit in innumerable ways as well. It should be clearly understood that the items which follow are merely a representative list. Others, equally valuable, may be found easily through the medium of the bibliographical aids.

17. Acosta, José de. *Historia natural y moral de las Indias.* Sevilla, 1590. There is a 1589 edition in Latin of part of this work, published at Salamanca, and there are numerous later editions in many languages; in English at London, 1604 and 1880. The last-named constitutes volumes LX and LXI of the Hakluyt Society *Works,* 1st series (see item 20). The 1792 edition (2v. Madrid) is the one quoted here.

 Born in Spain in 1540, Acosta eventually became a Jesuit, and spent seventeen years in the colonies, 1570–1587, mostly in Peru as a missionary and teacher. He also visited Mexico. In the *Historia,* he gives a most detailed account for all Spanish America of many things, such as climate, metals, plants, animals, native races, Spanish government, and the wars with the Indians. He even broached the subject of a canal at Panama. Because of the nature of his work he has been called the Pliny of the New World. The *Historia* (from which a passage was translated here) is one of the most important sources for the Spanish colonial period, but not more so, perhaps, than scores of other writings which might be mentioned.

18. Díaz del Castillo, Bernal. *A true history of the conquest of New Spain,* tr. ("From the only exact copy of the Original Manuscript") ed. by Alfred Percival Maudslay, in Hakluyt society, *Works,* v. XXIII–XXV, XXX, XL. 5v. London, 1908–1916. First published in Spanish at Madrid, 1632. Numerous editions in various languages since then.

 The Maudslay translation is the best English edition of the famous *True history.* Díaz was one of the companions of Cortés in the conquest of Mexico and a participant in numerous other adventures in that period. Displeased with the history of the conquest as told by Gómara, Díaz in his old age decided to write a history of his own, in which the companions of Cortés, overlooked by Gómara, should receive the credit due them. His work, in the colloquial Spanish of his day, is now generally adjudged the best of all the histories of the conquest, and it is also one of the most naïvely fascinating tales of those times.

19. Gage, Thomas. *A new survey of the West Indies*. London, 1648 (under diff. title). Many editions in various languages. Most recent English edition ed. by Arthur Percival Newton. New York, 1929.

The author of this valuable early narrative was an English Dominican, who was a teacher for many years in Guatemala, besides traveling elsewhere in Central America, Mexico, and the Caribbean. Returning to England, he became a Protestant, and wrote this volume, in which he told of the wealth of Spanish America, how poorly defended it was, and how easy it would be to conquer it. The English acquisition of Jamaica may be traced in part to the influence of this book. It may also be characterized as one of the most discerning accounts of seventeenth century conditions in the Spanish colonies.

20. Hakluyt society. *Works issued by the Hakluyt society*. 1st ser., 100v. London, 1847–1899; 2d ser., 71v. to date, 1899– .

This is perhaps the most famous of a number of great sets of volumes publishing in English the original narratives of voyagers and travelers in all parts of the world. It is a perfect mine of information about early Hispanic America. All accounts have been translated (when in a different language from English) and carefully edited by prominent scholars. About a third of the volumes so far issued touch upon the Hispanic American colonial field, mainly in the period of discovery and the early conquest. Two works in this set are given entry here (items 17 and 18). For one who already has a fair knowledge of the period, volumes such as these provide a fascinating and colorful picture of the events and times which they depict.

Among sets of similar material in English are the Burney, Churchill, Hakluyt, Harris, Kerr, Knox, Phillips, and Pinkerton collections, most of which contain items about colonial Hispanic America. There are still others, and also numerous separate publications of noteworthy voyages and travels.

Wilgus (item 6) lists much voyage material in English and other languages.

21. Humboldt, Friedrich Heinrich Alexander von. *Political essay on the kingdom of New Spain.* Tr. fr. orig. Fr. (Paris, 1811–1812) ed. by John Black. 4v. London, 1811–1822. The second edition (2v. London, 1814) is the one quoted here.

    One of the most frequently quoted writers about conditions in Spanish America as of the closing years of the colonial era is Alexander von Humboldt, famous German naturalist and traveler. From 1799 to 1804 he and Aimé Bonpland, a French botanist, were in Spanish America, ranging the territory from Peru to Mexico. Although the scientific contributions of Humboldt as a result of this long period of travel were especially important, his comments on social, economic, and political affairs are also an outstandingly valuable source of information. His most noteworthy work from this standpoint is the *Voyage de Humboldt et Bonpland* (23v. Paris, 1805–1834), of which the item entered here was (in the original French) one of a number of subordinate parts. The *Political essay* (included because it is in English and because a citation is made to it) is probably the most famous single item of Humboldt's of those which may be characterized as materials for history, but is by no means the only one. It is an exhaustive study of conditions in New Spain, or Mexico, in the years just prior to the outbreaks of 1810.

22. Juan y Santacilla, Jorge, and Ulloa, Antonio de. *Noticias secretas de América.* 2v. in 1. London, 1826. 2v. (*Biblioteca Ayacucho,* v. XXXI–XXXII). Madrid, 1918. An abridged English edition was published at Boston, 1851.

    This is one of the most remarkable documents of the whole colonial era, revealing much of actual Spanish administration not easily obtainable elsewhere. The two authors were Spanish mathematicians accompanying a French scientific expedition of 1735, sent to Peru to measure a degree of the meridian. They ranged all the territory from Panama to the Island of Chiloé, Chile, but made an especially long stay in Ecuador, which is the region more particularly described in the "Secret Notices." The work is so called, because their manuscript was prepared expressly for the secret instruction of the king and his ministers about the social and political conditions of the regions they visited. As Moses says of it: "It is the most frank and searching examination of the affairs of the colonies that has come down from the colonial period." It went into detail about the abuses and corruption of Spanish officialdom, being especially famous for its denunciation of the methods of the *corregidores*. Their report was buried, however, and not brought to light until many years later, when it was first published in England. A somewhat less severe characterization of conditions in South America is their *Relación histórica del viage a la América*, designed for the general public, and first published at Madrid in 1748.

23. Las Casas, Bartolomé de. *Breuíssima relación de la destruyción de las Indias*. Sevilla, 1552. Numerous later editions in many languages, including several in English. Several variants of title, notably in *Breve* for *Breuíssima*, or *Brevísima*.

    Historiographically important because of its oft quoted and exaggerated denunciations of the Spaniards for their treatment of the Indians, this volume of the celebrated Dominican friar, the "Apostle of the Indies," is less noteworthy as history than some of the other Las Casas works, especially the *Historia general de las Indias* and the *Historia apologética de las Indias*. Yet, Las Casas is remembered for his "Very Brief Relation" almost more than for the much worthier services he rendered in other ways. It is an ultra-partisan pamphlet, with scant regard for accuracy. Nevertheless, it developed a legend about Spanish cruelty which, ever since, it has been almost impossible to dispel.

24. Robertson, William. *The history of America*. 2v. London, 1777. Numerous later editions.

    The oldest of the histories of Spanish America written originally in English, this has some of the defects of the period in which it was published, and has been superseded in much, but is still valuable. It is primarily a history of the discovery by Columbus, and the conquest of Mexico and Peru, together with learned observations about the peoples and institutions of America, which to him seems to have meant Spanish America.

b. Later works

It is to this group that the general reader should first resort for materials on Spanish America prior to the wars of independence. Most of the works given here are in English. Only a few of the most vital of the others are included. The list of volumes in English is far from exhaustive; for example, just four of the numerous biographies of prominent individuals [1] and none of the national histories (which almost invariably have chapters on the colonial period) [2] are included; furthermore, many more items, a number of them of great merit, are excluded in order not to rob certain of the entered items of the stress which they deserve and to keep this essay within simple and readable bounds.[3] Nevertheless, the items given entry probably include the most essential volumes (although some of them are not more worthy of presentation than a number of those relegated to the footnotes), and they

[1] Among biographies or other books involving at least a portion of the career of some one person—most of them in English and by no means all there are—not given full entry are the following: Abbot (De Soto); André (Columbus); Beard (Toussaint L'Ouverture); Beazley (John and Sebastian Cabot); Benson (Magellan); Bolton (Crespí); Bolton (De Mézières); Bolton (Kino); Bourne (De Soto); Brion (Las Casas); Claudel (Columbus); Conner (Menéndez de Avilés); Coues (Garcés); Eaglin (Columbus); Graham (De Soto); Graham (Valdivia); Guillemard (Magellan); Hammond (Oñate); Helps (Cortés); Helps (Las Casas); Helps (Pizarro); Hildebrand (Magellan); Hill (Escandón); Irving (Columbus); Jane (Columbus); Johnson (Vespucci); Jones (De Soto); Kayserling (Columbus); King (De Soto); MacNutt (Cortés); MacNutt (Las Casas); Markham (Columbus); May (Inés Suárez); Maynard (De Soto); Mecham (Ibarra); Ober (Pizarro); Roberts (Henry Morgan); Robertson, J. A. (De Soto—the "Gentleman of Elvas" account); Robinson (Cortés); Sedgwick (Cortés); Shipp (De Soto); Vignaud (Columbus); Wassermann (Columbus); Waxman (Toussaint L'Ouverture); Wilber (Salvatierra); Wilmer (De Soto); Winship (Coronado); Young (Columbus). A number of these are translations of diaries or other documents of the individuals concerned, but usually have an introduction by the translator and editor. Still other volumes contain biographical chapters on important Spanish colonial figures.

[2] One writer, who sought in the main to set forth volumes in English, has a list of eighty-eight national histories. Rippy, James Fred, *Historical evolution of Hispanic America* (New York, 1932), 543-545. The reader is herewith referred to that volume for books of this nature.

[3] The following are some of the authors in this category, with a brief indication of the subject-matter of their volumes: Bandelier (The gilded man); Blackmar (Spanish institutions in the Southwest); Braden (Religious aspects of the conquest of Mexico); Brady (South American fights and fighters); Chapman (Founding of Spanish California); Coester (Literary history); Edwards (Peoples of old, i.e. colonial Chile); Fernández Guardia (Conquest of Costa Rica); Fisher (Intendant system); Fisher (Vice-regal administration); Fortier and Ficklen (Central America and Mexico); Graham (Conquest of New Granada); Graham (Conquest of the River Plate); Graham (Vanished Arcadia, i.e. Jesuit Paraguay); Hackett (Revolt of the Pueblo Indians of New Mexico); Haring (Buccaneers); Johnson (Pioneer Spaniards in North America); Keller (Colonization); Lea (Inquisition in the Spanish dependencies); Leroy-Beaulieu (Colonization); Lowery (Spanish settlements in the United States); Lummis (Spanish pioneers); Markham (Conquest of New Granada); Morris (Colonization); Richman (Spanish conquerors); Smith (Viceroy); Wagner (Spanish voyages to the northwest coast of North America); Zahm (El Dorado); Zimmerman (Colonization).

are probably representative of the field as a whole. Still other books can easily be found by those who desire them.

25. Aiton, Arthur Scott. *Antonio de Mendoza, first viceroy of New Spain.* Durham, N. C., 1927.[1]

The author of this volume, a professor in the University of Michigan, is one of the most active and soundest students of Hispanic American history at the present time. His *Mendoza* is a scholarly and delightful monograph about an official who was a distinguished man and who, in a sense, typified Spanish colonial administration at its best.

26. Altamira y Crevea, Rafael. *Historia de España y de la civilización española.* 4v. Barcelona, 1900–1911; 3 ed., 5v. in 6, Barcelona, 1913–1930. The earlier edition (the only one available to the writer) is the one cited here.

The crowded volumes of the great Altamira history cover the story of Spanish civilization from the earliest times to 1808. Through different periods of time there are successive chapters on the external political narrative, social institutions, the state, the church, economic factors, and intellectual life. Paragraphs on the Spanish colonies in the Americas appear at appropriate places within these chapters, and amount altogether to enough to make a volume in themselves. The author is not only one of the leading Spanish historians of recent times, but also has distinguished himself in various other fields of intellectual endeavor. For years he has been Spain's representative at the Hague Court, and also a professor at the University of Madrid. It would be possible to cite many other works of Altamira bearing upon Spanish colonial history, including several books which in a measure correct or amplify the *Historia.* This, however, is likely to remain his most famous work in this field, and may be allowed to stand as representative of his writings. It is certainly a most important source of information.

27. Bancroft, Hubert Howe. *Works.* 39v. San Francisco, 1882–1891. Many of the separate volumes were reissued in new editions.

While many of these volumes bear at least indirectly on Hispanic American colonial history, the following are especially noteworthy: *History of Cen-*

[1] Duke University Press, publishers.

tral America (3v.), v. VI–VIII; *History of Mexico* (6v.), v. IX–XII; *North Mexican states and Texas* (2v.), v. XV–XVI; *History of Arizona and New Mexico* (1v.), v. XVII; *History of California* (7v.), v. XVIII–XIX; *History of the northwest coast* (2v.), v. XXVII; and *California pastoral* (1v.), v. XXXIV. The volumes named include the wars of independence, but the pre-1810 matter is so much more ample in amount and notable as a contribution that entry is made here.

Written in fact by various authors under Bancroft's direction, the *Works* represents possibly the most stupendous compilation in the history of American historiography. The materials were chopped up according to the region to which they applied, and put together chronologically. Since they were not always studied critically before being used, literally thousands of errors appear in the Bancroft volumes. Nevertheless, they opened up hitherto unexplored fields, have by no means been superseded, and are still an indispensable starting-point for any investigation into the history of the Pacific coast countries of North America; whatever one wishes to take up, he is likely to find that Bancroft has touched upon it beforehand. His frequent and ample footnotes, with every manner of authority in them, good, bad, and indifferent, are also one of the most important bibliographical discussions in the field.

28. Bolton, Herbert Eugene. *An outpost of empire; the story of the founding of San Francisco.* New York, 1931.

This is entered as the most recent example in book form of Bolton's many writings in the Spanish colonial field. Cf. item 7. It was first issued as volume I in the five-volume *Anza's California expeditions* (Berkeley, Calif., 1930), the last four of which are translations, with learned editorial notes, of the diaries and correspondence relating to the Anza expeditions of 1774–1776. The *Outpost* volume is Bolton's own tale of the expeditions—expeditions which were to make Spain's hold on the precarious California settlements secure, thus avoiding a possible British or Russian conquest.

29. Bolton, Herbert Eugene. *The Spanish borderlands; a chronicle of old Florida and the Southwest.* New Haven, Conn., 1921.

If Bolton's "Epic" (see item 12) represents his

view of American history, this volume most accurately covers the field of his intensive studies, embracing the Spanish territories east of the Mississippi (old Florida), as well as Louisiana, the present border regions of the United States and Mexico, and the Pacific coast. In comparatively brief and highly attractive form, this is Bolton's story of the northern frontiers of Spain's American empire—a story which is almost wholly the work of Bolton himself and his many students. It is one of the most noteworthy of his formulated accounts.

30. Bolton, Herbert Eugene, and Marshall, Thomas Maitland. *The colonization of North America, 1492–1783.* New York, 1920.

Written with the idea of placing the history of the United States in a broader setting than it usually has in the narrowly local national volumes, this is, in a sense, an intermediate step toward the truly "American" history of the Western Hemisphere. Bolton (cf. items 7 and 12) designed the book, and wrote the parts which give it continental proportions (including all sections dealing with Spanish North America). Marshall, a brilliant scholar, who for many years has been a professor of United States history at Washington University, St. Louis, was responsible especially for the part concerning the English colonies. The volume is an extremely useful general survey.

31. Bourne, Edward Gaylord. *Spain in America, 1450–1580,* in *The American nation: a history,* v. III. New York and London, 1904.

Published early in the present century, this ranks with the works of Moses as one of the pioneer volumes by a United States scholar in the field of Hispanic American history. The dates in the title give an idea of the period covered, "from the birth of Christopher Columbus to the beginning of continuous activity in colonization by the English." But for the dates—often overlooked in references to this book—the title would be a misnomer, which it is to some extent, anyway, since the material included is only that which looks toward the eventual United States. Thus, it is mainly the voyages of exploration and discovery in North America, although there are also chapters on Vespucci and Magellan. Seven of the twenty chapters are concerned with "the

Spanish colonial system and . . . the first stage of the transmission of European culture to America."

32. Chapman, Charles Edward. *A history of California: the Spanish period.* New York, 1923.

Containing much material with reference to the methods of the Spanish conquest in the era of the "aggressive defensive," this volume has been used here, not for California history, but for the story of Spanish colonial frontier advance through the employment of missions, presidial soldiery, and civilians, after the day of the early and spectacular *conquistadores* had passed. Other volumes about the Texas, Louisiana, and Florida sectors of frontier activity, as well as a number concerned with the South American border lands, might equally well be included in a full list.

33. Cunningham, Charles Henry. *The audiencia in the Spanish colonies, as illustrated by the audiencia of Manila (1583–1800)*, in University of California, *Publications in history*, v. IX. Berkeley, Calif., 1919.

Although dealing with the *audiencia* of Manila, this volume is primarily, as the title indicates, a study of the Spanish colonial *audiencia* wherever found, and is exceedingly valuable in the field of colonial Spanish America. The author has supplemented the usual printed sources with an extensive use of manuscript materials in the archives of the Philippine Islands and Spain. As a result, his work is a veritable gold-mine of information on actual Spanish colonial administration.

34. Fiske, John. *The discovery of America, with some account of ancient America and the Spanish conquest.* 2v. Boston and New York, 1892.

Published a number of years ago, and supplanted in some respects by more recent works, this is still a worth while, as it is also a readable, account of the period of discovery and the ensuing Spanish conquest, to the middle of the sixteenth century.

35. Haring, Clarence Henry. *Trade and navigation between Spain and the Indies*, in Harvard university, *Economic studies*, v. XIX. Cambridge, Mass., 1918.

The work of a leading historian in the Hispanic American field, now a professor in Harvard University, this is the most important of his writings on the colonial period. It is a fundamental institutional study, the standard volume with respect to the subject-matter it covers.

36. Helps, *Sir* Arthur. *The Spanish conquest in America.* 4v. London, 1855–1861. Several later editions.

Helps approached this work because of his interest in the history of slavery, and so depicted "not conquest only, but the results of conquest,—the mode of government which ultimately prevailed—the extirpation of native races—the introduction of other races—the growth of slavery—and the settlement of the *encomiendas*, on which all Indian society depended." Helps made diligent use of source materials not employed before his time, and his work is one of the landmarks in the field. It is usually regarded, however, as too bitterly condemnatory of the Spanish system, especially of the *encomienda.* Cf. item 50. It is, nevertheless, one of the noteworthy surveys of the conquest in the era of the *conquistadores*, down to the middle of the sixteenth century.

37. Leonard, Irving Albert. *Don Carlos de Sigüenza y Góngora: a Mexican savant of the seventeenth century*, in University of California, *Publications in history*, v. XVIII. Berkeley, Calif., 1929.

An admirable and scholarly volume, this work is entered here, in part because a citation is made to it, and partly because it is representative of the studies in the intellectual history of the Spanish colonies. The author is a member of the Spanish department at the University of California.

38. Means, Philip Ainsworth. *Fall of the Inca empire, and the Spanish rule in Peru: 1530–1780.* New York and London, 1932.

Archaeologist, anthropologist, and historian, the author of this work has for many years concerned himself with pre-Spanish Peru—that is to say, with the territory "contained in the modern republics of Ecuador, Peru, and Bolivia, together with adjacent portions of Colombia, Argentina, and Chile." That is the field of the present volume, which is a sequel to his *Ancient civilizations of the Andes* (New York and London, 1931). A third volume is in contemplation: *The Andean republics in modern times.* This work, therefore, covers the Spanish period, down to 1780, when the Tupac Amarú revolt began. "From that year onwards events and developments were quite definitely shaping themselves toward a final break with Spain, having relatively slight connection with what had gone before." The author knows the materials for colonial Peru, and made capable use of them.

39. Merriman, Roger Bigelow. *The rise of the Spanish empire in the old world and the new.* 3v. New York, 1918–1925.

Volume I (*The middle ages*) has nothing bearing directly upon the Spanish colonies, volume II (*The Catholic Kings*) has only a little, but more than a third of volume III (*The emperor*) is devoted to the colonial period, with chapters mainly about Magellan, Cortés, Pizarro, and colonial administration. A fourth volume (*Philip the prudent*) has yet to appear. Merriman, a professor in Harvard, has in these volumes produced the best example of his scholarship and skill in political narrative. He has made an exhaustive study of the printed materials available, and within the limits of the story he tells has produced an account which is interesting and sound.

40. Moses, Bernard. *The establishment of Spanish rule in America.* New York and London, 1898. 2 ed. 1907.

This volume is especially important for historiographical reasons and as the first work on Hispanic America by a historian whose sum total of publications was to place his name in the front rank of those who have contributed to the field. Cf. item 4. Not overlooking the value of such earlier histories as those of Bancroft, Fiske, Prescott, and Winsor, several of whose volumes are entered here (at items 27, 34, 45, 46, and 52), it may be said that the *Establishment* was the first scholarly history of colonial Hispanic America by a professor of the material, with a student following, to be published in the United States. In a sense, it proved to be the head of a since great and rushing comet of publication in the United States on the subject of Hispanic American history. It is for that reason that Moses deserves the title of pioneer. This particular book is in the form of a series of somewhat disconnected essays, with little of the smooth and flowing style eventually developed by this gifted historian. It was a harbinger of better things, however. Omitting most of the detail of wars with the Indians, Moses in this volume covers the different areas of the conquest, emphasizing institutions.

41. Moses, Bernard. *Spain overseas.* New York, 1929. Despite the fact that the "light had failed" (cf. item 59), the venerable Moses was able to add this last of his volumes to an already long list. It is a thoughtful essay of only a little more than a hundred pages on the Spanish social order in the colonies in America and the Philippines, with two of its eight chapters devoted to their successors in both regions. It is a publication of the Hispanic Society of America.

42. Moses, Bernard. *Spain's declining power in South America, 1730–1806.* Berkeley, Calif., 1919.

In this volume Moses carries on the story of Spanish colonial South America from the point where he left it in his earlier *Dependencies* work (item 44, below). In the preface to the latter he spoke of the period from about 1730 to the battle of Ayacucho in 1824 as one which was "especially distinguished by the increasing social importance of the creoles and mestizos, the disastrous effects of Spain's commercial policy, the decline of loyalty to the mother country, and the successful struggle for independence." Except as concerns the wars of independence, that is the theme of this work, carried out in a discussion of the developments in each of the regions now embraced by the South American republics. This volume stands with the two-volume *Dependencies* history as among the best of the Moses contributions on colonial Hispanic America.

43. Moses, Bernard. *South America on the eve of emancipation: the southern Spanish colonies in the last half-century of their dependence.* New York and London, 1908.[1]

An earlier and less exhaustive work than the preceding item, this covers the same period of time, but in less detail and less connected fashion. Most of the chapters are in the nature of separate articles, but they are, nevertheless, noteworthy illustrations of the era embraced by the book.

44. Moses, Bernard. *The Spanish dependencies in South America: an introduction to the history of their civilization.* 2v. New York and London, 1914.[2]

This and the *Declining power* (item 42) are, on the whole, the most important of the many works on colonial Hispanic America by this prolific and schol-

[1] G. P. Putnam's Sons, publishers.
[2] Harper and Brothers, publishers.

arly writer. His *Dependencies* covers the history of Spanish South America from about 1550 to 1730, the important era when Spanish colonial civilization was in fact taking on its characteristic forms. To this period, "representing the origins and fundamental institutions of a new society," as Moses puts it, "one must refer if he would elucidate the civilisation [*sic*] of the nations that succeeded the colonial dependencies." These two volumes are sound in their scholarship and attractively written.

45. Prescott, William Hickling. *The conquest of Mexico.* 3v. New York, 1843. Numerous editions since.

A master of political narrative, with a somewhat florid style, Prescott in this work reached the peak of his reputation as a historian. Later writers have corrected or amplified his story, but it is still worth reading, not only because of the fascinating manner in which it is told, but also because it is, in the main, sound, based on materials (printed and manuscript) critically, if also enthusiastically, employed. Following introductory chapters on the Aztecs, it is primarily the story of Cortés and the taking of Mexico City.

46. Prescott, William Hickling. *History of the conquest of Peru.* 2v. New York, 1847. There have been a number of later editions.

The remarks made under the preceding item might be repeated here, except that this is a slightly less famous history. It deals with the Incas, the conquest by Pizarro, and the civil wars of the conquerors, until peace was at length established.

47. Priestley, Herbert Ingram. *The coming of the white man, 1492–1848*, in *A history of American life*, v. I. New York, 1929.

Some 209 pages, or over half of this volume, are concerned with colonial Hispanic America in the region of New Spain, or Mexico, and the Spanish border lands now part of the United States. The author, a professor in the University of California, and a leading scholar in the Hispanic American field, has brought to this book the ripe and mature judgment of his long experience, and has produced a work which, in the words of the editors of the series, is notable for philosophical analysis, picturesqueness of treatment, patient research, and imaginative reconstruction. It is not a detailed discussion of events, but rather an exposition of the culture of the regions with which it deals. As such, it is well adapted to the general reader. A "Critical Essay on Authorities" is a valuable feature for the scholar.

48. Priestley, Herbert Ingram. *José de Gálvez, visitor-general of New Spain (1765–1771)*, in University of California, *Publications in history*, v. V. Berkeley, Calif., 1916.

The first book of this well known scholar (cf. item 47), it is also one of the best on Spanish colonial institutions. While it is a biography of Gálvez for the years when he was in Mexico, it is even more a study of the financial institutions of the viceroyalty at that time, together with an account of the reforms and other activities of the *visitador*. Since the administrative institutions of New Spain, or Mexico, were in essentials the same as those of the other colonies, this volume amounts to a valuable contribution for the whole field.

49. Roscher, Wilhelm. *The Spanish colonial system*, tr. ed. by Edward Gaylord Bourne. New York, 1904.[1]

This little volume, only forty-eight pages long, is important out of all proportion to its size. It is a chapter, translated to English, out of the author's *Kolonien, kolonialpolitik und auswanderung* (3 ed. Leipzig, 1885). Broadly historical and thoughtful, it is a summary of the Spanish colonial system at its height in its social, political, and economic aspects. The footnotes of the editor have useful bibliographical information.

50. Simpson, Lesley Byrd. *The encomienda in New Spain: forced native labor in the Spanish colonies, 1492–1550*, in University of California, *Publications in history*, v. XIX. Berkeley, Calif., 1929.

Attractively written, this is the work of a sound scholar, a member of the Spanish department at the University of California, who has made a thorough study of the materials bearing upon his subject. He finds that in the light of sixteenth century conditions the *encomienda* "was a logical and wholly justifiable organization of society in the Spanish colonies," despite many evils attendant upon it, which, however, were due to other causes.

51. Thacher, John Boyd. *Christopher Columbus: his life and work*. 3v. New York and London, 1903–1904.

[1] Henry Holt and Company, publishers.

These enormous volumes represent one of the most detailed studies of the life of Columbus ever made. Each episode is discussed in minute detail. Other biographies of Columbus may be as good as this, or at least have cleared up some points which were still in doubt in Thacher's time, but this will long be a standard work on the subject.[1]

52. Winsor, Justin, *ed.* *Narrative and critical history of America, by a corps of eminent historical scholars and specialists under the editorship of Justin Winsor.* 8v. Boston and New York, 1884–1889.

Covering the entire Western Hemisphere, this devotes one volume (v. II, *Spanish explorations and settlements in America from the fifteenth to the seventeenth century*) and parts of several others to colonial Hispanic America. It is especially notable, however, for the critical bibliographical comments of the editor.

C. *The Spanish American wars of independence* [2]

a. Contemporary accounts

Again, the scholar (as in the case of the books cited above in section "B") will make use of this type of material, while the general reader should get to it only after he has perused a considerable number of the volumes listed below in section "b." There is a wealth of writings of this sort in Spanish, and a few in English, notably the memoirs of Dundonald (Lord Cochrane) and General Miller. None seem to require entry here.

b. Later works

As in the case of previous sections, the list here is primarily for the general reader, with most of the entered items being works in English.[3]

[1] Cf. *supra*, 366, n. 1, for a mention of other biographies.

[2] For an exceptionally important bibliographical item on the wars of independence, see the reference at page 350, n. 1, to the Bolívar *Bibliography*.

[3] Among authors of volumes in English whose works are not given entry—many of them decidedly worth while—are (noted briefly, as in previous footnotes of this essay) the following: Chandler (Wooster); Chisholm (Independence of Chile); Coffey (O'Higgins); Daniels (Makers of South America); Ducoudray-Holstein (Bolívar); Graham (Páez); Larrazábal (Bolívar); Latané (Diplomatic relations of the United States and Spanish America); Latané (The United States and Latin America); Lemly (Bolívar); Mehegan (O'Higgins); Noll and McMahon (Hidalgo); Parra Pérez (Bolívar); Petre (Bolívar); Rippy (Rivalry of the United States and Great Britain); Robertson (Francisco de Miranda and the revolutionizing of Spanish America); Schoellkopf (San Martín); Sherwell (Bolívar); Sherwell (Sucre); Vandercook (Black majesty, i.e. Christophe); Vaucaire (Bolívar); Washburn (Paraguay); Ybarra (Bolívar); and a plethora of volumes on the Monroe Doctrine.

53. Angell, Hildegarde. *Simón Bolívar, South American liberator*. New York, 1930.

There are numerous one-volume biographies of Bolívar in English,[1] but this is usually rated the best, although several of the others are not far, if at all, behind. By no means a biography of the Robertson's *Miranda* type (item 62, *infra*), it is, nevertheless, a work of good scholarship and a readable volume. Although unable to "get sight" of a collection of "two thousand letters from ladies" to Bolívar, the author appears to have made competent use of the more easily available materials.

54. Chandler, Charles Lyon. *Inter-American acquaintances.* Sewanee, Tenn., 1915. 2 ed. 1917.

Prepared "in the few spare moments of his life as a railway employé," the Chandler book is a brief work (187 pages) in six separate essays, four of which have some bearing on the period embraced by the present volume. Most important of its chapters, perhaps, is the one concerning citizens of the United States who took part in the Spanish American wars of independence.

55. Guido, Tomás. *San Martín y la gran epopeya*, in *Grandes escritores argentinos*, v. VII. Buenos Aires, 1928.

In this volume a number of scattered articles of Guido, a companion and intimate friend of San Martín, are brought together. They constitute one of the most important sources of evidence with respect to the career of the great Argentinian, notably so as concerns San Martín's reasons for withdrawing from Peru.

56. Hasbrouck, Alfred. *Foreign legionaries in the liberation of Spanish South America*, in Columbia university, *Studies in history, economics and public law*, no. CCCIII. New York and London, 1928.

This is a scholarly and interesting narrative of the foreigners who served in the armies of Bolívar in the wars of independence. It is therefore very largely concerned with the story of the British Legion.

57. Mitre, Bartolomé. *Historia de Belgrano y de la independencia argentina*. 3v. Buenos Aires, 1858–1876. 6 ed. (*Biblioteca de 'La Nación,'* v. XXVIII, XXX, XXXII, XXXIV). 4v. Buenos Aires, 1913.

[1] Cf., 350, n. 1, *supra;* also, 376, n. 3, *supra*.

In this work and his *San Martín* (item 58), Mitre told the story of the wars of independence in South America. Neither is a biography so much as it is a history of the wars, in which the person whose name appears in the title is the most important figure. The *Belgrano* work is less noteworthy than the *San Martín*, only in that the theatre of operations with which it is concerned was more restricted and not quite so vital as affecting the final issue of the conflict. It is, nevertheless, an outstanding treatise by a great historian.

58. Mitre, Bartolomé. *Historia de San Martín y de la emancipación sud-americana.* 3v. Buenos Aires, 1887. 3 ed. (*Biblioteca de 'La Nación,'* v. LXXXIII, LXXXV, LXXXVII, LXXXIX, XCI, XCIII). 6v. in 3. 1903–1907. The second edition (4v. 1890) is the one cited here.

As indicated by the full title, and as already set forth (at item 57), this is more a history of the wars of independence in South America than it is a biography of San Martín. The *San Martín* is easily the best history of those wars yet written, and it is also one of the best accounts of the career of Bolívar, as it is of San Martín. Cf. item 61. The author was one of Argentina's great men. Deserving to rank as the outstanding historian of his country, he was also one of its leading statesmen in the middle and later years of the nineteenth century, being president of Argentina from 1862 to 1868. All histories of the wars written since Mitre's time have been indebted to him for much they have to tell, and the present volume is no exception.

59. Moses, Bernard. *The intellectual background of the revolution in South America, 1810–1824.* New York, 1926.

A late volume of this great historian of colonial Hispanic America (cf. item 4), its failure to attain to the heights of some of his previous writings is explained in the first sentence of the preface. "This sketch might have become a book if the light had not failed." Moses was in his eightieth year when it was published. It is the work, however, of a man who still retained his intellectual powers, if not his eyesight. As Moses put it: "Behind the practical enterprises of the revolution there was a body of thought and opinion." The book is small, but is not equalled by anything else in English on the subject. Like several other Moses volumes, this was published by the Hispanic Society of America.

60. Paxson, Frederic Logan. *The independence of the South-American republics: a study in recognition and foreign policy*. Philadelphia, 1903.

An early work by one who described himself in a gift copy to me as one who might have been a "co-worker" in Hispanic American history (but whom circumstances directed otherwise), this is a volume which is in keeping with the high reputation for scholarship to which its author has since attained. It deals primarily with the policies of the United States and Great Britain with respect to the recognition of the South American governments engaged in the wars of independence against Spain. Paxson, for a number of years head of the department of history in the University of Wisconsin, is now Byrne Professor of American History in the University of California.

61. Pilling, William, *ed*. *The emancipation of South America*. London, 1893.

This is "a condensed translation," 499 pages long, of the great four-volume *San Martín* work of Mitre. See item 58. Naturally, it furnishes the best account of San Martín and one of the best on the wars of independence in South America as yet available in English.

62. Robertson, William Spence. *The life of Miranda*. 2v. Chapel Hill, N. C., 1929.[1]

Biography? This *is* a biography! The author, a professor in the University of Illinois, is one of the first-rank scholars in the Hispanic American field, famous for his meticulous accuracy and for his objective point of view. Of his many writings, this is perhaps the greatest piece of work. Robertson examined almost every scrap of information about Miranda, and made use of it in such a way that a reader can really know the subject. This is no biography through the medium of rhetoric and hyperbole on the part of the author, but one of *fact*, based on almost unlimited evidence. If one cared to criticize it at all, it would be because Robertson does not let himself go even a little bit in the direction of hero worship. It is, however, an outstanding

[1] University of North Carolina Press, publishers.

biography, and an exceedingly important study in wars of independence history.

63. Robertson, William Spence. *Rise of the Spanish-American republics, as told in the lives of their liberators.* New York and London, 1918.[1]

By the author of the preceding item, this is a broader type of work, being virtually a history of the Spanish American wars of independence, over the whole field, the only volume of its kind available in English. The lives of Miranda, Hidalgo, Iturbide, Moreno, San Martín, Bolívar, and Sucre are taken as the basis for chapters which are in fact not biographies so much as they are histories of the wars in the regions where these men were prominent. Otherwise, the choice of Moreno for Argentina might have been open to question. Like all the books of this distinguished scholar, this is a sound and valuable contribution to Hispanic American history.

D. *Portuguese Brazil*

There is by no means as rich a literature for colonial Brazil as there is for colonial Spanish America, whether in Portuguese, in English, or in any other language. Nevertheless, it would not be difficult to prepare a shockingly long list, which might well include histories of Portugal,[2] as well as of Brazil. Among the more noteworthy historians of Brazil who have written in Portuguese is Rocha Pombo, whose ten-volume work is possibly the most generally useful.[3] In addition to the items entered below, there are in English the colonial histories of Brazil by Grant and Henderson, both early nineteenth century publications, and a number of short general works on Brazil, mainly concerned with the independence era, however.[4] The chapters on Brazil in Dawson (item 16 above) are worthy of note.

64. Armitage, John. *The history of Brazil, from the period of the arrival of the Braganza family in 1808, to the abdication of don Pedro the First in 1831.* 2v. London, 1836.

[1] D. Appleton and Company, publishers.

[2] Among one-volume histories of Portugal in English are those of Bragança Cunha and Stephens.

[3] Other historians whose works are in Portuguese are Handelmann (originally in German), Mello Moraes, Oliveira Freire, Ribeiro, and Varnhagen, besides Oliveira Lima, one of whose volumes is entered here at item 67.

[4] Among authors of this group are Bruce, Buley, Carpenter, Cooper, Denis, Domville-Fife, Elliott, Fletcher and Kidder, James, Kidder, Nash, Oakenfull, Winter, and Wright.

The full title also contains the statement that this is "a continuation of Southey's history of that country." See item 68. The greater part of volume I is devoted to the period from 1808 to the end of the war for independence against Portugal.

65. Lannoy, Charles de, and Vander Linden, Herman. *Histoire de l'expansion coloniale des peuples européens: Portugal et Espagne.* Bruxelles and Paris, 1907.

Each of the two parts of this volume has six parallel chapters, dealing with the mother country at the beginning of the era of expansion, the story of the expansion itself, administration, economic factors, "*civilisation*," and results for the mother country. The section concerning Portugal, by Lannoy, is the more useful. On that account this item is entered here, although it also fits the subject-matter of the books in "B.b." The story told is a simple and conventional one, embracing the Portuguese colonies in the Far East as well as in Brazil. Both parts of the work are scholarly, however, with numerous citations to authorities.

66. Magalhaes, Pero de. *The histories of Brazil,* tr. ed. by John Batterson Stetson, in The Cortés society, *Documents and narratives concerning the discovery and conquest of Latin America,* no. 5. 2v. New York, 1922.

Two early works of Magalhães about Brazil are here translated and carefully edited. One of them, the *Historia,* was published in Portuguese in 1576. The other, or *Tratado,* existed only in manuscript. They deal with the topography, *flora* and *fauna,* Indians, missionary work, and *capitaneas* of early Brazil.

67. Oliveira Lima, Manoel de. *The evolution of Brazil, compared with that of Spanish and Anglo-Saxon America.* Stanford University, Calif., 1914. Also in Spanish and Portuguese.

Only 159 pages long, this is a general, non-factual work, in the form of six lectures delivered at Stanford University. In so far as they may be dated at all, they refer, for the most part, to the colonial era. The author's other works in Portuguese on Brazilian history are really much more important than this. He was one of the leading authorities among recent Brazilian historians.

68. Southey, Robert. *History of Brazil.* 3v. London, 1810–1819. 2 ed. of v. I. 1822.

The name of Robert Southey, one-time poet-laureate of England, is perhaps better known in other lines of literary endeavor than in that of Hispanic American history. Nevertheless, his *History of Brazil* has not even yet been supplanted in English, though frequently criticized from the standpoint of historical workmanship. It is concerned with the colonial period, from the discovery in 1500 to the arrival of the Portuguese royal family in 1808.

69. Watson, Robert Grant. *Spanish and Portuguese South America during the colonial period.* 2v. London, 1884.

As slightly more than half of this work is devoted to the Spanish colonies of South America, it might have been considered in section "B.b." Few other comparatively recent volumes have as much on colonial Brazil, however, and so it was deemed best to place it here. Not even remotely a great work of history, it nevertheless provides a reasonably good narrative of events from the discovery of the continent, in 1498, to the repulse of the British attack on Buenos Aires in 1806–1807.

II. MANUSCRIPTS

Despite the vast amount of material about colonial Hispanic America already in print, it is a mere bagatelle in comparison with the manuscript collections available for study, in addition to the incalculable quantity which has not yet found its way into public repositories. Although printed sources of information have by no means been exhausted, it is unquestionably true that manuscripts are the principal resort of the scholar in the Hispanic American field who wishes to set forth new evidences about the past. The general reader should know this, but will, of course, wait until the facts are presented to him in printed form.

ARCHIVE GUIDES

Most of the accessible manuscript material about colonial Hispanic America is in great public archives, of which the most famous and the richest is the Archivo General de Indias at Seville, Spain. There are also important groups of colonial material in the national archives of some of the Hispanic American republics. The public archives of the non-Hispanic countries have varying amounts of material on this subject. In addition, many private institutions, such as libraries and museums, have accumulated Hispanic American colonial manuscripts, either in the originals or in copies made from the papers in other archives. The Library of Congress, the Bancroft Library of the University of California, the Library of the University of Texas, and the Newberry Library of Chicago are examples of this type of institution. Although there are scores of printed guides to archive material, only a small fraction of manuscript sources are described in a way that is adequate for the purposes of the investigator; indeed, none of the great archives have even so much as a good catalogue of the material they contain, although meagre descriptions are usually available. The three items entered below are merely samples of existing guides.

70. Bolton, Herbert Eugene. *Guide to materials for the history of the United States in the principal archives of Mexico*, in Carnegie institution of Washington, publication no. 163, *Papers of the department of historical research.* Washington, 1913.

An early work of this prolific scholar (cf. item 7), this, like most of his other writings, was a pioneer task. Nobody before him had given much thought to the project, so it would seem, and there were virtually no facilities in the way of catalogues for the various archives he visited. These included, not only those of Mexico City, but also numerous others in different parts of the country. The materials found by Bolton are in the form of what he calls a "compilation of *notes*"—pertinent items in the *legajos*, or bundles, he examined. Vast in amount, they are particularly rich for the colonial period, when that part of the United States from Texas to California was a portion of New Spain, or Mexico.

71. Chapman, Charles Edward. *Catalogue of materials in the Archivo General de Indias for the history of the Pacific coast and the American Southwest*, in University of California, *Publications in history*, v. VIII. Berkeley, Calif., 1919.

This is but one of a score or more of guides to the papers of the Archivo General de Indias, most of them in Spanish. Among well known works in English are Roscoe R Hill, *Descriptive catalogue of the documents relating to the history of the United States in the Papeles procedentes de Cuba deposited in the Archivo General de Indias at Seville*, Washington, 1916; James Alexander Robertson, *List of documents in Spanish archives relating to the history of the United States which have been printed or of which transcripts are preserved in American libraries*, Washington, 1907;

and William Robert Shepherd, *Guide to the materials for the history of the United States in Spanish archives*, Washington, 1907. The *Catalogue* entered here includes 6257 items in a bulky volume (755 pages), but is really representative of some twenty thousand separate documents. It has been estimated, however, that there are perhaps 64,000,000 documents in the Archivo General de Indias, aggregating 160,000,000 pages. Thus, it would be possible to catalogue the archive, in the form employed in the Chapman book, in about 3200 volumes! The entire archive is devoted to the Spanish colonial period, including the Philippines, and coming down to 1898 in the case of Cuba and Puerto Rico. In the Chapman *Catalogue* there is a ten-page account of the Archivo General de Indias, fifty-nine pages more of broad description of the task in hand, and the detailed entry of materials.

72. Torres Lanzas, Pedro. *Independencia de América, fuentes para su estudio; catálogo de documentos conservados en el Archivo General de Indias de Sevilla.* 6v. Madrid, 1912. 1v. to date. 2d ser. 1924.

One out of a number of works by the learned gentleman who has for so many years been the head of the Archivo General de Indias, it is also another representative of the scores of manuscript guides, already published, which are attempting to reveal the almost unlimited wealth of the great Sevillian archive. For the wars of independence in Spanish America, this work is, of course, of outstanding importance, enabling the investigator to get a detailed idea from the Spanish point of view.

UNPUBLISHED THESES

Some of the most noteworthy analyses of colonial events are in the theses of graduate students who are candidates for the degree of Master of Arts or Doctor of Philosophy. Their works in most cases are not in print, because they would not have a ready sale, and because the writers do not have sufficient funds to bear the expense of publication. Three unpublished theses of University of California students (Lewis Winkler Bealer, Ferdinand Varella Custer, and Charles Edward Nowell) have been quoted in this volume. Altogether, there are approximately thirty doctoral theses and two hundred masters' theses at the University of California in the Hispanic American colonial field which are still in typewritten manuscript form only. Perhaps no other university could muster an equal number, but the sum total of all there are in the United States alone would probably run into the thousands.[1] Of varying merit, they nevertheless contain a vast fund of useful information. The value of the best of them may be measured to some extent by the quality of those volumes included in this essay which were originally submitted as a thesis in satisfaction of one of the requirements for a higher degree. Items 25, 33, 35, 37, 48, 50, 56, and 60 are examples in point.

[1] Pan American union, *Theses on Pan American topics*, bib. ser. no. 5, mimeographed (Washington, 1931), lists 502 theses "prepared by candidates for degrees in colleges and universities in the United States." The list is by no means complete, showing, for example, only eighty-one entries for the University of California. Nevertheless, this item is exceedingly useful in locating much otherwise fugitive, unpublished material. A revised edition (Washington, 1933) is about to be issued as this volume goes to press. It lists 1101 theses.

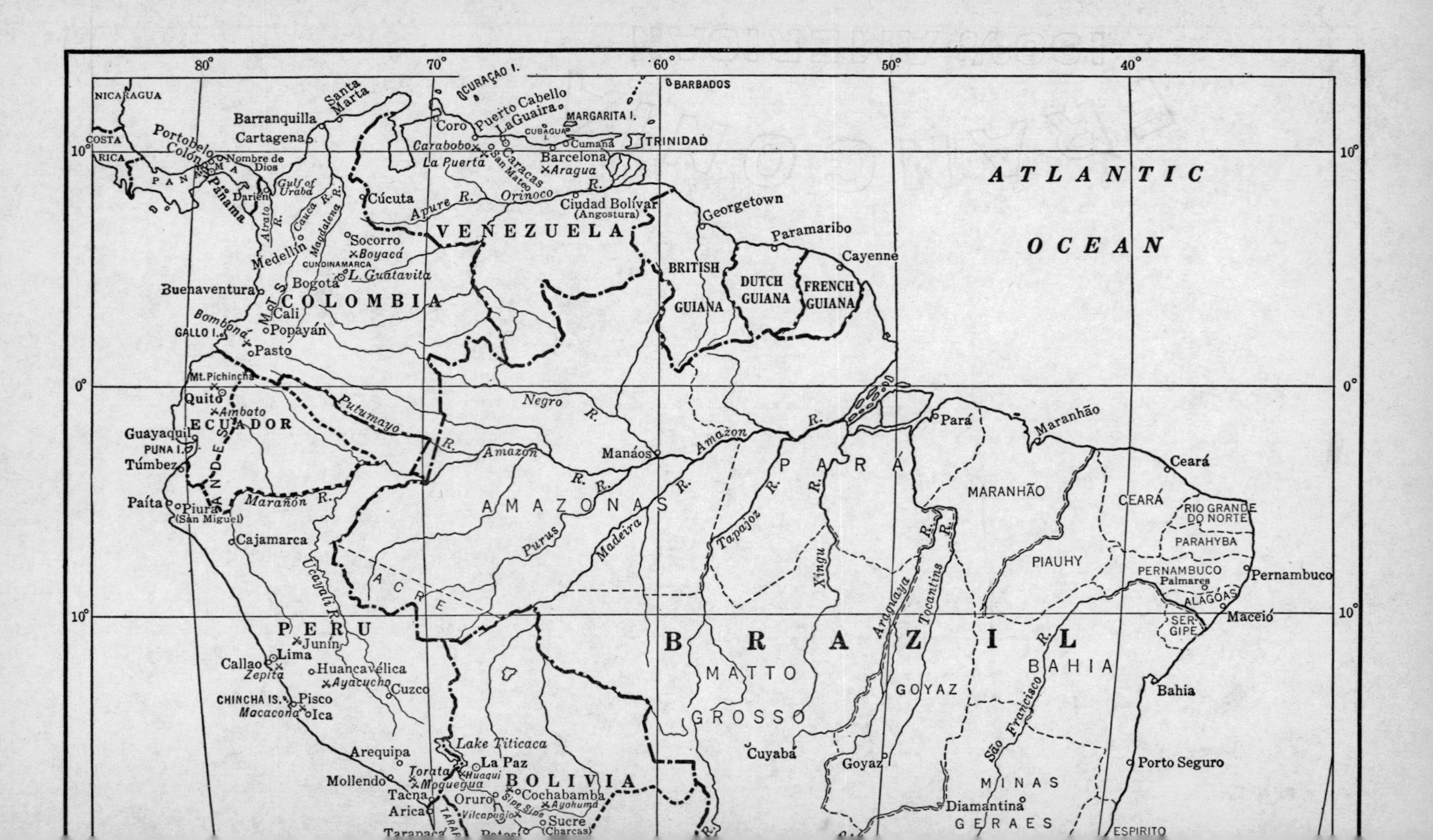

ATLANTIC OCEAN
VENEZUELA
COLOMBIA
ECUADOR
PERU
BOLIVIA
BRAZIL
BRITISH GUIANA
DUTCH GUIANA
FRENCH GUIANA
NICARAGUA
COSTA RICA
PANAMA
BARBADOS
TRINIDAD
MARGARITA I.
CURAÇAO I.
CUBAGUA I.
Santa Marta
Barranquilla
Cartagena
Portobelo
Colón
Nombre de Dios
Panama
Darien
Gulf of Uraba
Atrato R.
Cauca R.
Magdalena R.
Medellin
Cúcuta
Socorro
Boyacá
CUNDINAMARCA
Bogotá
L. Guatavita
Buenaventura
Cali
Popayán
Bombona
GALLO I.
Pasto
Coro
Puerto Cabello
La Guaira
Carabobo
La Puerta
San Mateo
Caracas
Cumaná
Barcelona
Aragua
Apure R.
Orinoco R.
Ciudad Bolívar (Angostura)
Georgetown
Paramaribo
Cayenne
Mt. Pichincha
Quito
Ambato
Guayaquil
PUNA I.
Túmbez
Paíta
Piura (San Miguel)
ANDES
Marañon R.
Cajamarca
Putumayo R.
Negro R.
Amazon R.
Manáos
AMAZONAS
Purus R.
Madeira R.
ACRE
Ucayali R.
Junín
Lima
Callao
Zepita
Huancavélica
Ayacucho
Cuzco
CHINCHA IS.
Pisco
Macacona
Ica
Arequipa
Mollendo
Torata
Moquegua
Tacna
Arica
Tarapaca
Lake Titicaca
La Paz
Huaqui
Oruro
Cochabamba
Sipe Sipe
Ayohuma
Vilcapugio
Sucre (Charcas)
Potosí
PARÁ
Pará
Tapajoz R.
Xingu R.
Araguaya R.
Tocantins R.
Maranhão
MARANHÃO
PIAUHY
CEARÁ
Ceará
RIO GRANDE DO NORTE
PARAHYBA
PERNAMBUCO
Palmares
Pernambuco
ALAGOAS
Maceió
SERGIPE
BAHIA
Bahia
São Francisco R.
MATTO GROSSO
Cuyaba
GOYAZ
Goyaz
MINAS GERAES
Diamantina
Porto Seguro
ESPIRITO
80°
70°
60°
50°
40°
10°
0°

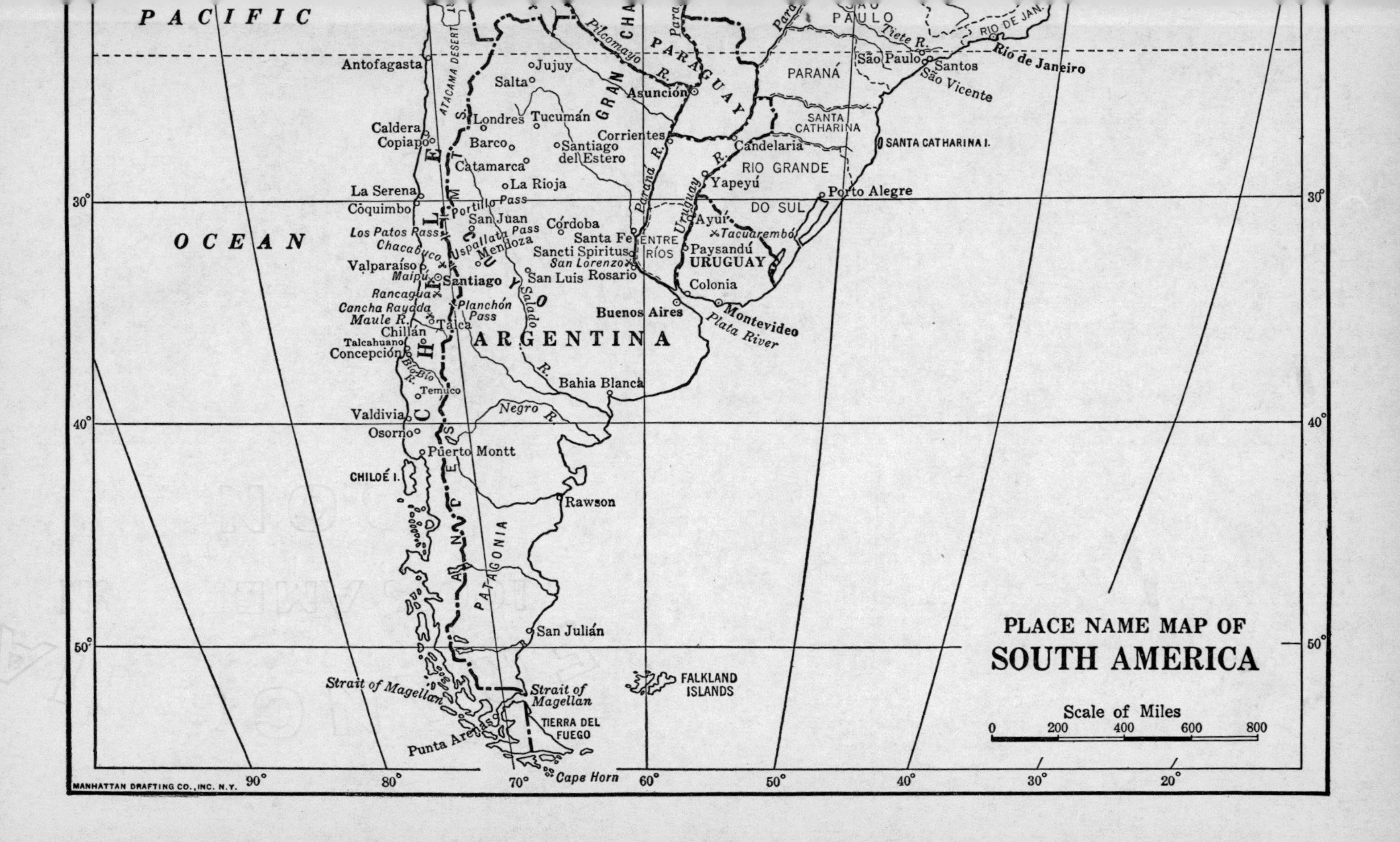
PLACE NAME MAP OF
SOUTH AMERICA
Scale of Miles
0
200
400
600
800
PACIFIC
OCEAN
ARGENTINA
PARAGUAY
URUGUAY
PATAGONIA
GRAN CHACO
Antofagasta
Jujuy
Salta
Asunción
Londres
Tucumán
Caldera
Copiapó
Barco
Santiago del Estero
Corrientes
Catamarca
La Rioja
La Serena
Coquimbo
Portillo Pass
San Juan
Los Patos Pass
Uspallata Pass
Mendoza
Córdoba
Santa Fe
Chacabuco
Sancti Spiritus
San Lorenzo
Valparaíso
Maipú
Santiago
San Luis
Rosario
Rancagua
Cancha Rayada
Planchón Pass
Maule R.
Talca
Chillán
Talcahuano
Concepción
Bio Bio R.
Temuco
Salado R.
Bahia Blanca
Buenos Aires
Valdivia
Osorno
Negro R.
Puerto Montt
CHILOÉ I.
Rawson
San Julián
Strait of Magellan
Punta Arenas
TIERRA DEL FUEGO
Cape Horn
FALKLAND ISLANDS
Pilcomayo R.
Paraná R.
Uruguay R.
ENTRE RÍOS
Yapeyú
Ayuí
Tacuarembó
Paysandú
Colonia
Montevideo
Plata River
Candelaria
RIO GRANDE DO SUL
Porto Alegre
SANTA CATHARINA
SANTA CATHARINA I.
PARANÁ
São Paulo
Tiete R.
Santos
São Vicente
Rio de Janeiro
RIO DE JAN.
ATACAMA DESERT
30°
40°
50°
90°
80°
70°
60°
20°
MANHATTAN DRAFTING CO., INC. N.Y.

INDEX